THE PHASE
By Michael Raduga

Michael Raduga

OOBE Research Center presents:

The Phase
A Practical Guidebook
(Version 2.0, October 2011)

By Michael Raduga

Translated by Peter Orange
Pictures: M.Raduga, E.Leontyeva, S.Buryak
Actress: Maria Forza

www.obe4u.com

PART I: GET PHASE WITHIN 3 DAYS..5
PART II: 100 PHASES...24
PART III: A PRACTICAL GUIDEBOOK..169
PART IV: CONSCIOUS EVOLUTION 2.0.....................................467
TABLE OF CONTENTS...499

2011 Michael Raduga. All rights reserved.

ISBN 978-1-300-55066-2

Proposals regarding translating and publishing this book and other works of M. Raduga may be sent to obe4u@obe4u.com

FOREWORD

The practice of phase states of the mind is the hottest and most promising pursuit of the modern age. Unlike in the past, the notions of "out-of-body experience" and "astral projection" have already lost their mystical halo, and their real basis has been studied in minute detail from the most non-nonsense approach. Now, this phenomenon is accessible to everyone, regardless of their worldview. It is now known how to easily master it and apply it effectively.

This guidebook is the result of ten years of extremely active personal practice and study of the out-of-body phenomenon (the phase), coupled with having successfully taught it to thousands of people. I know all of the obstacles and problems that are usually run into when getting to know this phenomenon, and have tried to protect future practitioners from them in this book.

This guidebook was not created for those who prefer light, empty reading. It is for those who would like to learn something. It contains no speculations or stories, only dry, hard facts and techniques in combination with a completely pragmatic approach and clear procedures for action. They have all been successfully verified by a vast number of practitioners that often had no prior experience. In order to achieve the same result, it is only necessary to read through each section thoroughly and complete the assignments. It gives each and every person something that previously could only be dreamt about - a parallel reality and the possibility of existing in two worlds.

The book is beneficial not only for beginners, but also for those who already know what it feels like to have an out-of-body encounter and have a certain amount of experience, as this guidebook is devoted not only to entering the state, but also equally dedicated to controlling it.

Contrary to popular opinion, there is nothing difficult about this phenomenon if one tries to attain it with regular and right effort. On average, results are reached in less than a week if attempts are made every day. More often than not, the techniques work in literally a couple of attempts.

Michael Raduga
Founder of the OOBE Research Center
January 11, 2009

Michael Raduga

PART I: GET PHASE WITHIN 3 DAYS

Quick Instructions for Novices

Success Rate:
For 1-5 attempts (1-3 days) - 50%
For 6-10 attempts (2-7 days) - 80%
For 11-20 attempts (3-14 days) - 90%

THE PHENOMENON

Way back when, people did not have consciousness. Yet once it developed, it gradually started occupying more and more of the waking state. However, nowadays consciousness is outgrowing the waking state, and has begun continuing its expansion into other states. Consciousness increasingly springs up during REM-phase sleep, giving rise to the most astounding phenomenon of human existence - feeling oneself in an out-of-body experience. It is probable that men and women of the future will have a conscious existence in two worlds. For now, however, this can only be accomplished using the special techniques described in this book.

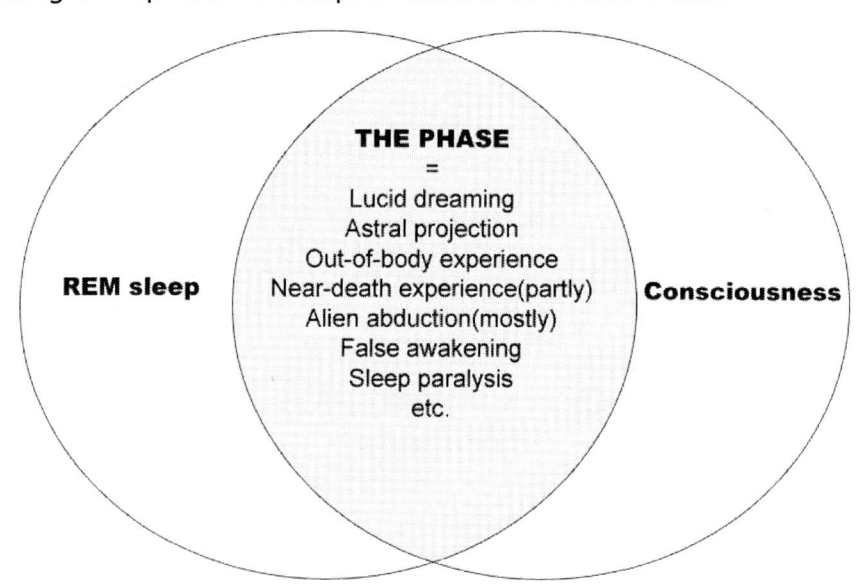

REM sleep ∩ **Consciousness** =
THE PHASE
=
Lucid dreaming
Astral projection
Out-of-body experience
Near-death experience(partly)
Alien abduction(mostly)
False awakening
Sleep paralysis
etc.

Hints at the occurrence of this phenomenon may be found in the Bible and other ancient texts. It lies at the foundation of other phenomena such as near-death experiences, alien abductions, sleep paralysis, and so on. The phenomenon is so extraordinary that many occult movements consider experiencing it to be an accomplishment of the highest order. Statistical research has shown that one person in two will have an intense encounter with it. Meanwhile, the existence of the phenomenon itself has been scientific fact since the 1970s.

The phenomenon is well-represented in many different kinds of modern practices, albeit under various names ranging from "astral projection" and "out-of-body experience" to "lucid dreaming". We shall use the pragmatic term "the phase" or "phase state" to refer to all the above phenomena, as there is no difference at all between them in their usual practice. We will also take as materialist an approach as possible, casting aside all theoretical tripe and concerning ourselves only with what works in practice.

As regards sensory perception of the phenomenon itself, this is not a mere visualization exercise. Reality itself is but a dull daydream in comparison to the phase state! You won't feel your physical body on the bed there, and all of your senses will be fully immersed in a new world of perception. You can touch and behold anything, walk and fly, eat and drink, feel pain and pleasure, and much, much more. And all this with even more realism and lucidity of perception than daily life! This is the reason many novices experience shock - or even mortal fear - upon entering this state. It's a true parallel world in terms of perception.

The practical side of the phenomenon holds even greater opportunity. In the phase, you can travel the Earth, the Universe, and time itself. You can meet any person you want: friends and family, the deceased, and celebrities. You can obtain information from the phase and apply it towards improving your daily life. You can influence your physiology and treat a number of ailments. You can realize your secret desires and develop your creativity. Meanwhile, people with physical impairments can release themselves from all fetters and obtain anything lacking for them in the physical world.

And all this is just the tip of the iceberg of ways to apply the phenomenon in daily life!

You may think that it's difficult to learn if you've read elsewhere that you need spend months, if not years, on it. Get those old wives' tales out of your head - we're in the 21st century! The instructions laid out in this section will help most people to experience this amazing state within only 2 to 3 days of trying. Remember: the techniques described in this book are the result of many years of experimental research at the OOBE Research Center. Thousands have participated first-hand in developing and perfecting the techniques presented here, and have proven that they can be used by absolutely everyone. **All that you need to do is follow these simple instructions as exactly and carefully as you can.** Then, you'll be able to literally live in two worlds!

There are three primary methods for leaving the body. They are used at different times of the day: after sleeping, while sleeping, and without sleeping beforehand. We will begin getting experience using the techniques by starting from the easiest ones - the indirect techniques, which are performed immediately upon awakening. They are quite simple. After mastering those techniques, you can then try to leave your body in the evening or during the day, without sleeping beforehand.

THE INDIRECT METHOD: STEP-BY-STEP INSTRUCTIONS

So, you have decided to experience out-of-body sensations and want to achieve this as quickly as possible. To that end, here we present a brief description of the easiest method - cycles of indirect techniques. This is a universal and most effective way to obtain a phase experience. It has been refined by the OOBE Research Center's work with thousands of people all over the world. The secret to indirect techniques is to perform them upon awakening, when the human brain is physiologically quite close to the phase state, or still in it.

Interesting Fact!
Indirect techniques are mainly to thank for our 80% success rate over only 2 days of attempts at three-day seminars, even in groups of 50 people and more. Once, more than half of the group had a phase experience by the second day, and most had two or more experiences.

Cycles of indirect techniques consist of attempts to separate immediately upon awakening, and if that is unsuccessful, then quickly cycling through techniques over the course of a minute until one of them works, after which it is possible to separate from the body. Usually, 1 to 5 properly performed attempts are all that is necessary to obtain results.

The techniques described below work extremely well both when awakening from *a daytime nap*, as well as in *the middle of the night*. However, we will be concentrating on the optimum strategy - *the deferred method* - which allows for numerous attempts to be had in a single day. This substantially increases the probability of success occurring in only 1 to 3 days.

STEP 1: SLEEP 6 HOURS AND THEN WAKE UP WITH AN ALARM CLOCK

On a night before a free day when you won't have to wake up early, go to bed at your usual time and set your alarm so that you'll only sleep for about 6 hours. When the alarm goes off, you must get up to drink a glass of water, go to the bathroom, and read these instructions once again. Do not attempt any techniques before going to bed the night before, no matter what the case. You just need to lie down and get some sound sleep. The sounder you sleep over these 6 hours, the better your chances of getting results.

STEP 2: GO BACK TO SLEEP WITH AN INTENTION

Deferred Method for Indirect Techniques

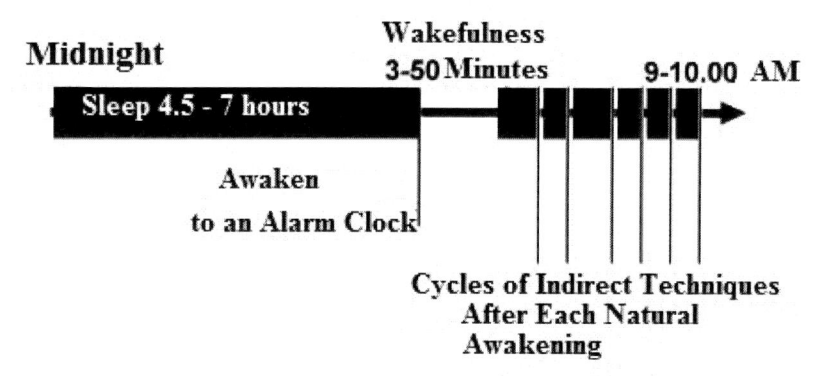

Midnight — Sleep 4.5 - 7 hours — Awaken to an Alarm Clock — **Wakefulness 3-50 Minutes** — Cycles of Indirect Techniques After Each Natural Awakening — **9-10.00 AM**

After 3 to 50 minutes of being awake, go back to bed and concentrate your attention on how you will perform cycles of indirect techniques upon each subsequent awakening in order to leave your body and implement your prepared plan of action. No need to set the alarm clock this time. Each subsequent awakening should occur naturally. If it's too bright in the room, you can wear a special eye-mask. If it's loud - use earplugs.

Meanwhile, focus your attention on how you're going to try to fall asleep without moving your physical body. This isn't mandatory, but it will substantially increase the effectiveness of the indirect techniques.

Now, sleep for 2 to 4 hours, but take advantage of natural awakenings that occur during this period of time. They will happen much more often than usual. After each attempt - whether successful or not - you must fall back asleep with that very same intention of waking up and trying again. In this way, you can make many attempts over the course of a single morning. Up to a quarter of those attempts will be successful, even for novices (70 to 95% of them will be successful for experienced practitioners).

STEP 3: SEPARATE THE INSTANT YOU AWAKEN

Each time you wake up again, try not to move or open your eyes. Instead, immediately try to separate from your body. Up to 50% of success with indirect techniques comes during this simple first step - one that is so simple that people don't even suspect that it could work.

In order to separate from your body, simply try to stand up, roll out, or levitate. Try to do it with your own perceived (i.e. subtle) body, but without moving your physical muscles. Remember that it will feel just like normal physical movement. When the moment comes, don't think too hard about how to do it. During those first moments after awakening, stubbornly try to separate from your body any way that you can and no matter what. Most likely, you'll intuitively know how to do it. The most important thing is not to think too hard and not to lose those first seconds of awakening.

Interesting Fact!

During the second lesson at School of Out-of-Body Travel seminars, participants are asked to explain in their own words how they were able to separate, but without using the words "easily", "simply", or "as usual". They are usually always unable to comply with this request, as separation nearly always occurs for them "easily", "simply" and "as usual" when the moment is right.

STEP 4: CYCLING TECHNIQUES AFTER ATTEMPTS TO SEPARATE

If immediate separation doesn't work out - which would become apparent after 3-5 seconds - start right then and there to alternate between 2 to 3 of the techniques that are most straightforward to you, until one of them works. When this happens, you can try to separate again. Choose 2 to 3 of the following five techniques so that you can alternate through them during awakenings:

Rotation
For 3 to 5 seconds, try to imagine rotating to either side along your head-to-toe axis as vividly as possible. If no sensations arise, switch to another technique. If a real or even slight sensation of rotation arises, focus your attention on this technique and rotate even more energetically. As soon as the sensation of rotating becomes stable and real, you should try to separate again using it as a starting point.

Swimmer technique
For 3 to 5 seconds, try to imagine as decidedly as possible that you are swimming or simply making swimming motions with your arms. Try to feel it no matter what, and as vividly as you can. If nothing happens, switch to another technique. There is no need to switch techniques if the sensation of swimming arises. Instead, intensify the sensations that arise. Afterwards, the real sensation of swimming in water will come to you. That's already the phase - and there's no need for separation when you're already in the phase. However, if such sensations occur while you're in bed instead of a body of water, then you will need to employ a separation technique. Use the swimming sensations as a starting point.

Observing images

Peer into the void before your closed eyes for 3 to 5 seconds. If nothing occurs, switch to another technique. If you see any kind of imagery, peer into it until it becomes realistic. Once it is, separate from the body right then and there, or allow yourself to be pulled into the imagery. When peering at imagery, it's important not to scrutinize details, lest the image wash away. You'll need to look through the picture, which will make it more realistic.

Hand visualization
For 3 to 5 seconds, imagine vividly and decidedly that you are rubbing your hands together close to your eyes. Try no matter what to feel them in front of you, to see them, and even to hear the sound of them rubbing. If nothing happens, switch to another technique. If any of the above sensations start to arise, then keep with the technique and intensify it until it becomes totally realistic. Afterwards you can try to separate from the body, using the sensations arising from the technique as a start-off point.

Phantom wiggling
Try to wiggle your perceived hands or feet for 3 to 5 seconds. Do not move a muscle under any circumstances, and do not imagine the movement itself. For example, try to intensively press down and then up, wiggle to the left and right, and so on. If nothing occurs, switch to another technique. If a slight or sluggish sensation of real movement suddenly arises, then focus your attention on the technique, trying to increase the range of motion as much as you can. Once you can move by at least 4 inches, immediately try to separate from your body starting off from the sensations arising from the technique.

All that you need to do for each attempt is alternate between 2 to 3 techniques for 3 to 5 seconds each. This leads to indirect techniques cycles, where the practitioner alternates one technique after another over the course of a minute in search of the one that works. It is very important to do no less than 4 cycles of 2 to 3 techniques during an attempt. Remember - even if a technique doesn't work immediately, that doesn't mean that it will not work on the very next cycle of techniques, if not just a bit later. That's precisely why it's necessary to stubbornly alternate techniques, performing no less than 4 complete cycles, but all within no longer than a minute.

For example, the entire process may take place as follows: a phaser goes to bed at 11:30pm and sets his alarm for 6:00am; at 6:00 he wakes up to his alarm clock, goes to the bathroom, drinks some water, and recalls the indirect techniques as well as his interesting plan of action for the phase (for example, to look in the mirror and fly to Mars); at 6:05am the phaser goes back to sleep with the clear intention of entering the phase upon each subsequent awakening; at 7:35am (or whenever natural awakening occurs) the phaser awakes unexpectedly and immediately tries to separate from his body then and there; not having separated within 3 to 5 seconds, the phaser begins to try to do rotations, but those also do not work within 3 to 5 seconds; the phaser performs the swimmer technique, but that does not work within 3 to 5 seconds, the phaser does phantom wiggling, but it doesn't work within 3 to 5 seconds, the phaser does rotation again, then the swimmer technique and phantom wiggling for 3 to 5 seconds each; then he once again does rotation, swimming, and phantom wiggling for 3 to 5 seconds each; on the fourth cycle he begins to do rotation and it unexpectedly starts working - the feeling of rotation arises; the phaser keeps with this technique, and spins as hard as he can and separates from his body right then and there using the sensation of rotation: he then runs to the mirror, all the while actively palpating and scrutinizing everything around him from a close distance, which intensifies his sensations; having already looked in the mirror, the practitioner employs the translocation technique and finds himself on Mars, but he is unexpectedly returned to the body; the phaser then immediately tries to leave his body again, but is unable to; he falls back asleep with the clear intention of repeating the attempt upon the next awakening and staying longer on Mars; and so on.

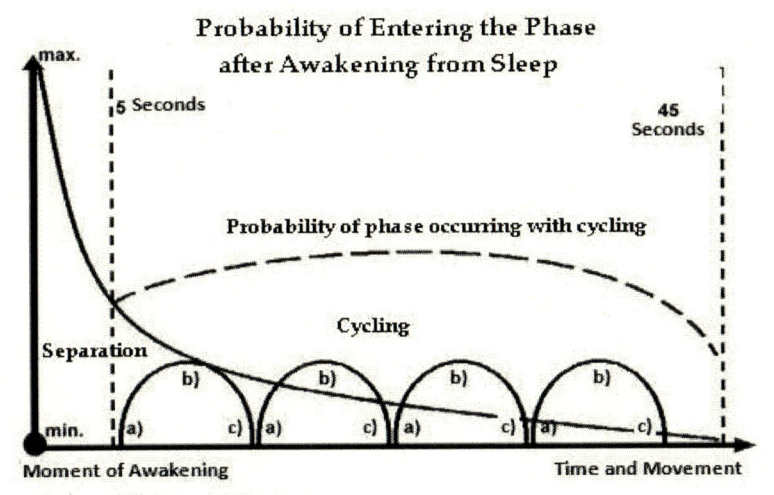

Probability of Entering the Phase after Awakening from Sleep

Cycles of Indirect Techniques:

1 – Attempt separation techniques for the first 5 seconds.
2 – If separation does not immediately occur, indirect techniques must be performed:
   -technique "a"
   -if technique "a" does not work, try technique "b"
   -if technique "b" does not work, try technique "c"
3 – If the technique cycle "a-b-c" yields no results, the cycle should be repeated at least 3 times.
4 – If all 4 cycles yield no results, the practitioner should go back to sleep in order to wake up again later and retry the entire procedure.

Just repeat the above using the techniques that come most naturally to you, and you'll open yourself up to a whole new universe!

If you take 20 to 30 minutes out of your day to simply train the techniques and the procedure, the method will be remembered and work better. This will substantially increase the success of attempts upon awakening.

Dream consciousness is also considered to be a phase experience. If you suddenly realize that you're dreaming while asleep, then that's already the phase. You should therefore proceed to implement your plan of action and stabilize the state. If dream consciousness does arise, it would be a side effect of doing technique cycles upon awakenings. This side effect is quite common - always be ready for it.

STEP 5: AFTER THE ATTEMPT

Fall back asleep if you can after each attempt (whether successful or not) in order to make another attempt to leave your body upon your next awakening. That way you'll not only be able to leave your body in one day, but also to do it several times on the very first day!

> ***Interesting Fact!***
> *At a School of Out-of-Body Travel seminar, a novice was able to leave his body for the first time in his life in 6 of 8 attempts upon awakening the very first morning.*

Even the most unsuccessful attempt should last no longer than a minute. If nothing happens over that period of time, it's much more effective to fall asleep and catch the next awakening, as opposed to stubbornly trying to squeeze results out of the current attempt.

PLAN OF ACTION IN THE PHASE

Before entering the phase, you should clearly outline what you are going to do there immediately after separation. This will increase both the quality of the experience and the likelihood of it occurring. Below is a list of the most interesting (if not the most straightforward) phase activities *for novices* (choose no more than 2 to 3 activities and remember them well):

Look in a mirror (a must for the first phase!)
Eat or drink something you like
Visit any tourist attraction
Fly over the Earth
Fly throughout the Universe
Fly to neighbors, friends, and family
Meet a lover
Meet a deceased relative
Meet any celebrity
Take medicine for treatment
Obtain information from phase objects
Travel to the past or the future
Walk through a wall
Transmutate into an animal
Drive a sports car
Ride a motorcycle
Breathe underwater
Put your hand inside your body
Feel vibrations
Inhabit two bodies at once
Inhabit another person's body
Move and set fire to objects just by looking at them
Drink liquor
Make love and reach orgasm

For your first phase, be sure to set yourself the goal of making it to a mirror and looking at your reflection. You should specifically program yourself to do this activity, as it will substantially facilitate your first steps in conquering the phase. You may then complete other items on your plan of action and never return to the mirror again.

If your sensations in the phase are dull (i.e. poor sight or numbed bodily sensations), try to touch everything around you actively and scrutinize the minute details of objects from up-close. This will allow you to have a more realistic experience. The same activities should be performed in order to maintain the phase when the first symptoms of a return to the body occur (for example, when everything becomes dim).

Returning to the body is something you needn't worry about. The state will not last more than several minutes in any case, especially for novices who are little-acquainted with techniques for maintaining the phase.

DIDN'T WORK?

Set yourself this goal: make 5 to 10 attempts to leave your body upon awakening. This procedure, when followed correctly, is sufficient for 50 to 80 percent of novices to get their first results. Turn back to this section if you run into a problem, as it describes the mistakes encountered in 99% (!) of unsuccessful attempts.

Never try these techniques every day, otherwise the success rate of your attempts will drop drastically! Spend no more than 2 to 3 days of the week on it, preferably only on days off. If you don't have an opportunity to sleep in long and with interruption, then don't forget that cycles of indirect techniques can also be used after any other awakening - in the middle of the night for example, or better yet, during a midday nap. What's most important is to establish the clear intention of trying them before falling asleep.

Despite the simplicity of these techniques, novices stubbornly deviate from the clear instructions, following them in their own way or only half-way. Remember what's most important beforehand: the more carefully and literally you follow the instructions in this book, the better your chances for success. Ninety percent will obtain results within one to three awakenings if they do everything correctly from the beginning.

Interesting Fact!

> At School of Out-of-Body Travel seminars, the main task consists not in explaining the proper procedure, but merely in getting participants to follow it to-the-letter. Even if that goal is only half-way accomplished, success is inevitable.

Typical mistakes when performing indirect techniques include:

- Lack of an attempt to separate
Forgetting to simply try to separate immediately after awakening before cycling techniques, even though this may lead to up to 50% of all experiences. Exception: awakening to movement, after which one may immediately proceed to the techniques.

- Lack of aggression
A desire to get a technique to work no matter what and really get into it is the main criterion for success in employing the indirect technique procedure. Meanwhile, determination should not be superficial, but intensely focused on the actions to be completed. Lack of determination can also manifest itself in passively falling asleep during an attempt.

- Fewer than 4 cycles
No matter what happens and no matter what thoughts occur, you should perform no less than 4 cycles of techniques, assuming none have worked so far. Not following this simple rule will scuttle more than half of your opportunities to enter the phase.

- Unnecessary Change of Technique
Despite the clear instructions given, novices will stubbornly switch techniques after 3 to 5 seconds, even when a technique has started working in one way or another. This is a serious error. If a technique has started working - however so slightly - you need to keep with it and try to intensify it in any way possible.

- Unnecessary Continuation of a Technique

If a technique hasn't begun working in the least after 3 to 5 seconds, it should be changed for another. The point of cycling is to quickly alternate between techniques until one of them starts working.

- Forgetting to Separate

When any technique starts working upon awakening - no matter to what degree - the practitioner is nearly always already in the phase, and is simply lying on his body while in it. That's why you should always try to separate immediately upon there being stable signs that a technique is working. If that doesn't work out, then you need to return to intensifying the technique and try to separate again. If you don't use the first seconds of a technique working, then the phase usually ends quite quickly and the necessary state goes away. Don't lie in your body while in the phase!

- Excessive Analysis

If you analyze what's going on when cycling through techniques upon awakening, then you are not concentrated on the techniques themselves and are sidetracking yourself. This will cause you to miss nearly all chances of obtaining results. The desire to experience the technique working should fully consume you, leaving no place in the mind for analysis or contemplation.

- Excessively Alert Awakening (no Attempt or a Sluggish One

Due to the perception of an excessively alert awakening (which will be not actually be alert, but only seem to be from 70 to 90% of the time) the practitioner will either forgo trying anything, or will make attempts quite unassuredly, which is equivalent to not trying at all. You ought to follow the instructions automatically, and not pay attention to such perceptions upon awakening.

- Attempting for Longer than a Minute
>If no result is obtained after one minute of cycling, then your odds of success will be much greater if you go back to sleep right away and catch the next awakening in order to make a new attempt, as opposed to stubbornly trying to continue on with the techniques.

- Incomplete Separation
>When attempting to separate, sometimes it doesn't come easily or completely. Sluggishness, stuck body parts, and being stuck in two bodies at once are some things that may occur. Never give up under any circumstances and do not stop separating if this happens. Full separation will occur if you counteract such problems with all your strength.

- Not Recognizing the Phase
>Practitioners often enter the phase but then return back to the body because they feel that what occurred is not what they had expected. For example, when observing images they are often pulled into the scenery, or they are spontaneously thrown into another world when rotating. Practitioners often think that they have to experience the feeling of separation itself, which is why they might return back to their bodies in order to obtain it. The same applies to becoming conscious while dreaming, as the practitioner is already in the phase and it only remains to deepen and implement his plan of action.

- Awakening to Movement (no Attempt or a Sluggish One)
>Awakening without moving is desirable, but not mandatory. There's no sense in forgoing most opportunities by waiting for the right awakening. You must take advantage of every awakening that you can.

- Wasting the First Seconds
>Try to develop the habit of immediately and reflexively proceeding to the techniques upon awakening, without losing a second. The more time

that elapses between awakening and the attempt itself, the lower the odds of success. It's best to learn to catch not so much the very second of awakening, but rather the transitional moment when "surfacing" from sleep. Separation is almost always successful during that transitional moment.

- Selection of Same-Type Techniques
There's no point in selecting techniques for your practice that are similar to one another or focused on the same sensation (when using techniques from other parts of this book).

- Use of a Single Technique
Cycling indirect techniques upon awakening is a universal method that can work for anybody provided they alternate several techniques. Completely different methods may work over different attempts. That's why using only a single technique upon awakening instead of cycling through at least two leads to substantially lowered odds of entering the phase.

- False Physical Movement
Sometimes separation is so indistinguishable from ordinary physical movement that novices are unable to believe their own success. They perceive separation as a physical movement and then disappointedly lie back down into their body. In such cases, one ought to carefully evaluate the situation and possibly perform reality checks.

THE FOUR PRINCIPLES OF SUCCESS

Do It No Matter What. When performing phase entrance and separation techniques, put your all into them and concentrate on them as if they were your life's goal and mission. Chomp at the bit to leave your body.

Be Aggressive. Put all of your enthusiasm and desire into the techniques. The desire to get the techniques to work should be coupled with full aggression in achieving that result.

Be Self-Assured. During attempts, be as sure as possible of the results. When making attempts, lack of assuredness in yourself and the results will substantially lower your probability of phase entrance. Nearly all phase entrances are accompanied by self-assured thought like "I'm going to do it now", while unsuccessful attempts involve thinking "I guess I'll try, but I doubt it'll work".

Do it Robotically. Don't think about anything when completing the technique procedure. You already have the instructions. Just carry them out, not matter what things may seem to you or what thoughts enter your mind. Robotically is also understood to mean exactly. The indirect technique procedure has been honed by work with thousands of practitioners all over the world, neglecting any detail isn't worth it.

IT WORKED!

If you were successfully able to employ the indirect techniques and enter the phase at least 3 to 5 times, then you can gradually move on to the advanced textbook in order to flesh out your practice. Now you're a man or woman of the future, and all that remains is to hone your new ability!

PART II: 100 PHASES

Real Experiences to Guide and Motivate

Chapter 1. My First Phase

Our inboxes receive a daily flood of phase entrance testimonials at the OOBE Research Center, School of Out-of-Body Travel seminars around the world, and all of our many-language websites and forums. A small selection of them are featured in this part of the book in order to vividly demonstrate how out-of-body experience occurs in practice. Of course, mere words can hardly convey even a tenth of the emotion people experience. However, they are enough to demonstrate how important and fascinating this can be for absolutely everyone. Thousands of phase experience accounts are also freely available on the "Practitioner Blogs" section of our forums.

We start with first-time novice phase experiences presented in order of entrance method and technique.

SEPARATION IMMEDIATELY UPON AWAKENING

Presented here are testimonials describing first-time phase experiences achieved during the first step in cycling indirect techniques: attempting to separate immediately upon awakening.

Johnny Asmussen
Silkeborg, Denmark

I woke up one morning without moving or opening my eyes, and it was a very good feeling. I then thought to myself that I should do my indirect technique. But instead, I said to myself, "Try to leave your body," and I thought that I would sit up on my bedside. I was lying on my back, but I had not yet moved at all, and so I decided to give it my all and thought, "Just do it!" Almost immediately, I was sitting up on my bedside.

I knew that I hadn't moved at all because I never get out of my bed that fast; it happened in a blink of an eye.

In my enjoyment of total freedom, I forgot my plan of action, and I forgot the most important thing to do next – deepening. While sitting there, I turned my head to look at my body, just to be 120% sure that I was out of my body. Just before, I had looked down at my bed (*M.R.: wrong reality check*). I woke up looking at the ceiling in my "real" body (*M.R.: no re-entering*).

It was short, it was quick, *but it was the phase*. I am hooked for life!

Alexander Dyrenkov
Moscow, Russia

My first entry happened at night. I was lying in bed and thinking about the phase, as I had been unable to fall asleep for a while. I dozed off for a moment and then awoke again, this time already in the proper state, and then easily rolled out (more or less unconsciously and reflexively). I went deeper by means of touching and then falling headfirst. It is a pity that I've already forgotten a lot of the experience, but I do remember that after deepening I fell right down onto the yard of my grandmother's house, but then lost consciousness, and so I returned into my body and rolled out of it several times (*M.R.: no plan of action*). I was unable to sharpen all my senses: When I deepened one sense (touch, for example), another (i.e. sight) would fade away. After that, I have a gap in my memory concerning my travels (consciousness and lucidity were weak, and I fell asleep and "resurfaced" several times), but I remember having been to a lot of places.

Here's how the episode ended: I dove headfirst into water from a high board (after first having deepened a bit), and then my sense of touch grew sharper: I felt "water" and hit my head against a very soft "bottom." I resumed the interrupted fall through willpower, but then it occurred to me that my grandmother wanted to wake me up. My level of awareness was not quite adequate, as it did not occur to me that I was actually sleeping in a dormitory, and not at my grandmother's house. That's why I decided that I needed to return to my body. A sharp fall occurred right after that thought, and was followed by sensations similar to those one experiences when hung-over.

Anthony Pucci

I had just had a slightly disturbing dream. (I can't recall what it was now, but it left me a little shaken.) I woke up, eyes still closed, and completely still. "Well, I'll give it a shot," I thought to myself. I tried to move my arms without using muscles. My right arm rose slightly, and I've had some experiences in the past that helped me remember the tingling sensations present during separation - *holy cow, it's finally working!*

I was still a little doubtful when it came time to get up, but I tried nevertheless and that "electric shock" sort of feeling coursed through me after total separation. "I did it," I said aloud. "I can go see her now." Who *she* is may be explained later if I feel up to it, but for now, I will call her Mia, since she is relevant and that name is easier for me to type. I regained my composure and recalled that I had to deepen, and did so. I felt the walls, the bed posts, and my clothes. I was wearing a very long shirt (down past my waist) and some boxer-briefs, instead of what I had gone to sleep in.

When I finally got my vision to return, everything seemed larger than it should've been, and I felt slightly anxious, sort of like that paranoia you feel after watching a scary movie. Regardless, I pushed through it. I went to my door. "Mia's behind this door," I thought to myself. It didn't lead anywhere unusual, just out into my hall. Again, things were a little larger than they should've been and a few places were covered in a very dim greenish light. I called her name, beckoning, "Mia?" My voice was quiet and shaken. I couldn't seem to regain my composure for some reason. I continued calling her name, and asked, "Where are you?"

I heard her voice in my head responding, "Huh? I'm right here." I went down the hall in a half-panic, checking various places in the house for her. Everywhere I went was extra-large and dimly lit in green. "Where is here?!" I cried. Her voice answered me again, "the usual place." I was getting frustrated now. I wanted to see Mia badly, asking, "Where's the usual place?!" I retraced my steps. Maybe she was behind me.

Unfortunately, that's where my story ends, because I returned to my body soon afterwards. I tried to leave it again, but I couldn't budge. The residual doubt and fear in my mind may have held me back. I know I made a few mistakes in my techniques, namely not being absolutely 100% convinced that my door would lead me to Mia, and not maintaining.

Svyatoslav Baranov
Perm, Russia

I woke up on my side. I didn't feel like sleeping anymore, but I closed my eyes anyway. When I lay down on my back, I immediately felt the sensation that I was about to fall from the couch (I was lying on the edge), and some kind of lapse occurred, as if I was being pulled somewhere. I lay down once again, and this buzzing started, and a green light appeared before my eyes. I lay back even further, and my eyelids started to flutter. I thought that I might fall from the couch at that moment, but then my vision came to me, and I observed that I was already lying on the floor next to the couch! I got up on my feet and noticed that the room was "spinning" as if I were drunk, but everything quite quickly went back to normal. At that very moment, I understood that this was it! The phase itself (*M.R.: no deepening*)!

In ecstasy, I forgot about all the techniques and went to look about the room (*M.R.: no plan of action*). Everything was just like in reality, but some things were out of place. I tried to levitate and bent backwards, and was somehow thrust outside. It was dusk out there, and there was a lot of snow on the ground. I went around the house and tried to levitate. I was able to soar upwards, and saw the horizon and sunset. But then I began to lose altitude. After having flown to the window on the other side of the house, I wanted to go up to the roof, but then a foul occurred (*M.R.: no maintaining*). In a fraction of a second, I had the sensation that I was "nowhere". But then, my real eyes opened (with difficulty) and there was once again the feeling of some sort of lapse (*M.R.: no re-entering*). Awareness was dim during the phase, apparently due to not having gotten enough sleep.

EMPLOYING THE INDIRECT TECHNIQUES

If separating upon awakening is unsuccessful or for some reason no such attempt is even made, then quick alternation through techniques is employed. Separation may be attempted once one of the alternated techniques starts working.

Dodd Stolworthy
Ventura, USA

I went to bed at 10 PM. I woke at 5:30, used the bathroom, and went back to bed. It took me a while to fall asleep. Once I did, I woke up a couple of times and changed positions each time. I felt vibrations come on and heard people talking as they came in my house. I also heard little footsteps near my bed and thought it might be one of my kids. Luckily, I remembered that this type of phenomenon happens when entering the phase (*M.R.: no separation*). I stayed still and strained the brain to increase the vibrations. This worked really well (*M.R.: no separation*). I then used phantom wiggling and got my left arm out. At this point I tried to separate by rolling out, but with no success. I then got my right arm out, but I thought I had actually moved my real arm. I was worried I had blown the whole thing, but decided to continue anyways. I tried to see both arms in front of me. They quickly appeared and I saw them through closed eyes! I started swinging my arms from side to side and rolled out of my body.

I was now on the floor next to my bed. I was so excited. I had just done what I had been reading about for 10 months! I remembered to stabilize the experience by rubbing my hands together. As I was doing this, I looked down and noticed my hands looked fat and swollen. I then saw my wife leave the bedroom and go downstairs (*M.R.: no plan of action*). I followed her and noticed the sun shining in through the windows. It was still dark in real life. My wife then went back upstairs, so I decided to go outside. I started for the front door but decided to fly through the window. I landed in the street and walked around for a bit. I started to go up to my neighbor's house, but noticed that everything was fading (*M.R.: no maintaining*). I had lost the experience and was now back in bed. I quickly spun around (in my mind) and noticed myself right back in the same spot I had left! I walked up to my neighbor's door, rang the doorbell, and waited for her to come. I then lost it again and tried spinning, but it did not work.

Maxim Shvets,
Moscow, Russia

I went to bed with the intention of entering the phase while dreaming or upon awakening in the morning. I woke up at about 6:30 am, and decided to try the method of visualization, as phantom wiggling had not worked over the past 2 days (*M.R.: no separation*). Vague images gradually created a scene in front of me, which I then found myself participating in. I felt myself separating from my body, and rolled out of it. I opened my eyes. Some guy grabbed me by the shoulder and said, "You've left your body, be cool." I told him that I was ready. He turned me around, and I saw my body...

My body was lying on its back with open eyes, even though I had started visualizing while lying on my stomach. Not assigning any particular significance to this, I decided to deepen right away. I squatted down and began to quickly palpate the floor and the walls with the palms of my hands. I then looked at my index finger, and could discern the lines in the skin. Figuring that this was all wonderful, I went to the kitchen in order to fly (*M.R.: no plan of action*). However, I remembered that it was best for novices not to attempt this. I returned to my bedroom door and pictured there being a sunny beach behind it. I opened the door and immediately woke up lying on my back (*M.R.: no maintaining and no re-entering*)...

Alan
Plymouth, UK

I woke up (*M.R.: no separation*) and immediately applied phantom wiggling on my left arm for five seconds, and my arm began moving freely (*M.R.: no separation*). I could at this point have had an OBE, but I wanted a lucid dream (*M.R.: wrong logic*). After five seconds of phantom wiggling I switched to five seconds of listening in (*M.R.: wrong action*). After about two seconds of listening in to the high pitched natural sound inside my head, it started to increase in volume (*M.R.: no separation*). After five seconds I still hadn't entered a dream, and so I switched to five seconds of observing Images. I didn't see anything, so I switched to straining the brain. Immediately the high pitched sound in my head became very loud, and so I immediately switched to listening in again (*M.R.: no separation*). I saw a purple pool of water and felt that its clarity was very good. Then, I found myself fully immersed in a lucid dream.

I was in a deep, beautiful valley with lambs frolicking about. I looked around and marveled at the ability to be able to have a lucid dream in a matter of seconds (*M.R.: no deepening*). I enjoyed my lucid dream...

Artem Arakcheev
Moscow, Russia

I did indirect techniques. While peering at images, I caught sight of the same dream episode that I had been watching until I first woke up. The picture was very realistic. It seemed to me that I could change everything in this dream. I tried to get out of my body, and immediately flew through my head right into that dream. I landed at the door of the home that I grew up in. I then found myself at a window on the second floor.

Having remembered about the deepening techniques, I quickly began to scrutinize the window itself. My attention then shifted, and I peered out through the window. Everything was in its place, like in real life. Some man approached the door. I don't know why, but I was sure that I needed to watch what he was up to. I instinctively took off from the second floor window, going right through the glass. I lowered to the level of the ground floor. The man walked in through the front door. I followed him, flew in through the door, and began to pursue him.

I then remembered that I had a plan for the phase. At precisely that moment, the phase space began to fade and disappear. I realized that I should apply the maintaining techniques, but did not manage to do so in time. Within a moment, I woke up to myself lying in bed. My body temperature went up. My breathing and heartbeat became more frequent. A second attempt to separate was of no use.

Wagner
Porto Alegre, Brasil

I was awoken by my cat and ended up accidentally employing the deferred method since I had slept some hours before this OBE. Then I did forced falling asleep, then cycled rotation, observing images, listening in, phantom wiggling etc. I can't remember which one led to vibrations. I amplified the vibrations once I felt them (they were an unknown sensation to me until then), but I couldn't remember what I was supposed to do then: to wait for sleep paralysis or try to separate. Then I decided to do just anything and tried to separate by floating upwards, as if me and my body had the same magnetic charge and would repel each other, because I've ruined some attempts before by trying to roll out and moving my actual body.

It worked, to a point. I felt as if I was floating about one foot high. Meanwhile, my plan was to separate, turn around, see my body and think, "Wow, man!" Then I would start rubbing my hands, palpating, peering and do a list of things while maintaining. But instead, I floated without seeing anything, I just felt the "thrust" pushing me up, which took about half a second or less and without sight. I simply "was" in a place that I hadn't consciously chosen, and I kind of forgot that I could make decisions at that point and started watching things passively. Earlier I had remembered all the techniques that I should employ, but at the moment it slipped my mind.

I went to a place where somehow I knew only musicians went to in order to find other musicians and play along with them. It had a great positive "vibe" to it, I the heard voices of people talking around. There was a female voice, and this girl walked from right to left behind me but somehow I "saw" her All Star shoes. She was commenting about what a cool and friendly place it was. There was a guy with a black trench coat and a shaved head playing something between a piston and a trombone - it was deep dark blue, and he played it with one hand and a guitar with the other, producing awesome music. The piston's keys were actually chromed Fender-type "elephant ear" bass tuners. He didn't put his mouth on the thing at any moment and played it pointing it towards his foot the whole time. The guitar was suspended out in front of him by a strap on his left side with its neck pointing upwards. It sometimes sounded like a piano. There were no amplifiers, pedals or cables at all.

When I felt he was about to finish his music, I wanted to applaud him and tell him that it was awesome, but he disappeared to I don't know where. This was strange because it was as if the music was still sounding, and I wouldn't dare open my mouth while he was still playing. It was beautiful.

Then, a man about 60 years old who was dressed somewhat like a sailor (at least that was what I thought) approached another guy who was playing some unknown instrument, resting the thing on his left shoulder like a violin. I think it was not an actual instrument, but rather something like a sewing machine or something oneiric in nature like that. The sailor stopped by the side of the sewing machine man and from inside of a worn out black, cheap looking plastic bag for which most people wouldn't give a penny, neither would I, pulled a barbed edged transparent acrylic plate which looked as if it was just sawn off of a jigsaw, as if it was a randomly cut plate which had fallen off while the actual piece, whatever it could be, was being made. The plate was about 1 foot by 1 foot 4 inches and was not exactly rectangular. I'd never suppose that thing would play music.

Actually, when he played perfectly accompanying the sewing machine guy, I asked myself, "what will he be playing with..." I lurched forward and opened my mouth in complete surprise: It was a Flexing Instrument. I had never thought of this obvious concept before, and probably wouldn't have without that experience. Everybody knows the bass, "pook" or "wok" sound that an X-Ray plate or some large plate like that - even made of different materials - makes when flexed, and most people know the high pitched, "kweek" sound of tiny steel lids about 2 inches in diameter that come in small cans of several types - the noise they make when folded in and out. Well, when the sailor held the plate with the tips of his fingers near the edges of the plate, the folding area was wider, and so the sound was bassier. When he held it with his fingertips close to the center, the folding area was smaller and so the sound was higher pitched. He could get his hands closer or farther as fast as choosing notes on any other instrument, and could play along with every note of the sewing machine man. It was impressive. I don't remember how this phase ended (*M.R.: no maintaining*).

HINTS FROM THE MIND

During some awakenings, the mind sends hints in the form of various sensations that can be easily used to enter the phase. You need only intensify those sensations and separate from the body. Such hints usually consist of images, sleep stupors, vibrations, noise, dream figments and real or false numbness.

Ivan Yakovlev
Antwerp, Belgium

I don't know what woke me up, but I knew right away that something was out of order. I could not open my eyes, and my body was almost just asking to rise up. I understood what was going on – all of this indicated that I was having an out-of-body experience. The first thing I tried was to lift my left hand up, and it worked. I understood that this was an astral hand, because I could see through it. I moved hastily and carefully to the other side of the bed (There was a strange sensation in my head at that time). I calmed down and tried to do something again. I levitated about half a meter above the bed. Vision came back to me right then and I saw what appeared to be my room, but not exactly it, as the rug on the floor was of a different color pattern and the door was closed for some reason (*M.R.: no deepening and no plan of action*).

I could not comprehend why everything was lit from behind my back. Then, I looked over my left shoulder and saw a small bright white ball behind my shoulder blade at a distance of 8 inches. It was lighting up the room up. Then I tried to go through the door, but was unable to (*M.R.: no maintaining*). Out of the fear that I would never return to my real body (*M.R.: wrong logic*), I woke up in the everyday world (*M.R.: no re-entering*).

Natalya Kozhenova
Shchelkovo, Russia

When I was about 17 or 18 years old, I read some esoteric articles on astral projection. They seemed quite interesting to me, but no more than a curiosity – I did not particularly believe in such things.

One evening, I went to bed as usual. I woke up in the middle of the night, but was unable to move my body and there was a loud noise in my head. Having been reminded of those articles, I simply tried to levitate and I managed to do so, as if through my forehead somehow. The sensation of flying was very realistic, to my great surprise. The first thought that occurred to me was, "Wow, these astral guys weren't lying!" I hovered above my body for some time in the dark. I thought of vision, and it started to appear. I then flew towards the window, and upon turning around in to face my body (*M.R.: no deepening and no plan of action*), I saw it in its proper place. I decided to fly back to it and touch it. When I finally poked it, it sucked my back into it, causing a quite strange sensation (*M.R.: no maintaining and no re-entering*).

Alexander Furmenkov
Saint Petersburg, Russia

I woke up at early in the night after some difficulties with falling asleep. Blurred images started to float before my eyes and I realized that I could enter the phase. I started to discard unnecessary images, and after getting ahold of one of them, I emerged in some kind of a yellow corridor. The level of general realness and awareness of the experience was about 80% to 90% of that of reality. I remembered about the methods for deepening, which is why I started to look at everything going on around me, but this did not yield any serious results. I started to touch myself, but all sensation seemed somewhat dampened. I realized that I was losing awareness. I came round, but nevertheless fell asleep in about 20 seconds (*M.R.: no plan of action and no maintaining*).

BECOMING CONSCIOUS WHILE DREAMING

If you become aware that everything around you is but a dream while you are in one, then everything from that moment on is already the phase. All that remains is to make it a full phase experience by enhancing your sensations and carrying out your plan of action.

Evaldas
Lithuania

I was sitting on a bench, just thinking and doing nothing, when suddenly a woman showed up and said to me, "Maybe you are dreaming". I was in shock. It struck me like lightning: "Oh my God! I am in the phase!"

A plan, a plan, I had a plan. What should I do next? Since I'd just finished reading Michael's book, I knew all about deepening and maintaining, and so I touched everything around me, looked closely at my hands and rubbed them. My vision and other senses got stronger and so I moved on to my plan.

I wanted to try flying, walking, teleporting, diving into the ground and jumping through walls. First of all, I tried flying. I jumped up as high as I could and then floated down. I jumped again and started flying. I felt the wind and the sun. I could see far into the distance. When my vision got blurry, I decided to teleport into my room and do some maintaining and deepening.

In my room I found that same woman, and she told me: "try going through walls". I touched the wall and was a little bit afraid. After forgetting my fear I started running towards another wall and jumped through it. The feeling was amazing. The woman advised me again: "Try diving into the ground, but don't forget to imagine where you want to end up". I walked into the middle of my room and started falling down. I closed my eyes and imagined a beautiful rice field. It felt like

I was falling forever, and then - BOOM! I was falling down from a very far height. I was falling towards a huge table full of delicious dishes which had rice as the main ingredient. I started laughing and thought: "Wow, my subconscious played a hell of a joke on me". That's when I woke up (*M.R.: no maintaining and no re-entering*).

Ssergiu
Reşiţa, Romania

I don't think that I needed to realize that I was dreaming because as soon as I fell asleep, I became lucid. I couldn't see anything but the screen of an iPhone and I knew I had to choose the place I wanted to be in. I chose a weird place that I had never seen before and then I saw a white door. I opened the door, wondering where it would bring me to (*M.R.: no deepening and no plan of action*). I got in a weird room and there were a lot of skeletons on the floor, so I freaked out and then teleported somewhere else.

I remembered having been in many other places when I woke up next to my bed. I wasn't sure what had actually happened, I thought it was still a lucid dream.

I was next to my bed and could see almost everything in my room, even the turned-out TV - but I couldn't bring myself to look in my bed's direction. I didn't want to do that at all.

After a while, I started to feel my breath. I was scared because I was breathing too slowly and I thought I was going to die if I didn't start breathing faster (*M.R.: wrong logic*).

I wanted to wake up, but each time I tried I got back in my body but only for a second (in SP) and then again next to my bed. I had tried to wake up about 7 times before I finally woke up (*M.R.: wrong action*). I was scared but also amazed of what had happened to me. However, I could consider myself "lucky" because I had experienced sleep paralysis before and I knew how to get out of it.

After the experience I didn't even bother trying lucid dreaming again, I got all interested in OOBEs.

Roman
Rostov-on-Don, Russia

My first time entering the phase. I dreamt that I was hurrying somewhere, and constantly thinking about something. At a certain wonderful moment, I hit upon the idea that I was dreaming, and decided to try to exit (*M.R.: wrong action and no deepening*). I lay on the ground and began to exit, imagining how I was separating from the body. During the transition, I nearly was thrown out of the phase due to tension and fear. I was nonetheless successful. I saw myself at a doorway after having crawled through a wall. It was like coming out of a bog. The sensation of separating was very vivid.

I suddenly noticed a person there. He helped me to get completely out (*M.R.: no plan of action*). He introduced himself, and started telling me some particulars about the world that I had landed in (I don't recall well what he said, as I was looking around the whole time and couldn't tear my eyes off my surroundings - I was spellbound). In the end, I became worried about my body, and decided that it was time to return back (*M.R.: wrong logic*). Returning was like a nightmare. There were voices, sounds, and strange sensations. I had the feeling that time had stood still... I was so happy upon waking up that I couldn't sleep for the rest of the night.

Josh
Australia

One night I was dreaming of travelling in a car with a friend and thought she was driving way too fast and then I got bizarre rushing sensations that enveloped my entire physical body and it felt like I was being turned inside out.

The sensations stopped, and then I was fully awake and completely aware and I opened my eyes. I was in my bedroom lying on my back and my body had a blue hue or tint to it (*M.R.: no separation and deepening*). I felt my arms moving around and I realized what had happened and

panicked. I asked to go back to my body and then with a slight tingling I opened my eyes for real (*M.R.: wrong action*) and I was actually lying on my side facing my partner.
Then I knew the experience was real.

Alexei Bakharev
Sochi, Russia

This was the first time that I managed to become conscious while dreaming. Before falling asleep, I concentrated on the darkness before my eyes and tried to remain consciousness as long as I could. All of a sudden, I dreamt that I was levitating to the ceiling, which resulted in my becoming conscious that I was dreaming. My phantom body responded poorly to attempts to control it, and simply hovered beneath the ceiling (*M.R.: no deepening*). There were two people sitting on the floor below. They were looking in my direction, but it seemed that they did not see me (*M.R.: no plan of action and maintaining*). At this point I woke up and felt some sort of tingling and itching in my legs (*M.R.: no re-entering*).

DIRECT EXIT FROM THE BODY WITHOUT PRIOR SLEEP

Direct entrance into the phase without prior sleep (or after a period of full awareness) is achieved by bringing about shallow dips out of conscious awareness. All that remains is to separate from the body on the way back up from such a dip.

Phil B.
New York, USA

I woke up at 6 AM today, went to the bathroom, and then lay back down immediately to try to sleep. I usually have difficulty falling asleep, so this time, for the first time, I put in earplugs and wore a facemask. After about an hour, I was still quite awake and running through ideas for my class in my head.

After an hour I wasn't falling asleep yet, but I was very relaxed physically, and so I tried forced falling asleep. After about 10-15 seconds, I felt a strange dislocation and numbness settle over my body (*M.R.: no separation*), which felt unusual. I immediately tried listening in, and heard a very loud ringing sound, like fire alarms going off. I listened to it and it got louder and then seemed to peak. It was very loud (*M.R.: no separation*), but nothing else was happening and so I switched to observing images for a few seconds. Still nothing. The ringing got even quieter, and so I went back to listening in. It got louder again, and again it seemed to peak.

Then, I realized that it was so loud that I was probably already in the phase but didn't realize it. I tried rolling over with a sudden jerk, and BAM! I was out of bed, standing on the floor! I can't describe how unexpected this was: I had no idea what rolling out would feel like, and it turned out to be kind of like climbing out of a pool, about that much resistance. Michael's advice to not worry and just DO IT was right on the money.

I was very excited, but I remembered the SOBT advice to immediately deepen. Everything was grey and I felt nothing, heard nothing, saw only grey silhouettes around me. I started rubbing my hands together firmly in front of my face and they slowly came into view, along with everything else in my room. I started peering at my hands and fingers, and my vision became crystal clear. My room came into perfect lifelike focus. I walked around my room peering and palpating everything I could find. Since it was my first time in the phase, I examined all the random objects lying around on my shelves and table and they all appeared perfectly real, even the writing on them (I didn't stop to try to read the individual words because I didn't want a foul). I continuously reminded myself that I was phasing, so as not to lose consciousness and fall asleep (*M.R.: no plan of action*).

www.obe4u.com

After spending about a minute looking at everything and being amazed by the simulacrum of reality, I decided to try to do something with the experience. I didn't have any plans beforehand because I was not really expecting success, but I decided on the spur of the moment to try flying. I looked up at my ceiling, then down at my feet, took a deep breath and tried to levitate while looking at my feet. They slowly rose a few inches off the floor, and as I exhaled they went back down. Perfectly controlled, as I expected. I tried again, with another deep breath and this time a jump, and I launched myself through my ceiling like superman, fists extended. I didn't want to pass through my ceiling insubstantially, I wanted to blast out, and I did, through about 10 floors of brick and plaster which exploded in front of me like a multistory pratfall in reverse.

Then I was out, above my house. I was not in my neighborhood, but in some kind of huge cave that housed an entire city. I didn't recognize anything and didn't have any plans of where to go, so I just flew around a little bit and eventually zoomed in on a window where some "friend" of mine (I don't know who it was, they were just labeled "friend" in my dream consciousness") was watching a movie on television. At this point, since I didn't have anything to do, and I was just hovering outside the window with a pause in my actions, I fouled and woke up in bed.

I hadn't moved and I wanted to immediately try to enter the phase again, but I was just too excited and I felt my physical body very clearly. I decided to get up and record my experience, and when I stood up it confirmed that I was completely awake and not the least groggy or relaxed since I was able to turn on my computer and write clearly and lucidly right away.

Anna
Barnaul, Russia

I was in my bed imagining that I was leaving my body and soon I felt that I was pulled by someone out of my body.

I decided not to resist it though the vibrations were strong and frightened me a little. And in less than no time I found myself standing on the floor out of my body. The room was luminous with sunlight. I felt free and extremely happy, as if I got rid of something unnecessary which always troubled me.

My new body had no legs but there was no need in them (*M.R.: no deepening*). And I had thought that it was necessary to bring something from the other room as the fact confirming that I was in Astral (*M.R.: wrong logic and no plan of action*). I flounced out of the room, seized a bag and brought it to my bedroom. (In the morning the bag was in its former place again).

Then I watched something strange: my new bed and room existed simultaneously with my old bed and room. Everything had mixed up and I hastened to return to my body. I saw my body lying in my bed and became suddenly very upset. I thought: "How such a young soul can return to such an "old" body?". Then, I felt a pity to myself and I tried to join my body (*M.R.: wrong action*), but did not manage it. Fear overwhelmed me.

At once I recollected, that I had read somewhere that one should make a turnabout to join his body. I did so and soon found myself in my physical body.

John Merritt
Houston, USA

A friend of mine found *A Practical Guidebook* on the net and sent me the link. I read the book, and soon it finally happened.

I went to sleep around 10 or 11 and woke up at 4. I stayed up for 30 minutes and lay back down. I started meditating, and then going over the techniques and separation in my mind. I fell into a free floating state, going in and out of consciousness. I started observing images. And soon vibrations started. I had already experienced vibrations once or twice. The first time I felt them I was scared and they went away after a few seconds. The second time I tried to intensify them and it seemed to work for a few seconds, but then again nothing. This time I used straining the brain and the vibrations got stronger and stronger. And this time I didn't lose them. They intensified and came to a crescendo, and when they were over, I felt different. My next thought was I was already separated from my body. All I had to do was just stand up! And I was right.

I rose up out of my body and sat up and stepped off the bed and I was out! I hadn't really planned what I would do (*M.R.: no deepening and no plan of action*). The room was dark, and my first thought was to turn on a light. I was in my bedroom so I walked into the bathroom in my bedroom and flipped the light switch on. Nothing. I vaguely thought to myself, "maybe the light is burned out", so I walked out into the hallway and into the other upstairs bathroom and turned on that light switch. Again nothing. But I remembered then from reading lucid dreaming books that light switches don't work in dreams. And since I was in my astral body turning on the light switch wasn't going to work either.

I decided to go back to my bed and look at myself. I ran into the room saw my bed and literally jumped up on the footboard and looked. And there I was. Or there my body was. And it was the most incredible feeling I'd ever experienced in my life. I was outside my body and I knew it. I was wide awake, fully conscious, with all my essence, memories, all of me. But there it was asleep on the bed. My physical body. I even saw one of my arms jerk a little. After that I felt the need to verify what had just happened, and see if I could remember it. Soon I was back in my body and wide awake (*M.R.: no re-entering*). And it was true. It had really happened. At last I had done it. And it was real. And I remembered every second of it.

Artem Mingazov
Ulyanovsk, Russia

I lay on the couch and tried to directly exit. Everything was going along well when my consciousness suddenly "checked out" for a moment. When I returned, I realized that I was lying on the bed and felt a phantom body. I tried rolling out to the side, which worked, albeit with some difficulty.

Here I began to palpate the bed and myself (I did everything a bit hurriedly). I couldn't see yet. I decided that I could deepen and I dove head-first into the floor (that is, more exactly, into the void). I flew down a little bit, and found myself in my neighbor's apartment below. I then flew back up to my own apartment and stood on the floor. Trying to restore vision, I opened my eyes. It felt like trying to open the eyes after a long period of sleep deprivation, my eyelids were heavy and yielded grudgingly. I looked around: I was standing in my room, it was sunny outside. I decided to try to fly (well, I love flying) (*M.R.: no plan of action*). I was able to fly up to the ceiling, but immediately began to gently fall back down, being pulled backwards. Upon touching down on the floor, I bounced back up. This was comparable to when a balloon falls and hits the floor, springs back up, falls again, and then bounces up again. I was only able to remain standing on the floor after repeating this process several times.

Suddenly it became difficult to breathe, and I tried to go back to my body (*M.R.: wrong action*), but was somehow unable to. At first panic arouse, but then I realized that giving in to the fear would do me no good, and that I would have to stick it out. But as soon as I calmed down and relaxed (*M.R.: no maintaining*), I had a foul (*M.R.: no re-entering*). All of the above sensations lasted for about a minute.

Matthias Holzer
Vienna, Austria

March 13th, 2001 - This was my first OBE. There were two experiences with the "vibrational state" before, but I didn't have the guts to go through with it since at the time I believed the essential soul would leave the body, which could be dangerous. Nevertheless, this time I decided to do it for real. I was 20 years old at the time. I awoke at five o'clock in the morning, but felt very tired and knew that I'd fall asleep again as soon as I lie down. As soon as I relaxed the vibrational state set in, my body felt paralyzed like it was asleep and I heard the roaring noise I already knew. The state seemed to be not very deep because as soon as I tried to move, I moved the physical body and awoke.

However I immediately started a second attempt, which worked. I waited a bit longer this time, suddenly my "body perception" changed and then I just carefully moved like I would get up in my physical body. The next moment I was standing up and knew I was out of body. I couldn't see very well, only a bit (*M.R.: no deepening and no plan of action*). I was curious if the "silver cord" I had read about really existed (*M.R.: wrong logic*). I felt for it and true enough, there it was, extending out of my astral back. I tried to look at my physical body on the bed, but I couldn't see it. Then I tried to look at myself, my astral body, and could see my left hand shimmering in a light purple color. At this point I decided to end the experience and got back into the bed in order to reenter my physical body (*M.R.: wrong action*). This didn't work at first, but there was no fear, my consciousness faded into a dream and I awoke about an hour later well rested and very satisfied.

Oleg Kudrin
Moscow, Russia

I woke up. It was still dark, I answered "nature's call", and I looked at my watch: 4:15 am. I got into bed and lay on my left side, closed my eyes, and... It felt like something was shining into my eyes. I realized that that was impossible: it was 4:15 am, and I was the only one awake. There was no-one else in the room besides my wife. Meanwhile, the light steadily intensified. I experienced some slight fear, mixed together with curiosity - what would happen next? And then the light became brighter and brighter, I felt I was in danger (*M.R.: no separation*). But at the same time, an instinct to investigate took the upper hand. I knew that something unusual was happening, but knew that all this was impossible - a bright light of an unknown nature piercing my eyes through closed eyelids! Then, the idea occurred on its own that they were coming to check on me. And after that - I'LL GO ALL THE WAY!

The next moment, I found myself in a small, rectangular room with subdued light. There were ledges along the wall that you could sit on (I figured they were benches). One wall had round portholes of about three feet wide. I looked through them and realized that I was in deep outer-space (*M.R.: no deepening and no plan of action*). There was an impressive construction outside the room that I was in. What I saw there could not exist in even the most fantastic environments on Earth. It was a lattice construction, but the elements had no logical structure and gave the appearance of a beehive. It seemed to be a dual tube construction of such colossal proportions that the diameter of only one of those tubes could be compared to the diameter of a stadium. Bustling and scurrying around the structure were small spacecraft, which appeared to be doing some kind of work.

"It's a docking portal" - sounded the answer in my head. I turned around, and in the far corner of the room sat a beautiful young woman dressed completely in Earthling fashion, wearing a skirt and jacket. Strange as it may be, she looked like a famous pop singer, although the similarity was incomplete. This woman was much more interesting than that artist.

I shall formulate the one question dogging me at the time as follows: "What is the emptiness that the Buddhist masters speak of?" I framed that question to the good-looking person in the room with me. For some reason, I didn't come up with the idea of doing something else... Besides, I'm married. But my question was heard, and the answer followed ...

What I then experienced has no parallels in everyday life. Moreover, those feelings cannot be expressed in words - human language simply lacks the ability to communicate such concepts, but I'll try. It was as if I were turned inside-out. Everything outside of me turned out to be inside of me, including the starts, galaxies, and other worlds - in short, the entire material Universe. And this ALL was collapsed to such small proportions that it all could have fit into the eye of a needle. And I, being outside this material universe, was looking at it simultaneously from all sides, even though I do not have hundreds of millions of eyes. I was one large field encompassing the space around this compressed universe, and able to take it all in at once visually! I myself was endless, I had no boundaries in space or time. All around was stillness, and I myself was this stillness. Contemplating this universe brought the realization that through effort, I could turn into NOTHINGNESS. Next thought - but then there would be nothing to do the contemplating?

Then, I became like a funnel collecting in from the perimeters of my universe, whirling inside it, pulling all in deeper and deeper, until I lay on the bed as I had been after having "answered nature's call" (*M.R.: no re-entering*). This vision moved me so much that I already couldn't sleep, I just wanted to run outside and jump for joy and delight. I wanted to tell everyone about my experience, and simply share it - but I realized I would be taken for a schizophrenic.

And that's more or less how I lived from that point on, often recalling that vivid experience, and treasuring it in the depths of my soul. I dreamt nearly every day about having a similar experience again - until I discovered the indirect techniques.

Roman Reutov
Samara, Russia

Truly, the most interesting things almost always happen unexpectedly.

After a sufficiently long break in my attempts to go to the other world, tonight I decided to try it again. I threw in the towel after yet another unsuccessful attempt, rolled to my other side, and decided to simply get a good night's sleep. I do not know exactly how much time passed while I lay down and thought about what I was still doing wrong while observing interesting images that my imagination was drawing. But at one fine moment, I suddenly felt the phenomenon that is commonly referred to as vibrations. I started to intensify them (I should add that the feeling is indescribable), but I could not levitate, though I really wanted to take a look at myself from the outside. I decided to simply stand up, and that's when it all became most interesting! The entire process of transitioning from a horizontal position to a vertical one was accompanied by increasingly palpable vibrations and a louder and louder roaring sound in my head. The sensation was the same as that experienced after going to bed after not having slept for 24 hours and then being suddenly roused by somebody: my head spun, everything started crackling inside of it, and I was about to lose consciousness. Then, a flickering picture started to appear. It stabilized after one or two seconds, the roaring in my head died down, and I realized that I was sitting on my bed.

    I was in my apartment, thought it was noticeably altered. My room seemed more or less the same, though the interior was indeed different upon detailed examination (*M.R.: no deepening*). For example, my mobile phone, which is always within a reach, was somehow an older and different model. It turned out to be the first object that I tested, as I suddenly wanted very much to find out what time it was and check which day of the month it was (*M.R.: no plan of action*). I distinctly felt the phone in my hand, but upon attempting to concentrate on and look at the display, I was thrown back into the reality.

    I immediately climbed back out of my body and decided to simply pace around the apartment while trying to remember what I could experiment on. I tried to conjure an object, but that didn't work and resulted in some mental activity. This caused the phase to fade and my being thrown back into reality. In total, there were about five successive entries into the phase that lasted for 2 to 3 minutes each. The experiences were not stable at all, which is why I was examining my surroundings in a hurry, always trying to get ahold of anything I could get my hand on. However, there were a good amount of impressions, considering that it was my first entry.

SPONTANEOUS EXPERIENCES

Sometimes a person does nothing to reach the phase or even knows nothing about it - but it nonetheless occurs spontaneously for him. This usually happens during relaxation, slumber, awakening, a dream episode, or the like. Analysis of mistakes in these accounts has been kept to a minimum in consideration of the fact that their authors lacked prior knowledge regarding the phase.

Jaime Munoz Lundquist
Orange County, USA

My first out-of-body experience was very dramatic. I fell asleep around 4-5am. I experienced a sensation all over my body, I was in a meditative state of sleep, but at the same time I was aware of what was going on with me. I had this feeling of a tingling sensation all over my body followed by paralysis.

Suddenly I found myself levitating from the bed and wound up in a standing position. I got very scared and started praying, asking the lord to protect me. Then I got back into my body, quick like a flash. When I woke up I had this feeling like I needed to understand what just happened to me. I did some research and I was told that you can travel places, and go to the moon so I couldn't wait to try again. That day, I was feeling so good with myself, I felt I have discovered something new and exciting!

Oksana Ryabova
Moscow, Russia

I seemed to me that my deep morning slumber had been interrupted by the discomfort and mild pain of numbness in my left arm, which my head had been lying on while I slept. The desire arose within me to get rid of that discomfort. I moved my numb arm in front of me and opened my eyes. But I couldn't see the physical arm in front of me, even though I clearly felt it there and could curl and uncurl my five fingers and bend the arm at the elbow. This all made me somewhat confused. I clearly understood that something like this could not happen in the normal physical world. I decided that this was a very realistic dream, and that in order to wake up, I would simply need to close my eyes and strain my brain with the desire to awaken. That thought was followed by action. I opened my eyes shortly thereafter, thinking that I had finally woken up.

Before me was the daily reality that I always observe upon awakening: a large window through which sunlight pours onto my bed in the center of the room, a desk and chair, a bookcase of academic literature, and a wardrobe with clothing in it. Just like always. I decided to spend this weekday-off (I had a lot of days off that week) getting calm, easy rest.

I sat up Indian-style in bed with my elbows on my knees. I squinted, enjoying the rays of May sun massaging my face. It was warm, and the air was fresh. And I felt a sense of peace pour through my body like a sort of unearthly sweet nectar. I turned to look around. And suddenly, that state of relaxation abruptly changed into cold and shivering, the sense of peace transformed into terrible fear - my body was lying behind me! Panic. I glanced at those hands in front of me that I could feel but not see. They were lying peacefully on the bed alongside my body. I touched them and felt their velvety skin, yet not feeling the sensation with my physical hands. I tried to return to my body. I lay down into it, closed my eyes, straining in an attempt to wake up. I opened my eyes and got up, but the body was still lying there. Fear, otherworldly mortal fear. Tears. Perplexity. Incomprehension.

www.obe4u.com

The question, "what next?" And all around me was that bright and sunny day.

I became more and more afraid. The desire to leave that state grew exponentially. All of my attempts to return to my body brought no result. Frightened and scared, I sat on the bed like a figurine. Suddenly, out of the silence, I heard steps in the room. But I couldn't see anybody. The fear grew worse and worse. I began to scream at that invisible man wandering in my room, bidding him to stay away from me. I then asked the question, "Who is he and what does he want here, and why can't I see him?" I got an answer: "Don't be afraid, this is all normal". He appeared a moment later, standing beside my bed. He was about 6 feet tall and a little over 30 years old, with a stocky muscular physique. His hair was dirty-blond and cut short, his eyes were gray-blue. He was wearing only a black bathing suit. Around his neck was a thick gold chain. He began to explain something to me about a certain city, calling it a transfer point. Then he said that many go through such a state and that it was a normal thing. He took my hand and said, "let's go." A moment later, we found ourselves on some sort of old-town street. The house that we stood in front of had a blue rectangle on its corner with the name of the street and house number. I was easily able to read everything, and was surprised at what I saw.

We stood almost naked in the middle of the street, but passersby paid us no attention. I realized that they didn't see us. I didn't stop looking around, shocked and scared by what was happening. My head was filled with what was at the time a terrible question: how to return?

The young man abruptly ran towards the corner of the house in front of us. Entering through its wall, he said that it was time for him to return, as his friend was due to arrive. He disappeared. I stood in same place for some time, watching people pass me by. I didn't know how to get back to my room, because the place from which we entered the street turned out to be a wall. What a bad break, how was I to go through the wall? I closed my eyes thought about my room, and recited, "whatever will be, will be," stepped forward, and found myself on my bed.

Sweeping my eyes over the room, I discovered that nothing had changed in it. The sun shone into it just as it had before. Breathing in a sigh of relief and closing my eyes in great hope that I would wake up, I rushed to open them. To my horror, I instead found a table with medical instruments on my bed. Waves of fear swept over my body with renewed intensity. I gulped that I would not make it through if they put me under the knife. I closed my eyes once again, and started to pray. The fear gradually receded, I calmed down..... and finally woke up. The first thing that I did was to make sure that the table with the medical instruments was not there. I jumped up and started knocking on the dresser, the wall, and on the window in order to make sure that it really was all over.

Andre Sanchez
theandresanchez@gmail.com

I was in my bed and I noticed two plastic objects in my right hand. I thought it was weird for them to be there so I got up and threw them on the floor. The first one did not make any kind of sound. The second did, likely because I started expecting it after noticing that the first one didn't. I thought it was odd so I went to the light switch near the door and tried turning the light on. It didn't work. I had two thoughts: "very strange... could I be in 'the phase'?"; and, "did the power go out?"

I left the room and went into the hallway, walking towards the living room, but it was very dark (which would be normal if the power had gone out during the night). I was thinking about how this was all somewhat odd, but felt too "real". I started to worry and tried calming myself down by thinking that if something really strange and/or scary happened, I could be sure I was in the phase, and shouldn't worry. I vaguely remember a weak yellow-greenish light starting to appear from the living room, but I did not see anything.

Dmitry Markov
Moscow, Russia

My first time was the most terrible event in my life. I had never experienced such terror. It happened in December, 1990. I was falling asleep in my bed at home. Suddenly, I heard someone enter my room, but I did not pay attention to the "intruder". Then, two female hands grabbed me from behind, and while pressing my belly, started to lift my body up. I distinctly felt thin fingers with long nails on my belly, but was completely paralyzed and absolutely unable move any part of my body or put up any kind of resistance. I felt my body go through the ceiling, but then was pulled still higher and higher.

I got scared that this could be death. I was afraid not so much of death as of the unknown. All of this happened so swiftly that I found myself unprepared for such a crossover. I started to pray. I asked God to help me free myself and go back. I panicked. I can't say how many seconds my forced levitation lasted or how high I was lifted above my house, but the moment came when I instantly returned to my bed.

April L. Alston
Raleigh, USA

I had my first OBE experience by accident. After my morning workout at the gym, I felt exhausted and came home to my dorm for a nap. When I was awaking from the dream, I felt a tri-location of myself. I was aware and could feel everything in my dream, and I could also feel everything in my body lying on the bed. I also felt a third consciousness falling through the bed. My third one was what I believed to be an OBE to the "real-time zone (RTZ)". My energy body felt like it was separating from my physical body by falling through the bed. This happened by accident.

I felt like I no longer had a body, but that I was a floating sphere of consciousness. I could sense things 360 degrees around me but I couldn't see with my eyes because I had no eyes. I could perceive where things were around me though. I had an intense burning sensation in my head and the more I tried to focus my awareness into the astral body, the more the pain worsened. Eventually, I woke up from the experience. I kept lying still and tried to reenter the trance but I was unsuccessful.

Tatyana Kiseleva
Vancouver, Canada

That particular evening, I finally decided to deal with the outside noise that had ruined a few previous attempts and got myself a set of nice, bright orange ear plugs.

I plugged my ears and went to bed with an intention to wake up in the morning and practice the deferred method. Also, just before going to bed, I read a few forum posts on Michael's website about people's first experiences. All of this led to the following:

I woke up in the middle of the night because of a very loud "thump" I heard somewhere in the building. I was sitting in my bed, thinking that the thump must have been really loud because I could hear it perfectly even with my ears being plugged. I decided to go to the front door and peek into a peep hole in hopes of seeing what was going on. I heard the loud "thump" again. It sounded a bit scary. I lowered my feet to the floor, stood up and walked out of my bedroom towards the front door. I could feel the cold floor with my bare feet. As I was approaching the front door and could see the bright peep hole in the darkness, it hit me: "I am in the Phase!"

I did not believe myself. "I did not do any techniques", I thought, doubting.

So I decided to test if it was indeed a phase. I lifted both of my feet up - that made me 'sitting' in the air - then I grabbed, with my right hand, the edge of a sliding door of a closet and pushed against the door with my both legs. I flew backwards, all the way to the other side of my living room, really surprised that I was still feeling my hand holding the closet door! My arm must have stretched like 10 feet (*M.R.: no deepening and no plan of action*)!

I was floating right by my fireplace, seeing both of my feet in the air in my pajama pants. And I still did not believe that I was in the phase, so I decided to fly up, but I could not push against the floor because my feet were in the air. So I concluded that it's not the phase (*M.R.: wrong logic*) and I decided to go back to sleep.

At that moment I found myself sitting on my bed, again realizing that my plugged ears were bothering me tremendously, and so I took the plugs out. However, a second later I realized that my ears were still plugged. "Hmm", I thought, "that's weird. I just took the plugs out, didn't I?"

And that's when I realized I was lying in my bed and feeling my real ears. I jumped in excitement, as I realized what had just happened. It was my first real out-of-body experience, although I did not believe it! I was 100% aware of the experience, but I was about 90% conscious, otherwise I would clearly know that I was indeed out-of-body.

I took a notepad and as I was writing everything down, I vividly remembered the vibrations that I felt before leaving the body. It was exactly as they are usually described - like being electrocuted without pain.

Joshua Rachels
Belleville, USA

I found myself struggling to fall into a full sleep, with what felt like "naps" and the last recognizable time occurring in reality was at 4:30 a.m.

I had once again rested my head back down and what felt like almost immediately after doing so the next thing I was "aware" of is that I am in a field walking toward what I had recognized as an old comic shop I used to visit. Not having any notion as to how I may have gotten there, I remember staring at the ground of the field beneath my feet and questioned if I had been dreaming. I then tried jumping as high as I possibly could, which initiated a leap several feet high and long, cueing the realization that I was in fact dreaming.

Now this is where things get a little broken (sequence-wise) for me, so please bear with me:

The next thing I recall is being inside of the building I was heading towards in what I was told was a rehabilitation center. Everyone around me was dressed in white. None of the faces where completely recognizable except for two: a good friend of mine named Dan and a women with no name (in the phase I referred to her as "the one I love") and even the woman's face blended back and forth between what I can only describe as a mix between Natalie Portman and one of my ex-girlfriends.

I remember Dan leaning against a doorway next to me while I was staring into a mirror (I could see myself, but my hand kept touching my face as it was blurred – the only visible portion was my white clothes and hair) as he began answering what I can only assume was my subconscious question of why I was there and for how long. I told him I could not remember how I got there or why I was there and I remember his response as clear as day:

Dan: "Do you know why you're here man?"

Me: "I can't even tell you how I got here. Marijuana?"

(keep in mind I was in a "rehab center")

Dan: "Haha - you can't remember? That's probably why you're here in the first place. You're here for like a month dude. Go check the schedule."

At this point I believe my subconscious began to panic about possibly becoming stuck, because time in the phase seemed to begin to narrow. People began crowding me around the "schedule". I remember specifically an African-American man shouting beside me, "who's Josh, who's Josh!" soon after leading me outward toward the front door where "the one I love" had been leaning, gesturing me to come closer.

I then remember walking with "the one I love" when she began crying, begging me not to wake up, screaming that we could be happy there together if I stayed. During this tantrum, chains developed on her arms and legs and I began to feel heavy.

I then began thinking of my family, my mother specifically and thoughts of getting stuck in a coma, which I do believe led to my subconscious to panic further because time seemed to narrow even further.

"The one I love" then led me into a back room and well, not to get vulgar, but we began having sex and right before my "orgasm" she started screaming at me not to go, at which point I felt myself being pulled away - and in fact I was being pulled away.

Now here's what really blew my mind about the whole experience: I then awoke to daylight and rushed out of my room to find my mother and stepdad standing in the living room. I began explaining my experience to them both. However, my stepdad began pre-guessing my whole experience dead on, which I questioned. I then took out my phone and noticed there were scratches and dents all over it. I handed my phone to my mom to look at the damage and as she hit the back light button I WOKE UP!!

I shot up almost immediately after opening my eyes, it was still dark outside I looked at the time..5:17 a.m.

Chapter 2. Full-Fledged Travels in the Phase

Here we will concentrate not on the fact of out-of-body experience itself, but on the activities carried out during it: translocation within the phase space and controlling it, finding objects, and experimentation.

These practitioners occasionally apply their out-of-body experience towards some goal or another, and these experiences are on a wholly other level than simply appearing in the phase. The phase travels introduced here exhibit a greater degree of skill - and in some cases luck - than those of the first section. This, however, does not save the practitioners from making a slew of mistakes, which often prevent them from experiencing maximum success. Analyzing these mistakes will allow the reader to avoid them in his own practice.

Rudolph
The Rocky Mountains, USA

I was moving when I woke up, and I tried various positions for FFA (forced falling asleep) and they did not work so finally I lay out flat on my back and began going through the relaxation routines and then when it felt right I started the brain squeeze, phantom wiggle, listening in, etc.

Within three to five minutes I found myself immediately in a phase. I was at a mall. I decided to get up from the bench I was sitting on and go to the men's room (*M.R.: no deepening and no plan of action*). As I was walking I noticed as the tiles on the wall started changing from a dingy white to a sparkling, bright white and black checkerboard. My feet dissolved and I floated up a few feet and began float-flying. I went past a rounded wall and thought, "there should be a chocolate shop behind this wall". But as I started to go through it I stopped and thought I wanted to get out of there and do something better.

I went to the front entryway and it was a fine piece of architecture with shiny marble reaching to much higher heights than would be expected for a mall. I was floating up to the top but gave up and just went through the wall to the outside. I had tunnel vision so I started doing my Qi Gong and then "Clarity Now!" exclamations and my vision improved. I then remembered my 'to do' list and began flying off into the clouds (this time was a Sufi level of Heaven). I reached a place of orangey, creamsicle like clouds and there was a black speck sort of shaped like the Polo logo guy in the middle of it and I thought, "that's me".

Nothing else was happening, so I came back to my body (*M.R.: wrong action*) and started writing it down.

Rudolph
The Rocky Mountains, USA

I think I may have had three very long OBEs last night. I woke up around 3:45am and began the brain squeeze and then phantom wiggling and suddenly it was as if I had projected into the phase. I spent a long time with my brothers enjoying a nice visit. Then, I landed back in my body. I was thinking about getting up to write it down but I wanted to project again and I did. It only takes a few seconds once I have managed the first exit. I immediately landed back in the exact same place with my brothers as though nothing had changed (*M.R.: no deepening*). We were doing a project together but I told them I had other things to do and that I was going to take off alone (*M.R.: wrong action*). They nodded to me and I turned to run and then began flying.

I went to a large building and interacted with some attractive women (*M.R.: no plan of action*) for a while but local security came to stop me and I flew up to an upstairs room (*M.R.: wrong action*) and I wanted to fly through a window but it felt very real -- so real I wondered if I would be able to go through it. I affirmed to myself that I was OBE but slowed down as I approached it and then flew through with no trouble.

Then I went to a room with a large table where men were gathered and talking. It felt like an exclusive club of sorts. There was a banquet laid out with delicious food prepared in ways I had never seen before and I dove in and was having a great time. I was conversing with a couple guys and I mentioned that I was OBE and that I had a body far away in another state. They just looked at me with blank stares and one quickly looked down and walked away. Then I began speaking with the man across the table from me and he mentioned something that reminded me of one of my "Action Plan" items. I told him what I wanted to do and he motioned to a woman standing behind me and I could hear her talking to someone. He said, "Well then, she is the one you should talk to". I turned around and tried to introduce myself but landed back in my body (*M.R.: no maintaining*). I made the decision to leave the journal aside and project again, hoping that I would remember all this in the morning.

I projected again and arrived immediately at a busy street corner. I asked someone if he knew how I could find this woman I had been directed to in the prior OBE and he pointed her out in the crowd. I went over to her and we sat down on the curb and began speaking and she gave me a nickname that I could call her and it wasn't until after I had gotten up and was having coffee that I laughed and made the connection to something I had journaled on a few days ago.

My alarm went off and I got up... otherwise I think I could have gone on for another hour or more.

Jorge Antonio Becerra Perea
Hidalgo, México

After waking up around 8:00 AM (on a holiday, of course), I had breakfast and went back to sleep. Then, after having an extremely weird dream, I managed to awaken without movement. I immediately tried to separate by rolling, and failed. Then I tried forced falling asleep (FFA) followed by phantom wiggling, but this time I tried to move my legs slowly and feel the movement. Suddenly, I noticed that I was already standing next to my bed, but with my blanket still over my body. After taking it off, I started to deepen in the phase, touching and peering at everything, and immediately after feeling myself in a hyper-realistic environment, I started to explore my own house (*M.R.: no plan of action*).

The time was changing constantly between day and night, and in the next room I found my uncle, watching TV. I was so excited about the phase and so curious that I tried to explain to him that everything was non-physical, just to watch his reactions. He said I was crazy, ignored me and continued watching the TV. Then I threw the TV. through the window and continued to the next room.

Suddenly, I came back to my body (*M.R.: no maintaining*) and started the separation again. I separated again in my room. This time, it was night. I started to call a woman I was looking for by name, but I started to have problems with my voice, so I decided to trans-locate to my school. I closed my eyes, and imagined the place. Suddenly I started to feel a sensation of flight, and after opening my eyes I was already there. The place was pretty different than in reality, but I enjoyed it a lot more than if it were as usual. I spent a lot of in-phase time looking for that woman, asking people, calling her name, with no results.

In the end, I lost consciousness and fell into a normal dream. Anyways, it was a wonderful experience.

Jorge Antonio Becerra Perea
Hidalgo, México

I got conscious during a dream when I was about to go upstairs at home, just after a false awakening. The stairs where so freaking scrambled that I immediately got lucid. Suddenly, the phase faded out, and before I could realize what was happening, I went back to the dream. I appeared in the middle of a huge street (*M.R.: no deepening*). I didn't have any plan, because I was not expecting this experience, and so instead of thinking about it I decided to explore running and jumping between cars and buildings in a kind of extreme parkour style.

It had been one of the most vivid and fun phase experiences I have ever had. I have no words to describe the feeling of complete freedom I had at those moments. After exploring half of the entire city (I was running really fast) I started to have some serious problems with the phase stability, and so I decided to awaken by myself before falling into a normal dream and losing the precious memories of this experience (*M.R.: wrong logic*).

Jorge Antonio Becerra Perea
Hidalgo, México

Everything started as a normal dream. In my dream, I was trying to fall sleep in my bed, with no success. Suddenly, I started to hear strange and loud noises outside, so I turned my head to the window in order to see what the heck was happening, and what I saw really scared me.

There was a UFO flying through the city, as if it were looking for people to abduct. It stopped right over my house. I closed my eyes and pretended to be asleep. Suddenly, I awakened, with absolutely zero movement, and I had the idea of trying the abduction method or the fear method. I started to recall the fear I was having a few seconds earlier and also tried to imagine the abduction. Sounds and vibrations started to arise and I immediately tried to separate by just standing up.

It worked.

After deepening by palpation, I noticed that three of my best friends were with me. They were watching TV. It's funny that although my native language is Spanish, the TV program was narrated in English, and I could understand everything.

Then I moved into the living room, and, following my action plan, I tried to translocate to London. I had a lot of problems with translocation this time. I started to visualize Big Ben in front of me, and while the image was forming behind my eyelids, it stopped and the tower morphed into a weird Japanese building.

A lot of samurai soldiers started to jump out of the building in order to attack me. I thought that it was because I was losing lucidity, so I used peering to deepen the phase, closed my eyes, and suddenly the image of a switch appeared before them.

I focused my attention on the light switch, and while translocating I tried to visualize London, but I ended up in a kind of formal meeting on the coast.

Now I realize that I was at The Hague, Holland. I tried to do an experiment. I took out my iPod Touch and suddenly it morphed into my cellphone. I took a look to the screen and the only thing I was able to see were strange symbols. Then, I walked through the crowd of people. My father came and asked me what I was looking for. I told him that I was looking for a person very important to me. I kept looking for Victoria (that's her name) with no luck, and suddenly the phase vanished. Once back in my body, I separated again. One of my friends was still in my room.

I translocated myself to my school, and I suffered such a loss of lucidity that I entered my classroom, sat in my desk, and paid attention to the class lesson. Suddenly, I stood up and said to myself "WHAT THE HELL ARE YOU DOING?!" I left the classroom, did some deepening, and threw my backpack away. A friend came up to me and said, "hey, your backpack!" I told him, "you can have it".

I can't remember what happened next. I probably fell asleep (*M.R.: no maintaining*). The next thing I remember is that I was at a car-wash station. I had a bottle in my hands and started to experiment with it. I poured the bottle onto the floor while trying to feel the bottle still filled up with water. As a result, I had a bottomless bottle in my hands...

April L. Alston
Raleigh, USA

I was sleeping, minding my business in a dream one day, when all of a sudden lots of ninjas started attacking me throwing knives at me. I deflected one of the knives and then I realized I was dreaming. Now lucid, I began flying around and deflecting knives, having fun (*M.R.: no deepening*). I didn't have time to experiment in the astral plane because I was busy deflecting knives. More and more ninjas started attacking me. When I ran away and came to an opening outside (*M.R.: no plan of action*), a large army of ninjas stared me down, and I knew there were too many. I started shooting ice balls out of my hands in a flowing motion as I began to freeze the entire army of ninjas. As I was freezing them, I felt a sharp pain pierce my back. I had been stabbed by a sword. The fun was over. I forced myself to wake up (*M.R.: wrong action*).

After awakening, my boyfriend called me. Before saying hello, he said, "April, please go back to sleep so I can take my sword out of your back." I told him about my dream, and he said that he sent the ninjas into my dream to distract me so that he could put a sword blade into my back to test my intentions regarding him. This proves to me that the movie, *Inception*, is VERY POSSIBLE!

Tatyana Kiseleva
Vancouver, Canada

Deferred method. About 7 AM. Ears plugged, wearing a mask. Trying to do the techniques: phantom wiggling, observing images, listening in. Nothing is working. I feel too awake but I am still trying and alternating each technique with forced falling asleep.

At certain point I realize that I am still in my bed watching TV. I have a TV set in my bedroom but not this one and at a different spot. The TV that I see is my old one and now is at my mom's house.

As soon as I see this I realize that I am in the phase. I am looking at the screen and thinking about my plan (*M.R.: no deepening*). Now, one of the items on my 'phase to-do list' is to find out what happened to my dad who disappeared a long time ago and I don't even know if he is alive or not. So on TV I see a person walking away. The person looks like one of the singers my dad liked very much and also resembled a lot. So I start calling him, dad, dad. The person on the screen turns his head and start transforming into my father and I feel the sensation of being pulled into this picture. In a second he and I are standing in front of each other in the middle of my bedroom. He is wearing a cap and a light colored jacket with a yellow sweater sticking out of the jacket. Later I asked my mom if he ever wore anything like that. She said no, however she mentioned that this description matched more my dad's brother, my uncle, who I never met. So I am hugging my dad and telling him that I am so happy to see him and starting to explain that I learned to leave my body. No dialog, however, took place. He was there but that was it, he wasn't responding, wasn't doing anything and finally he disappeared.

Then I remember looking at myself in the mirror, there was me exactly as I was at that time in reality, in a t-shirt and pajama pants.

I remembered that I need to do deepening techniques, but first I decided to find a pen and notepad and write everything down, right there in the phase, so I won't forget. I found a notepad (I have it in reality) and a thick red pen (don't have it in reality). Now, because I was wearing a sleep-mask, in the phase I sometimes had normal vision, and sometimes my sight was blocked by the mask. So as soon as I was all set to write everything down, I realized that my sleep-mask was blocking my vision. I started to pull it off my face thinking that I should not open my eyes because I might wake up... and bingo, I woke up (*M.R.: no re-entering*).

Tatyana Kiseleva
Vancouver, Canada

I am in LA right now, participating in an experiment at the OBE Research Center that Mike is leading.

Today's assignment was: using the differed method and cycles of indirect techniques, roll (or levitate, or climb) out of the body and meet the aliens that are waiting for us there (this was a goal for this experiment).

Again, I woke up a bit disappointed because it was time to get ready for our second session and none of the techniques worked. I was in my LA hotel room. It looked different from how my room looks in reality but I guess in my mind it was just a different room (not my bedroom at home), so I was not really paying attention to the fact that the main door and windows had switched places, it was much lighter in color and overall amount of light in the room, there were some staff around, a camera that I don't have, and knickknacks everywhere.

So I started becoming aware when I was in the shower and noticed that the water drops on the shower walls were dark in color. I decided to stop showering and then when I was back in the room, getting ready, everything felt so real that I don't even know why I decided to check if it was the phase.

Imagine it yourself: yesterday you went to bed, then you woke up this morning, showered, got ready, did this, did that and then decided to check if it was the phase - and it turned out that IT IS (!)

So I decided just for the heck of it to test if it might be the phase by "breathing with the nose pinched" technique and of course it did not work at first, because I had been doing it with the "how can it be the phase, everything is so real" thought. But I kept trying and after a third attempt air got out from somewhere behind my ears and I happily confirmed for myself that I was totally in the phase.

I felt very happy. I started rising in the air and flew in a couple of circles under the ceiling. Then, I felt the need to deepen and I really focused on that. I looked a few times at my palms. I looked at myself and noticed I was wearing a towel wrapped around me. Then I started touching everything in the room. I took a camera and put it on the floor, thinking that I will check later it it's going to be on the floor in reality. (don't know what had gotten into me, that's a pointless test, I guess I just remembered someone doing this once) At first it felt that my hands were numb, but as I was touching everything I got back my sense of touch.

Since perception was back to 100%, it was time to go look for aliens. They were not in the room. I looked outside of the hotel window and saw some road with huge fallen branches on it, a chain-link fence and some greenery and trees behind it. Aliens were not there either. So I decided to get into the corridor, I opened the door, it was really dark inside, even the light from the room could not penetrate it. I thought, aliens must be there, so I stepped into the darkness... At least 3 tiny hands touched my shoulder... I totally freaked and woke up... (*M.R.: no re-entering*)

Craig P.
Los Angeles, USA

I took a nap from 10:40 am to 11:20 am. I tried to fall asleep so I could practice upon awakening. I was having difficulties in falling asleep so I thought nothing was going to happen. After awhile I must have fallen asleep as I noticed a floating type of sensation. I then decided to separate however I felt like nothing was happening. Then I noticed I was looking down at some drinking glasses that are on the top shelf. I realized I was out of the body.

Things were not very clear so I tried to start looking at objects and feeling them. I told myself to go see aliens. The next scene I was near a mountain in a clearing with trees around it. There was a space ship. There were two aliens with helmets on. They also had a type of robot with them. It was about 7 ft tall and was silver in color. The aliens did not appear to be friendly. When the alarm went off I felt like I was 100 miles away and it was difficult to come back to the physical body.

Bo
Antwerp, Belgium

I entered the phase this morning. More or less like the previous times, only this time I rolled deliberately over to the other side of the bed. I came down on the floor, which became visible when I opened my eyes.

I touched the sheets. Everything turned very real and I thought to myself, "where am I" because I was so overwhelmed by the vividness.

The light was dim and I asked for more light but it didn't change. The room was a combination of our room now and my room when I was a child.

I pinched my nose and blocked my airways but I could breathe normal. I stood up and went to the door (*M.R.: no plan of action*). I opened it. It was dark outside. Then I saw that there was a drawing on the outside of the door. It was a little figure and when I looked more closely it began to move his head.

I wanted to touch it, but I felt paralyzed. My arms felt very heavy. Once I had almost touched it, I woke up (*M.R.: no re-entering*).

Bo
Antwerp, Belgium

This morning I had a difficult phase entrance. Without feeling much -nearly no vibrations- I tumbled out of bed. It was very dark and my consciousness was unstable. I made several weird movements, still half unconscious. After a few moments I ended up sitting against the bed (*M.R.: no deepening*). It was still dark, but consciousness was better and I spoke to myself, saying something about *the envelope*.

I crawled on my hands and knees to the other side of the bed where my bedside table was. Everything looked realistic and *the envelope* was in its place. I picked it up and felt that there was something small and thick in it. I ripped it open and in it was a shiny packaging of a cookie or something like that.

I opened it and found that it was a chocolate. I bit into it and it was delicious. It had coconut in it.

As I was chewing on the chocolate, I closed my eyes for a moment to concentrate on its taste. The taste remained the same and there was of course my smacking, but I felt pressure in my head, which was building up. I opened my eyes again and the pressure disappeared.

I now came across a little dilemma. Should I eat the whole chocolate, or should I start my mission of translocation? I decided to do the latter and threw the chocolate away.

I stood up and started running with eyes closed. The running didn't feel natural but I was moving anyway. I felt no walls, no resistance of any kind.

Because of the closed eyes, I again felt a foul coming so I opened my eyes - but everything remained very dark and I was afraid of losing it.

Normally, my experience would have ended there. Instead of giving up, I kept running and opened my eyes as wide as I could.

This apparently helped, because suddenly a light appeared at the end of some tunnel (no NDE tunnel) When I came out of the tunnel I was filled with joy!

I saw a blue ocean with big waves striking against the rocks. I was on a road hugging a beautiful rocky coastline. The sight was magnificent.

I was on a bus or something - I saw trucks on the road that had problems because of the big waves. Shortly after this I woke up (*M.R.: no maintaining*).

Note:

When I was running in order to translocate, I didn't think of a particular location. A few days ago I fantasized about where I would translocate. In my fantasy, I would end up in a 17th century sailing ship on the blue ocean.

Jason
New York, USA

I woke up not trying to move but that was unsuccessful. I decided to try some cycles anyway and began with phantom wiggling. To my surprise I felt my body go into sleep paralysis and get numb (*M.R.: no separation*). Then I switched to listening in, but then I decided to try and separate by rolling over. There was resistance, but it ended up working and I stood up. I was skeptical as to whether I was really in the phase, even though I have had lots of experiences before. I guess it was because the transition between waking and dreaming never felt so conscious and self-induced before. Not to mention that it only took about one minute.

I hear my mother in the kitchen. I do a reality check by trying to put my right index finger through my left palm. It was a struggle, but it worked - so I know I am in the phase. I walk out into the kitchen and my mother says good morning, I give her a kiss on the cheek and continue down the hallway (*M.R.: no plan of action*). I touch the walls as I am walking to stabilize the experience, even though I don't need to. It's pretty dark inside the house but I can see that it is sunny outside. I am in my shirt and boxers, although normally I just go outside and clothes appear on me without me noticing.

I open the front door and see all of the upstairs neighbors outside on the porch. I close the door back just to double check that I am phasing before I go outside in my boxers, I do the reality check and it works again, so I go outside. By this time the neighbors were going upstairs. It is indeed sunny outside and there is a little kid outside sort of nagging me, but I ignore him. I half-heartedly try to create a portal and teleport by going through the floor but neither of those work. I walk down the block and I try this hopping thing that I read about to get around faster, but I don't like it. I fly upwards and don't have much control... I keep going higher and higher and have to grab on to these power lines to prevent me from leaving the atmosphere.

It was a long phase and for some reason I lost a chunk of memory here (*M.R.: no maintaining*). I don't remember where I landed, I remember bits and pieces but my memory kicks in when I am in a department store and I see a guy that looks familiar. I ask him, "don't I know you?" He shakes his head "no" and keeps walking. He looks suspicious so I keep an eye on him. He meets with another guy and he points at me and they start running after me. I duck behind some people as they run by and I go the other way. I go out of an emergency exit expecting the alarm to sound, but it doesn't. There are two locked gates leading to stairs that go to the roof. I melt through both gates and go to the roof. I fly away and they come out and start flying after me. I use mental energy to fly faster but it isn't enough. We battle for a while, and then I end up in a portal inside some sort of spaceship.

I am driving it through these tunnels that remind me of *the Matrix*. I crash into the walls a little but for the most part I am good. I pull up into the place that these tunnels lead to. This part is boring so I will skip it.

I walk out of this building and I am in a cityscape full of people. I walk down this block and my vision gets sort of different, almost movie like. I walk in this hotel lobby and people are sitting around. I decide to look for someone to have to sex with to end the experience because I want to remember everything. All of the females around are either not attractive or too young. I look back at the hotel door and there is a lady looking at me but she turns away quickly. I was curious why she was looking at me and who she was so I go outside. She is kind of in a panic running towards a black van. I run after her and pull open the door before they pull off. There is a guy in the driver's seat and she is crying in the passenger's seat. She said that when my friend got his promotion (from the boring part of the experience I skipped earlier) she was forced to set him up and that this is the guy that made her do it. I started punching him in the phase and this caused me to lose my proper frame of mind to maintain and I woke up (*M.R.: no re-entering*).

Jason
New York, USA

I wake up to slight consciousness and I'm unsure if I have moved or not. My first thought is to go back to sleep, but then I decide to try to enter the phase. I apply forced falling asleep and immediately start to feel vibrations. They fluctuate between strong and mild and I start to feel them subside. I then remember what I always tell myself: if I get vibrations, then I'm already in the phase. So I try to roll out of my body... There is resistance, but I am able to do it.

I stand up in my current apartment and it is completely dark. As I am walking to the front door, I try to put my right index finger through my left palm to make sure I am in the phase. It works, and so I open the door to the hallway but it looks nothing like my actual hall. It is still very dim and there is another gentleman there. I point to different areas and say the word "lights", and sure enough, one-by-one they come on. I keep touching things to engage the senses as I am walking. I walk into a room with a young boy in it and he is watching TV. I think about my plan of action and remember that I wanted to try the teleportation technique in SOBT. I had previously been teleporting by melting through the floor but it was unreliable and I would end up in darkness sometimes. I had read in EWLD that closing your eyes in a dream can cause you to wake up, but I figured that if Michael does it all the time then this isn't fact.

I ask the boy where should I go... to a football game? He says yes, but then I figure that since I have never actually been to a football game, I should go to a basketball game instead. I close my eyes and concentrate on where I wanted to go. I start to feel movement and even get the feeling you get when going down a huge drop on a rollercoaster. When the movement stops, I open my eyes. It has worked, and I am standing in the middle of an arena while a basketball game is going on. I take a step onto the court and immediately the referee blows the whistle to stop the game and get me off of the court. I go sit in the stands and began talking to one of the prettier girls. I don't remember what we were talking about, but after a short while she wants to exit the main arena and go towards the concession stands and bathrooms. You can guess where the rest of the experience went.

**Matthias Holzer
Vienna, Austria**

I had a lucid dream. It was a dream I have quite often: going home from work and realizing I'm missing my suitcase. As soon as I got home in my dream, sure enough my suitcase was standing there. I then became aware of a discontinuity: I remembered that I had punched the flextime clock at work when leaving, but the card for this was in my suitcase. How could I have done this if my suitcase was at home? This must be a dream! I became lucid, and as usual at this occasion I immediately woke up in my excitement. However, I instantly entered the vibrational state, which seemed very strong and stable. I tried the rolling out method and it worked perfectly.

As usual, I reached for the silver cord, but only felt something like mild electrical energy in my neck where the cord is usually located (*M.R.: no deepening*). First off, I decided to walk into my mother's room with whom I was living at the time (*M.R.: no plan of action*). I expected to see her in bed and for an instant I thought I'd see exactly this, her face on the pillow (I couldn't see very well however), but then I realized that she must have been in the living room since she always got up very early and must surely have been awake at this time - it must have been a reality fluctuation. Next, I looked into one of the mirrors in my mother's room, wondering what I would see. What I saw were several distinctly separated body parts of mine floating around - like a photograph of me had been cut into a jigsaw puzzle!

Then I looked at my hands, they started to melt until the stumps looked cut off, just like the picture in the mirror. Next I continued into the living room, looking for my mother, but I didn't see her. Now I decided that I finally had to leave my apartment, something I had never accomplished in all my years of OBEs. Without any difficulty I walked through the closed main door and out into the corridor. The light out there seemed to be on, but I realized that I was having some sort of tunnel vision, a very narrow field of view. I demanded more energy and better sight, but this didn't help much. As I walked down the corridor, physical reality disappeared more and more towards the end of the hallway (where in reality the door to my grandmother's apartment was located, where I wanted to go), there was just some kind of rectangular portal. Now only half conscious, I decided to return to my body and end the experience because I didn't want to risk losing my memory of it (*M.R.: wrong logic*). That very instant, I awoke physically in my bed (*M.R.: no re-entering*).

Oleg Sushchenko
Moscow, Russia

Last night I spent about an hour developing the interplay of images in my mind after I no left felt any feeling of kinesthetic sense. I was lying on my back in an uncomfortable position. After sliding towards sleep for some time, I felt slight vibrations and echoes of sounds from the dream world, but the uncomfortable position still hindered me. In the end, I thought the heck with it, and decided to lie down however was comfortable, and turned over to lie on my stomach. Despite the fact that the movement upset the process, after about five minutes the state began to return and build up. I was able to get a little vibration this time, although I was unable to amplify it. I drew a picture of my kitchen in my mind, and because the images in that state were really vivid, strong, and realistic, after some time I understood that not only were my attention and awareness there, but so were my bodily sensations. I was quite surprised that the phase had been so easy to fall in to (there was no doubt that this was the phase).

I jumped out through the window and began to fly around the courtyard. Actually, it was the first time that I had flown only upon a single mental command, without any physical effort (*M.R.: no deepening and no plan of action*). The courtyard bore only 10% similarity to its real-life counterpart, but I was not at all surprised by this, and I simply enjoyed it as much as I could, as I was able see and was not immediately thrown out. But, after having looked at and taken in the city, the thought of whether or not this was the phase and not just a lucid dream occurred. I was so conscious in the dream that I was able to know about and comprehend such terms, and differentiate between them - can you imagine?! I have to add that I gave little attention to my memory, so I can't say how much of my "self-awareness" was there, but I was aware enough to be able to differentiate between the phase and a lucid dream (or at least think about the difference).

I even went and asked people around if it was the phase or a lucid dream. Sounds funny, doesn't it? The funniest thing was that they answered that it was a different world, and they refused to discuss the topic any further with me. Then, I decided to not get my mind all mixed up and just go with the plot, which turned out to be quite long and uninterrupted! I recalled a moment from the day before how I had lain down and induced the phase while lying on my back, and how I had turned over and flown away. I recalled all this periodically during the course of the phase, and realized that I should try to ask about what had been going on with me on the forum later.

Then, later in the phase, I found myself in a basement. As there was just a really nasty smell there, I decided that I had already had enough and that it was time to go back. That happened even more easily, as soon as I thought about going back (*M.R.: wrong action*), a vibration as light as a breeze went through me and then I was back in my body with full awareness and a well-rested body and mind. I was completely refreshed! And that's despite the fact that I remember everything, every second of the dream, from the moment I started flying!

Jaime Munoz Lundquist
Orange County, USA.

I got up at 7 am, made coffee then I went back to bed around 7:30 am. I started relaxing and putting myself in a meditative state and doing the breathing techniques (from Michael Raduga's book) to induce myself into falling asleep. Suddenly I felt a jolt, right there and then I knew that it was the moment I have been waiting for to be aware of the phenomenon. I continue to relax, inhaling and exhaling. Suddenly, I got up from my bed, looked around, and proceeded to scan my bedroom. I then started to do the deepening technique that I had learned and was starting to apply: touching the walls, textures, rubbing the palms of my hands, looking at my arms, and saying to myself, "is this a dream, or am I out of my body?" (*M.R.: wrong logic*)

The texture of the fabric of the thermo I was wearing was real, I touched the wall and it was solid (*M.R.: no plan of action*). I knew from hearing it that you can go through walls, but this didn't happen. I looked again around my room and suddenly everything turned green, like a forest-green color, even my thermo shirt. It was a very intense emerald-green color. Peaceful and yet so intense, I was fully aware of what was going on, and at the same time very excited.

I remembered that I needed to be very aggressive in my deepening technique, and so I continued touching everything in my surroundings and continued to rub my hands, touching my arms and trying to look at myself. I knew it was me. It was so real, it was awesome! I don't understand why, but I was thinking of my brother and out of nowhere, he appeared in my room. I didn't panic, I then proceeded to open the door in my bedroom and everything was so different. I was going downstairs and everything was still green around the house. It looked like an old 1920s house.

I continued going to the next level and saw 3 black dogs and their hair was luminating like neon blue lights, it was incredible. I was thinking to myself, "okay, this is enough (*M.R.: wrong logic*) of the experience for right now," and went back to my body. When I woke up, I started to write down everything as I didn't want to forget anything, since I was told to document my experience and progress.

Karen
New York, USA
(www.karen659.blogspot.com)

Meeting with OBE friends in California and sharing their excitement motivated me to want to try something new and see if I could get OOB while traveling on the plane to home, since I knew it would be a long trip and I could sleep. I was concerned it might not happen, as I have never attempted this in a noisy, bumpy, moving environment, but still wanted to try.

I used my usual affirmations and visualization before sleep, and remember being surprised to feel my left knee floating up as I sat in the plane seat. (I was in a window seat, next to the wing of the plane.) It didn't bring me to awareness of possibly being OOB, as my mind registered it as something interesting but not that unusual.

It was at that point that we had to have hit some turbulence, or maybe my seatmate moved slightly to bump me, but I felt my astral leg quickly and heavily sink back into my physical body, enough to startle me to more awareness.

I realized, "hey wow! I WAS starting to get OOB!" Without waking completely, I settled back in and soon found both knees now floating up, to the point where I felt totally squished in the seat! I wondered how do I get out fully while sitting in this plane seat?!?

I thought a change in position might help, so I leaned back, falling through the back of the seat, and then used a "floating" visualization to try to lift. My next memory is of seeing the ceiling of the plane only inches from my face!

I now realized I was out!! I was so thrilled, yet I told myself not to get too excited. I remember thinking I should verify it by moving my hand through the roof of the plane (*M.R.: no deepening*). As I placed my hand partially through the ceiling successfully, I fearfully remembered I was in a moving airplane and maybe shouldn't disturb some important "wiring" or such and so pulled my hand back in quickly! (This shows me how strong my beliefs were that you just don't go outside or mess with a moving airplane!)

Next, I was doing handstands on the back of the seats, flopping myself into unsuspecting passengers' laps, and then moved to the front of the plane. I found two open seats next to a young male and thought I'd just stop here to check out first class. While there, the stewardess made some announcement, and I realized that no one was too happy about her disturbing their quiet. I could feel the passengers' 'irritation' and even sensed some 'discontent' from the stewardess as she performed her job.

At that point we did hit turbulence, and I awoke fully from my experience. I was so happy to have succeeded! I knew I had felt 'confined' to the inside of the plane by my fear of causing problems should I have exited it.

Karen

www.obe4u.com

New York, USA
(www.karen659.blogspot.com)

I found myself "awake" lying on the couch, and being aware of a sense of FEAR! Not so much a sense of me being fearful, but fear that was associated with someone quite close to my body as it lay on the couch (*M.R.: no separation*)!

I didn't really see this person at first, I just felt the fear energies emanating from him or her, which of course, to be honest, made me just a little bit concerned. My fear dissipated immediately when I realized this was a very small child standing next to me! (He couldn't have been more than 2 years old, likely less...)

I was at first caught off-guard, wondering "Now what do I do?!" (*M.R.: no deepening and no plan of action*) Then I sensed an adult presence also nearby at the bottom of the couch area. This was a female, clearly seen, short sandy-colored hair and small glasses and a petite frame. I somehow knew she was waiting for this child to know she was there.

I'm not sure how I did it, but turning to face the child, I sent love and even tried to hug him with my energies. He calmed immediately and I told him, "look who's here!" as I picked him up and handed him to this woman. I have no idea how I knew what to do, or if I was doing the right thing, I just did what felt to be right.

The woman smiled, the child's energies calmed and changed, and then they both disappeared!

LucidDreaming
Lithuania

I was on my one-and-a-half week dry spell and I was not trying to get into the phase. But I broke my dry spell by becoming conscious within a dream. Once I understood that I was in the phase, I immediately tried to do deepening, but I failed and got thrown back into my body. Refusing to surrender, I somehow managed to reenter my phase - YAY! So, after successfully reentering my phase, I performed deepening and throughout all of the phase I did maintaining.

My plan was to talk with my subconscious and ask for my talents and a quick way to earn money. After summoning my dream character to talk with me, I started the conversation. It was a very strange conversation, because she kept asking non-related things which I can't remember. After finally asking the question I had wanted to ask, she answered, "Eating". She said this and nothing more after that. That's when my phase ended (*M.R.: no maintaining and re-entering*), after about 10 minutes of being in it.

LucidDreaming
Lithuania

My break from the phase was still on, so I decided not to try indirect techniques. I found myself awake after about 6 hours of sleep but without using an alarm, although I ignored this and went to sleep again. Then, I had a conscious awakening and it already felt like I was in the phase. Indeed, a very strange feeling. I thought, "Well, I should try using a separation technique". And I did. It worked and I separated.

I was standing in my room, but my body was not in bed, so I started doubting if I was really in the phase, even though separation had felt very real. I immediately pinched my nose and I could breathe in through it. I rubbed my hands and touched everything around me. Once I felt that my phase had good quality, I started acting as planned. In the end, it was very nice phase experience , but I had forgotten to do maintaining and woke up after about 10 minutes.

LucidDreaming
Lithuania

The alarm clock on my phone broke (don't ask how that happened), so lately I've been trying to wake up after 6 hours of sleep without any kind of device to help me. And I succeeded today. I woke up, went to the bathroom and went back to sleep. The thought of conscious awakening was going through my head as I drifted into a dream. I managed to exit that dream, and so I woke up without moving (*M.R.: no separation*). And then I had to face my biggest difficulty - loud noises (my family was up very early preparing to go to work and they were shouting for no good reason). I decided not to let this chance slip away and performed observing images. It worked immediately and there was no need to perform separation technique. I ended up in the phase.

After successfully entering the phase, I immediately performed deepening. I also performed mainitaing throughout the phase. My plan was to try shapeshifting and turn into a wolf. I tried imagining myself becoming one and started running on my hands and legs like a dog, but I failed, and so I tried again. After a few unsuccessful tries, I started hearing loud noises and thought that it was my parents, so I had to do something. I performed deepening, but to no end... I lost control and woke up. I tried to re-enter, but failed.

Shaun
Minneapolis, USA

After awakening without moving, I begin indirect techniques. I am still very sleepy. In an "imagined movement" cycle I begin to feel very real sensations and lose all connection with my physical body. I am blind somewhere in the phase.

I rub my hands, arms, legs, and face until I get sight. Oddly, at first it is only imagined sight like in a normal dream, but it quickly becomes complete sight like in real life. The phase is still very weak, but I begin my plan of action. I should have deepened further through peering or other options, but didn't. I will pay for this shortly.

I am in my bedroom. My wife is there but, thankfully, no one else is. No strangers milling about like usual. Normally she isn't there. I'm still groggy so I begin to talk to her, but then remember my plan of action and go downstairs.

I walk through my living room on my way to the kitchen and touch the wall to change its color. It turns yellow, even though I had meant the walls to turn blue. I should have deepened since this was an indication I didn't have complete control. Instead, I continue into the kitchen.

There are two strangers in my kitchen at our breakfast nook. This isn't uncommon. They ignore me.

I open the refrigerator with the intention that a small vile of a liquid will be in it. This liquid will help deepen and lengthen the phase (I tell myself this to induce a placebo type effect). The fridge is full of food, but the only drinks are 7-Up and milk. We never have 7 Up. I close the refrigerator and open it again with the placebo intention. Once again, it is full of food and the 7 Up and milk. I drink the 7 Up telling myself it is my "phase potion."

I should have deepened further once again since my lack of control over my refrigerator items and general groggy state showed a very weak phase.

I continue my plan of action by going outside to our garden. When I step outside, my vision goes away. I'd never lost vision before in the phase. I then begin rubbing my hands and try to deepen, but I am so groggy and the phase is so weak I am already close to exiting into sleep like I do all too often.

In the end I do restore vision, but now it isn't as realistic as it normally is. It is nowhere near real life.

I walk to one of my grapevines and make it grow out the full year's growth and produce ripe fruit. The fruit is very sickly looking and tasteless. This lack of control should have signaled me to deepen, but I continue on.

Suddenly, I'm not in my yard. I am in a random place with two people I know from my past. They are talking to me.

I have almost entirely lost lucidity and no longer have control over my phase. We are by a pool and one friend throws the other in. This is very dream-like and not very lucid, but I do have a little lucidity.

I do find a tree that looks like my chokecherry and it has mature fruit. I take a berry and eat it. Unlike the grapes, it tastes just like a chokecherry, which is to say it tastes very bitter and awful. I start spitting it out everywhere and thinking, "why would I taste this and not my grapes, this is awful, but my grapes are awesome!"

Then I return to my body. It is now 8 AM (*M.R.: no re-entering*). My memory of the entire experience is somewhat diminished. I am fairly certain I had slipped into a complete dream state somewhere in there because it didn't quite feel completely real like a normal phase experience should.

Shaun
Minneapolis, USA

I had a regular separation, but no vision. I felt around, but the furniture I felt wasn't my furniture. I thought it would be cool to be in a mountain cabin, and when I gained vision I was in an unfamiliar mountain cabin. Again, I was alone.

It was completely real again, like my last experience. I was so excited I started running around (after doing deepening). I ran around the house exploring for a while until I was out breath (*M.R.: no plan of action*). Then, I was afraid that all the heavy breathing would wake me up.

This time, the thought of having a real body instantly made the phase experience weaken, so much so that I was afraid I would fall asleep. I began to deepen.

Then I saw a jug of a drink in the kitchen and told myself it would help me deepen.

It was the most delicious thing I've ever tasted. I've eaten and drunk in the phase before, and it always tasted like whatever I thought it would. I didn't have any expectations, only that of deepening. It was like a sweet carbonated drink, only without any bite. It was truly indescribable.

Strangely, the drink did deepen me back to complete realism, and I was so excited that I ran around exploring again. Then, once again, I became afraid of waking. This time, that thought brought me back to bed.

I attempted to separate, but then my wife called for me and so I got right up. After a few moments I realized that I was still in the phase. I actually only got up in the phase, but it took me a few moments to realize this. I was back in my house.

After some time in my house, I awoke in my bed for real, but quickly re-entered the phase into my house once more.

I was going to do a fourth reentry, but my real wife shook my arm during separation to get me up for the day, because it was well past the time I normally get up.

I'm not sure how long I had slept for before I entered the phase the first time. I do remember having a very vivid normal dream during that time. I may have also fallen asleep between phase experiences, but I still remember them being so real that I doubt it.

I got up for the day 1.5 hours after first waking up for the deferred method (the phase likely happened just in the last few minutes).

Alexander Lelekov
Saint Petersburg, Russia

When I'm dreaming I usually move by taking great leaps, much further than a kangaroo, about 100-300 yards. This happens regularly in my dreams, and I usually immediately realize that I'm in a dream. During one of the leaps, I realized while airborne that I was dreaming and also realized that I was able to land in a small dirty pond. As expected, I landed right in the pond and went deep under the water (*M.R.: no deepening*). And at that very moment, I found myself in the stencil, with my hands and head half stuck in it.

I got a little nervous that this attempt would also be unsuccessful, and so I immediately tried to separate from my body. I was unable to get my head or hands out, and for the first time I tried to turn around round my axis and managed to get out. Then I either slipped down or fell from the bed, but I did not feel any pain. I crawled for 1-2 meters and then felt that I could go back. I started to touch the rug and some other thing, though I don't know exactly what it was as it was dark, and, lo and behold: within 20-30 seconds I probably felt what small kittens feel when their eyes open for the first time. Everything was foggy and blurry at first, but then a picture started to appear, the room filled with light, and colors became bright and vivid. I tried very hard to restrain my excitement, and, to my surprise, was able to.

I walked around my apartment thinking about what I should do (*M.R.: no plan of action*). Realizing that I did not have that much time, I decided to talk to an elderly man who would answer my questions. I decided that there would be an omniscient elderly man behind the apartment's front door, which I was about to open. And there he was, half-bald, about 60 years old, in a grey coat waiting for me. I asked him the question, "What should I do to get into the phase more often?" But he started to tell me about how he was raped as a child. And to be more precise, this was already not an elderly man, but an elderly woman. I was not very interested in hearing her story, thus I tried to move away from her, suggesting that we could talk later. But the elderly woman was persistent, and I did not want to offend her, because I thought that this was an unusual phase with its own set of rules, and namely that once you have asked an old woman a question, you are supposed to be courteous and listen to the entire answer (*M.R.: wrong logic*).

I went with her to the kitchen of my apartment. The telephone suddenly rang. I got scared that the telephone was ringing in my apartment and would wake me up, which is why I immediately started to look at my hand in order to maintain. But the sensations were quite stable, and I stopped doing that. Then, me and this lady wanted to cook something in my kitchen. She said that I could heat a frying pan without gas. But I instead decided to try the technique of putting the hands together and blowing on them, and returned back into my body (*M.R.: no re-entering*).

Daniel
Bistrita, Romania

I set my alarm for 5 AM, as I had gone to bed at midnight! The alarm went off, I silenced and got out of bed at 5:10 AM, went to the kitchen, ate something, smoked a cigarette, and then got back to bed with *intention*.

So, I do not know how I got into the phase again, I think I just woke up into it.

I remember very well being in a strange room again, and my vision was blurry. I remember the place as being very colorful. I had shouted aloud, "I need clear vision", and then repeated myself. And as I had shouted, I found myself peering at the walls of the room before me. After few seconds, everything was a crystal-clear as the picture from a Bluray disc.

I deepened by punching the walls. This time, like every other time I observed the details of my fist entering into the wall, I felt it so realistically. It was as if the wall was made from rubber. I saw and felt how it moulded tor my fist. The wall even changed color: it went from yellow to bluish. As is typical of me, I had no plan of action. Even when I have a plan of action, I do not recall it very well when in the phase.

So I found a mirror. I looked at my reflection, everything was normal. Then I closed my eyes and intended to see my muscles as being larger. When I opened my eyes, my chest seemed pretty big, but it looked like it was the chest of a 70 year old. I thought, "what the heck?"

I closed my eyes again and created my intention, more intensely this time. When I opened them again, to my surprise I was like Vin Diesel: big chest, well defined, big arms etc. I said, "damn I look awesome!"

So from there on I think I pretty much lost it (*M.R.: no maintaining*). But it was great anyway...

Robyn
Australia

I had an awakening and immediately attempted to roll out. That didn't work, so I tried brain strain, but still nothing... So I phantom wiggled, not sure which part of my body, just something - anything, as I was determined to separate.

It worked, and I felt myself moving upward and forward and then I seemed to get a little stuck, and so I thought, "Oh, I am just going to stand up - they say that works when you are stuck." I immediately stood up, my legs from the knees down went through my bed. It was very pleasant to be free of my body. The whole movement of separation had a slight, effervescent tingling sensation (as you see on Star Trek when they are translocating, i.e. "Beam me up Scotty.")

I moved to the side of my bed, but I hadn't opened my eyes yet as I was a teeny bit anxious (excited) about what I would see when I did. I naturally started touching everything within reach: the wall, the bed, and the stool at the end of my bed. I then opened my eyes.

I immediately felt and saw a small dark shadow at my feet. I knew it was Tsar, my Mother's Blue Russian cat. Although he does not live with me at the moment, I knew it was him. As I moved away from room, I caught a glimpse of my body lying in my bed: my mouth was slightly open and I could hear myself softly snoring. I had no desire to look directly at my body.

I was thrilled to be out. I stepped into my living room (*M.R.: no plan of action*). To my left was a lamb and a sheep and several brownish-black geese. I was delighted to see them there in my living room. I felt Tsar at my feet again.

My attention was drawn to what was outside through the window. There I saw colorful, twirling carnival rides. The colors were not brilliant as I had hoped they might be, however when I looked directly at one it twirled faster. There were a multitude of birds in the sky, passing overhead. It was quite surreal. I got the same feeling as I got when watching the scene when birds flew by in the movie *Jurassic Park*.

Back in my living room, the animals had gone but I noticed wet, sloppy bird droppings on the carpet (naughty geese!). I looked at my hand it was not normal. Half was natural flesh, and the other half was like moulded, skin tone plastic, as in the mask the Phantom of the Opera wears. I was not at all perturbed at its appearance. I just thought, "oh, that's interesting." My next thought was, "I am going poke my finger through my hand." I did, and then quickly removed it, thinking to myself, "eewww! It works." Again, I was not perturbed.

I moved into the kitchen. It was as if burglars had been there. There was broken glassware and crockery all over the bench. I am presuming it was those naughty geese again. Anyway, I turned to the refrigerator and saw a broken mirror on the floor and wondered where it had come from. The refrigerator door was ajar, I opened it further and discovered that the vegetable crisper drawer had a mirrored front and it had been smashed. I opened the freezer door to see about 8 cups of ice cream (the commercial kind, something like Cornetto). Their lids had been peeled off and sticky ice cream had run and dripped everywhere. Was it those birds again?

I turned back into the living room to see more runny bird droppings than there were before. Puzzled, I wondered how I was going to clean up this mess.

I then heard people outside and looked down through the window. (I live upstairs.)

There were half a dozen people dressed in dark blue workman's clothes down there talking. One of them was a woman who shot me an unpleasant look and said something that I couldn't hear. I felt threatened. A little nervous, I waited for them to pass underneath my apartment, but they didn't appear on the other side of the building. Phew! (In reality, my apartment is suspended between two buildings, cars and pedestrians pass under.)

Standing on the threshold of the living room and kitchen, I decided to fly and see how that felt. I zoomed around the ceiling a couple of times.

Now standing in the living room, contemplating what I should do next, I felt a little bored. I figured I might as well go back to my body (*M.R.: wrong logic*). I moved to my bed and crawled into my body. I felt a little disheveled and

www.obe4u.com

crumpled in there, but as soon as I felt smooth and comfortable I opened my eyes.

Nina
Brisbane, Australia

I woke up. I needed to go to the bathroom, but decided to ignore the need. I felt light vibrations and did forced falling asleep. I knew I was in the phase. I could feel myself moving, but the vibrations weren't there anymore. I thought to myself, "that's odd... oh well, just roll out!" So I did!

I was on my husband's side of the bed and I couldn't see properly. My eyes felt stuck together. After some straining, I could see out of my left eye fine and noticed a whole lot of pillows and blankets piled on the floor. I thought, "how did all that get there??"

I tried to open my right eye, but the eyelids were stuck together. I tried physically opening it with my fingers, but it was stuck like glue. I thought, "what if I rip my eyelid," but knowing full well I couldn't. Then, I realized that the reason my eye was not opening was because I had to deepen! I closed my eyes and frantically started touching everything I could. I touched the walls, my husband's bedside table, and knocked over everything. I could hear glass hitting the table. I'd knocked over a glass of water. I still couldn't see! I sort of stalled, and didn't know what to do.

Then, I remembered that while in the phase, I had wanted to stick my head out of my *closed* bedroom window, look out, and jump! (my bedroom is on the 2nd floor) I ran excitedly to the window and stuck my head out! *Argh!! It works! So cool!*

I jumped out, and before I hit the ground I said, "I want to fly." I took off and flew around my house and the others around it. *Ahhh so this is what it feels like.* It was amazing! Then all of a sudden - SPLAT! I fell out of the sky! *How rude!*

I jumped up and tried again. I didn't take off, but sort of hovered and then fell again. I did this twice, and on the third time I took off. I flew down the road. I still couldn't see out of my right eye, and thought, "I wonder if I can make it rain?" I said, "I want it to rain," and it started raining! As soon as it had started raining, I could see out of both eyes. I wiped my face. There were beautiful cool rain drops as I was flying! It was so peaceful. I didn't want it to end.

It did however end, and I found myself sitting on the side of the road a block over from my house. I realized I needed to go to the bathroom! *Damn it!* I woke up.

This was the coolest thing I have ever experienced in my life - so much fun! I can't wait for more OBE's - bring it on!

Boris Bender
Moscow, Russia

I became conscious in my dream almost immediately after falling asleep. I was in my apartment standing in the corridor. Being surprised by having so suddenly found myself in the phase, I started to touch the walls with my hands to test their firmness or, "realness," as well as to intensify the phase by touching. I entered the room (*M.R.: no plan of action*). There was a bed standing next to the wall, with my mother sleeping on it. I could not see her face, only her body under the blanket. The room and corridor were exact replicas of their real-life counterparts.

While thinking about my sleeping mother, I suddenly started to feel somewhat uneasy. When I approached the window, I saw a grotesque landscape behind it that was similar to pictures from movies about catastrophes: a wasteland, houses in ruins, odd pileups of building materials, slabs of concrete, garbage, craters from explosions here and there, and I noticed human figures in some places.

Fearing a foul caused by the fact that I was taking in a panoramic view (the view from the window spanned 180 degrees and cut off at the horizon, which is in fact almost exactly as the view from my apartment is in real life), I turned back into the room and started to touch the wardrobe, and then knelt down to touch the floor. All the while, my fear had been growing stronger and stronger: both out of thinking about my sleeping mother and due to the view from the window. Anxiety turned into real fear within a matter of several seconds, and then graduated into terror and panic. I lost the ability to think critically. I had only one thought: I had to go back to my body (*M.R.: wrong logic*). I darted back to my bed and suddenly found myself lying on it. I closed my eyes, but could not understand if I were in my real body or still in the phase. My terror grew even stronger when I half-opened my eyes and saw that my mother was getting up from her bed. She looked like a character from a horror movie and apparently was hostile to me.

I wanted to disappear, dissolve, and wake up! I hectically tried to recall the techniques for an emergency exit from the phase, but with poor results: I tried to freeze, relax and touch my fingers to my toes in order to feel a connection with my real body. At some moments I felt like I had it, thinking, "The connection had been restored!" I opened my eyes, but realized that I was still in the phase when I saw that the room had changed, and was now awash with garbage.

The fact that the attempts kept ending with false awakenings was driving me crazy. I was especially shocked when I got up after one of the false awakenings and saw my mother standing at my bed, still looking threateningly at me, like a vampire or a zombie from a horror movie. Plus, she started to reach out toward me with her hands!

I nevertheless kept on and tried to freeze and wiggle my toes, this time without opening my eyes, and not checking where I was. I started to calm down after some time, but I was unable to feel my real body, which was confirmed by the fact that sounds were coming in from the phase: I heard sparrows chirping outside the window, though it reality it was too late for sparrows to be out. However, the chirping and the associations that it brought (i.e. day, warmth, sparrows, and sun), probably helped me a lot and calmed me down, as I finally managed to sense my real body and found myself in reality. Nevertheless, after I got up, I immediately started to verify for about half a minute that I was no longer in the phase by touching objects, making sure that they were hard, and feeling all of my bodily sensations.

Sumer
sumer.phase@gmail.com

All my entries into the phase were spontaneous via lucid dreaming or in a state of very dim consciousness. This was my first fully conscious separation. Because of this, it felt like REAL FUN.

I returned from a business trip and went to bed with an eye-mask on at 3 PM. I attempted to enter the phase by direct methods, but fell asleep. I woke up in about 3 hours without movement, but with a feeling that I had woken up completely (*M.R.: no re-entering*). Nevertheless, something told me to try to move my arm - in case it was my phantom arm. The arm started to rise together with the duvet. I had a feeling that the duvet was covering my head as well (which was not true), and therefore decided to raise the arm higher to test whether it was my phantom arm or not, as at some point there would be light from the window if it indeed was my real arm. No, there was no light and I realized it was my phantom arm. I tried to roll out with the arm. At first, separation was partial. I tried again and rolled out form the bed and ended up on all fours on the floor. Vision appeared almost immediately. I started palpating the floor, walls, and window shades, feeling the texture. Then I rose and started clapping my hands. There was sound. Then I went to explore the rooms (*M.R.: no plan of action*). I passed by a mirror. I looked at myself and saw myself there with dark glasses and a wide smile, although I was not smiling at the time. I went into a room and saw a beautiful partition wall made into an aquarium. I saw people behind the partition and went there – and then, a foul! (*M.R.: no maintaining*)An attempt to separate again did not work.

My main mistake in the phase was in not taking the clues that the deepening was not sufficient. The clues were: no change in perception of realism after application of deepening techniques, the weak sound of my hands clapping, and the strange reflection of myself in the mirror.

John Merritt
Houston, USA

I already had a few successes with astral projection, but they hadn't lasted long, and I had never made it out of my house. I consulted with a friend and she told me there was a sort of gravity that tended to pull you back into your body if you stayed too close to it, and that what she did was try to immediately leave the location of the physical body so that the pull would be weaker.

So, I set my intentions on leaving my house as quickly as possible on my next successful attempt. After a few days I had a projection. And I remembered that I had wanted to get out of the house this time, and so as soon as I rose up off the bed I started running down the hall, down the stairs, and to the front door. I opened the door (or at least it felt like I opened the door) and ran outside. I had done it. Within seconds of leaving my body, I made it outside the house. I hadn't really planned what I would do once outside and I just started running through the yard and towards the street. I happened to look back toward the house, and I saw a couple of little red eyes in the darkness. And those eyes were moving too! I could see that it (whatever it was) was running too, and I was afraid that it was running after me! I got scared and immediately found myself back in my body (*M.R.: no maintaining and no re-entering*).

This projection was special because it was the first time I was able to leave the house and the first time I encountered another entity while outside my body.

Alexei Teslenko
Moscow, Russia

Actually, I was not planning to travel that night, but when I woke up around midnight I decided to try to enter the phase nevertheless. I started to perform phantom movements with my arms, but then a strong sleepy lethargy overcame me and I suddenly wanted to give up my attempts to enter the phase and simply fall asleep. However, I was persistent and continued to perform phantom movements with my arms. Instead of feeling the usual vibrations that occur when this technique is performed, I simply fell asleep and continued the phantom movements while dreaming. Because of that, my consciousness apparently did not fall asleep completely, and I became aware that I was dreaming.

I immediately climbed out of my body. There was no vision, conscious awareness was no more than 50%, so the phase was not that deep. In order to maintain the phase, I immediately started chaotically touching everything around me. It helped. Vision came, though it was murky. I then found myself in my apartment. I decided to strive to deepen. After I had achieved a stable phase, I decided that it would be good to grab a snack and headed for the fridge (*M.R.: no plan of action*). I should add that I was on a strict diet at the time and was craving something sweet or fried. However, when I opened the fridge, I was quite disappointed. There was a lot of food in the fridge, but all of it required preparation (raw meat, fish, dill, etc.). However, there was a bottle of sparkling mineral water on a special lower shelf in the fridge. Without giving it any thought, I took the bottle and started to chug it.

All of the sensations were just as in real life: I felt the bubbles from the carbonation, that peculiar taste that mineral water has, and also how the water went down my throat. In general, everything was quite realistic, though there was no sensation of my stomach filling up with water and, moreover, the water felt somewhat dry. It sounds funny, but that very feeling of water's dryness spoiled my overall impression somewhat. After a foul, I realized that a possible reason for this might have been dryness in the mouth of my real body.

Usually, if there are, for example, candies in the kitchen or in the fridge, I actually take a handful of them and consume them while traveling through the phase.

After going to the fridge, I wanted to see something interesting. I decided to employ the technique for creating objects and people, and so I closed my eyes and focused on the image of a girl whom I wanted to see at that very moment. I affirmed my desire, and I then opened my eyes, concentrating on the area to my side. The air grew misty at first, and then the person I was expecting materialized out of the air, and came to life, seemingly fully autonomous and with free will - she had the same manner of speaking as in real life, and acted in the same way...

Dodd Stolworthy
Ventura, USA

I set my alarm to go off in 6 hours, but I woke up to vibrations after 5 hours of sleep (*M.R.: no separation*). Straining the brain worked really well and the vibes got stronger and stronger (*M.R.: no separation*). While they were getting stronger, I told myself that if I heard any kids coming in the room or felt the bed shake, that it was fake! This is because I've been fooled too many times.

My body started getting loose and floaty and before I knew it, I was just out! Didn't have to separate!

My neck has been messed up since April and the last couple weeks I've made it my goal to do something about it in the phase (I got the idea from the thread "Healing in the phase" by Jeff on the obe4u.com forum). I wanted to try some kind of manual stimulation, but I did not see my body on the bed. Instead, I noticed my sister-in-law was sleeping with my wife in my bed.

I wanted to accomplish my goal before I fouled. Since I didn't see my body, I recalled Michael talking about taking pills. I was a little worried about taking random pills, so I did a reality check first and then went for it.

When I woke up I noticed weird tingling, vibrations in my neck and I feel pretty good today!! I'd say a 20% improvement! AWESOME!

Dodd Stolworthy
Ventura, USA

I was waking up and felt a strange feeling in my hands and feet. I also noticed I was sleeping in the baby's bed but, like most dreams, did not think anything of it. Meanwhile, *I felt the presence of someone standing by my bed*. It was a strange feeling and the presence that made me question lucidity, so I stuck my hand through the wall, and BAM! I was now lucid.

So I grabbed my 7 year old son, put him on my shoulders and told him we were going flying. I jumped up but nothing. So I decided to walk through the wall. As I did so, everything went black and I knew I was losing the phase. I rubbed my hands together and waited patiently for the phase to return. To my surprise, it did! I've been able to recover phases before, but none after losing them as long as I had here. So this time I decided to not do anything until I was able to make the phase more stable. I rubbed my hands some more and everything became so vivid! I still had my son on my shoulders, and decided to just jump through the wall and I gently floated down to the street - man, what a rush! I then took another huge leap and slowly floated down again (*M.R.:*

no plan of action). Everything faded and I did not feel any hands that I could rub together, and so it ended (*M.R.: no maintaining*).

I've heard of people lying still after phases and being able to re-enter the phase, but I was not able to do it.

Matthew Shea
Canada

I was having a dream, and at the end of the dream, I could feel the shift in consciousness as I came back to my bed (*M.R.: no separation*). I attempted rubbing my hands together, and I decided to incorporate rubbing my face as well. It began to start to feel realistic, so I starting putting more work into it. Then, I tried to get up. Immediately after trying to get up, I questioned whether this was the physical world or not. Regardless, I kept on trying. I had to put in a large amount of effort into it, but I eventually managed to get myself out of bed.

I couldn't open my eyes. I tried to force them open with my hands and got a little bit of light in. Then I remembered that sometimes you don't have vision, and that you need to do grounding techniques. I began feeling the walls and soon enough my vision began to come to me. In the process, I could hear a woman I know giving orders to someone. When my vision came, she was gone. I projected into my brother's room instead of my own, but now the whole house was different. There were people everywhere dressed in hunting uniforms. I walked into one room and there was a desk with a girl I know behind it (*M.R.: no plan of action*). She seemed to be in charge of what was going on around there. We talked for a minute and then someone came in with a dead moose in a huge bag. It was quite strange.

I proceeded to walk somewhere else, but I don't know how I got there. It was a huge room, with shelves full of VHS tapes on one side and someone playing the piano. They were playing Jewish music, I think, and people were all around, listening. We walked into another room and someone started dancing. I began to dance with them, just fooling around. Everybody came into the room and watched us dance or joined us. I started to lose the phase, and could partially feel myself lying in my bed. I felt around trying to ground myself again but it was too late. I could feel the sides of my bed. I tried to get out of my body once again but it never worked.

Matthew Shea
Canada

I felt as if I was lying in my bed at first, but at the same time I felt like I was in a dream. I could hear a game show or something on a television, so it was definitely in my head. I relaxed and knew I was either in a dream, or about to be. All of a sudden, I was thrust into the phase. I landed in a grassy field in a place like my town, but having a bit of a different appearance. I walked along, and felt the grass and other things as I did. I crossed a road as a huge vehicle came down the road. The vehicle hit me and knocked me down, but luckily it didn't hurt. I felt as if I was observing a movie. It felt great. Suddenly, I realized what my plan was.

I really wanted to try and fly and go visit someone that I know. I jumped a couple times to no avail. Then, I jumped and began to fly a little. All of a sudden, the police came and pulled me out of the sky (*M.R.: wrong action*) and accused me of terrorism! I ended up being let off because they really don't know what the heck they were talking about. I went home after this. I really wanted to try and visit my friend again, so I went and put my shoes on. At that point, I started thinking about my physical body, and so I immediately stopped thinking about it and continued with the shoe thing.

I walked outside, and then I start thinking about what the world around me looked like. I gazed up behind my house, where there are usually a few hills. They were huge now and very grassy instead of rocky. This amused me and I looked around some more. Now there were hills in my front yard. As I gazed up at the sky, I noticed something amazing. There were moons of every different shape and size, differing from the normal color. Some were pale blue. Some of them were oval and some were round. It was a really fantastic sight. After this, I continued on my way to visit my friend. I started walking down the road, trying to fly again and again.

My brother showed up and I told him what I was doing. He suggested that he give me a boost. I told him that I might end up hurting myself like that, and so he doesn't do it. I kept trying. I even jumped off someone's head when I saw them coming up the road. I guess I finally gave up on it. There was a small lapse between then and when I ended up in my house (*M.R.: no maintaining*). Once I did end up in my house, we were having something to eat. As I was sitting at the kitchen table, I all of a sudden woke up (*M.R.: no re-entering*). It feels really interesting to just wake up peacefully in your bed after an experience like that.

Chris
Chrille_pk@hotmail.com

I woke and started to apply the indirect techniques after an attempt to separate. Nothing happened...

I remembered to keep doing cycles, and once I reached the fourth cycle and was really struggling to not fall asleep, I noticed that I was hearing a beeping noise, and so I started listening in. I don't really remember, but I think I tried to separate in my bedroom at that point. I teleported and suddenly found myself standing in a shopping mall.

I sort of knew it was a dream, but my mind couldn't accept it, and so I was both aware and unaware at the same time. But then my "aware half" decided to touch the ground and everything I saw around. The dream was now perfectly clear.

I tried to summon a person. I thought, "around that corner I will meet my friend Johanna." Once I walked past it, I saw her! She had on different clothes than usual, but her face looked all the same. I talked to her while simply admiring the vivid world and projections of people I know. She then gazed at me for several seconds and kissed me! I was shocked, because I don't have feelings for her. However, here I lost lucidity (*M.R.: no maintaining*)...

Dmitry Bolotkov
Moscow, Russia

The following all occurred after I woke up, and then began to doze off again. I lay on my side and was beginning to fall asleep, when I saw some fuzzy images from a previous dream. My body began to fill with heaviness, I practically stopped feeling it. Mild vibrations arose. I immediately remembered about the phase, and just relaxed... Imagine my surprise when I felt that I was separating. My heartbeat abruptly increased during the process. I separated, and found myself suspended in the air (I still couldn't see yet). So I started flailing my arms and legs, spinning in the darkness, trying to fly as far away as possible from my body. I came up against something solid (the ceiling, I think). My legs then swung down to the left, and I assumed a vertical position. I started rubbing my hands, trying to see them. My vision gradually came to me.

I finally saw my own hands. They were smaller than in reality, and seemed to have a green hue to them. Then I reviewed the situation: I was in my old apartment, but the furniture was chaotically arranged. I began to palpate and scrutinize everything. My vision was incredibly sharp, much clearer than in reality (I've become quite nearsighted over the last two years). Strangely enough, I felt as if my eyes were closed, but that I could nevertheless see. I then was somehow able to turn off my vision. I dove into the floor (*M.R.: no plan of action*).

I flew down for some time. Then, I stopped and turned my vision back on. I was in outer space, and saw totally strange planets. Because I'm afraid of heights, I turned off my vision again and wished to find myself in another place, one where I'd have something solid to stand on. After a few moments, I felt I was standing on something. I turned my vision back on. I was in the desert. Strange animals were grazing, there were pigeons everywhere, and poker chips scattered all over the sand. For some reason, I figured I was near Los Vegas. I walked around a bit. Once I started looking around, my field of vision began narrowing. As soon as there was nothing but a small peep-hole of vision left, I began rubbing my hands together and looking at them. My vision returned after several seconds. Then, a pigeon ran up to me with the clear intention of biting my leg. I began running away, kicking up sand at the bird (*M.R.: wrong action*). That's when it all ended. I found myself back in my body, and opened my eyes (*M.R.: no re-entering*).

Yan Gvozdev
Moscow, Russia

When implementing the counting technique, I thought about parks, and an image of a photograph of an autumn park appeared before me. I tried to bring the image to life, as if I were moving the details of it. Inside, I felt that I was in a state suitable for trying to enter the phase, and was able to dive into the picture upon my first attempt.

I now found myself in that autumn park, it was very beautiful. In an effort to deepen, I started to palpate everything around me: leaves, the bark on the trees, and my own hands. The state stabilized, and I went for a walk around the wonderful park. It was full of birds singing and crisp leaves.

As previously planned, I decided to play it by ear.

The first thing that came to mind was the question of how my future home would look, something that I had been thinking a lot about. I concentrated, and transported to that home using the method of closed eyes.

I found myself near a very beautiful house. I had never even daydreamed about so beautiful a house in real life. I walked towards it, rubbing my hands together all the way in order to deepen the state. Once I got closer, the home began to change and take different forms at a speed commensurate with the thoughts in my head.

Then, walking around the house for some time, peering at and touching the furniture, I had the thought that the house somehow reminded me of a beautiful hotel, and then the house turned into a hotel. It stood before me like one of those huge beach-side tourist resorts in Egypt.

I entered the enormous hotel. It was full of guests. I walked among them, talking with some, and touching at others out of curiosity. Then I went into the restaurant, and saw there a variety of dishes. I sampled some of them. Then, I went out for a walk inside the hotel, continuing to talk to people I encountered along the way.

Internally, I had been asking myself about the near future in real life, and trying to figure out who or what could tell me about it. My wife Alexandria appeared, and we started to wonder together about our near future, as we were quite interested to know about it. My wife's double behaved exactly like my spouse in real life, with the same character traits.

Alexandria proposed that we try to enjoy ourselves, and think of something to do by the sea. For example, we could go down the great water-slide at the hotel's water park.

We went up to the highest water slide, which was so high up that I became short of breath. I realized that going down such an enormous water slide would be good for maintaining and stabilizing the phase state. It absolutely wasn't clear why there wasn't a swimming pool at the end to land in. I figured that it perhaps wasn't such a good idea to slide down, as we were quite high up. But Alexandria went first, and I, like a real gentleman, slid down after her. But then, as I had guessed, the slide ended 50 yards from the ground. At the bottom was asphalt. There was no time left to concentrate and imagine that there would be a swimming pool at the end of the slide. I flew right onto the asphalt. 110% Realism. While I was still flying, I figured that the landing would be quite painful. I landed with a thud right on my feet. The pain ran up my entire body, especially my shins and knees. Once the realization came that I had modeled that pain before my descent merely by thinking about it, the pain immediately vanished.

Then Alexandria decided to have more fun - she was already in a painfully playful mood. She found some kind of amusement-cannon that would shoot us quite far into the sea.

She again decided to go first, and I went right after her. It shot us 300-400 yards out from the shore. While I was flying behind Alexandria, I became quite afraid. Why so far out into the sea? Would we be able to swim back to shore?

I often mentally compare the phase space to the real world, and can state that they are often indistinguishable from each other. This is especially true of a very realistic phase when you ask yourself the question, "And exactly where am I right now?" At such moments, the only thing that helps is a deep analysis of the situation and thinking about the body, but doing so risks fouls occurring.

She went first into the water, and I after her. Due to the height and speed from which I fell, I dove quite deeply into the water. I felt like I was suffocating. I could not breathe underwater, and started looking for Alexandria. I spotted her courageously swimming down in the ocean depths.

I came to my senses, and started concentrating on breathing underwater. I was successful, but the weight and depth of the water unnerved me. I swam down to catch up with Alexandria. We swam deeper and deeper, overcoming the water pressure with difficulty. We went down to 1500 feet below sea-level. Impressed by what I saw, I was at loss for thoughts, as the events taking place were completely indistinguishable from reality.

We swam even deeper, and something caught our eye. We swam up closer, and saw something like a cave in the coral reef. When we went down a little deeper, the seabed was clearly visible.

We spotted a tunnel that led into a cave, and swam towards it. Alexandria seemed to have already known the way. I followed behind her, not quite understanding where we were going, but trusting her completely. We swam into the cave, and surfaced inside the pool of water inside it into an air-filled space. The chamber had windows like those of an aquarium. One could watch all kinds of beautiful fish swimming right past this sea-cave. We were greeted by four women in the cave, who appeared to have been waiting for us. They sat us down next to each-other. They looked like journalists and anchorwomen.

I stopped moving once I sat down, and started to fade out. I began to focus on issues concerning our future, forgetting to maintain the phase.

I started asking them my questions once the newscast started. Then, I accidentally thought about my body, and a foul occurred (*M.R.: no re-entering*). I nevertheless obtained a lot of visual information, which I later distilled into events and images.

Two weeks later, I went on vacation to a big hotel in the real world, where I saw the same images that were described above and occurred in this phase. Of course, the correspondence was not 100%, but the overall picture of the situation completely coincided in terms of meaning and significance.

breadbassed
cabeludo@hotmail.co.uk

So last night after about 4 hours of sleep, I woke up and did a few little things, went to the bathroom, lit some incense, and then went back to bed. As I was falling asleep, I started to observe dream images coming in and out of my awareness. Once I felt that one was strong enough, I just got up and fell off the end of my bed. I was now in the phase.

I was in complete darkness, which happens to me a lot when I exit my body, and so I started deepening techniques untill I could see. Here's the interesting part: I've been wanting to do an OBE "test" for a while, and so before going to bed that night I had shuffled a deck of cards and put one high up in my room where I couldn't see it (I hadn't looked at it). As soon as I could see after deepening, I climbed up and looked at the card. What I saw was the 8 of diamonds.

After doing this I jumped out my window and explored a "phase" garden. Two alien-like creatures drove up and pulled out guns on me, but I disarmed them quickly. I stole their car and drove around crashing into things for fun. Then I had a false awakening. I was back in my room, but had woken up in a standing position, and I so instantly knew I was still in the phase.

This time, I decided to try something else I had wanted to try. It might sound a bit crazy, but I spoke to the plants in my room, I made them grow huge and they filled my room. It looked spectacular. Then, the spirit of the plants manifested as my bag, which was strange, and he spoke like an old English man. I don't really remember what he said.

Shortly thereafter I woke up for real, and it took me a little while to remember what I had done in the phase, but once I did I jumped up and checked the card to see if I was right. It turned out to be the 8 of clubs, so I got the suit wrong but the number right! I was still pretty happy - even though I didn't get it 100% correct, it was close enough for me!

breadbassed
cabeludo@hotmail.co.uk

So I woke up at 6.30 this morning, did a few things, and went back to bed. I didn't do any techniques as such, but it took me so long to get back to sleep that I felt myself enter sleep paralysis, and so as soon as I felt the moment was right I got up and fell off the end of my bed (seems to be becoming my standard exit procedure these days). After some deepening I walked out my room and saw my reflection in a mirror: I was wearing a hat, which was confirmation for me that I was now in the phase, as I haven't worn a hat in years.

So I wanted to repeat my previous test in a slightly different manner. I got my sister to write down a 3 digit number and put it in her room to see if I could read it in the

OBE state. I walked in her room and her boyfriend was asleep, I called out his name a few times and tried to convince him it was a phase but he seemed sleepy and didn't respond. The results from looking at the number were inconclusive, as I perhaps hadn't deepened enough and it wasn't very stable. I'll tell my sister what I saw anyway and let you know if the results are worth hearing about. Anyway, after also telling my sister that this was a phase and they could both do what they wanted, I dived through the floor to relocate.

I ended up in an old library and tried some deepening, and the normal method of touching everything worked. There was also a CD on the floor, I wanted to use more senses than touch to deepen further, and so I licked the CD. At first it didn't taste of anything, but after a few licks it kind of tasted how I suppose a CD would. This did seem to make my surroundings more realistic.

Last night before bed, I was reading a highly interesting website on the Illuminati, actually made by some members. I figured I would try to find out more about them in the phase, and so I called out, "Illuminati". Before I finished the word, 3 chairs moved by themselves into a small row and a voice said, "take a seat", and so I did. The walls of the library opened up into a stage and many robed figures began to put on a show and sing (nothing like I was expecting!). Shortly after it began, I thought to myself, "if I just sit here and watch I will probably wake up soon", and lo and behold after thinking that I pretty much woke up straight away (*M.R.: no re-entering*).

Perhaps just having the thought of waking up made me lose the phase quicker?

Also, I've noticed that if I have an idea of what I'm going to do in the phase, it generally comes with some expectations of what will occur when I try it. Not on one occasion has trying an idea out ever met my expectations (I'm not saying it has been better or worse, but just completely different to what i would expect). In the phase I would expect happenings to occur based on expectations, but clearly this isn't quite the case.

breadbassed
cabeludo@hotmail.co.uk

Last night I had what seemed like a very long phase experience. I went to bed at 1:00 AM and as I was falling asleep I started to notice some visuals, and eventually found myself in a room that was dark and dull. It seems my experiences from falling straight asleep always seem to be this way. In addition, it felt very unstable and I felt some invisible force pulling me around like it was trying to get hold of me.

Since I haven't had luck using sensory amplification to enhance my visuals in previous direct experiences, I decided to try something slightly different. I sat in my normal meditation position and took some deep breaths. As I first sat down, the "force" was strong and I kept moving around, like on a ship in a storm, but after a few deep breaths the force weakened and my visuals enhanced. I flew out the window and shortly thereafter awoke again in darkness.

I realized it was a false awakening, and remember feeling uncomfortable again and so I started to sing my favorite Bob Marley song. I remember a man in a suit who was "coming after me" as if I didn't belong there and was trying to take me away. I tried to make him disappear, but it didn't work, and so I went for him. He then deflated like a balloon and fell to the floor.

I was in what seemed like a club, and I asked one woman "what is the truth about this reality?" She replied, "It's all statistics." I found this confusing, and so walked around a little trying to decide what to do (*M.R.: no plan of action*). I remembered a website someone posted on a while ago with some "tests", one of which was to draw the infinity sign on a door then walk through it. I found a door and scratched the "omega" sign on it and walked through. It was just another room in the club, with a bar, and two men. One of them seemed very busy (I assumed he was the manager) and the other was sitting and drinking. The manager walked past me and I asked him to tell me something wise. He said, "bad socks"!

I spoke to the other man briefly but can't really remember the conversation. I went out of the room and sat with some people. I picked up a tissue and transformed it into a cheesecake, it tasted so delicious, so good in fact in made me want to have sex, and so jumped on a nearby lady, as we began we started to fly through the air, I remember flying through trees and could feel the leaves caressing my skin as we flew. At the point of climax I awoke again, in darkness.

I was still in the phase, this time in some sort of factory, with a huge green machine, I'm not sure what its purpose was. The phase characters told me that it required a special cog to work; I think they called it a *trigadore* (?)cog. After this, I remember a friend of mine coming into the room, upset, and I gave him some advice. I told him that sometimes you have to forgive yourself and not be too hard on yourself. This seemed to cheer him up.

Again I was shifted into darkness, almost hoping I was awake this time - but no, I was still in the phase. I decided to attempt to wake myself up (I thought it might not work, but I tried anyway), and just ended up feeling a sensation of movement and re-appearing in darkness. I found myself back in the club where I was previously, at this point I was starting to get concerned as it had felt like I had been in the phase for too long. I walked around the bar and asked a woman, "If I was lucid for the whole night, how long would it feel like?" I then realized it was a foolish question, as time in the phase cannot really be established. I re-phrased the question, asking when I might wake up, and she said "sometime today". Shortly after this, I awoke for real.

This phase felt like it went on for ages, and more happened that I haven't written here or have forgotten. When I eventually woke for real, I looked at the time: 1.43 AM. I had only slept for about 40 minutes but it felt like much longer. I tried my hardest to remember as much as I could, I wanted to write it down then, but I didn't want to wake my girlfriend, and so I decided against it.

Arlindo Batista
London, UK

This is my very first OOBE in which I could seemingly see the physical world as it is. I saw myself and my partner lying in bed and everything was crystal clear. I had the sensation of being catapulted out of my body as I heard a noise like a stone knocking the inside of a bucket. I watched my white ceiling approaching me very quickly, and just as I thought I was going to crash into it, I slowed down right up against it. I never actually remained in one location. I moved constantly. The movement was gradual, as though I were moving in frames of space - if this makes any sense to the reader. Then I could see everything in my bedroom. I was near the ceiling, and a feeling of excitement caused me to bounce all over the place at amazing speed, without actually touching any objects.

I wished to inspect my body closely, and instantly I found myself next to it as if by teleportation (*M.R.: no plan of action*). It was very weird. Initially I had felt like I were just a "floating head", but upon seeing my physical body, I started to look around for my new body. Suddenly, a transparent version of my hands and arms could be seen. Inside my new limbs, I could see moving patterns and could make out something like transparent veins and what looked like a fluid running through them. However, this was unlike what I have seen thoroughly illustrated in human anatomy books.

I then flew out of my bedroom window, and saw the landscape outside in the early hours of the morning. I was hovering 15 feet above the ground and as I moved I saw a little girl in my neighbor's window looking at me. I flew towards her, a bit confused because she could see me, and I asked her, "can you see me?" It seemed like I had projected this to her as a thought form. She shook her head in denial, which contradicted the fact that she had responded. She seemed terrified, so I hovered away and back to my room. When I woke up (*M.R.: no re-entering*), I thought to myself, "Was it an intense lucid dream? Was it very accurate about the reality I know?"

After all, I knew my neighbors and had never seen that little girl (she seemed to be about 5 years old) before. Then, in the following days, I noticed that my neighbor's daughters had friends around and they seemed to stay over. On one particular day, my partner sent me to the fish-and-chip shop. On the way there I went past our local Baptist church. I saw my neighbor talking to some people outside, and suddenly I saw the little girl! She was real as she came running out of the church with other children. She never saw me as she was having fun running around the adults with her friends. Then I realized that I was probably seeing her for the first time with my physical eyes. But how could I have a visual memory of her?

Arlindo Batista
London, UK

After an eventful day at the park with our children, Stacey and I went to bed around 12.30 PM. I'd had a glass of milk and a couple of chocolate digestive biscuits before going to bed. I was so tired that it didn't take me long to fall asleep. I woke up at 3.50 AM to use the bathroom. My sleep inertia symptoms were strong and it felt like the perfect opportunity for an out-of-body excursion. I lay down feeling like a dead weight and just relaxed. Soon I entered a familiar state of clarity and the hissing pulsation returned. I remember thinking that perhaps the "pineal engine" had ignited and was revving up to a rollercoaster of rushing sounds. What followed was a sensation of detachment from everything, but I was still conscious of lying in bed without visibility.

Suddenly, I could hear voices as though a radio had been switched on in my head. I couldn't understand what they said, but somehow the audio focused on a particular female voice which spoke as though it were delivering a lecture (*M.R.: no separation*). The subject-matter appeared to be consciousness itself, and a sentence stuck out to me: "The 'I' is the center of consciousness; therefore we are all centers of consciousness." The voice then proceeded to divulge a deep secret about reality that made me experience an epiphany, and yet I don't recall what was said. The voice turned into a whisper and was drowned out by orchestral music and clapping. This was followed by a vibrational surge, and subsequently I appeared to have separated from my body solely by willing myself out.

Vision was hazy, but I could distinguish my bedroom environment (*M.R.: no deepening*). I shifted in midair into the hallway and towards the mirror on the wall, which looked grey and absolutely non-reflective. I glided through it as I wished to see Marge, Stacey's deceased grandmother. What is unusual about what followed is that I was not traveling through a dark void as is typical when I plunge into the hallway mirror. Instead, I was zooming past treetops, rooftops, roads and vehicles. When I came to a halt, I saw that I was at ground level, skittering through an alley littered with rubbish in broad daylight. The colors of the environment were dull and I tried to make them brighter with my mind, but to no avail. Involuntarily, I teleported to another setting.

Initially, it was hard for me to see where I was because I kept laterally zapping from surface to surface, unable to fixate on a particular location. I managed to slow down my movement near the ceiling of what looked like a large bathroom. I saw a little girl, who appeared to be eight or nine years of age, in a tub full of dirty water, and her groggy face was barely sticking out. I could see her swallowing water and lots of hairs until her head was completely immersed. A scowling man entered the room. He was tall, stocky, and his hair was short, dark and spiky. Wide-eyed and in a frenzy, this character drowned the child by pressing her head further down using a plunger. Neither characters took any notice of my presence. The intensity of the experience was alarming and I was literally in fight-or-flight mode as I witnessed that crime.

My perspective changed galvanically and I appeared to be in the tub now. The room was the same but the lighting was different. The same scowling man came in and proceeded towards me. In a reflex action, I ascended to the ceiling and, when I looked down, I observed a naked boy in the tub, screaming in sheer horror. Mercilessly, the man drowned the boy, and, as he did so, he blamed the child for what was happening to him and accused him of being the reason why he was a monster. He growled and shook the boy underwater. The child's efforts to break free were futile. I moved about the room uncontrollably as I attempted to see what else was going on.

I regained physical awareness in sleep paralysis, hoping that what I had experienced was imagined. My head hissed again. I heard more voices in my head as though they were engaged in dialogues with classical music intervals. I separated again, but this time, into a dark void. I wished to see Marge and felt hands gripping me on either side and leading me somewhere. I saw light ahead and found myself in a crisp environment. Sharp colors defined a surreal scenery composed of what appeared to be Roman ruins in a forest. I set out to look for Marge there but encountered a bald black man instead. I asked him who he was and he told me his name was either Simão or João Figo. We spoke in Portuguese. I asked him where we were and he told me that we were in the same place all the time. The conversation then became more vague and dreamlike. At times I had the impression that he could say what I was thinking and vice versa. It was as if we were somehow connected. I was unsure whether I could at times control his speech, or if the fact that I was thinking what he said at times was coincidental.

As I regained physical awareness, I heard mild showers in my head and my body felt cold. It was 7:30 AM.

Dmitry Plotnik

Moscow, Russia

Returning from a night out, we wandered into a shop called "The Magic Stone". We bought a druse piece (small crystals encrusted on the surface of a rock or mineral, in our case, amethysts). According to my girlfriend, the rock helps one to "tune in to one's dreams". To that end, one simply needed to put the piece on the headstand of one's bed, and just go to sleep. That's just what we did. We had to get up really early the next morning (at about 5 am) in order to make it for an excursion. As it were, we didn't have time to waste, but I nevertheless made an attempt to "tune in" to my dreams. I feel asleep at some point, but continued on to dream that I was lying on the bed and trying to tune-in for an exit from the body. At that very moment, I felt a light tingling in my back, a kind of life energy. I even tried to facilitate the sensation, thinking, "great, it's coming, so act!". It intensified, and now felt like waves going up and down my spine (*M.R.: no separation*). A characteristic sensation, long forgotten, went through my body. The sensation could not be considered pleasurable in any way, and that's when I thought to myself, "now I remember why I had stopped intentionally trying to enter the phase." However, it was already too late to turn back. At some moment I was lifted up, barely having time to look back at the couch.

I soon found myself in a spacious room (*M.R.: no deepening*). It was so large that the only thing that I could see clearly was the wall next to me. There were also some people in the room. They all wanted something from me and kept coming up to me with stupid pretexts. I kept telling them to "buzz off", and tried to drive them away. I had only one thought in my head: "I've got to find my girlfriend". I tried as hard as I could to remember where we had fallen asleep, but my memory kept failing me. Different characters constantly distracted me the whole time, one of them was especially persistent. At one point, he even insisted that I help him to open his bottle of wine with a corkscrew. I decided to help him, and once I had opened the bottle, I thought: "Why not?

I've never tried out wine in phase," and put the bottle right to my lips. The wine tasted really funny, more like watered-down blackberry jam with pieces of fruit floating around. The unfinished bottle somehow was no longer in my hands, and I continued trying to get out of that room.

The only thing I could find to deepen with was the wall of a strange construction made of wooden planks. It was whitewashed with what seemed to be an oil-based paint (more than anything else, it reminded me of an outhouse). I was about to poke my head in when an assertive type warned that, "... it's a portal from which uninvited guests are able to crash in..." Not eager myself to climb in there, I contented myself with taking off a small dark mirror from the outer wall. I played around a bit with my reflection (which did not always want to follow when I moved my head), but those characters milling about stuck to me like glue. I then decided to have some fun, and began looking into the mirror together with those companions, in pair with one at a time. However, their reflection was quite different from their outward appearance. I got quickly bored with this game, and told everybody to go away again.

I finally decided to get out of that building, concentrating on where the place at which we were sleeping might be. I abruptly opened a door, but was disappointed. There was an unfamiliar outdoor scene on the other side. It seemed to be just before dawn outside, the darkest hour. Single cars went down the street. I began to peer at the cars parked at the curb. They had quite a funny-looking appearance. Suddenly, a car swerved off the street and towards me. It drove up to me, and I could see an interesting-looking woman sitting behind the wheel. She was wearing mostly green. We talked, and I couldn't get past the idea that she was speaking "bookishly", as if quoting the lines from a character in 19th century literature. I told her, "Now you're saying all that and so on..." She looked at me, and I noticed her strange eyes. She had green ladybugs instead of ordinary pupils. I realized that I was beginning to return to reality (*M.R.: no maintaining*).

I woke up (*M.R.: no re-entering*). I realized that I was lying on my back with my arms at my sides, and holding my girlfriend's hand in mine. She suddenly woke up too, and began to relate her experience...

Nadezhda Maslova
Moscow, Russia

We were already a bit stressed out on the night that it happened, because we had to wake up very early the next day in order to go on an excursion. We were afraid that we'd oversleep. I had woken up several times over the course of the night, and finally decided to use the nocturnal awakenings to enter the phase.

I successfully "exited the body", and stood up on the pull-out bed (*M.R.: no deepening*). I was in the same room that I had fallen asleep in, but discovered that there were two mirrors on the wall that weren't there in real life. Peering into one of the mirrors, I noticed that I wasn't wearing the same clothes that I had fallen asleep in. I then recalled my "idee fixe" - to whisk my boyfriend into my own phase experience. I went over to the couch he was sleeping on, pulled him up by the arm, and took him up to the mirror. I was then thinking, "So maybe he'll see himself in the mirror and become conscious while in my phase?"

We stood in front of the mirror, and I saw our reflections diffusing. I figured that I had been unsuccessful once again, and so I let him go. But I resolved to crawl into the mirror myself in order to translocate. I got up onto the table, put my hand into the mirror, and started moving in head-first. I suddenly realized that the mirror was "closed" - that there was nothing but darkness and a wall behind it, and thus I wouldn't be able to translocate anywhere. I then opted to employ the technique of "rotation". I started turning and imagining a favorite birch-tree forest from one of my travels in the phase. I really wanted to go there again.

I turned and turned, but could not enter into the forest, even thought it was vividly flashing before my eyes. I was unable to come to a halt in time. In the end, I landed in my mother's apartment. There was a toy stuffed rabbit lying on the floor. I took it by the hand, figuring that if I started to lose the phase, I would fiddle with it in order to stay in. Then, I saw another mirror on the wall, and decided to have a look at my reflection. I looked, but the reflection was not of me, but of some blurred creature, like a ghost. I even became somewhat frightened. That fear returned me back to the body (or so I thought while still in the phase), with the stuffed animal still in my hands.

I found myself back on my bed, but I didn't give up there. I decided to try another way to get my boyfriend to join me in the phase (after all, it gets lonely walking around all alone there!). I grabbed his hands and started sliding out of bed. We actually fell off the bed, but did not land on the floor. It was as if we had fallen from a cliff, and were suspended in air. Even though it was dark in the room that we were sleeping in, there was daylight all around us during our fall. Everything was really bright, much brighter than in the experience that I had just had. I was sure that I had been successful in pulling him into the phase with me! But then I saw that the arms holding me were clearly not his. I lowered my eyes, and saw that I was embracing another man!

He looked somewhat like my boyfriend, but his face was more aged and a bit different, while his hair was longer and gathered in a ponytail. I push him away and asked, "Who are you?" And he responded, "Well, I've already told you my name. Or maybe you're just seeing the future?" I calmed down a bit and told him, "I need a dress, I don't want to run around half naked." He replied, "So let's go buy one". I turned around, and saw a shop. We went in - actually, we hovered in about a foot off the ground. We were greeted by a mulatto shopkeeper, he showed me all the dresses hanging on the rack. I was in ecstasy! I stepped towards the rack... and instantly found myself back in my body (*M.R.: no re-entering*)!

What a shame, not to have been able to wear those cute dresses at least in the phase!

Chapter 3. Journeys of Well-Known Practitioners

Presented next are out-of-body experience accounts from the most famous authors and researchers in the field: Muldoon, LaBerge, Monroe, Castaneda, and Bruce. However, if their experiences are to be compared with some of those from the previous section, it would turn out that some humble freshman from the countryside is able to exceed all of them in terms of understanding how to use techniques to control and apply the phenomenon - with the possible exception of Stephen LaBerge.

The explanation for this is simple: the knowledge we have now could only have arisen thanks to the foundation they laid, whatever its quality. It is no exaggeration to state that their work was revolutionary for its time. But now we live in a completely different era, with contemporary advances in technology and technique. A time will come when our currently up-to-date knowledge becomes antiquated.

In order to give the reader practice at independent analysis, these experiences are provided without commentary regarding mistakes. Gather your courage and, using the analyses in previous sections of this book as a guide, comb the experiences of the authoritative figures for what modern knowledge now recognizes as the most typical and common mistakes:

- *no separation;*
- *no deepening;*
- *no plan of action;*
- *no maintaining;*
- *no re-entering;*

Sylvan J. Muldoon
***The projection of the Astral Body* (1929)**

A few mornings ago, I awoke at about six o'clock and lay awake for about twenty minutes. Then I dozed off to sleep again, and dreamed that I was standing on the same spot which I occupied in the metronome dreams-in the instances I told you about before.

I dreamed that my mother was sitting in a rocking chair, and she said to me: "Do you know you're dreaming?" I replied: "By gosh, I am, aren't I?" That ended the dream, and it seemed that I had no sooner said" By gosh, I am" than I awoke in the physical body, in bed. I was conscious, but unable to move; I could not utter a sound, could not move my eyelids. This condition prevailed for about three minutes, and all the time my entire body kept twitching, especially the limbs . Then I suddenly became normal.

About two seconds later a loud rap sounded-as if some one had struck the iron of the bed a blow with a heavy mallet. The noise was so loud that I "ducked," as it rather frightened me... Remember, I was perfectly conscious for about two seconds before this rap sounded. No one was anywhere near, and this occurred in full light. These physical manifestations are certainly Interesting to me, at least-as I never before have experienced such things. But then, neither have I ever tried; these things came about by themselves...

Robert A. Monroe
Journeys Out of the Body (1971)

...I woke up early and went out to have breakfast at seven-thirty, then returned to my room about eight-thirty and lay down. As I relaxed, the vibrations came and then an impression of movement. Shortly thereafter, I stopped, and the first thing 1 saw was a boy walking along and tossing a baseball in the air and catching it. A quick shift, and I saw a man trying to put something into the back seat of a car, a large sedan. The thing was an awkward-looking device that I interpreted to be a small car with wheels and electric motor. The man twisted and turned the device and finally got it into the back seat of the car and slammed the door. Another quick shift, and I was standing beside a table. There were people sitting around the table, and dishes covered it. One person was dealing what looked like large white playing cards around to the others at the table. I thought it strange to play cards at a table so covered with dishes, and wondered about the overlarge size and whiteness of the cards. Another quick shift, and I was over city streets, about five hundred feet high, looking for "home" Then 1 spotted the radio tower, and remembered that the motel was close to the tower, and almost instantly I was back in my body. I sat up and looked around. Everything seemed normal.

Important aftermath: The same evening, I visited some friends, Mr. and Mrs. Agnew Bahnson, at their home. They were partially aware of my "activities," and on a sudden hunchr I knew the morning event had to do with them. I asked about their son, and they called him into the room and asked him what he was doing between eight-thirty and nine that morning. He said he was going to school. When asked more specifically what he was doing as he went, he said he was tossing his baseball in the air and catching it. (Although I knew him well, I had no knowledge that the boy was interested in baseball, although this could be assumed.) Next, I decided to speak about the loading of the car. Mr. Bahnson was astounded. Exactly at that time, he told me, he was loading a Van DeGraff generator into the back seat of his car.

The generator was a large, awkward device with wheels, an electric motor, and a platform. He showed me the device. (It was eerie to see physically something you had observed only from the Second Body.) Next, I told about the table and the large white cards. His wife -was excited at this one. It seems that for the first time in two years, because they had all arisen late, she had brought the morning mail to the breakfast table and had passed out the letters to them as she sorted the mail. Large white playing cards! They were very excited over the event, and I am sure they were not humoring me.

In this morning visit to Mr. Bahnson and his family, the time of visit coincides with actual events. Autosuggestion hallucination, negative; no conscious intent of visit, although unconscious motivation possible. Identical reports with conditions of actual...

Robert A. Monroe
Journeys Out of the Body (1971)

...The vibrations came quickly and easily, and were not at all uncomfortable. When they were strong, I tried to lift out of the physical with no result. Whatever thought or combination I tried, 1 remained confined right where I was. I then remembered the rotating trick, which operates just as if you are turning over in bed. I started to turn, and recognized that my physical was not "turning" with me. I moved slowly, and after a moment I was "face down," or in direct opposition to the placement of my physical body. The moment I reached this 180° position (out of phase, opposite polarity?), there was a hole. That's the only way to describe it. To my senses, it seemed to be a hole in a wall which was about two feet thick and stretched endlessly in all directions (in the vertical plane).

The periphery of the hole was just precisely the shape of my physical body. I touched the wall, and it felt smooth and hard. The edges of the hole were relatively rough. (All this touching done with the non-physical hands.) Beyond-through the hole—was nothing but blackness. It was not the blackness of a dark room, but a feeling of infinite distance and space, as if I were looking through a window into distant space. I felt that if my vision were good enough I could probably see nearby stars and planets. My impression, therefore, was of deep, outer space, beyond the solar system, far in an incredible distance.

1 moved cautiously through the hole, holding onto its sides, and poked my head through carefully. Nothing. Nothing but blackness. No people, nothing material. 1 ducked back in hurriedly because of the utter strangeness. I rotated back

180°, felt myself merge with the physical, and sat up. It was broad daylight, just as when I had left what seemed a few minutes before. Lapsed time: one hour, five minutes!..

Robert A. Monroe
Journeys Out of the Body (1971)

...This was a most unusual and vivid experience, and I don't know if I want any more like it. I went to bed late, very tired, around two in the morning. The vibrations came in promptly without induction, and I decided to "do something" in spite of the need for rest. (Maybe this is rest.) After moving out easily, and visiting several places in quick sequence, and remembering the rest need, I attempted to get back to the physical. 1 thought of my body lying in bed, and almost immediately, I was lying in bed. But I quickly realized something was wrong. There was a boxlike contraption over my feet, evidently to hold the sheet off my legs. There were two people in the room, a man and a woman dressed in white whom I recognized as a nurse. They were talking softly a short distance from the bed.

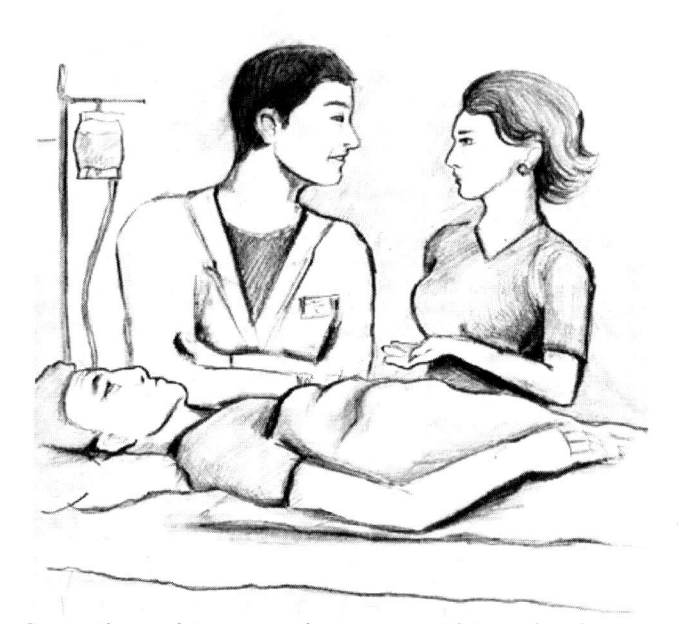

My first thought was that something had gone wrong, that my wife had discovered me in some kind of coma and had rushed me to the hospital. The nurse, the sterile atmosphere of the room, and the bed all supported this. But something still didn't feel right.

After a moment, the two stopped talking and the woman (nurse) turned and went out of the room, and the man approached the bed. 1 grew panicky because I didn't know what he was going to do. I became more so as he bent over the bed and held gently but firmly onto each of my arms at the biceps, and looked at me with bulging, glistening eyes. Worst of all, I desperately tried to move, but could not. It was as if every muscle in my body were paralyzed. Inwardly, I writhed in panic, trying to get away as he brought his face down closer to me.

Then to my utter astonishment, he bent over further and kissed me on each cheek, and I actually felt his whiskers; the glistening in his eyes was tears. He then straightened up, released my arms, and walked slowly out of the room.

Through my terror, I knew that my wife had not taken me to the hospital, that this man was a stranger, that I was again in very much the wrong place. I had to do something, but all the will I could muster didn't have any effect. Slowly, I became aware of a hissing in my head, much like a strong steam or air hiss. Through some dim knowing, I concentrated on the hiss and began to pulsate it, i.e., modulate it soft and loud. I made the pulsating go faster and faster in frequency, and in a few moments it had accelerated to a high-order vibration. I then tried to lift out and succeeded smoothly. Moments later, I was converging with another physical body.

This time, 1 was cautious. I felt the bed. I heard familiar sounds outside the room. The room was dark when I opened my eyes. I reached for the place where the light switch should be, and it was there. I turned on the light and sighed with great, great relief, I was back...

Stephen LaBerge
Lucid Dreaming (1985)

...As I wandered through a high-vaulted corridor deep within a mighty citadel, I paused to admire the magnificent architecture.

Somehow the contemplation of these majestic surroundings stimulated the realization that I was dreaming! In the light of my lucid consciousness, the already impressive splendor of the castle appeared even more of a marvel, and with great excitement I began to explore the imaginary reality of my "castle in the air." Walking down the hall, I could feel the cold hardness of the stones beneath my feet and hear the echo of my steps. Every element of this enchanting spectacle seemed real—in spite of the fact that I remained perfectly aware it was all a dream!

Fantastic as it may sound, I was in full possession of my waking faculties while dreaming and soundly asleep: I could think as clearly as ever, freely remember details of my waking life, and act deliberately upon conscious reflection. Yet none of this diminished the vividness of my dream. Paradox or no, I was awake in my dream!

Finding myself before two diverging passageways in the castle, I exercised my free will, choosing to take the right-hand one, and shortly came upon a stairway. Curious about where it might lead, I descended the flight of steps and found myself near the top of an enormous subterranean vault. From where I stood at the foot of the stairs, the floor of the cavern sloped steeply down, fading in the distance into darkness. Several hundred yards below I could see what appeared to be a fountain surrounded by marble statuary. The idea of bathing in these symbolically renewing waters captured my fancy, and I proceeded at once down the hillside. Not on foot, however, for whenever I want to get somewhere in my dreams, I fly. As soon as I landed beside the pool, I was at once startled by the discovery that what from above had seemed merely an inanimate statue now appeared unmistakably and ominously alive.

Towering above the fountain stood a huge and intimidating genie, the Guardian of the Spring, as I somehow immediately knew. All my instincts cried out "Flee!" But I remembered that this terrifying sight was only a dream. Emboldened by the thought, I cast aside fear and flew not away, but straight up to the apparition. As is the way of dreams, no sooner was I within reach than we had somehow become of equal size and I was able to look him in the eyes, face to face. Realizing that my fear had created his terrible appearance, I resolved to embrace what I had been eager to reject, and with open arms and heart I took both his hands in mine. As the dream slowly faded, the genie's power seemed to flow into me, and I awoke filled with vibrant energy. I felt like I was ready for anything...

Carlos Castaneda
The Art of dreaming (1993)

...As I was watching a window in a dream, trying to find out if I could catch a glimpse of the scenery outside the room, some windlike force, which I felt as a buzzing in my ears, pulled me through the window to the outside. Just before that pull, my dreaming attention had been caught by a strange structure some distance away. It looked like a tractor. The next thing I knew, I was standing by it, examining it.

I was perfectly aware that I was dreaming. I looked around to find out if I could tell from what window I had been looking. The scene was that of a farm in the countryside. No buildings were in sight. I wanted to ponder this. However, the quantity of farm machinery lying around, as if abandoned, took all my attention. I examined mowing machines, tractors, grain harvesters, disk plows, thrashers. There were so many that I forgot my original dream. What I wanted then was to orient myself by watching the immediate scenery. There was something in the distance that looked like a billboard and some telephone poles around it.

The instant I focused my attention on that billboard, I was next to it. The steel structure of the billboard gave me a fright. It was menacing. On the billboard itself was a picture of a building. I read the text; it was an advertisement for a motel. I had a peculiar certainty that I was in Oregon or northern California.

I looked for other features in the environment of my dream. I saw mountains very far away and some green, round hills not too far. On those hills were clumps of what I thought were California oak trees. I wanted to be pulled by the green hills, but what pulled me were the distant mountains. I was convinced that they were the Sierras.

All my dreaming energy left me on those mountains. But before it did, I was pulled by every possible feature. My dream ceased to be a dream. As far as my capacity to perceive was concerned, I was veritably in the Sierras, zooming into ravines, boulders, trees, caves. I went from scarp faces to mountain peaks until I had no more drive and could not focus my dreaming attention on anything. I felt myself losing control. Finally, there was no more scenery, just darkness...

Carlos Castaneda
The Art of Dreaming (1993)

...It seemed at that time that every breakthrough in dreaming happened to me suddenly, without warning. The presence of inorganic beings in my dreams was no exception. It happened while I was dreaming about a circus I knew in my childhood. The setting looked like a town in the mountains in Arizona. I began to watch people with the vague hope I always had that I would see again the people I had seen the first time don Juan made me enter into the second attention. As I watched them, I felt a sizable jolt of nervousness in the pit of my stomach; it was like a punch.

The jolt distracted me, and I lost sight of the people, the circus, and the mountain town in Arizona. In their place stood two strange-looking figures. They were thin, less than a foot wide, but long, perhaps seven feet. They were looming over me like two gigantic earthworms. I knew that it was a dream, but I also knew that I was seeing. Don Juan had discussed seeing in my normal awareness and in the second attention as well. Although I was incapable of experiencing it myself, I thought I had understood the idea of directly perceiving energy. In that dream, looking at those two strange apparitions, I realized that I was seeing the energy essence of something unbelievable.

I remained very calm. I did not move. The most remarkable thing to me was that they didn't dissolve or change into something else. They were cohesive beings that retained their candlelike shape. Something in them was forcing something in me to hold the view of their shape. I knew it because something was telling me that if I did not move, they would not move either.

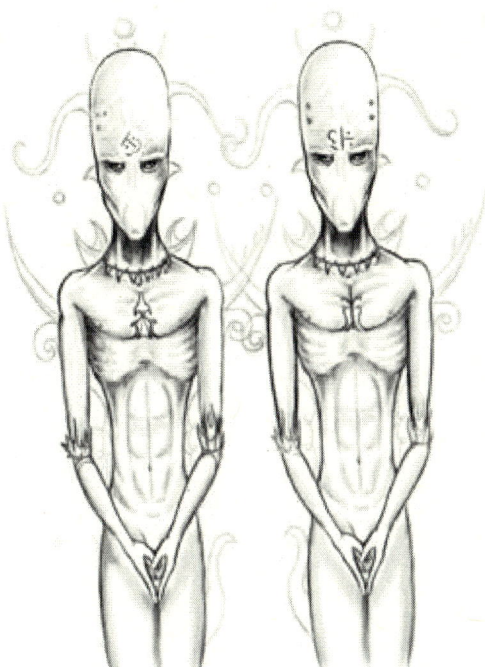

It all came to an end, at a given moment, when I woke up with a fright. I was immediately besieged by fears. A deep preoccupation took hold of me. It was not psychological worry but rather a bodily sense of anguish, sadness with no apparent foundation.

The two strange shapes appeared to me from then on in every one of my dreaming sessions.

Eventually, it was as if I dreamt only to encounter them. They never attempted to move toward me or to interfere with me in any way. They just stood there, immobile, in front of me, for as long as my dream lasted...

Carlos Castaneda
The Art of Dreaming (1993)

...I had a most unusual dream. It started with the appearance of a scout from the inorganic beings' world. The scouts as well as the dreaming emissary had been strangely absent from my dreams. I had not missed them or pondered their disappearance. In fact, I was so at ease without them I had even forgotten to ask don Juan about their absence.

In that dream, the scout had been, at first, a gigantic yellow topaz, which I had found stuck in the back of a drawer. The moment I voiced my intent to see, the topaz turned into a blob of sizzling energy. I feared that I would be compelled to follow it, so I moved my gaze away from the scout and focused it on an aquarium with tropical fish. I voiced my intent to see and got a tremendous surprise. The aquarium emitted a low, greenish glow and changed into a large surrealist portrait of a bejeweled woman. The portrait emitted the same greenish glow when I voiced my intent to see.

As I gazed at that glow, the whole dream changed. I was walking then on a street in a town that seemed familiar to me; it might have been Tucson. I gazed at a display of women's clothes in a store window and spoke out loud my intent to see. Instantly, a black mannequin, prominently displayed, began to glow. I gazed next at a saleslady who came at that moment to rearrange the window. She looked at me. After voicing my intent, I saw her glow. It was so stupendous that I was afraid some detail in her splendorous glow would trap me, but the woman moved inside the store before I had time to focus my total attention on her. I certainly intended to follow her inside; however, my dreaming attention was caught by a moving glow. It came to me charging, filled with hatred. There was loathing in it and viciousness. I jumped backward. The glow stopped its charge; a black substance swallowed me, and I woke up.

These images were so vivid that I firmly believed I had seen energy...

Robert Bruce
Astral Dynamics (1999)

...I awoke at about two in the morning, lying on my back with my whole body vibrating. I could feel myself about to spontaneously project. My arms and legs were already starting to float out. However, I did not want to project. I was tired and had a busy day ahead of me, and just wanted to go back to sleep. I'd been having a very interesting dream up until then and wanted to go back into it if I could. I felt heavy and sluggish but managed to roll onto my left side. The vibrations stopped immediately and the heavy sinking feeling soon left me. Happy now, I snuggled down and relaxed back into myself, concentrating on the dreamscape I had just left and the name I had given it: "Advantage". I hoped this would take me back into it, as this trick often seemed to work.

After only a few seconds, I popped directly into the dream I'd left earlier. The transition was breathtaking. There was a full continuance of waking consciousness. I did not fall asleep and then wake up within the dream, but projected directly into it from the full waking state. I suddenly appeared in a busy, brightly lit department store, just like the one I'd been dreaming of earlier.

In front of me, a dark-haired young woman was setting up a dining room display. I saw people everywhere, shopping, serving, packing shelves, etc. Everything looked and felt real, stable, and solid. It was simply mind-blowing! I jumped up and down few times to feel the weight of my body, then pinched myself, "Ouch!" This hurt just as it would in real life, and my body weight felt normal. I was fully dressed and could even feel the texture of my socks when I wiggled my toes inside my shoes.

I glanced at my hands. They looked normal and did not melt. I tried creating an apple in my hand, but nothing happened. The dreamscape I was in did not waver in the slightest. Curious, I thought, in a normal lucid dream the environment can be altered and anything can be created by imagining it. Regardless, I was fully aware that I was dreaming.

I walked over to the young woman and asked her what she was doing. She told me they were getting ready for the big day, whatever that was. I picked up a large vase of flowers from the table in the middle of her furniture setting. The china felt like real china and the flowers smelled like real flowers. I pulled a rose petal off and ate it. It tasted dry, scented, and faintly bitter, just as a rose petal should taste, but the taste did not linger in my mouth as it normally would, I tipped the vase and splashed some of the water into my hand. It felt cold and wet, just like real water.

I braced myself, hoping that I was truly inside a lucid dream as I believed. I yanked the linen tablecloth from under the main table setting in the display. It almost worked, but the vase and a couple of plates smashed noisily on the floor. A few people looked, but no one seemed to care about the breakage, not even the shop assistant whose display I had just ruined. She went on unpacking and arranging things as if nothing had happened, shaking out another linen tablecloth as she busied herself resetting the table.

More confident now, I walked down an aisle and pushed over several large pieces of cheaplooking pottery from the top shelf, one at a time. I looked around to see if anyone noticed. These made very loud smashing sounds and broken pieces flew in all directions. A few people looked over, but no one seemed to care. Reassured by this, I walked over to the checkouts and jumped up onto one of the benches. A few people looked at me, but no one seemed to care and no one said anything.

I slipped back into my body and rolled onto my back thinking, "Wow! That was incredible ... so real!" I fought to control my excitement and settled back into myself again, trying to get back into the dream. This was getting really interesting. I held the store and its name in mind again and tried to sink back into it, but to no avail. The vibrations started up again and I felt myself starting to project. This time the projection reflex caught hold and buzzed me out of my body. I came to rest at the foot of my bed. The house was dim and quiet as I floated around my bedroom deciding what to do. I took a quick look at my hands. They looked strangely elongated and started melting away.

Not wanting to continue the OBE, I dove back into my body and opened my eyes. I lay there for a moment, then closed my eyes and tried to get back into the dream. The vibrations started up again and another wave of falling, floating heaviness came over me as I started projecting again. I fought it off and rolled over onto my right side. The projection symptoms stopped, but I couldn't get back into my dream. I rolled over onto my left side and settled back into myself again. This position felt much better. Holding the image and name of the dreamscape in mind again, I soon found myself back there.

I reappeared in the store where I had started during my last visit, several minutes ago. The same shop assistant was busily setting up the same dining display. The vase I'd broken earlier was whole again and back on the table where it had been earlier. I walked through the store, looking for signs of damage from my earlier visit. Everything I had broken earlier was whole and back on the shelves again. It was like nothing had ever happened. This was incredible! No matter what I did, the scenario restored itself.

I slipped back into my body again and rolled over to my back, trying to settle myself and get back into my dream. I think my excitement had interrupted it. The vibrations started again, so I rolled over to my left side again. I was getting the hang of this now, and realized that projecting into the dream was much easier from my left side. Settling back into myself and holding the store's image and name in my mind again, I slipped back into the store. Everything was normal and I was back where I had originally started from again, with the same young lady busily setting up her dining display. She

looked up and smiled as I waved, then happily went about her work. I decided to explore further afield before anything else happened, and walked out past the service desk into the mall. I walked for some time, exploring the huge mall. There were a fair number of people around.

Everyone seemed very busy shopping, or preoccupied with whatever they were doing. Of note, all the children I saw were very quiet and well behaved, walking like polite little robots beside their mothers.

There was some light background organ music playing and the usual noise of people quietly bustling about. A few people were talking on telephones here and there, but no one seemed to be chatting or talking to each other. People answered when questioned, but their replies were uninteresting and not very helpful. It seemed impossible to start a conversation that did not involve talking about the person's immediate task at hand.

Everyone seemed to lack personality, like background characters in a movie. On the surface this dreamscape was incredibly real, maybe too real, but beneath the surface it lacked something.

This looked like real life, but was definitely not the same type of real life I am familiar with.

I had decided to look for a way out of the mall and do some further exploring when I suddenly felt weak and heavy. The strength flowed out of me and I felt like I was moving in slow motion. My legs floated slowly upward as I fell ever so slowly to the floor, settling there weak and paralyzed.

People stepped over and around me as I lay there, but no one paid any attention to me. I felt like a child's balloon bobbing about on the floor. I was weak and heavy and could no longer feel the normal weight of my body, nor could I feel the floor beneath me.

I slipped back into my body again, coming wide awake this time. I rolled over to my back and lay there pondering the significance of these experiences. The vibrations did not start up this time, probably because I was pretty much wide awake now. It was obvious to me that my resting position had been affecting the different types of experiences I'd been having. I was far too excited and wide awake by now to do any kind of further exploration with this phenomenon, so I gave up and went to get a drink and record this experience in my journal...

Chapter 4. The Author's Experiences

Below, the author presents the most interesting excerpts from his phase travel log: it happened to him for the first time in the fall of 1999, when he was a senior in high school. One of the interesting things about these excerpts is that they describe the development of a personal practice from the teenage years through the present day.

It's worth noting that my many years of experience and thousands of phases logged have had a strong effect on the practical side of my practice. I long ago realized those desires and wants that everyone has, and at that - many times over. Nowadays, I mostly do technical experiments, research, and hone my skills, all while obtaining elementary satisfaction from the practice itself and the vividness of sensation in it. That's why even the most recent excerpts from my log are not characteristic of the phase as it is usually practiced. They are merely the most illustrative examples. An unprepared audience would simply not understand ordinary phases.

As with the previous section, the reader is encouraged to exercise his theoretical knowledge by undertaking an independent and critical analysis of the experiences described.

October 1999
False Alien Abduction

I went to bed with a feeling that I had lost another 12 precious hours of my life. Then I suddenly woke up. Unfortunately I can't say exactly for how long I had been asleep, but, probably, for two or three hours. My mind was clear. And there was something else.

Before I could determine anything else, a sudden thought paralyzed me: I was being taken away, I was being abducted by THEM! That thought struck me. What I felt that moment could be compared to the greatest shock, the only difference is that I had all the symptoms of shock at once. My world turned upside down, as did my insides. At that moment I couldn't explain even to myself why I was so sure that I was being abducted by extraterrestrials, but I had no doubt that my guess was right. I knew it, I simply knew it. And what happened next proved that I wasn't going mad. When that thought came to my mind, I got a feeling that high-tension current went through my body. It didn't harm me, but made every cell of my body vibrate. And, the most important thing was that I could not move. Only my eyelids obeyed me. I had never been so scared in my life. All the sensations were more than real, and so my last doubts disappeared.

In my mind I kept asking those creatures to postpone my journey, saying that I wasn't in the mood, and that everything would be fine the next time. At the same time, I damned myself for my weakness. I understood that such things do not happen every other day. I was lying on one side facing a wall, and so I could not see the rest of the room, although I didn't hope to see anybody because I decided that they were doing it from their ship, but for all that I was sure that they did hear my thoughts. Meanwhile, it seemed that my mood didn't bother them as something lifted me up from my bed.

My heart could not have been beating faster. I pleaded them to stop. And they did. As cautiously as they had lifted me up, they put me down. I couldn't have been happier. I felt that I was born again. A sigh with relief escaped my lungs. But it was too early for champagne.

Not giving me a chance to enjoy my lucky escape, they lifted me up again and carried me to the window. I still could not move, no matter how hard I tried. Then something roused my interest and I almost forgot how frightened I was. I was moving feet first towards the window but I could see that it was closed. So, I became curious about how they were going to drag me outside. Everything was so real that I did hope that they wouldn't use me for glass breaking. And I knew that they wouldn't do it. Being the representatives of an advanced kind, they would find the way to spare me from unpleasant experiences and save the windows. When I was near the window I closed my eyes in order to intensify the new sensations and not to break the window (I don't know or why I decided this would help). But I felt almost nothing, only some imperceptible plane went through my body from toes to head.

I opened my eyes. I was outside, on the level of the third floor just opposite my window. The cloudless sky was studded with stars. I'd never looked at the stars from that position, and it was unforgettable. By that time I had managed to beat my fear, and so what was the point? I decided to make the most of it. I was even glad that the aliens hadn't listened to me and had dragged me out of bed, because I would never have dared to do it myself.

My fear subsided and I managed to relax, and even complained about the weather, as it was rather cold and I was wearing Adam's costume. I just managed to reconcile myself with destiny and started to look at the bright side. The next moment, I was already in my room and in my bed.

Only after 1 to 2 years would I start to understand that it was just my first spontaneous phase experience, and that it had nothing to do with aliens.

February 2001
A Glass of Juice

I awoke at night and thought of the phase. That thought evoked strong excitation bordering on fear, thanks to which I fell right into the phase. I began experimenting with vibrations, but was still afraid to separate. The vibrations gradually became so powerful that they simply threw me out of my body. After having overcome my fear with great difficulty, I then floated about the room. As my sight returned, night turned to day. I then came back down and stood on the floor, extremely frightened by the realness of everything going on.

However, there was a table at the window of the room that shouldn't have been there. But I didn't even stop to think about that, as I was nevertheless still in shock over what was going on. Concentrating on the situation at hand, I noticed a glass with some kind of liquid in it on the table. I got the idea of testing out how real the sense of taste would be. Still totally surprised by the realness of everything, I went up to the table, picked up the glass, and held it up to my eyes in order to get a better look at it. I then hesitantly brought it to my lips, and took a sip. My God! I didn't expect it to be that realistic. It was a glass of tomato juice. I could feel its texture with my lips, tongue, and palate. By the time it hit my throat, I was already savoring the taste. I felt the cold from the glass on my hands and lips - everything was indistinguishable from real life.

Relishing both the taste of the juice and my triumph in entering the phase, I quietly thought about the new frontiers opening up before me while quenching my thirst. However, I completely forgot about the need for concentration, and had a foul. I was in a great mood all the next day after having discovered this experience.

May 2001
Maximum Deepening

Right after dinner, I decided to enter the phase using the direct method. To that end, I started implementing the dotting technique (concentrating my attention on different parts of the body). However, I encountered difficulties during relaxation: I could not stop my mind from getting distracted with other thoughts. Only with great difficulty was I able to concentrate on the task. I kept to relaxation. Then, I once again employed dotting for about 20 minutes, but nothing worked. However, weak vibrations arose from time to time. Meanwhile, I became more and more sleepy. At one point my conscious awareness checked out, but then quickly came back (this didn't seem to last more than a minute, which was confirmed by my alarm-clock upon returning to the body) under the influence of my preliminary intention not to fall asleep. I then began to feel alert and was enveloped by vibrations, which occurred on their own in amid the transition between physiological states. I was easily able to amplify the vibrations.

Then I rolled out. However, the vibrations began to die down, and I was returned back to my body. I tried to separate again by climbing out. I was able to do this despite great difficulty. I was now suspended in an indeterminate space of vague sensation. While separating, I felt a strong feeling of discomfort that nearly persuaded me to cut the attempt short. However, I knew that that this sometimes happens and always occurs before plunging into a more stable phase. In order to deepen this phase, I decided to employ levitation.

It succeeded, and I derived real pleasure from this process. For some reason, the levitation did not lead me into the deepest phase, and so I began to fall head-first in order to further deepen it.

The movement and deepening brought a feeling of slight uneasiness that bordered on fear, but I was able to keep it under control from the outset. I soon realized that I was in the deepest state that I had ever been in. This increased my anxiety. For the sake of experiment, I kept going deeper and deeper. I began to have thoughts about the impossibility of returning to the body from such depths. My vision faded in and out, because I was made uncomfortable only by my feelings, and not by what I could see around. Once my vision came to me, what I saw cannot be described in words. That's how uncommon, indescribable, and realistic it was. It was as if I were seeing with some other organ of sight, one far more advanced than the human eye. I couldn't feel my body (neither my real or phantom one).

For the first time in my life, I physically felt my thoughts: when I started thinking about something, I begin to automatically move through space. Meanwhile, I could clearly tell that my thoughts were causing this movement. My brains were somehow being wracked by thought. (this was the first time I had ever had this experience, and so I can't say how realistic it was, or if it could actually be experienced in a normal state. Nonetheless, the sensation was quite realistic). Realizing how deep I was in the phase, I decided to get out of there, as I was afraid for my life. As it is easy to suppose, this was, to put it lightly, not easy. I began to feel fear. I was completely unable to enter my body or get control of it. Once was finally able to feel it, it felt like someone else's. Contrary to my expectations, even concentrating on my big toe did not help. Instead of getting me out of that state, relaxation deepened it. Then, I got completely lost: what normally helped wasn't working, and there were no other effective methods to employ. After long desperate attempts, I finally managed to enter my body. This only happened thanks to attempts to move any body part I could, in addition to concentrating on breathing.

June 2001
A Domed Paradise

I suddenly became aware that I was in a dream. I felt joy and satisfaction. The positive emotions were so plentiful that, having become aware of my presence in a world outside of reality, I tried to share my emotions with passersby. I didn't even care that there was no point in doing this. It should be noted that I did not have to return to my body in order to deepen the state and separate once again, as is normally to be done, as there was an immediate and atypical realism to my surroundings. It was that very realism that had led me to become aware that I was dreaming in the first place.

I was in a very interesting place: there was no sky - instead of it there was a low, large blue dome, which distributed a strange light across the entire space; the scenery all about recalled a corner of paradise: there were a lot of fountains, streams, and numerous architectural curiosities of unknown purpose. There were flora and fauna everywhere: all the streams were teeming with myriad types of fish, all the trees were alive with the chirping of flocks of exotic birds (from simple green parrots to those of fantastic appearance). There was so much to take in all around. Wherever one looked, there were beautiful flowers and trees of all different shapes; many people milled about on all kinds of business, paying not the slightest degree of attention to me, and there were many objects with unfamiliar objects around.

All was distinguished by a rich display of life in all its manifestations. Everywhere was crowded, peopled, and there was practically no free place to stand. Everything literally teemed. However, there was room enough to move about. I was seized by intense emotion arising from such an uncommon, and, most importantly, realistic and vivid landscape. Everything could be taken in visually, and in minute detail. There was a lot of everything around to observe, I did so with relish. In other words, I performed the technique of concentration, I didn't even have to think about procedures for maintaining. I didn't feel at all like carrying out my previously planned tasks. I didn't need anything else but to enjoy the simple pleasure of observing this little corner of paradise. I felt like a stranger in a strange world, and was very happy to have landed in such a place, and been able to experience it firsthand. For this, I was sincerely grateful for the phase. Something like this would never have happened in real life. The thought occasionally came to me that this was not simply my inner world, but actually some real one. However, the laws according to which it operated went against this. The only thing that could have startled me was the realness of the situation. My inner world could not accept such things, as I had already grown accustomed to thinking about reality in a different way over the course of my life.

My presence in this paradise was threatened by the possibility of my conscious awareness checking out, and me subsequently falling asleep. I started to become quite worried about this, and so had to perform some active exercises in order to keep my awareness from submerging. Without thinking twice, I decided to start talking with people there, because this was always one of the most interesting things to do. Unfortunately, everyone present there was unfamiliar with me from reality. But that did not bother me too much, because an interesting scene started to develop before my eyes.

The two men started singing some songs, before that they had been quietly sitting on a bench and enjoying some unknown liquid from wineskins. From the tone of their voice and their appearance, one could easily guess at the alcoholic inspiration for their vocal concert. After singing the refrains of some well-known songs, they graduated to obscene limericks and jokes. That's when it got really interesting. I expected them to recite only things that I already knew, but to my total surprise, this was not to be the case. I stood there and listened very carefully to everything. Even though the limericks were funny, I was more shocked than amused, as I had never heard any of them before. This meant that at that moment, my brain was literally composing quite high quality stuff on the fly, without any intervention in the process on my part. Perhaps I had once been unwittingly exposed to everything that I heard in that world, and simply not paid attention to it, and now it was coming back to me in this form.

Then, I suddenly got the idea that I should enjoy myself in a more active and unusual way. After all, one ought live in the moment...

March 2002
Healing Myself

After one of many morning awakenings, I hadn't moved at all physically, and immediately began trying to separate from the body. I realized after a couple of seconds of trying that separation would not happen right then, and so I peered into the void before my eyes, trying to discern any images. There weren't any, and so after a few seconds I started with phantom wiggling, which manifested itself somewhat in the feet: both feet inched up somewhat, and them came back down. Meanwhile, my ears were filled with a soft noise, and there was a slight "buzz" in my body.

    I tried to increase the amplitude of the motion for 5 to 10 seconds, but was still unable to achieve anything. In order to overcome this barrier of some sorts, I decided to switch to the technique of observing images for some time, and then continue with phantom wiggling. However, the images came on so strong that I realized that I could skip phantom wiggling, as it would be much easier to simply use the images. Before my mind's eye appeared a river, and behind it a steep hill wooded with tall trees. I began to peer into it, trying to take in the whole picture. It immediately became sharper and sharper. I realized after 2 to 4 seconds that I was viewing the picture just as if from a window in real life. As soon as that realization came, I rolled out of my body and into the room.

    I quickly got to my feet and started palpating and trying to see. My vision returned at once. The phase was sufficiently deep that I could see everything as clearly as in reality. Meanwhile, using the deepening techniques led to everything becoming much more visually intense and colorful than I was accustomed to in real life. This startled me a bit. The thought of returning to the body even flashed through my mind, but I was able to overcome it, and immediately concentrated on the goals that I had set: treating high blood pressure, conducting an experiment on the viscosity of fluids, and some items of fun to improve my mood.

    I opened the door of my wardrobe, which in reality contained a box of medicines. I looked for the drug that was to help me lower my blood pressure or at least make it easier to deal with my condition. Delving into the package, I took out the various tubes of ointments, packages, and spray-cans, peering at them in order to maintain the phase. I also tried to figure out what the medicines were, and whether or not I needed them.

It took some time, as for 15 to 20 seconds I couldn't find anything worthwhile. Then I suddenly pulled out some blue bottle with pills. On it was written, "LifeMix - Life without Hypertension. All the best products in one". This was very close to what I was looking for, so I immediately took two tablets, chewed them, and swallowed. They were awfully bitter and distasteful. At one point, that bitter taste even made me forget that I was in the phase and that I definitely needed to do something to keep it from being over. Instead of letting that happen, I bent down and covered my face with my hands.

Suddenly, a strange wave of unusual sensations coursed through my body. My head and entire face started to fill up with blood, causing swelling in my lips, nose, cheeks, and eyelids. It goes without saying that this was an unpleasant sensation. It was more than unusual. This was especially true of the sensations I felt inside my head. It was as if it were heating up and expanding. I figured at that point that I had done something wrong.

As soon as I thought that, I felt as if a balloon filled with cold water had burst in my head. Here the heat turned to cold, and my head and body "decompressed" back down to size. I felt an uncommon lightness and freshness inside. I had the sensation of having tapped a new reserve of strength and life-energy.

In order to not have to search for that blue bottle again, I set it on the right corner of the lower shelf. Afterwards, I decided to cement the effect by performing a physical exercise that had always caused pain in my head due to heightened blood pressure. I ran into the hallway and sat on the floor, with my back against one wall and feet towards the other. I pushed off with my legs while pressing my back against this wall, thus simulating bearing a physical load. All the while, I tried to peer at all around me, concentrating on my position. The wall wouldn't give, and I had to make Herculean efforts to somehow straighten my legs. I bent my legs back again, and then returned to trying to straighten them out.

I had physically exerted myself more than once in the phase, which had always been accompanied by increased blood pressure in the head. This was often painful, and the discomfort would even last throughout the morning after awakening. This time, my head felt easy and light. I just concentrated on the physical effort, and not on how hard this exercise was to perform. In addition, I tried to deliberately relieve my head of that heaviness and pressure, trying to create subconscious programming for the physical world. In addition to all of the above, I did my best to give myself hypnotic suggestions.

That done, I moved on to the next items in my plan of action....

April 2002
A Phase Gone to Wasted

...After another awakening, I decided to try to enter the phase. Even though there were no symptoms of the phase being close, I was immediately able to roll out. Surprised at how easy it had been to roll out, I began to deepen by palpation: first I ran my hand along the length of the bed, and then started patting down objects near it. The sensations gradually became increasingly real. But still I could not see. So, I decided to continue with palpation, hoping that vision would come by itself, as it always had before in such cases. After taking several footsteps about the apartment, vision came back to me somewhat blurrily. I was easily able to deepen it by concentrating on my hands.

Instead of doing anything productive like conducting research, I decided to have some fun. To start with, I skyrocketed through the apartments above mine, experiencing the unforgettable feeling of flying through concrete floors. I then repeated the motion in the opposite direction, all the way down to the ground floor. I could see how my neighbors had decorated their homes through that flight up and down the apartment complex. There was a great temptation to cause havoc in the apartment on the first floor, but I was even more interested in flying. So, I blasted off headlong at an angle up through the wall and out into the open air. I flew about 50 yards out and hovered over the apartment complex's playground. In order to stay in the phase, I would look at my hands from time to time, and only then take in the landscape in between doing so. My heart leaped at the height. I could feel wafts of air coming from birds flying by. This all gave me a real high. At one point I faded somewhat and almost lost the phase, but managed to create vibrations through straining the brain. I was long able to maintain the phase after that by controlling the vibrations, without having to resort to concentration.

    I then came up with a brilliant idea - I decided to try to test myself in the role of a fighter pilot. It was not easy to concentrate on this goal. I quickly picked up speed, and yawed to the side. The higher the speed I flew at, the louder the screaming in my ears. I felt the maddening velocity and G-force with every cell in my body. Of course, I could have chosen to feel only the movement itself, but I deliberately tuned in to the sensation of all the aerodynamic effects. Air whistled by with increasing warmth as it flowed around me. It was only with difficulty that I overcame instinctual fear that I had brought in with me from the real world. Clouds whizzed by above, and below me were homes, forests, and people - everything was so real that I had to really ponder what was going on, and what to make of it...

January 2004
A Journey into Outer Space

    My body was still very tired, even though I had already been able to sleep for several hours that night. As soon as I lay down, I almost immediately felt vibrations occurring, but was not relaxed enough to bring them up to full force. At the moment, the best way to relax and enter the phase seemed to me to be through "trans-awakening" (the free-floating state of mind). I turned out to be right, as after the fifth or sixth time I felt intense vibrations enveloping me from all sides. In this case, there was no need to amplify the vibrations or deepen the phase, as my body was tired, and it would create a most deep state all on its own in order to more quickly restore its vital energies. I just lay for some time and observed the changes occurring within me. However, I could not remain idle for long, lest I unintentionally fall asleep.

I spent some time on fixing my secondary attention on avoiding falling asleep and involuntary exit from the phase. I rolled out. As usual, I rolled out of the bed as if for real, but not hitting the floor. Instead, I hovered above the floor as if I had fallen on a one-foot high invisible air mattress. I have rolled out hundreds of times, but I always experience doubt in the back of my mind that I am actually falling out of bed in reality.

A multitude of ideas flashed through my mind on how to use this position. I immediately formulated an approximate plan of action, which included those senseless things that I save for a rainy day. However, I first decided for the umpteenth time to observe outer space scenes. I took up my goal: the Cosmos. Here I was immediately picked up by a mysterious force that whisked me away at breakneck speed. My vision quickly came back to me, and I found myself floating in an unknown part of the Cosmos. I don't know how true-to-life the sensations were, as I have never been in outer space. Nonetheless, I probably experienced it just like it would be in real life. Sight was the predominate sense here, I stopped paying attention to the other four. Taking in the galaxy within my field of view brought fantastic pleasure. The unusualness in the visual perception consisted in the uncommon way that my eyes had to focus, as we rarely use our eyes in that way in real life. Taking in the galaxy required my eyes to fully uncross and look at the sight in parallel. The galaxy seemed as if it were alive, and I said to myself that this was probably the most beautiful thing that I had ever seen.

However, I couldn't stay there for long, as there was nothing to concentrate my sense of sight on, because the objects were very far away. I returned to the void, and, suspended in a static position, created strong vibrations. For a while, I simply enjoyed this uncommon sensation. It was interesting to observe the characteristics of this phenomenon. When I raised my arms and brought my palms towards my face, I felt strong, warm wind streaming from them to my face. Noise filled my ears. When I palpated my head with my hands, it seemed as if I was touching my unprotected brain, but there was no pain.

I enjoyed this state for some time, plunging in some unknown direction. After a short flight, I was ejected back into my room at home. This time everything in it corresponded 100% to reality, enough though I had not set myself that goal. Nothing interested me in the room, and so I walked through my bedroom door into the other rooms, with everything as in real life. I didn't have to look long for adventure, as I found my mother and brother in the other room, both of whom I had not seen for a while. I spoke with them about anything that came to mind, just for the sake of hearing their voices and getting a chance to look at them. This was a real gift for me. But I faded out a bit, and was only able with great difficulty to regain control over the state through the infamous technique of falling head-first ...

October 2006
A Murdered Friend

Don't watch the morning news and eat at the same time. I vomited all today's breakfast into the toilet after watching the news report that someone I knew, far from a passing acquaintance, had been brutally killed that night. He had he tried to call me a couple of weeks before, but I hadn't been in the mood to accompany him on another one of his drinking bouts. For my own peace of mind, I decided to somehow try to make amends.

I lay down. With great difficulty, I calmed down and began to focus my attention on phantom wiggling with my arm. No wiggling occurred at first, but once it came, it started quickly increasing in amplitude. A short lapse in consciousness occurred after about 10 minutes, and I was able to easily get up out of bed.

I didn't need to deepen. After closing my eyes, I immediately focused my attention on the image of my friend. Then, something picked me up and moved me in an unknown direction. After several seconds, I was literally thrown into the kitchen of his apartment. As usual, he sat in a chair at a table cluttered with cognac. He didn't pay any attention to me. He didn't look good, with many bruises and cuts on his face and arms. Although there was almost no blood, it was all awful to look at due to the hyper-realism, and I began to feel nauseated again. When I came closer, he turned to me and sobbed... I tried to ask him what had happened, because they didn't say exactly what had occurred on the news. It turned out that his lifestyle lay at the cause of it all. He started shouting that he wanted to live, and that he would no longer act like that if he could only live again. I apologized for not having picked up the phone. I looked at him for the last time. And, acting against my beliefs, I returned to my body.

By evening, his explanation of what had happened was confirmed. As for his behavior and external appearance, they were understandably triggered by my still raw emotions. I think that if I meet him in several months, he'll look and act differently.

December 2008
Tyrannosaurus Rex

I woke up during a daytime nap. While still in a drowsy state, I tried to roll out of my body and fly up into the air, but nothing happened. However, I felt that I was in a state very close to that of the phase. I tried forced falling asleep, and then felt lapses of consciousness, during which images flickered before my eyes. A few seconds later, I decided to try separating from my body again. Meanwhile, I knew that if that didn't work, I could switch to observing images, as they were already there. However, that turned out not to be necessary, as I was easily able to simply get up out of my body. My vision immediately came to me. I was quickly able to make the state that I was in extremely realistic by palpating and peering at objects around me. I also managed to quickly palpate my body, all the while creating and amplifying vibrations in order to cement myself in a deep phase.

    While I had a clearly-formulated plan of action regarding studying the phase, I had already re-thrashed its details several times that week. At that moment, I really just wanted to use the phase for my own personal enjoyment, and do something I was looking forward to for a while. At one of my seminars about a week before, I had told my students about how it was possible to go for a walk among dinosaurs. A desire to do so now burned within me, as I had not done anything of the sort for a long time. So I scrapped my previous plan of action, closed my eyes, and concentrated my attention on the Tyrannosaurus rex. I then felt the sensation of movement. The translocation took longer than usual. This was normal for such a situation, because it was simply psychologically difficult to believe one would see dinosaurs, even though I had succeeded in doing so many times before. The rational brain tends to have difficulties with things like encountering dinosaurs.

    I nevertheless managed to get myself together and concentrate my attention. Then, I landed on something soft. It was a patch of moss in the forest. I began to scrutinize the moss and palpate it with my hands. Vision almost immediately came to me, and became incredibly sharp. I crouched on all fours and stared for a while at everything right in front of me - mainly small twigs of various shapes and decayed leaves. There were also all kinds of insects crawling around.

I then focused my attention on my own feelings and perceptions. I was still wearing the same t-shirt and shorts that I had fallen asleep in. My body itself seemed unusually pale. However, I was most surprised at how hard it was to breathe. Not only was the air saturated with indescribably-repugnant odors, it also turned out to be quite hot and humid. Trying to breathe in only through my nose made me dizzy. Meanwhile, the air was so hot that breathing in through my mouth hurt my throat. In the end, I decided to breathe in through my mouth, and was able to banish the pain.

I turned my attention to my surroundings. There was forest all around. Very little sun made it through the canopy. The trees were very tall, and had long straight trunks. There were plants all around that looked like ferns, but they were nearly my height. I had found myself in a small clearing without trees. The whole place was filled with sounds that were unnatural for a forest. Instead of birds chirping, I heard whistling and croaking. I heard roaring from time to time coming from somewhere in the distance. I kept hearing crackling and then something crashing to the ground. I could hear a lot of rustling and dull thuds coming from somewhere behind the bushes about thirty yards away from me. I immediately understood that that's where my objective was.

By the time I decided to head for my dinosaur, I was already itching from constant attacks by exotic insects of all colors and sizes, both terrestrial and airborne. While heading for the target, I all the while scrutinized my arms and the leaves that I had ripped off with my hands. I intentionally made right for the tree trunks ahead. I kept special tabs on the hyper-realism of the experience, as this was the most important factor here. The vibrations didn't die down one bit, as I constantly kept them going right from the start.

I went up to the bushes and cautiously peered through them. There was a stream flanked by a muddy bank, from which an enormous patch of horsetail shot up. My objective was wading right in the middle of the stream, I almost shouted out in ecstasy at the sight of it. I kept quiet only out of a desire to not attract its attention. That could have ruined everything. I tried to avoid drawing its attention not so much because I was somewhat afraid, but more out of a desire to simply watch this magnificent creature from the side, and feast my eyes on its beauty.

I had already seen a T. rex at least five times before, but this one was much larger than all of the previous ones. Even the the color of its skin was different - slightly darker and with fewer spots. For some reason, this one seemed to be a female. The giant paused at some point, apparently reacting to me. I immediately returned my attention to peering at the leaves and the insects on them, so as not to interfere in the situation with the dinosaur, and also remain in a deep phase.

I was quite afraid that this phase might not be sufficient for more sensations - and so instead of sticking it out, I quickly ran up behind the T. rex. It immediately turned in my direction, but I concentrated as much as I could on the thought that it would see me as a friend and not a foe. Risking the phase, I even stopped in order to program the situation. Its huge head looked at me for several more seconds, and then calmly bent down. It seems that it had a victim there.

I ran up to its massive tail. I quickly peered at it up close, and then moved to its face. I was meanwhile in a panic over the phase and its depth, and so made great effort to amplify the vibrations I was feeling. Also, I petted the reptile the whole time, for now moving my hands down its side, and stepping into the cool water up to my ankles. Everything was already so extraordinary, and I didn't want to be ejected into reality by making a stupid move. Fear of the monster had already completely subsided, but I started to grow a little concerned over the great depth of this phase. The unwholesome idea of staying there forever suddenly came over me. However, the instinct of self-preservation kept me to my senses.

Pulling up the reptile's massive and muscular frame, I got up to the front of it. I had not seen tyrannosauruses up so close that often before, so I was a bit amused by how helplessness its forearms appeared, almost like puny unwebbed flippers (Tyrannosauruses only have two clawed limbs). They are generally considered to be vestigial, but this reptile was clearly using them to help itself to the carcass of another big lizard, holding it up. In turn, the prey seemed to be quite ugly and bony. Its innards were hanging out of the large jaws of the dining reptile. I squatted down just a yard away from the dinosaur's muzzle and watched the scene. It didn't pay me any attention, even when I grabbed the gnarled leg of its victim (it looked like a chicken-leg, but a hundred times larger), and threw it aside. The T. Rex, still ignoring me, raised its head and went straight for the delicacy. Its movement seemed to require a lot of effort, and all the muscles of its haunches simply pushed forward when exerted. I could see that the beast was incredibly strong.

  After going halfway towards its prize and scanning its surroundings, the lizard turned again to the carcass. It began to go at it again. I had already made up my mind to feed him by hand, but then some kind of alarm went off. Quickly realizing that it was coming from outside the window in the physical world, I immediately dunked my head underwater in order to get rid of that sound by programming the qualities of the space around. It was indeed quieter underwater, but the alarm was still audible. While observing the pebbles at the bottom of the clear water, I plugged my ears with my fingers. The sound became even quieter. Employing the straining the brain technique made the vibrations still stronger, creating a noise that I began to listen in to. The alarm sound went away. I surfaced, took my fingers out of my ears, and then it occurred to me that it could have been a car alarm. "And what if that was from my car?" - I thought. Cursing all earthly matters, I recalled my body in order to return back into it. And it was only just upon feeling the physical body that I remembered that my car had already been at the mechanic's for several days now... I heard the alarm again, but it wasn't coming from my car. And so, there was no point in cutting the phase experience short. I tried to get back into the phase once again, but the wail of the alarm did not stop, and so all of my attempts to return to the phase were in vain.

August 2008
An Experiment and a Love Story

I woke up at about 8:00 am and took a cold shower, but was still unable to get into work mode. I decided to go back to sleep. Given that this would be a good time make attempts to enter the phase, I decided to try make a go of it. However, I wasn't in the mood to try anything but phantom wiggling. Not really expecting anything to come of it, I half-heartedly and monotonously tried to "rock the boat" with one hand. That hand, in turn, quickly yielded and started moving, though initially with little amplitude. Already having practically fallen asleep, I noticed that the amplitude had increased dramatically and my hand began to literally slip out of my body. I decided to monitor the situation more closely, and was able to move my forearm further and further to each side. At some point, I was able to trace a full circle with it. It then occurred to me that there had been a marked change in my sense of bodily perception. Something clearly started to occur. I tried to roll out. That did not work, but vibrations arose upon attempting it. This served as a signal to try more actively to roll out. I tried again - and it worked. Granted, there was some difficulty and sluggishness involved, but it worked.

I rolled out off the bed, but the state was unstable: there were no distinct sensations, and I was drawn back into my body. I began erratically palpating everything. The pull on my body gradually disappeared, and after 5 to 10 seconds my sight started to return. I used it to deepen by peering. That proved to be the decisive factor. The phase became hyper-real.

I remembered right then and there what needed to be tried in this phase, and I began from the most important item - experimenting with translocation. I had wanted to check once again how difficult it was to translocate in space using the door technique. First, I closed the door. I focused my attention on there being an auditorium behind it in which I was to give a lecture. I opened the door, walked into the auditorium, and closed the door once again behind me. I then focused my attention on the other side of the door being the weight-room of the gym that I go to. I opened the door, and looked in to the weight-room. Then, I shut the door and opened it again - the weight-room was still there. I went into it and closed the door behind me. I then focused on deep outer-space being behind the door. I opened the door, which led into the hallway that would have been there if I were really in the weight-room. I closed the door and concentrated even harder on outer-space being behind it. I started to open the door, but something seemed to be holding it back from the other side. I had to use force to get the door to budge. After that, it opened all the way easily. At that point, I noticed that the phase space began to blur. However, I managed to concentrate and restore its realism by straining the brain. Behind the door was deep outer-space.

    I stood at the entrance to the weight room, and literally a step in front of me was endless expanse without beginning or end. I could breathe freely. An icy draft came in through the door. Experiments have shown that unless one is simply going from one room into another, translocating using doors is one of the more difficult methods. Such difficulty is probably only due to the internal psychological blocks that people have. While standing and analyzing what was happening, I was sucked into a stencil. The only thing that I could do at that very moment was grab at the door handle, which I did almost automatically.

    I then felt myself lying in my body. However, my hand was clearly still grasping the door handle. I began moving the phantom hand on every plane, and soon felt that I would be able to separate. I easily rolled out and found myself in my room.

I quickly brought the state to a level of hyperrealism through peering interspersed with palpation. Realizing that I had already achieved my primary objectives, I gave in to a desire to meet with a girl whom I had not seen for a while, but still had feelings for. I went to the bathroom door, and opened it without a shred of doubt that she would be on the other side. And that's just how it happened. I opened the door and saw behind her the interior of my old apartment where she used to visit me. I had of course hoped to have seen her naked in the bathtub, but this scenario was not bad at all.

She was sitting on the couch and looking out the window. I felt that she understood that I was close-by. I went up and sat down on the floor next to her. I cuddled up to and started being affectionate with her. Thanks to the hyper-realism of the experience, the sensations were incredibly intense and amazing. Simply stroking her skirt and jacket was a stunning experience, as it once was in reality. It was extremely pleasant to feel her soft and warm body under her clothes, pantyhose, and knee-high stockings.

Once I brought my hand to her head and began taking her hair away from her face, she turned toward me and smiled. After seeing the gaze of those same very eyes and that same smile, there was nothing I could do in response but smile. I continued to move my hands over her face, head, and body in order to maintain the phase. Her eyes were sad, her smile seemed to be amid tears. But all the while, her expression was more open and sincere than it had ever been in reality.

She also started to smooth my face and hands. She then came to ask me how I was doing and what I had been up to. Understanding that such communication was only a formality of secondary importance in the phase, I answered only in monosyllables, all the while enjoying the fact that I was next to her, could feel her touch, see her eyes, and hear her painfully familiar voice. Surprisingly, I was not overwhelmed by the unbridled sexual instincts that usually arise when contacting the opposite sex in phase.

After spending some more time with her, I decided that it was time to bring the meeting to a close, as I could see her another time. Before me still remained the task of entering and exiting my body multiple times. Practicing that skill had been a part of my preliminary plan of action.

I intentionally returned to my body and immediately began trying to exit it. I was easily able to roll out. I returned back to my body, and then rolled out of it again. However, my connection to reality greatly increased after that last return, and it took a fair amount of effort to literally fly out of my body. I would also have to employ the technique of forced falling asleep.

Having found myself floating once again in the center of the room, I clearly understood that there was no point in returning back again to the body. Without even bothering to strengthen the phase through deepening, I nevertheless intentionally rushed back to my body in order to discover the limit of my own capabilities, and further refine my skill at exiting the body. Caught in a stencil, I was at first barely able to move, but then I was seized by a wave of awakening. I switched to forced falling asleep, and then on to observing images when forced sleep did not work. No images appeared. I again began to try to divide, but then arose the feeling of having fully awakened.

I started trying to move my hands down along my body and back. Phantom movement arose after several seconds, and my consciousness immediately submerged deeply, sinking away from the outside world. I focused even more on movement, and it occurred even further. I started to try to get up. I was able to, but very sluggishly. My body seemed to be several times heavier than it really was. Any relaxation on my part immediately nailed me back to the stencil. At some point I managed to completely separate, and found myself next to the bed. I tried chaotically to use all available deepening techniques, but nothing helped, and I was returned to my body. I was done for that session.

January 2009
Obtaining Information

Once I got into bed, I found myself in the mood to try entering the phase using a direct technique. After having laid down for a bit and some end-of-the-day reflection, which calmed and relaxed me to some extent, I began to concentrate my attention on imagined rotation along my head-to-toe axis. I was unable to rotate more than halfway for the first minute. But then I was able to rotate all the way around, and it got easier and easier with each minute. I rotated in one direction, and then another. I periodically lapsed into sleep and shallow dreaming. I did not even try to attempt separation when surfacing, because I did not feel any phase symptoms. At one point, conscious awareness sank into unconscious for a longer period of time than before (I almost completely fell asleep). When I came to, the rotation was somewhat sluggish. I intensified the rotation, which then spun me around like an electric motor: my whole body was abuzz with vibrations, even though the rotation was still imaginary, and not as perceptually real as usual. I also heard noise. It became clear that if I was not already in the phase, then I was close to it, and so I tried to roll out for the first time. It worked like a charm. However, I did not fall onto the floor, but floated an inch or two above it, as it seemed to me.

Wasting no time, I abruptly stood up in the middle of the room. I couldn't see the room around me, but clearly understood that I was in it. I quickly began to palpate the floor, closet, bed linen, my own torso, and so on. On the whole, I could immediately tell that the phase was deep, even though I couldn't see. I did everything more out of habit, and in order to ensure a long and confident phase. Moreover, the lapse in consciousness was recent, and it would be necessary to fully regain consciousness before going into action, otherwise I might easily drift out of the phase. After 5 to 10 seconds of palpation, my vision returned. As soon as it did, I stared at my hands, peering at all the lines on my palms and fingers. The phase became not only real in terms of perception - it became hyper-real.

At that moment, I quickly defined my goals: to obtain information about phase training, and to conduct an experiment on the connection between the body perceived in the phase and the physical body left behind on the bed. I didn't initially recall what else had I wanted to do, but figured that I'd remember the other tasks while completing the first two.

All that thought on my plan of action did not take more than two seconds. I then closed my eyes and concentrated on finding a wise old man. I abruptly flew off, and quickly enough found myself in a hut, entering as if staggering in after flying through the wall. The wise man sat facing away from me, so I quickly walked around to face him, and then asked him how I could improve my teaching methodology at seminars. I expected that he would once again propose certain tricks-of-the-trade and special techniques. Instead, he unexpectedly said that it was worth working more actively on the emotional factor and especially motivation, as many simply do not make the necessary effort, mainly because they don't understand what awaits them and how interesting it is. Even though their technique should be corrected, there's not point in doing so when they aren't always motivated and do not perform the techniques thoroughly.

Having obtained what I needed and having set its analysis aside for later, I took advantage of the opportunity and asked a question concerning my personal relationships with people that I care about in my life. However, the response caused me to fade out, and my mind wandered for a couple of moments, which was enough for everything to become blurred. Realizing that directly employing maintaining techniques would be useless at this point, I just tried to maintain the phase by grabbing the sage's beard. I ended up in my body, but with my hand still holding his beard, which I strongly clutched in my hand in order to amplify the flow of sensations as much as possible. Rubbing my hand with the beard, I was able to almost effortlessly get out of bed. After palpating the nearby space with my free hand and realizing that the state was stable enough, I began trying to scrutinize the hand with the beard, holding it close to my eyes. My vision started to return, and within several seconds I was already able to see the space and my hand itself quite clearly. In it lay a thick clump of gray hair. This made me laugh. I tried not to get distracted, and was able to contain myself.

Then, I began to study the connection between the body that is visible on the bed from the phase, and the real physical one. Perhaps the phase space itself came to my aid, because it was precisely at that time that I saw my body indeed lying on the bed. I had been enjoying this sight less and less frequently, though at the beginning of my practice I experienced it with nearly every exit from the body.

Watching myself from the outside was once again not very pleasant, something jostled me inside and aroused mixed feelings. This was perhaps because the person I was looking at did not exactly correspond to how I experience myself to be. I began to touch his feet, stomach, and head. Contrary to old wives' tales, this did not cause any getting pulled into a stencil - this process deepened and maintained my phase, as it was a type of sensory amplification. At some point, touching and examining the face, I all too clearly realized that it was me. Everything faded for a moment, and I even felt someone's hands on my face. But I was then able to go back to what I was doing, and continued on with the same clarity of purpose. I wrapped up the experiment.

Here it dawned on me that I could not remember what else I had wanted to do. Quite disappointed, I now had to go on with doing the first thing that popped into my head, so as not to waste the rest of the phase as a result of my poor memory...

March 2009

An Unexpectedly Long Phase

I had put a lot of work into the book the day before, wrapping up a three-day session. My brain was still very tired, and would need more than the previous night's sleep to recuperate. After working another hour from 8 to 9 am, I fell asleep. I woke up around dinnertime, ate, and was once again unable to resist falling asleep. After about another hour or two of sleep, I woke up motionlessly to partial conscious awareness after a vivid dream. I realized that my mind was clear and relaxed enough to try to enter the phase. Moreover, I had an intense desire to do so. I tried separating - and nothing. I began observing images. At first they were quite dull. I could make out a forest landscape somewhere in the distance. It quickly became more and more realistic, and seemed to be sucking me in. However, I didn't feel like waiting for it to pull me in, and so I tried once again to roll out. I was only able to make several degrees of movement, and then I was stuck again. I returned to my body, and once again rushed to force myself to roll out. I was able to move significantly farther, but was still stuck. I returned again, and even more forcefully started rolling out, this time meeting no resistance.

I felt the phase to be fairly weak. Even deepening techniques hardly helped. I had no vision, and the sensations had less than 50% the stability of those of real life. I was nearly pulled back into my body. I tried palpation on the objects in my room with double effort, and meanwhile ran around in order to obtain more sensations. It took effort, but the situation started to stabilize. Once I could feel that I was stably in the phase, I put my hands to my eyes and aggressively tried to see through the darkness. Sight quickly came, and I could see the whole room no less vividly than in real life.

Since the phase still seemed unstable to me and destined to be short-lived, I decided to put aside my plan of action and instead practice skills that I had not used in a while. First, I went up to the wall and started to forcefully knock on it with my knuckles. I immediately felt sharp and unpleasant pain. I concentrated my attention, and the pain quickly subsided. I knocked even harder. There was no pain. I punched the wall several times with all my strength, breaking the surface of the drywall and leaving a dent. There was no pain at all.

    I then looked at my slipper lying next to the bed, and tried to move it just by looking at it. After some hesitation, the slipper started to move a bit, though reluctantly. I noticed that the realism of the space around me sagged somewhat and everything seemed to fade a bit - afterwards, the slipper bent to my every will. I moved it across the floor and made it move through the air. I finally dashed it against the window, shattering it. A cold draft blew in. I then telekinetically flipped the bed over and installed it on the ceiling, all by staring at it. I then focused my attention on the light-bulb of the lamp, trying to turn it on by force of will. The light bulb flickered on, and then off. I increased the depth of the phase to a hyper-realistic state through peering and palpation, and then tried illuminating the light-bulb again. This proved to be more difficult. It didn't particularly want to obey my will. But after a few seconds, it gently reddened, and then lit up.

    I finished my phase skills training session by concentrating on the bed, willing it to catch fire. It immediately started smoldering. Then, small tongues of fire erupted here and there. Within a few seconds, the whole bed was on fire, filling the room with a sulphuric smell and a lot of smoke.

    Rubbing my hands together in order to deepen the state, I went up to the broken window, startled that the phase had lasted so long, as it had initially been so unstable. I decided to use the last moments of it to take off into outer-space in one of those ultrafast machines featured in the move "Star Wars". I focused my attention on the idea, closed my eyes in anticipation, and immediately felt myself moving. I gradually felt the sensation that I wasn't standing, but sitting on and sinking into a comfortable chair that had just appeared. I now felt that I was dressed in some kind of spacesuit, and holding a pilot's joystick in my gloved hands. As soon as I focused my attention on that tactile sensation and had already decided to bring back my sight, a horribly loud sound started blaring. A force of titanic proportions pulled me from the chair and cockpit that I was in, its safety restraints nearly tearing me apart. The shock forced my eyes open.

Fortunately, my eyes did not open to the physical world. But unfortunately, I saw that I was approaching a huge spaceship at high speed, with sparks flying about all around me. There was already nothing that I could do. After another second, there was nothing but darkness, and I was weightless. Vexed at the interruption of such an interesting adventure, I totally forgot to employ further techniques, and soon realized that I was lying in bed, and could feel daylight through my eyelids. I figured that it was time to get up and continue writing the book. Without attempting to get back into the phase, I went to the bathroom to wash up, meanwhile reflecting on what had happened. I looked in the mirror, and did not immediately realize what was happening: I had huge beer-belly. At first I was in shock, because I had devoted so much energy to getting rid of this "trophy" that I got from "bulking up" and heavy weight training. Taking the belly in my hands, I squeezed and rolled the layers of fat. I then realized that I had never had a belly like this before. And then came the epiphany - I was still in the phase! One can only imagine my relief ...

January 2010
A Long Way for a Short Phase

I woke up sometime at about 9 am, and my first thought was that I had woken up too alertly to do anything with the phase. As always, I forced myself to still try to do something. The awakening was so alert that it was somewhat difficult to convince myself to this end. The situation was aggravated by physical movement - I was lying down uncomfortably on my stomach.

I immediately performed forced falling asleep for a few seconds, causing me to feel a sharp plunge in my mental state, as if I were retreating deep into myself. I tried to separate right then, but nothing happened: neither levitation, nor rolling out, nor getting up. I started performing one of my favorite techniques: phantom wiggling. No movement arose. A few seconds later, I tried visualizing my hands. Then observing images. There was no result, but I noted that my hearing was fading out: I already couldn't clearly hear sounds coming from outside the window or the room. That definitely meant something. I again tried phantom wiggling, but nothing happened after several seconds of trying.

I decided to do visualization of the hands together with forced falling asleep. I started waving my hands in front of my face, and then rubbing may palms together, trying to distinguish all this visually. Meanwhile, I feel into a deeper state, leading my conscious awareness into the void. It was right then that I noticed that I sensed my hands to be less under the pillow, and more in front of my face. Once my conscious awareness got distracted by this, everything stopped right then and there. I again began to fade out, and then tried to feel and see my hands in front of me. With my remaining remnants of awareness, I began to notice that my hands' presence in front of my face was increasingly palpable, and I even began to be able to make them out visually. As soon as I realized that I could see them, I reactivated my conscious awareness, and started trying to discern the hands as clearly as possible. And after a couple of seconds, they became as clearly visible as they would be in reality. Now I could feel them 100%, and even forgot about where they were lying in reality. Not more than 30 seconds had elapsed so far from the moment of initial awakening.

After that, I just got up off the bed, quickly mentally running over my plan of action. But then, the telephone lying on the floor next to the bed unexpectedly started ringing. I picked it up, and could feel not only its physical features, but even how it vibrated out the ring-tone. My colleague from work flashed on the caller ID. I wondered what he would say to me in the phase, and so I pressed the button to take the call. To my surprise, the phone kept on ringing. I became confused. I again pressed the button to take the call, but to no end. I realized that the phone was probably also ringing in reality.

As soon as that realization hit me, I was instantly back in my body. The phone was really ringing. And indeed, it was my colleague from work calling. The question remains as to why that sound didn't immediately knock me out of the phase. Perhaps because the phase space was overlapping the real world in a completely logical way.

December 2010
Turning into Lenin's Mummy

It was an exhausting day: flying into Seattle from LA, and then driving out to Yelm just in time for the first session of a seminar. That's why the plan wasn't to enter the phase, but to at least catch up on some sleep.

I awoke quite early the next morning, and went right for the kitchen to get a taste of the delicious treats that my hostess had baked. It was already fairly light outside, and I got a chance to enjoy the beauty of the brook and pine forest outside the window. I thought about how nice it must be to live in a place with such scenery. After having enjoyed some tasty treats with a glass of milk, I went to go back to bed. As I lay down, I nearly immediately heard some noise. This was puzzling, as the phase rarely comes to me so quickly and without lapses in consciousness. Meanwhile, such noise is a definitive sign that a phase is already in progress. Something wasn't right...

Then, it finally dawned on me: up in these northern parts at this time of the morning, it simply couldn't have been as light outside as it had seemed to me when I was walking about the guest story of the house. It had all happened in the phase! The treats, the milk, and taking in the landscape. And even I, with all of my experience, would have never figured that out if it weren't for that noise which betrayed the fact that I was in the phase once I returned to my body. Incredible...

I rolled out of my body right away and got on with a series of experiments...

As soon as my obligatory plan of action had been completed, I was returned back to my body. I rolled out again with ease and decided to just run through the beautiful environs of the fabled little town of Blueberry Hill, upon arriving there by force of will. The place was quite impressive. I rushed through the window and began sprinting around the house from a distance of 100 yards, intently scrutinizing everything I came across.

My secondary plan of action complete, I was returned back to my body. I couldn't recall anything else important to do. But I had to squeeze everything out of this phase, and use it for still more. For some reason, out of the blue I got the strange idea of turning up inside Vladimir Lenin's mummified body at his tomb in Moscow's Red Square. Without first separating, I began trying to feel myself being him. My body immediately shortened in stature. I began to feel myself in the exact body position that his mummy lies in, as well as in its clothing. For the first time in a long while, once I began to feel the surrounding environment, being in the phase felt very scary. The incredible realness of sensation evoked some strange terror that made me decide to cut the phase short, against my own advice. I returned to my body with only minor difficulty. I opened my eyes. It was pitch black all around me. The time was 2 am.

I went back into Lenin's body, but the terror did not return. This was unfortunate, as I would like to experience such extraordinary feelings again. Seeing as the nearly dumbfounding account of my adventure was illustrative of many items on the curriculum, I decided to share it and everyone at the next day's seminar got a good laugh out of it.

May 2011

A Typical Investigative Phase

I awoke at 6 AM, turned on CNN, and had a bite to eat, as is my custom. After catching the latest news, I turned off the television. I then began to attentively review my plan of action for the day's upcoming phases and add in new details. The morning's first phase was to be devoted to an experiment on maintaining by means of assuming an extremely uncomfortable or even painful position with the perceived (subtle) body. The second phase would be needed to undertake an experiment on the consistency of bodily perception: somehow separate or cut off an arm and see what happens with sensations. Other items on the plan of action for this and subsequent phases consisted of more down-to-earth and everyday goals.

At 6:20 AM I closed the balcony door, inserted earplugs, and put on a sleeping mask to keep sunlight from interfering. After lying down in a comfortable position on my stomach, I once again thought about my plan of action. I decided to enter the phase using a direct technique. I didn't start off with the technique right away. Instead, I decided to reach the edge of sleep first. I got lost in thought at some point, and my imaginings turned into episodes that enveloped me. My mind was then abruptly returned to the body, and I tried to separate, but unsuccessfully. I then began to do the rotation technique quite slowly and passively. My awareness once again began to fade, and another shallow lapse in consciousness took place. On the way back up, neither standing up, nor levitating, nor rolling out were successful as separation techniques. Meanwhile, I could clearly sense an approaching phase. I started doing sensory-motor visualization, imagining that I had already separated and was walking about the room while deepening the phase. Those imagined sensations started becoming real after another micro-lapse in conscious awareness about three minutes in.

As soon as the sensations had become true-to-life, I rapidly made them hyper-realistic through a mix of palpation, peering, and focused intention. Then, I fell backwards to the floor and folded my legs underneath, trying to recreate a pulling feeling in my hips that had once helped me to stay in the phase for a long time. This time, however, my legs bent quite flexibly, and so no pain or strain arose. Feeling that the phase would soon end anyway, I began to twist my legs even more intensely. Mild pain finally came. Realizing that I couldn't hope for much more at that point, I decided to see whether such weak sensations were enough for maintaining the phase. Now fading, I kept my legs in as painful a position as possible. I started counting the seconds that went by, all the while enjoying a tranquility uncharacteristic of the phase. After all, staying in the phase for as long as possible usually requires chaotic action in order to stimulate all of the senses. At 26 seconds in, the sensations abruptly began to dissipate, as did the pain. Several seconds later, I was back in my body. I was unable reenter the phase state, which meant that it had fully run its course.

I began falling back asleep with the intention of repeating the test during my next phase experience, and only then moving on to the other activities on my plan of action. The indirect method would bring me twice more into the phase that morning, allowing me to continue on with the experiment. Yet another phase would come thanks to becoming conscious while dreaming, and all this by 9:30 AM.

PART III: A PRACTICAL GUIDEBOOK

Only for Experienced Practitioners

Entering the Phase State

Chapter 1 – General Background

THE ESSENCE OF THE PHASE PHENOMENON

The term phase state (or simply phase) encompasses a number of widely known dissociative phenomena, many of which are referred to by various terms, such as astral travel or out-of-body experience. This concept also includes the more pragmatic term lucid dreaming, but is not limited to the sense and form implied by that expression. Hence, the term phase has been introduced to ease the study of phenomena that exist beyond habitual – and often inaccurate- associations and stereotypes. The term out-of-body experience is accurate to the extent that it describes the sensation felt by a person experiencing the phase phenomenon.

A phase has two primary attributes: 1.) practitioners possess full, conscious awareness during the experience, and 2.) practitioners recognize a genuine separation from the physical body.

Simultaneously, the degree to which practitioners perceive the phase environment affects the level of sensory experiences therein, which often occur in a higher form than the sensory experiences of wakefulness. This concept is difficult to imagine without firsthand experience of the phase. And so, it is not without reason that this practice is considered to be a higher state of self-hypnosis or meditation, and is often referred to under different names as the highest possible human achievement in various religious and mystical movements (yoga, Buddhism, etc.).

How the Phase Differs from Wakefulness and Dream

	Wakefulness	Phase State	Dream
Consciousness, Self-Awareness	✓	✓	
Realism of Perception	✓	✓	
Stability of Surrounding Space	✓		
Effort Necessary for Entry		✓	

In essence, the phase is an unexplored state of mind where one is unable to control or feel the physical body. Instead, space perception is filled with realistic phantom experiences.

Interesting Fact!

Sensations in the phase state can be so realistic that practitioners who unintentionally enter it often believe they are still in the physical body, and that the experience is occurring in the waking state. These types of unintended excursions most often occur at night or early in the morning.

www.obe4u.com

It is believed that one person in two on this planet will encounter this phenomenon at least once in his life. However, when the variability and differing levels of depth of the state are taken into consideration, practically everyone has encountered it in one way or another. Since the phase is a rare subject of study, many who inadvertently enter it do not realize what has taken place once they return to wakefulness. Many do not assign any significance to the occurrence of a phase environment that is not fully formed because shallow phases don't leave the same jolting impression as deep states. Elusive as the phase may seem, this is an extremely common phenomenon, accessible to anyone willing to consciously learn and apply the correct methods of achieving and maintaining it.

> ***Interesting Fact!***
> *9 and 75 year-olds have studied at School of Out-of-Body Travel seminars. Meanwhile, even as many trouble themselves over the issue of how much age hinders or helps in the practice, these people demonstrated some of best results in their groups.*

Even a scientific approach to the phenomenon states unequivocally that the phase is accessible to all, barring serious brain pathologies. This has been unambiguously confirmed by experimental research. Therefore, there's no sense in reasoning that the phase is something difficult, accessible only to a small circle of people, or out of anyone's reach. Difficulties in mastering it attest only to technique-related mistakes, and not to the inaccessibility of the phenomenon.

SCIENCE AND THE PHASE

Science first accepted the possibility of the phase state within the dream consciousness context with Keith Hearne's 1975 experiment at England's Hull University. Over the course of the experiment, practitioner Alan Worsley was able to make deliberate and previously agreed eye movements at the same that an EKG monitor indicated his brain was in a state of sleep. Several years later, Stephen LaBerge would perform a similar experiment at Stanford University that became well known due to his active contribution to the development of this field of study.

Quite a number of scientific experiments have been conducted worldwide to prove the existence of the phenomenon and investigate its nature. For example, experiments on three phasers at the Max Plank Institute in Frankfurt (2008) demonstrated the following: the largest difference between the states of wakefulness, the phase, and rapid-eye-movement (REM) sleep is observed at the 40 Hz frequency, and is concentrated in the frontal parts of the brain. Essentially, it was demonstrated that the phase is something in-between wakefulness and REM sleep. Notably, those very parts of the brain that are very much responsible for consciousness and whose development distinguishes humans from primates turn out to be the most active while in the phase. This work was undertaken by J. Allan Hobson, Ursula Voss, Romain Holzmann, and Inka Tuin.

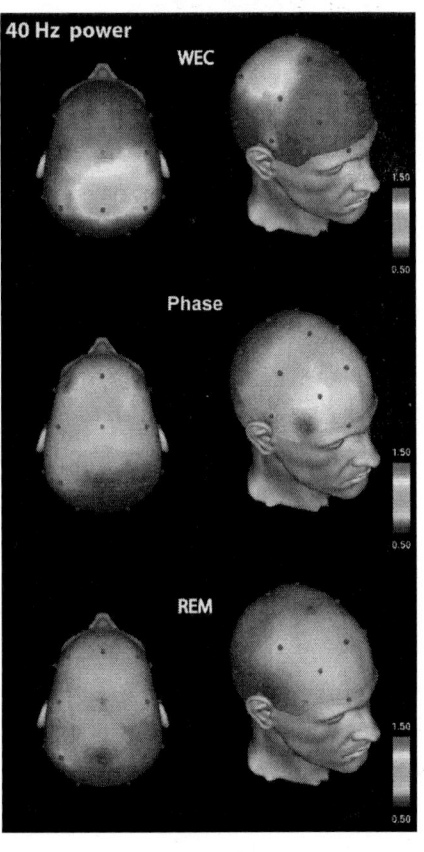

They are credited with demonstrating the difference between states of consciousness at 40 Hz.

More in-depth explanations of the nature of the phase state phenomenon remain to be discovered. With each passing year, the scientific community increasingly realizes how important the study of this state is, recognizing that it enables a better understanding of the mechanisms responsible for consciousness and how varying states of wakefulness and sleep arise.

There is also a theory which states that the phase is a product of the evolution of human consciousness: consciousness first arose in and occupied wakefulness, and then gradually began to seep into the REM state, the next-closest state still free of conscious awareness. Possibly, conscious existence in two worlds - wakefulness and the phase - will be as commonplace for men and women of the future as being aware only during wakefulness is today. However, there is also a completely opposite theory which maintains that phase ability used to be inherent, but is gradually disappearing. It points to the frequent ease with which younger children enter the phase, but later lose the ability with age due to its neglect.

ESOTERIC AND MYSTICAL EXPLANATIONS

Although the general tone of this learning material has so far kept to a sufficiently materialist tack, it is not theorizing about the phase that brings people together, but its practice. Practice is indisputable, while theory always leads to contention. For that reason, it makes no difference at all what the practitioner considers the nature of the phenomenon to be, including if he sees esoteric or mystic motifs in it. Everyone has the right to their own outlook and it is by no means the aim of this book to influence any life philosophy or encourage it towards some theoretical bent. What's most important is that the reader be able to get real practice with the phenomenon.

Unfortunately still, there is no clear definition of the phenomenon in esoteric culture, nor an unambiguous term for it. Depending on the esoteric practice, the phase state is alternatively lumped in with astral projection or out-of-body travel, and sometimes with lucid dreaming. Postulated is some essence (the soul or astral body) leaving the physical plane and finding itself somewhere in a) the physical world, b) the dream world, or c) the astral plane, etc. Meanwhile, the number of worlds that can be visited varies depending on the mystical school. For example, the astral plane can be the higher one or the lower one, or also the mental plane, etheric plane, and so on and so forth. In some mystical schools this is considered a higher experience in terms of one's personal practice and state of being, while in others it is equated to the physical world, and is but a layer between more ethereal realms. Just the same, explanations of the nature of the phenomenon and its significance also vary widely.

It is also often considered to be the same state that people experience when dying. In many Eastern practices and religions, like Buddhism for example, where the main goal is to stop the cycle of reincarnation through remaining conscious while dying, it is believed that conscious dying can only be accomplished through ability to enter the phase, which would be a form of training for the moment of death and remaining conscious during it.

There are endless disagreements regarding how lucid dreaming (i.e. dream consciousness) actually differs from so-called "out-of-body travel" and whether its classification under the phase is justified. The same controversy extends to another esoteric term - astral projection. *However, such doubts only trouble novices and those whose acquaintance with the phase is superficial. Not a single experienced practitioner can unequivocally differentiate these phenomena, although explanations for this may vary.* For example, when classifying all these phenomena together, one practitioner will conclude that it's indeed a parallel world, while another might maintain that it's all generated by the mind.

There are many reasons to classify lucid dreaming (i.e. dream consciousness) together with out-of-body travel. This is not only because existing research and a massive number of peoples' experiences easily prove it. There are a number of questions that adherents of dividing phase phenomena into various states cannot answer. First, why do lucid dreamers and out-of-body travelers use the very same techniques to achieve their states, but merely call the result by different names? Second, why are the fundamental properties of the out-of-body plane and lucid-dreaming world exactly the same? Third, if the world of dreaming can take on any external form with any properties, then how does one differentiate real exit of the soul from the body into the physical world - or a parallel astral one - from a simulated dreamscape? Many can offer theoretical explanations, but not one that can be applied or proven in practice.

People usually encounter extreme physiological difficulty in leaving behind the idea of there being a myriad of worlds that they can fall into. This is usually tightly interwoven with their life philosophy and worldview, which can be pulled at the seams by such questioning. However, even opponents of classifying phase experiences together can easily use the techniques to achieve them in a way compatible with their outlook. This again demonstrates the secondary role of theory and the overriding importance of practice.

WHY ENTER THE PHASE?

Such a question can only arise from not fully understanding the properties of the phenomenon and its nature. When one suddenly understands at a certain moment that he is just as real as he normally is, and is standing somewhere that is not in the physical world with his same hands and body, and can touch everything around him and discern fine details, such much emotion stirs up inside him that no questions arise at all. *This is the most amazing experience that a person can attain!*

The initial phase encounter is always jolting and sometimes frightening. Depending on the individual, fear experienced during initial encounters with the phase occurs in about one-third of all cases. Even veteran practitioners encounter fear, which speaks to the profound nature of the phase state.

With time, as rapture ebbs and emotions wane, thoughts turn from the fact of the phenomenon itself towards how to somehow use it. And here, a fantastically diverse field of practical application opens up before the practitioner. These applications – which this book communicates – are not to be associated with the many unproven and dubious methods often described in sundry esoteric literature. The information presented herein is verifiable, practical, and attainable.

Whatever the nature of the phase - a state of mind, or perhaps an external experience - this is the sole opportunity to: visit any part of the world or universe; see people who are out-of-reach in real life, including relatives, the deceased, celebrities, and various creatures; communicate with the enormous resources of the subconscious mind and obtain information from it; realize desires that are unattainable in real life; model artistic productions; influence physiology, and more. These are not dull experiences. They are eminently personal and real.

THE LIFESTYLE OF A PRACTITIONER

It must be said that various diets, exercises, rituals, and so forth do not produce noticeable supplementary effects to proper practice of the phase. Naturally existent psychological and physiological comfort is of the utmost importance. Thus, methods recommending overeating, under-eating, or tormenting oneself with various diets and strange exercises are useless and ultimately detrimental to a practitioner's wellness and balance, invariably producing a negative impact on the effectiveness of techniques taught in this guidebook. Additionally, no meaningful association has been found between practice of the phase and what may be construed as "bad habits". Regardless of a lifestyle's null effect on phase achievement, a healthy, active lifestyle will always be recommended to enjoy a good quality of living.

> ***Interesting Fact!***
> *If one believes that it is necessary to position one's bed with the headboard facing the northwest or some other direction in order to have more effective out-of-body experiences, then doing so will invariably have a positive effect on results. However, the issue at hand is not the positioning of the body, but a belief that is akin to an intention, which in turn is enormously important.*

It has been observed that a regular and orderly lifestyle increases the frequency of genuine, lasting phase experiences. Sleeping normally and soundly is the most basic example of a lifestyle choice that produces direct, positive impact on results, especially when a practitioner commits to a full night's rest several times a week.

In order to better understand the proper approach to the practice, it's worth enumerating four types of people who usually have the quickest and best results. First, people who are mathematically inclined. The more exactly the instructions given in this textbook are followed, the greater their effectiveness. People with mathematical minds immediately get and clearly understand the whole procedure in its entirety, which is why they have better success in carrying it out. Next are the athletes. Their practice is facilitated by their clarity of purpose as well as ability to focus and push themselves. Third are those who love to sleep. A successful practice can definitely be predicted for a person who falls asleep easily and can slumber for 10 to 12 hours, often waking up and then falling back asleep throughout. Finally, children. Their success is ensured not only by physiological factors, but also in much part by a clarity of mind yet to be encumbered with useless knowledge and hamstrung by excessive analysis. Practical instructions reach their minds unhindered and are easily followed unerringly.

There is absolutely no requirement to fall into the above categories in order to take up the practice of phase states. You need only separate out and understand what exactly helps these types of people, try to find similar traits in yourself, and then accentuate them in your own practice.

Similarly, certain types can be singled out who often have difficulties in beginning their practice of the phase. First are those who have light, brief, or fitful sleep due to physiological traits, lifestyle, or their work. Next are active practitioners of esoteric techniques with many years of experience. The minds of such people are so weighed down by various theories and practices that it can be simply impossible to convey even the basics regarding techniques to them, as they immediately interpret everything in their own idiosyncratic way and synthesize it with other accumulated knowledge. Then there are people who are simply inattentive. Their problem consists in frequently focusing on secondary matters, all while blatantly ignoring what's most important.

If a practitioner fits into one of the above categories, that doesn't mean that nothing will work for him or that he's better off not taking up this practice. The truth is that this practice works for everybody, it's just that some of the habits of the above groups can interfere with their developmental path. If you recognize such tendencies in yourself, all that you have to do is to try to overcome or mitigate them.

One of the main criteria for a successful start to one's out-of-body practice is to approach it with a blank slate. If a practitioner has read, heard, or tried out even something having to do with this phenomenon, he's better off forgetting about it or at least putting it aside for now. And that blank slate should be carefully and exactly inscribed with these instructions, which have been proven to work by thousands across the globe.

A number of practices and pastimes have been found to have a positive effect on the practice of out-of-body travel. *Sports* help one learn to focus on goals, push oneself, and overcome weaknesses. The practice of *stopping internal dialog* allows one to concentrate intensely and avoid needless analysis when desired. *Self-hypnosis* and *meditation* also allow one to learn to concentrate, as well as have control over the mind and body. However, you should never exhaust your energies and enthusiasm by taking up an excessive number of practices at once. That usually leads to overall lack of results.

There should be no neuroticism or obsessiveness in approaching the phase - as they reduce odds of success to zero. All actions should be cool and self-assured, without letting the importance of the end-goal stir one up into a frenzy.

Sound sleep is one indicator of correctness of approach and following the instructions. If all of the methods are implemented correctly, the practitioner will always enjoy sound sleep. Conversely, fitful and chronically light sleep, as well as insomnia, always serve as symptoms of errors in one's very approach to the practice. One's general feeling of well-being is also a good indicator. Correct practice of the phase will never cause fatigue, nor bring out emotional or physical exhaustion. To the contrary, the phase should be emotionally invigorating and energizing. To put it simply, the practice should not cause any discomfort, even during unsuccessful attempts.

PRACTICE REGIME: 2 TO 3 DAYS PER WEEK

It is never recommend to practice the phase state more than 2 or 3 days a week! This is categorically forbidden for novices and is motivated by external factors, in addition to a whole slew of other reasons, mainly psychological. Ideally, over the first months or even years, it's best to only concentrate on attempts before days off from work, when there's no need to wake up early or it's possible to take afternoon naps. *Never make any attempts at leaving the body on other days. During them, try to divert yourself from the phase and busy yourself with matters and other practices far removed from it.*

Of course, if the phase starts to occur spontaneously during such breaks, then there's no need to run away from it. Take advantage of those opportunities, making use of your entire technique repertoire and practical skill.

Over time, only experienced practitioners will be able to set themselves an ideal schedule that does not affect the quality of their attempts. Some may even do it every day. However, there's no sense in forcing yourself to that level. It's simply not possible for the average novice, no matter how well he has picked up on the all the most important aspects of the practice.

Interesting Fact!
Even the School's beginner seminars take the form of 3-days of lessons with two nights of practice in a row. For a large number of reasons, this is just as effective as if the seminar lasted for an entire 5 days, for example.

If a practitioner has been trying phase entrance techniques every day or almost every day, he should take a break for 1 to 2 weeks in order to start doing them on the right schedule- two or three times per week.

You should try to enter the phase only 2 to 3 days a week, regardless of whether or not your attempts are successful. This should be a simply mandatory rule, so that you don't suffer from emotional exhaustion or hit a wall with your practice. When correctly following it, you can have many phase experiences over a single day, which is why even 2 to 3 days a week is totally sufficient for making constant progress.

Ignoring this rule can lead to quite severe consequences for one's practice: phase entrance will simply not happen at all, and a block in one's practice may arise due to the lack of success. That block will worsen until complete loss of faith in one's own abilities or even the phenomenon itself occurs. The only cure is an even longer break during the week, which it is helpful to take periodically anyway, even when one's practice is successful. To put it bluntly, a phaser should keep to a certain rhythm and cycle during good times and bad, as does the rest of the world.

ALGORITHM FOR MASTERING THE PHASE

A novice practitioner must understand the procedure for learning and mastering phase entry. This procedure consists of several primary steps, each of which is a unique science unto itself.

1. The first and most important step addresses the techniques used to enter the phase state. It is not necessary to master every type of entrance technique (direct, indirect, dream consciousness). Learning and applying the easiest techniques provides the necessary prerequisites to more advanced methods.
2. Contrary to popular opinion, the need for conscious techniques does not cease upon phase entrance. It is absolutely necessary to learn and apply methods for deepening the phase to achieve a consistently hyper-realistic environment. Failing to apply deepening techniques almost guarantees that experiences will be dull, uninteresting, and subsequent practice short-lived.

Practitioners should immediately learn and apply deepening techniques after mastering any one entrance method.
3. The third step involves mastering techniques for maintaining the phase, as without them the average person would have phase experiences of much shorter duration than is possible. When in the phase, the question of how to leave it almost never occurs. On the contrary, one is normally thrust from it in the course of several seconds if one simply does nothing.
4. After learning all the necessary techniques for mastering the phase state, it is time to learn and apply methods of control, which encompass the ability to translocate, find and interact with objects, influence surroundings, and so forth.
5. Once the previously noted steps have been accomplished, a practitioner may proceed to apply phase experiences to enhance everyday life. Over the course of this guidebook, we will examine dozens of these valuable applications in great detail.

ALGORITHM FOR MASTERING THE PHASE

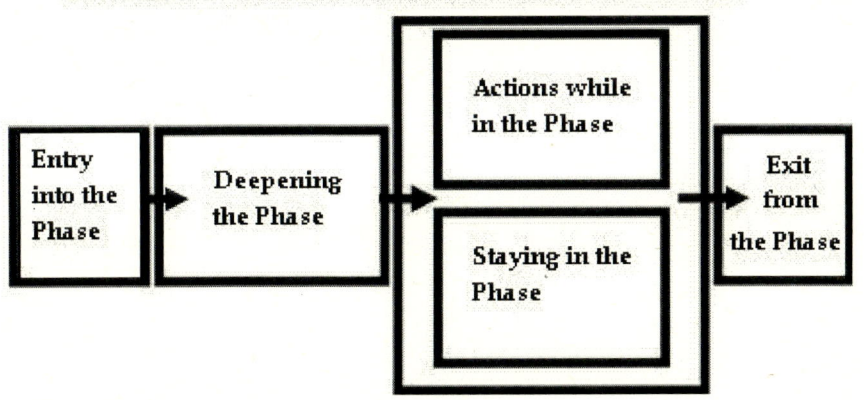

Entry into the Phase → Deepening the Phase → Actions while in the Phase / Staying in the Phase → Exit from the Phase

With basic skills mastered, remember that practicing the phase is worthwhile and effective only when the results are consistent. If a practitioner enters the phase only once a month, the experience will be too emotional to allow for observation of important principles and methodologies. The phase should be encountered at least once a week. Working toward a level higher than a weekly phase entry is ambitious, even beneficial. Realistically, two to four phase experiences per week might be considered the level of a master, but this is far from the upward boundary (2-6 phases per one day!).

As a rule, novice practitioners achieve the phase less often than is desired. However, with regular attempts, success occurs more and more frequently, which should help alleviate any frustration resulting from failed attempts.

Every budding phaser should realize that the instructions given in this textbook are the best tools for the average person to achieve the phase state. However, many have their own physiological and lifestyle idiosyncrasies, and so something might not suit them or might be counter to their nature. Minor adjustments to the instructions are permissible from the very beginning. As long as they're minor. Substantial changes are only for people with substantial experience, and should only be made using tried and true methods. The methods work for everyone in any case, but for the experienced practitioner they are merely a template that can be fine-tuned to further improve results. If nothing at all works for a practitioner, then it's not a question of method but a question of how well the method is being applied. This is why introducing substantial changes at beginning stages is categorically forbidden.

The aim of this book is to lay a strong foundation for individual practice that is devoid of any dubious elements. Some things might not be as fancy or fantastical as one might wish. On the other hand, everything described here is backed up by the facts. Everyone has the right to choose their own path, personal-growth philosophy, and interpretation of what is going on when building the foundation of their nascent practice.

TYPES OF TECHNIQUES

There are three primary types of techniques that make it possible to enter the phase: *direct*, *indirect* and *dream consciousness*. These methods are performed while lying down or reclining, eyes closed, and the body in a state of total relaxation.

Interesting Fact!
Often, people have an out-of-body experience without prior knowledge or belief in the phenomenon. It just happens, and a large body of evidence has been gathered to support this fact. Even more interesting is that spontaneous experiences often occur after a brief study of material about the topic, like this guidebook...

Direct techniques are performed without any noticeable lapse in consciousness. While practicing direct techniques, a lapse into sleep for less than 5 minutes is not considered a breach of the technique.

By definition, direct techniques encompass the performance of specific actions for a pre-defined interval of time. Successfully applied, direct methods result in a phase entrance without passing through any intermediary states. For 90% of the population, these techniques are the most difficult because the mind naturally exists in an excessively active state. It has been clearly proven within the School's student body that novice practitioners do not benefit from beginning a training regimen with direct techniques. This is because direct techniques require a thorough understanding and masterful application of indirect techniques in order to be effective. The incorrect notion that the phase state is extremely difficult to enter is due to the fact that people are more often drawn to the more difficult direct techniques. It is always better to approach direct techniques only after becoming expert in the use of indirect techniques.

Indirect techniques are techniques that are put into practice upon awakening from sleep.
The effectiveness of indirect techniques is not dependent on the length of the prerequisite sleep cycle. Indirect techniques can be used while exiting a full night's sleep, after a daytime catnap, or following several hours of deep sleep. The most important thing is that there is a lapse of consciousness into sleep before implementing the techniques.

Indirect techniques are the easiest techniques to practice, which is why many practitioners use them to enter the phase. Sleep naturally provides the mind with deep relaxation, which is often difficult to acquire by other methods. Since sleep is required to perform indirect techniques, it is a convenient, oft-occurring means to conduct experiments with the phase. Novice practitioners benefit greatly from the use of indirect techniques, and learn firsthand the possibility of phase entrance.

Dream consciousness is acquired by techniques that allow entrance to the phase through what is commonly referred to as lucid dreaming.
In this case, the phase begins when the awareness that a dream is occurring happens within the dream itself. After becoming conscious while dreaming, several types of actions can be performed, including deepening or returning to the body and rolling out, which will be described later. When deepening techniques are applied in the context of a conscious dream, the sensory perceptions of the phase surpass those of normal wakefulness.

Techniques that facilitate dream consciousness are usually categorized separately from methods used to perform out-of-body travel; in practice, however, it is apparent that the characteristics of dream consciousness and out-of-body travel are identical, which places both phenomena directly in the phase. These practices are difficult because, unlike other techniques, they do not involve specific actions that produce instantaneous results. A large measure of preparatory steps must be observed that require time and effort without any guarantee of results. However, dream consciousness techniques are not as difficult as direct techniques. Moreover, the majority of practitioners, whether using indirect or direct techniques, experience spontaneous awareness while dreaming without having to apply techniques aimed at dream consciousness.

Every phaser finds their own balance between all of the methods for entering the phase based on their abilities to work on them, their individual predispositions, and their very understanding of how to perform them. Some work with only one type of technique. Most often it's the indirect method or dream consciousness. However, whenever possible it's best to strive for balance and diversify phase entrances as much as possible. Moreover, practically everything becomes achievable with practice, and in this field nothing is impossible. With a balanced approach and all things being equal, the direct method will account for about 15% of all experiences, the indirect method 50% (half of those being immediate separations upon awakening, and the other half using the techniques), while the remaining third of experiences will be had thanks to dream consciousness. However, at times the boundary between methods is so hard to pin down that it sometimes appears impossible to assign a phase entrance to a specific method.

In addition to the techniques described above, there are also non-autonomous means and tools: various devices, programs, external influences, and so forth, which can be used to enter the phase. It is necessary to mention that these are only useful to practitioners who are able to enter the phase without supplementary assistance.

Various chemical substances and herbal supplements have been recommended to assist phase entrance, though using them is unlikely to do any good, and use of these has never yielded the effect that can be achieved through unadulterated practice. As such, the use of a chemical crutch is regarded here as completely unacceptable.

CONTRAINDICATIONS

Exact scientific proof that entering the phase is dangerous – or even safe - does not exist; there has never been an exhaustive, controlled study to prove either supposition. However, since the phase exists at the fringes of naturally-occurring states of mind, it can hardly be assumed dangerous. Notably, the phase is accompanied by rapid eye movement (REM), which every human experiences for up to 2 hours each night, and this begins to explain the phase experience as entirely safe and natural.

Already confirmed are the psychological influences of the phase on the physical mind and body; namely, the emotional effects that can occur during the onset of the phase state.

Phase entry is a very profound, incredible experience that may induce fear, which is invoked by a natural instinct for self-preservation. The phase can create stress. This is especially true for novices and those poorly acquainted with the nature of the phenomenon and techniques used to control it. Without knowledge and proper practice, a fear-induced reaction can escalate into full-blown terror. After all, while in the phase, fantasy quickly becomes reality, and reticent fears can take on hyper-realistic qualities. When this occurs, it's not the phase environment, but the fear that is treacherous. It goes without saying that fear is a toxic influence, especially to sensitive souls, the elderly, and people with physical ailments, like certain cardiovascular conditions. This does not mean that persons in these groups should abstain from practicing the phase. The solution is to learn about and avoid common stressors associated with the practice, know the mechanics of controlling objects, and understand the principles of making an emergency exit.

Given the possibility of negative phase experiences, it could be advised that practitioners limit the time in phase to fifteen minutes, though it is quite exceptional to maintain the phase for such duration. Proposed time limits are entirely theoretical and motivated by the fact that natural REM does not normally last longer than fifteen minutes, and, at the risk of side effects due to the alteration of natural cycles, experiments directed at unnaturally prolonging REM are not recommended.

RECOMMENDATIONS FOR USING THE GUIDEBOOK

During classroom instruction at the School of Out-of-Body Travel, several key factors are known to produce positive and negative effects on the likelihood of success during individual practice:

Positive Effect on Practice	Negative Effect on Practice
Attentive, thorough study of the course material.	Hasty and inattentive study of course materials.
Consistent work with practical elements.	Inconsistent application of techniques.
Diligent completion of technical elements.	Approximating the techniques outside of recommended guidelines.
A relaxed approach to the subject matter.	A hysterical approach to the matter, "idée fixe".
Keeping a journal of all initial attempts, followed by recording successful phase entrances.	A lack of personal analysis when problems or a lack of success are encountered.
Adhering to the	Excessive number of attempts

recommended number of daily entrance attempts.	per day.
Regular attempts and practice.	Sporadic practice regimen.
Understanding that the author knows his field well.	"I also know everything I need to and will do as I want". This attitude is good only for those who have a great amount of real practical experience. Reading a lot on the subject or simply having knowledge of it is not experience.

EXERCISES

Questions

- Which alternative states are included in the term "phase"?
- How does the phase differ from out-of-body travel?
- Is the perception of reality different in waking life than in the phase world?
- Does the phase have applications for day-to-day life?
- What skills must be learned before proceeding to practical use of the phase?
- How many types of autonomous phase entrance techniques are there?
- What is the difference between direct and indirect techniques?
- Which techniques are easiest for the majority of practitioners?
- Is it worth trusting various devices and programs that promise to be able to help one enter the phase state? Why or why not?

- Should one eat meat when practicing the phase?

Tasks

1. Try to remember if you have experienced phase encounters in the past.
2. If you have encountered the phase, what type of technique gained entrance; direct, indirect, or conscious dreaming?
3. If possible, ask some friends and acquaintances about the subject of out-of-body travel or conscious dreaming. Do any of them remember a similar experience? What was it like?

Chapter 2 – Indirect Method

THE CONCEPT OF INDIRECT TECHNIQUES

Genuine practice of phase entrance is best begun with the easiest, most accessible methods: indirect techniques, which are conscious actions performed upon awakening from sleep. Some critics incorrectly assume that indirect techniques are not ideal, and prefer to start with direct techniques. However, doing so provides no guarantee of success and results in a large amount of wasted time and effort. *Starting practice with indirect techniques guarantees entrance into the phase.*

A specific universal technique that suits every practitioner is a myth since individuals differ widely in personality, psychology, and learning speed. However, there is a relatively easy universal algorithm, or procedure, that accounts for the characteristics of each person and allows for the most rational, effective way to attain the initial phase entrances. This algorithm encompasses cyclic practicing of the indirect techniques covered in this chapter. Without exception, these techniques - despite their varying degrees of difficulty - are suitable for every practitioner who wishes to experience the phase.

Results can be expected immediately following the first few attempts; however, to achieve measurable results, an average of five conscious attempts must be made. Making more than five attempts even over the course of a single day is fine, too. There is nothing difficult to understand about performing the techniques since they are clearly laid out and based on real internal processes. *Remarkably, due to correctly practiced indirect techniques, more than half of students at the live school attain phase entrance after only two days.*

Interesting Fact!
Many experienced practitioners prefer to bypass the effort associated with direct techniques and hone their skills through the sole use of indirect techniques.

In order to ensure that one's efforts are most fruitful and productive, we are going to individually examine each step and principle behind the actions in great detail. Let us start from a description of the techniques themselves, which will actually apply practically just as much to direct techniques as to indirect techniques; as they only differ in character and length of application.

There are plenty of techniques, so after practicing all of the indirect techniques presented in this chapter, a practitioner should be able to choose three or four of the most straightforward, individually effective methods.

Separation techniques will be examined later. They are completely different from usual techniques, which only bring one into the phase, but do not necessarily themselves lead to separation from the body. It is often also necessary to know how to stop perceiving one's physical body after employing these techniques.

It is necessary to understand when to employ these techniques, and the importance of waking from sleep without opening the eyes or moving the body. Attempting to enter the phase immediately upon awakening must be learned and practiced to mastery since it constitutes the main barrier to successful practice.

After examining the peripheral information surrounding indirect techniques, the cycles of indirect techniques will be examined, including what they are, how they work, and how they are best used. Successful phase entrance is the direct result of performing these cycles. However, there are exceptions, and it is not completely necessary to proceed with these cycles if one's own mind somehow hints what exactly one should start from, which we will also examine separately.

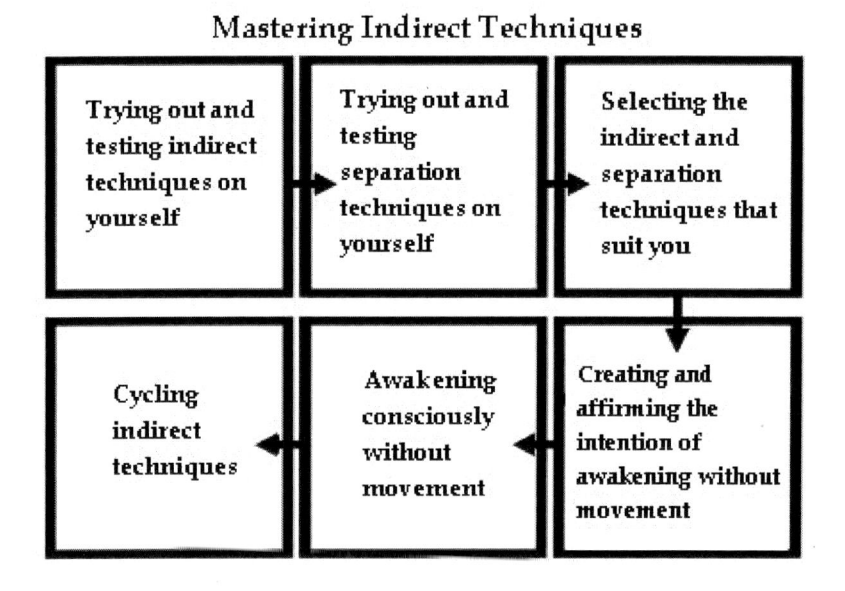

Mastering Indirect Techniques

Trying out and testing indirect techniques on yourself → Trying out and testing separation techniques on yourself → Selecting the indirect and separation techniques that suit you ↓

Cycling indirect techniques ← Awakening consciously without movement ← Creating and affirming the intention of awakening without movement

PRIMARY INDIRECT TECHNIQUES

Nota Bene! The techniques described below are the simple components of indirect technique cycles. Merely implementing each technique's description is far from effective. Of the list given below, it behooves the individual practitioner to choose the most comprehensible and interesting techniques, then actively study and apply the instructions for use.

Observing images
Testing Individual Effectiveness. Immediately after waking from sleep, remain motionless, eyes closed. Observe the blank space before the eyes for 3 to 5 seconds and try to

locate recognizable pictures, images, or symbols. If nothing appears during this exercise, the technique should be substituted. If something appears, continue to passively observe the images. Meanwhile, the images will become increasingly realistic, literally enveloping the practitioner. Do not aggressively examine the details of the image, or it will vanish or change. The image should be experienced as a panorama, taking everything in. Observe the images as long as the quality and realism increases. Doing so yields two possible results: the practitioner becomes part of the surroundings, and has achieved the phase, or the image becomes borderline or absolutely realistic, and separation from the physical body is possible.

Training. To train the use of this technique, lie down in the dark, eyes closed, and observe the blackness for several minutes, identifying any specific images that may arise from simple spots or floaters, and then gradually transition to whole pictures, scenes, or scenarios. With practice, this technique is very easy and straightforward. A common mistake made during practice of this technique is when the practitioner aggressively attempts to conjure images versus passively observing what is naturally presented.

Phantom wiggling (movement)
Testing Individual Effectiveness. Immediately after waking from sleep, remain motionless, eyes closed. Try to wiggle a part of the body for 3 to 5 seconds, but without using any muscles. If nothing moves during the attempt, try a different technique. If a sensation of wiggling occurs, even in the slightest, continue to employ the technique, striving to increase the range of movement as much as possible. This technique should be performed very aggressively, not passively. As soon as the range of movement nears or exceeds four inches - which may take just several seconds - the following situations may arise: one momentarily finds oneself somehow in the phase, or the wiggled part of the body begins to move freely. The occurrence of movement

during practice of this technique allows the practitioner to transition to a separation technique and attempt to leave the body.

While practicing phantom wiggling, strong vibrations may occur, amid which separation may be attempted. Sounds also often arise, allowing the opportunity to practice listening in, which can lead to phase entrance.

The phantom wiggling technique is not meant to produce an imagined movement by a phantom body. The point of the technique is to attempt the movement of a physical body part without using muscular action. That is, the focus should rest upon an internal intention of movement without physical action. When the sensation occurs, it differs little from its real counterpart and is often accompanied by heaviness and resistance. Generally, there is very little range of movement at first, but with concentrated effort the range of movement noticeably increases.

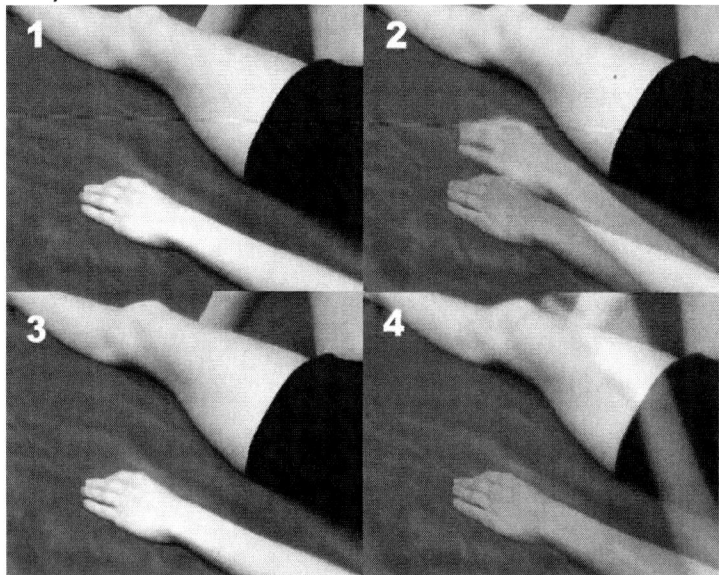

It does not matter which part of the body is used to exercise phantom movement. It may be the whole body or just one finger. Neither is the speed of the movement important. Increased range of perceived movement is the aim of the technique.

Training. To train the technique of phantom wiggling, relax a hand for several minutes while lying down, eyes closed. Then, aggressively envision the following hand movements, without moving any muscles, for two to three minutes each: rotating, up-down, left-right, extending the fingers and drawing the fingers together, clenching and unclenching a fist. No sensations will occur at first. Gradually, the sensation of muscular action will become so apparent that the perceived movement will be indistinguishable from real movement. During the first training attempts, practitioners are often tempted to open their eyes to see if actual movement is occurring – that's how real the sensation feels.

Visualization

Testing Individual Effectiveness. Upon awakening without moving your body or opening your eyes, try to peer at something previously determined and close (4-6 inches from the eyes) for 3 to 5 seconds. For example, this may be your own hands rubbing together, or an apple. If no imagery arises within 5 seconds, switch to another technique. If even dull imagery arises, keep with the technique and try to scrutinize it as best you can. The image will then become more vivid and color saturated. As soon as it is becomes perceptually real, you can separate from the body.

When performing the technique, avoid the most common mistake: only imagining seeing the object, instead of having a real vision of it. The key difference between observing images and peering is in the active desire to see something previously determined, instead of passively peering into the void in search of some spontaneous imagery.

Training. In order to practice the technique, lay down with your eyes closed in a dark room and try to spot various predetermined images in the void before your eyes, starting from the simple (apples, candles, an X, etc.) and moving on to the complicated (landscapes, room interiors, action scenes, and so on). Try to be able to see all of the details of the visualized objects as clearly as possible. The more vivid and the more detailed they are, the better the end result. It's also desirable to try to see objects that are just above eye-level, across from the forehead.

Imagined movement
Testing Individual Effectiveness. Upon awakening, without first moving your body or opening your eyes, try to feel some imagined movement for 3 to 5 seconds. For example, this may be running, pulling a rope, etc. If no result occurs after several seconds, switch to another technique. If the sensation of movement is feeble, or the feeling of being in two bodies at once arises, keep with the technique and increase the degree of realism of the sensation as high as possible: to the level of real feeling. At that moment, the imagined sensation will become dominant, and you can try to separate from your body, as you'll be already in the phase. When implementing this technique, spontaneous translocation often occurs to some place or another - after which separation is already unnecessary.

Training. In order to practice the technique, lie down with your eyes closed in a dark room and try to feel, as authentically as possible, imagined movement of various kinds: swimming freestyle, running, power-walking, pedaling with your hands and feet, pulling rope, rubbing your hands together in front you, etc. Such training will help you to learn to quickly create the intention of feeling a specific sensation, which will play a key role right when it counts.

Listening in
Testing Individual Effectiveness. Immediately after waking from sleep, remain motionless, eyes closed. Try to listen to noise in your head. Do this for 3 to 5 seconds without moving and without opening the eyes. If nothing happens during this period of time, switch to another technique. If any sounds like buzzing, humming, raving, hissing, whistling,

tinkling, or melodies occur, listen attentively. With results, the sound will increase in volume. Listen in as long as there is some dynamism in the volume of the sound. When the sound stops, or the noise becomes loud enough, a separation technique may be attempted. Sometimes, the noise itself throws one into the phase while listening. At a certain stage, sounds may be extremely loud and have even been described as comparable to the roar of a jet-engine.

The action of listening in consists of actively and attentively exploring a sound, the whole of its tonality and range, and how it reacts to the listener.

There is an optional technique known as forced listening in, where it is simply necessary to strongly want to hear noise, and meanwhile make intuitive internal efforts, which, as a rule, are correct. Performed correctly, forced sounds will intensify the same way as those perceived with the standard listening in technique.

Training. In order to practice listening in, lie down in a silent place, eyes closed, and listen for sounds originating in the head. These attempts are usually crowned with success within several minutes of trying, and one starts to hear that noise that absolutely everyone has within. One simply has to know how to tune in to it.

Rotation
Testing Individual Effectiveness. Immediately after waking from sleep, remain motionless, eyes closed. Imagine the physical body is rotating along an axis for 5 to 10 seconds. If no unusual sensations occur, try another technique. If vibrations occur during rotation or the movement suddenly feels realistic, then continue the rotation technique as long as there is progress in the sensation's development. There are several possible outcomes when rotation is practiced. The imagined rotation is replaced by a very real sensation of rotating along an imagined axis. When this occurs, a practitioner may easily leave the body. The other outcome is the sudden presence of strong vibrations or

loud sounds, amid which separation from the body is possible. During rotation, separation has been known to spontaneously occur and the practitioner enters the phase.

Training. To practice rotation, imagine revolving around the head-to-foot axis for several minutes while lying down, eyes closed. It is not necessary to focus on the visual effects of rotation or minute sensations in the body. The key factor is the vestibular sensation that arises from internal rotation. As a rule, many practitioners experience difficulty performing full rotation. One person may be limited to 90 degrees of movement where another experiences 180 degrees. With consistent, correct practice, full 360 degree rotation will occur.

Several dozen secondary and mixed techniques are presented in a separate section at the end of the textbook (Chapter 12).

SELECTING THE RIGHT TECHNIQUES

The next step to mastering indirect techniques Is choosing the right techniques that suit individual predispositions. There is no point in going for one technique or another only because they look interesting and because someone wrote a lot or spoke a lot about them. The choice should be based strictly upon what suits an individual practitioner.

Out of all of the enumerated primary indirect techniques, practically only straining the brain works easily and quickly for 95% of practitioners. All other techniques work immediately for only about 25% to 50% of practitioners during initial training. However, after several training sessions, each technique yields results for 75% of engaged practitioners.

One way or another, every practitioner should identify a certain set of techniques that works best. A set should consist of no less than three techniques; four or five is even better to allow more options and practical combinations. Non-working techniques should not be discarded wholesale by the individual, because they afford an opportunity to achieve success through new, previously unresponsive experiences.

To ensure the correct selection of techniques, each should be separately practiced over a period of at least three days. To this end, one should experiment with each of the primary techniques for 2 to 10 minutes during the day. This regimen allows a precise determination of the techniques that will yield the best results for the practitioner. During the process of selecting personalized techniques, a practitioner learns and retains the techniques in an intimate, personal way, which positively affects how techniques are used during critical moments. Don't put off attempts to enter the phase on weeks when you're training. Instead, do both in parallel.

However, before going to sleep, never ever train if that you plan to use techniques the next morning. In this case, it's much better to train techniques during the day or in the morning. This is one of the most critical errors that novices commit. Training the night before an attempt brings internal exhaustion in its wake and dissipates intention. After a result, a practitioner will have far fewer attempts at night and in the morning, and they will be much less focused and of lower quality.

It is worth noting that the final selection of techniques should be varied. For example, choosing both straining the brain and straining the body without using muscles is pointless because they are practically one and the same. More often than not, they will both either work or not work. This is why techniques should involve various types of sensory perception: visual, audio, kinesthetic, vestibular, imaginary sense perception, and internal strain. Remember that priorities and goals change with time, and that a technique that fell flat during initial attempts may unexpectedly prove valuable later on. Be flexible. No set of techniques should be carved in stone. In fact, the set may change several times over the first few weeks as the practitioner discovers what produces the best individual results.

To close this section, a list detailing the most effective indirect techniques has been provided. This list was compiled with classroom data from the School of Out-of-Body Travel and may prove helpful in determining an effective set of indirect techniques.

The Most Effective Indirect Techniques at School of Out-of-Body Travel Seminars (2010-2011)	
Swimming Techniques (Imagined Movements)	25%
Phantom Wiggling	20%
Observing Images	20%
Rotation	20%
Other Techniques	15%

SEPARATION TECHNIQUES

Let us begin with a totally shocking fact: during 50%(!) of successful indirect entries into the phase, it is not necessary to perform any specific phase entry techniques, as separation techniques are immediately successful... This has been statistically proven at School of Out-of-Body Travel seminars and in the analyses of other sources. Conversely, an incorrect understanding of separation techniques may lead to undesirable consequences. It is possible for a practitioner to enter the phase state and be unable to separate from the body. Therefore, it is very important to understand how separation techniques work since they are often a key to success.

Interesting Fact!
Relatively often, a practitioner will try to employ separation techniques to no

effect. However, he will later unexpectedly understand that he had been lying in a different position than he sensed that he was in, and in fact, it had only been necessary for him to stand up. This happens mostly among beginners and is indicative of an incorrect understanding of separation techniques.

At times a practitioner need only think about separation, and it happens. This is a rarity, which explains the existence of a whole series of auxiliary techniques. The most important separation techniques are rolling out, getting up, climbing out, and levitation.

Rolling out
While awakening, attempt to roll over to the edge of the bed or the wall without using any muscles. Don't worry about falling out of bed, hitting the wall, or be concerned with the details of how this technique should feel. Just roll.

Getting up
Upon awakening, attempt to get out of bed without physical exertion. This should be performed in a way that is most comfortable for the practitioner.

Climbing out

While awakening, try to climb out of the body without using any muscles. This technique generally comes to mind when a partial separation has been achieved through the use of other techniques, or one part of the body has completely separated.

Levitation
Upon awakening, attempt to levitate upward, parallel to the bed. While attempting to levitate, do not wonder how it should be accomplished; everyone intuitively knows how to levitate from their experiences in dreams.

Falling out
Practically the same as levitation: upon awakening, try to sink down through the bed.

Pulling out
Here, upon awakening, try to exit the body through the head, as if escaping from a lidded cocoon.

Backwards roll
After awakening, try to perform a backwards somersault over the head without using any physical muscles.

Bulge the eyes
Upon awakening, bulge out or widen the eyes without opening them. Frontal movement toward separation may result.

Imagining Yourself Already Separated
You can imagine yourself already separated and inside your room, trying to feel your separated body as intensely as possible. Your sensations will gradually flow into your subtle body from your physical one, and become just as realistic.

Translocation

You can try to employ the translocation technique without first separating, which will lead to both translocation and separation occurring at once. Teleportation with eyes closed works best for this.

Flight
You can try to feel yourself flying at high speed.

Separation techniques are united by a singular idea: nothing should be imagined, movement should be attempted without the use of physical muscles. The techniques produce the same sensations of movement felt in real life. If nothing happens immediately after trying, then the technique is not going to work, though it may deliver results at a later time. A practitioner will instantly be able to recognize if the technique has worked. However, people are often unprepared for the realness of the sensations and think that they are making a physical movement instead of realizing that a part or all of the body has separated. After this unfortunate failure, careful analysis helps to understand what happened and plan for a successful retry.

If separation was incomplete or took place with some difficulty, this is a signal that the technique is being performed correctly, but that strength and aggressive effort are required from this point to achieve complete separation. For example, if some movement began and then stopped after having made some progress, then one should go back and move even harder once again in the same direction.

In order to practice separation techniques, lie down with the eyes closed and attempt all of them over the course of several minutes. A separation attempt has likely been accomplished if no muscles twitch or strain and a sensation of movement occurs. There will be a strong, almost physically palpable internal effort to perform a movement. Naturally, no physical movement actually occurs and the practitioner remains prone and immobile; however, at the right moment, these actions will lead to an easy entrance into the phase.

Interesting Fact!
Approximately 1% to 3% of the time that the phase is practiced, one realizes immediately upon awakening that one has already separated. This means that one may already go somewhere and stand, lie down, sit down, etc. This is not however becoming conscious in a dream, but an actual awakening.

It is also worth discussing how to conduct yourself upon separation if one of the phase creation techniques starts working. In such a situation, it's important to realize that separation should be done with the same body and same sensations that were obtained when performing the technique. For example, when rotating, you need to stand up using the same sensations of rotating, and when observing images you need to separate using the same body that sees the images, etc.

Additionally, it's important not to completely return back to the body if your phase creation technique involves the sensation of partial separation from the body. For example - if rotation worked, then before trying to separate, there is no need to fully turn back into the body and merge with it. Separation would immediately become much more difficult. It's better to do it on the fly after halting rotation in a position perpendicular to your physical body. The same temptation can arise during phantom wiggling, when separation should begin from the arm that began to move - i.e. do not move it back into the physical body. The same goes for all of the partial separation techniques.

If a novice has learned through practice what phantom wiggling is and how it feels, then he may proceed to separation like he would to phantom wiggling, but this time moving his entire body. That is, this is an attempt to move with the perceived (i.e. subtle) body; not a muscle is to be moved in the physical one.

The most important thing is to immediately realize that logically speaking, if indirect techniques have worked or awakening has just occurred, then the practitioner is already in the phase. All of his sensations are no longer coming from his physical body, although it may seem that they do. All that remains is to stand up, roll out, and levitate, as if doing so with the physical body.

Novices and the inexperienced often try to discover some tell-tale sign of separation, and expect to encounter it in practice. Actually, there are a whole variety of sensations that occur during this process. Those who do not know this often waste a large number of experiences when they encounter unexpected situations. That's why it's good to always be prepared for any eventuality and know the primary separation scenarios observed in 99% of all cases.

Types of Phase Entrances (Separations) Listed by Sensation:

- **Ordinary movement**
Here, separation usually seems like a completely ordinary movement, as if it were made with the physical body. The practitioner simply stands up, rolls out, or levitates as if he were doing so in reality.
- **Separation**
Actual direct separation of the subtle body from the physical one, as if the practitioner were actually exiting something. Despite the fact that this sensation gave its name to the entire process of entering the phase ("separation"), direct separation occurs quite rarely and the term is inaccurate in terms of sensation.
- **Pulling**
A feeling of a mass of gummy rubber stretching from every part of your subtle body and pulling it back

into your physical one. Forcefully overcome that feeling of being pulled in, and it will dissipate.

- Sluggishness

The subtle body becomes quite heavy, as if it weighed several times more. The sluggishness will dissipate in proportion to the counteracting force applied.

- Awakening to Separation

The practitioner awakens or surfaces from a lapse in consciousness in an already separated state, and does not need to separate or use a phase creation technique. Simply get up and go forth.

- Stuck Body Parts

Some parts of the subtle body can become stuck in a physical stencil during the process of separation. For example, this often occurs with the legs, trunk, head, and pelvis. In such situations you need to fully break free with all your might by changing the direction of your exertion.

- Being in Two Bodies at Once

A feeling arises of not really being in the phase and not really lying in bed, but of truly being in the phase and also truly lying in bed at the same time. You need to try to press on through with the situation, transferring all of your sensations into your phase body, which will become the only one perceived.

- Spontaneous Full Separation (When Performing Techniques)

When performing any technique, you may spontaneously find yourself having already fully separated into your room or into any other place in the phase. There's no need to return back into your physical body in order to "properly" separate.

- Being Pulled Out by Someone or Something

In this case, separation occurs not fully by one's own will, but due to help from a phase object. For example, someone starts pulling at your legs or lifting up your entire body. The important thing in this situation is not to relax, but to start moving on your own as soon as possible. Such a situation often occurs with so-called ""alien abductions", which are actually spontaneous and unrecognized phase experiences the majority of the time.

- Suction

When performing techniques like observing images or visualization, practitioners are often completely sucked in to the imagery being observed, with all the accompanying sensations. This imagery then becomes a full-fledged phase space of its own. There's no need to return back into your physical body in order to "properly" separate.

- Putting Your All into a Technique

When performing sensory-motor visualization and several other techniques, a convergence between separation and the technique itself occurs. This leads to there no longer being a need for separation in the traditional sense. For example, during sensory-motor visualization, the practitioner initially begins by actively imagining that he is walking about a room, but that imagined perception gradually morphs into the real sensation of actually being in the room. Meanwhile, when phantom wiggling it only remains to stand up from the body in which wiggling is felt, and so on. There's no need to return back to the physical body in order to separate "properly".

- Dream Consciousness

Becoming fully consciousness while dreaming with full cognizance of what is occurring is also a separate phase entrance method, but one that does not involve direct or indirect techniques. There's no need to return back to the body in order to separate "properly", although many do so in order to obtain more vivid sensations.

THE BEST TIME TO PRACTICE

The key to practice is the quantity and quality of attempts made that hone a practitioner's skills. There are several windows of time best suited for employing indirect techniques.

To begin, it should be stated that sleep follows a cyclical pattern. We awaken every hour-and-a-half and then quickly fall asleep again, which gives rise to sleep cycles. Furthermore, we experience two primary stages of sleep: rapid eye movement (REM) sleep, and non-rapid eye movement (NREM) sleep. NREM sleep includes many internal stages. The more we sleep, the less the body needs deep NREM sleep, and the more time we spend in REM sleep. Phase entrance is most likely to occur during REM sleep.

The best way to implement indirect techniques is by *the deferred method*. The aim of the method is to interrupt a sleep cycle during its final stage and then disrupt it again after falling back to sleep, which makes sleep light during the rest of the sleep cycle. Sleep accompanied by frequent interruptions can be put to productive uses.

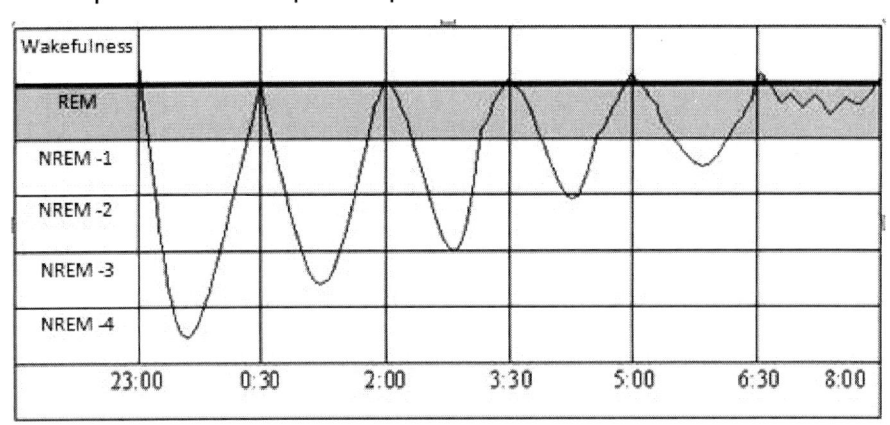

Interesting Fact!
When the deferred method was first made mandatory at a 3-day School of Out-

of-Body Travel seminar in June 2008, the overall success rate immediately doubled.

For example, if a practitioner (let's call him Jack) goes to sleep at midnight, then Jack should set an alarm for 6 o'clock in the morning. Upon awakening, Jack should engage in some sort of physical activity, like going to the bathroom, getting a drink of water, or reading a few pages of this book. Afterward, Jack should go back to bed thinking about how, within the next two to four hours, he will wake up multiple times and make an attempt to enter the phase during each awakening.

If Jack goes to bed earlier, then his alarm clock should be set back by that amount of time, since six hours of initial sleep is the optimal length of time. If Jack sleeps less than six hours, then the second half of his night's sleep will be too deep. If Jack sleeps longer than six hours, then there will be little time remaining for attempts, or Jack may not even be able to fall asleep.

If a practitioner naturally wakes up in a forceful manner, it will be difficult to regain sleep. Thus, it will not be necessary for the practitioner to get out of bed with the aid of an alarm. The practitioner should attempt to go right back to sleep.

If a practitioner is able to fall back asleep after as much as 45 minutes of being awake, then it's better to keep to that very interval, as it allows one to obtain the highest probability of success during subsequent awakenings.

Naturally, the deferred method is most applicable in cases where it is possible to sleep as long as a practitioner desires, without having to wake up early. Not everyone enjoys such luxury on a daily basis, but nearly everyone has days off when time may be set aside to practice the deferred method. *It is in large measure due to the deferred method that classroom courses at the School of Out-of-Body Travel allow up to 2/3 of class participants to enter the phase in the course of a single weekend!*

The second most effective window of time for entering the phase is *ordinary morning awakening*. This generally occurs during light slumber following a full night's sleep.

Another effective time to practice indirect techniques is after awakening from a daytime nap. Once again, this type of sleep will be light and short, which provides the body needed rest while allowing memory and intention to be kept intact through the moment of awakening. Again, not everyone has the luxury of taking daytime naps, but if such a chance arises, then it would be very beneficial to take advantage of the opportunity.

Nighttime awakenings are the least effective times for phase experimentation because the brain still requires a lot of deep sleep at this time. Awakening at night, the mind is quite weak and hardly capable of any effort. Even if some results are observed, awakening often ends with quickly falling back asleep. This is not to say that normal practice of the phase cannot occur at night; it just won't be as effective as at other times. The nighttime option is best for those who lack an opportunity to use other windows of time for practicing the phase.

Understand that we awaken at night every 90 minutes, which is why a minimum of four awakenings is almost guaranteed when sleeping, even for just six hours. When the practitioner knows about this and strives to seize those moments, with time he will actually seize them and take advantage of them.

CONSCIOUS AWAKENING

Conscious awakening is waking up with a particular thought in mind; ideally, a thought about indirect techniques. In order to start using indirect techniques upon awakening, it is not sufficient to have a cursory knowledge of the techniques to be used when waking. Due to the peculiarities of the human mind and its habits, it is not always easy when waking to recall any particular motive or idea. The goal of conscious awakening is to practice instant action without being idle after waking up.

Interesting Fact!
There exists a belief that the phenomenon of out-of-body travel is practically unattainable, and is accessible only to an elect few through practices that require secret knowledge. However, the greatest difficulty when trying to experience out-of-body travel in a short period of time lies only in immediately remembering about the techniques upon awakening without moving. This is all simple and straightforward. But it is precisely this trifle that is the largest stumbling block when trying to experience such an uncommon phenomenon.

This is not difficult at all for approximately 75% of the population. However, for the other one-quarter of the population, this is a difficult barrier to entry that can even seem insurmountable. If such thoughts arise, one should simply understand that this cannot be so, and that persistent attempts and training are the key solution.

The reasons why people are unable to remember practicing the phase upon awakening are: not being in the habit of immediately doing anything upon awakening, a desire to sleep longer, a desire to go to the bathroom, being thirsty, a desire to suddenly start solving day-to-day problems, and so on.

Conscious awakening with the intent of attempting an indirect technique should be a practitioner's primary goal, which should be pursued at every cost. The speed at which the phase is learned and experienced depends on this.

There are several effective tricks to learning conscious awakening:

Intention upon falling asleep: This is the very important to successfully achieving conscious awakening. A very clear scientific fact has been proven by somnologists (scientists who study sleep): upon awakening, people usually think about what they had been thinking about before falling asleep. This phenomenon is easy to observe if the sleeper is experiencing a serious life problem; they fall asleep with the problem and wake with it. So, in a case like this, if difficulties at the front of the mind are replaced with a desire to practice the phase, this will produce the desired effect. It is not necessary to think solely about conscious awakening while falling asleep. It is sufficient to simply affirm the intention clearly and distinctly, even stating the intention out loud. Practicing these types of conscious actions while entering sleep will do much to promote the success of indirect techniques upon awakening.

General intent: The more clearly a practitioner concentrates on the importance and necessity of waking up and immediately remembering to practice the techniques, the more solid the intent will become, and the more likely the process will fulfill its role and actually lead to results.

Affirming desires: Sometimes an internal intention is simply not enough for some people, or they are unable to properly affirm one by virtue of individual characteristics. In this case, an affirmation of desires should be introduced at the physical level. This could be in the form of a note with a description of a goal placed next to the bed, under one's pillow, or hung on the wall. It could be a conversation with friends or family about the particular desire, or by repeatedly vocalizing the actions that need to be performed upon awakening. It could even be an entry in a diary, blog, or texting on a mobile phone.

Interesting Fact!
There are known incidences of practitioners "programming" food and water to induce phase entrance. They are essentially employing both auto-suggestion and the placebo effect by programming their subconscious mind to perceive that food as bringing not only satiation, but also a high probability of entering the phase.

Analyzing unsuccessful awakenings: Analyzing unsuccessful attempts at conscious awakening is extremely important. When remembering the failed attempt after several minutes, several hours, or even later in the day, focus on it and resolve to succeed during the next attempt. Deep exploration of the failure is highly effective and practical since the practitioner is learning what works, what doesn't work, and making healthy resolutions toward success.

Creating motivation: The greater the desire to enter into the phase to accomplish a goal there, the quicker successful conscious awakening is achieved. Motivation is be created by a great desire to do or experience something in the phase. In general, previous visits to the phase are great motivation, but an uninitiated person does not know it and will need something to which they can relate. For some, this could be a childhood dream of flying to Mars, for others it could be the opportunity to see a loved one who has passed away, for another it could be the chance to obtain specific information, or influence the course of a physical illness, and so forth.

Aside from natural methods to achieve conscious awaking, there are various devices and tools that facilitate a measure of success. These will be covered in Chapter 5 in the section describing non-autonomous ways of entering the phase.

The best moment for conscious awakening is while exiting a dream. This is the most effective and productive time to attempt separation or performing the techniques. At this moment, physical awareness of the body is at a minimum. Awareness at the very end of a dream often occurs after nightmares, painful experiences in the dream, falling dreams – any dream that causes a sudden awakening.

With time, one should develop a reflex that enables one to perform planned actions at the moment of awakening, but when consciousness itself has not yet had time to return. This type of reflex is highly beneficial to seizing the most fruitful of opportunities to enter the phase.

Due to various psychological and physiological factors, it is not possible for every person to achieve conscious awakening after every sleep cycle. Thus, there is no point in becoming upset if conscious awakening does not occur every time. Experiencing only 2 to 3 awakenings per day is normal; this is sufficient enough to attempt phase entrance 2 to 5 times per week when practiced daily.

It is not worth getting carried away with an excessive number of attempts. During the School's courses, it has been noted that doing 10 conscious awakenings or more (some students try 20 or even 30) over the course of one night and morning rarely yields results. This is due to the fact that if one sets oneself a goal that is desired so much that its realization breaks the natural rhythms of the body, one deprives oneself of the intermediate, transitional states that make the phase effective. A practitioner may also quickly become emotionally exhausted from the large number of attempts and be unable to push limits in the right direction. The upside is that one will simply tire out. If that starts to happen, it is better to calm down and try to approach the matter in a more relaxed manner, evenly and gradually.

Michael Raduga

AWAKENING WITHOUT MOVING

Alongside remembering the phase immediately upon waking, another important requirement is awakening without moving, which is difficult since many people wake up and move. Upon awakening, scratching, stretching, opening the eyes, and listening to real sounds should be avoided. Any real movement or perception will very quickly disintegrate the intermediate state and introduce reality, the activation of the mind and its connection to the sensory organs.

At first, awakening without moving seems difficult or even impossible. However, it has been proven that this is remedied for through active attempts and the desire to achieve set goals. People often claim that they cannot awaken without moving, that it's an impossible experience. However, after several attempts, it will happen, and it will occur more and more frequently with practice.

Thus, if there is difficulty in awakening without movement, do not despair, just keep trying. Sooner or later, the body will yield to the practice, and everything will happen smoothly.

Awakening without moving is very important because, for the majority of people, experiments with the phase are not possible except in the first waking moments where waking without moving sets the stage for successful indirect technique cycles. Often, a practitioner will make 10 unsuccessful attempts and move while awakening. Once the practitioner learns to consistently wake calmly and gradually, success quickly follows.

However, if an awakening is conscious, but with movement, that does not mean that the practitioner cannot immediately make an attempt to fall into the phase. Such attempts, although they will be about 2 times less effective than usual, should nevertheless be made. Any opportunity to practice while waking should not be wasted. It must only be kept in mind that one must first neutralize the effects of the movement in

order to once again fall into an intermediate state. In the case of movement, it is extremely helpful to begin practice with forced falling asleep. Listening in also works well, as does observing images. After performing these, cycling may begin.

WARNING!!! IF YOU WAKE UP AFTER OR TO PHYSICAL MOVEMENT, IT WOULD BE A SERIOUS MISTAKE TO FORGO AN ATTEMPT! YOU HAVE TO TRY ANYWAY! NOVICES OFTEN GET THEIR FIRST EXPERIENCE TWO TO THREE TIMES LATER THAN THEY NORMALLY WOULD DUE TO THIS MISTAKE.

After physical movement, the success rate for attempts using indirect techniques is usually substantially lower merely due to the fact that practitioners lose confidence in both themselves and the success of the current attempt. As a result, the attempt itself simply becomes poor in quality and lackluster. However, if the attempt is nevertheless performed self-assuredly and as if no movement had occurred, then odds of success will remain practically undiminished.

Awakening without movement, despite all its importance, is not a goal in and of itself, and also not worth suffering over. When awakening, if there is great discomfort, something itches, a need to swallow arises, or any manner of natural reflex, it is better to deal with it and then act according to practices recommended when movement upon awakening happens.

Not all movements upon awakening are real and, if only for this reason alone, when movement occurs, indirect techniques should follow.

Interesting Fact!

Up to 20% of sensations and actions that happen upon awakening are not real as they seem, but are phantom.

False sensations occur in widely diverse ways. People often do not understand what is going on with them without having experienced the phase. For example, a person may think they are scratching their ear with their physical hand when they are really using a phantom hand. A person may hear pseudo-sounds in the room, on the street, or at the neighbor's without noting anything unusual. Or, a person may look around the room without knowing that his eyes are actually closed. If a practitioner recognizes such moments for what they are, they may immediately try to separate from the body.

CYCLES OF INDIRECT TECHNIQUES

Thus far, indirect techniques used for phase entrance and techniques for separation in the phase have been covered. Conscious awakening and the best times to practice it have also been examined. Now, a specific algorithm of action for indirect techniques will be presented. Following this algorithm promises quick and practical results.

It ought to be clearly understood that the more natural and sound sleep preceding an attempt is, the better the effect from awakening and the higher the odds of success. What is needed is to fall soundly asleep and sleep sound thereafter, after which a sound awakening can be put to good use. Cycles of indirect techniques can occasionally be successfully used during fitful sleep, but in most cases this is a pure waste of time and energy. When sleeping poorly, it's better to do no techniques at all and await sound sleep, as opposed to spending all your time trying to snatch the phase from the jaws of a wearisome and hardly salvageable situation.

Algorithm of Action upon Awakening:

1 Testing Separation Techniques within 5 Seconds

As noted above, 50% of success with indirect techniques is immediate due to the fact that the first seconds after waking up are the most useful for entering the phase. The less time that has elapsed after awakening, the better.

Conversely, if one lies down expecting something to happen, chances quickly dissipate.

Thus, upon awakening, preferably without first moving, a practitioner should immediately try various separation techniques, like rolling out, getting up, or levitation. If a technique has suddenly started to yield results for approximately for 3-5 seconds, then separation from the body should be attempted up to full separation. Sometimes inertia, difficulty, or a barrier will arise during a separation attempt. No attention should be given to these problems. Instead, resolve to separate - decidedly and aggressively climb out of the body.

Keep in mind that trying to immediately separate upon awakening is a skill of the utmost importance; one that is worth honing from the very beginning, never forgotten.

Interesting Fact!

For some practitioners having trouble reaching the phase, one motivation for separating without using any techniques is an unwillingness to "bang their heads against techniques" any further. This forces them to catch the right moment of awakening much earlier on and push themselves much harder during it. The result is that they are practically always able to achieve the phase upon that first step.

2 The Cycle of Indirect Techniques to Use if One is Unable to Separate

If separation does not occur after several seconds, it most likely means that separation will not occur, regardless of elapsed time in effort. This is where the practitioner must resort to other techniques.

The practitioner should already have chosen a minimum of three primary or secondary techniques that suit a practical repertoire. Here is where the techniques are put into action.

Nota Bene! In order to give a specific example, we will examine the use of three specific techniques, which should be replaced with a tested and chosen set of techniques. The following operational techniques shall be used as examples: observing images (a), phantom wiggling (b), and listening in (c).

After an unsuccessful attempt at separating, the practitioner immediately starts observing the void before the eyes. If images begin to appear within 3 to 5 seconds, observation should continue without scrutinizing the images in detail, or the image will evaporate. As a result of this action, the image will quickly become more and more realistic and colorful, engulfing the practitioner. If everything comes together correctly, a sudden translocation into the picture will occur, or, when the picture becomes very realistic, attempt to separate from the body. If nothing happens after 3 to 5 seconds, then the practitioner should transition to the technique of phantom wiggling.

For 3 to 5 seconds, the practitioner quickly searches the entire body for a part that can be wiggled. Or, the entire period of time is spent in an attempt to wiggle a specific body part: a finger, hand, or leg. If the desired effect occurs, then the practitioner should continue with the technique and achieve the maximum possible range of movement. During this process, a number of things can happen, including spontaneous separation, a successful separation attempt, free movement of the wiggled part, or the presence of sound or vibrations. All of these events are of great advantage. If nothing wiggles over the course of 3 to 5 seconds, then the practitioner should move on to listening in.

The practitioner should try to detect an internal sound. If the sound is there, listen and try to amplify it. As a result, the noise may grow into a roar and spontaneous separation will occur, separating through the use of a technique will be possible, or vibrations will occur. If no noise occurs over the course of 3 to 5 seconds, then the entire cycle should be repeated.

It is beneficial to examine the reason behind the use of a set of three indirect techniques. This is motivated by the fact that the body often reacts to techniques in very peculiar ways. For one person, a technique may work one day and not work on another day, which is why if only one technique is used, even a very good technique that works often, a practitioner can miss out on a lot of different experience through the lack of variety in practice. Thus, a practical repertoire should consist of several techniques.

Interesting Fact!
Sometimes, the first technique that works for a practitioner never results in a repeat of phase entrance again, although other techniques that were not immediately effective at the novice stages of practice later begin to work regularly and successfully.

It is also important to understand that the techniques themselves will work quite poorly and rarely if performed merely for the "sake of appearances". You need to give them your all, trying to get into them with all of your sensations and all of your being. Try no matter what to have all of your sensations become one with the techniques. A phaser's mind must be fully focused on every aspect of each technique being performed. In this case cycling indirect techniques is an easy way to exit the body, as everything starts off quite right and works with ease. If the practitioner doesn't remain aware of this, he risks wasting his time and energy.

3 Repeating the Cycle of Indirect Techniques
If the first cycle of 3 techniques does not yield any clear results, this does not mean that all is lost. Even if the techniques do not work, they still draw the practitioner closer

to the phase state and it is simply necessary to continue using the techniques by again observing images, phantom wiggling, and listening in – and repeating this process at least three times.

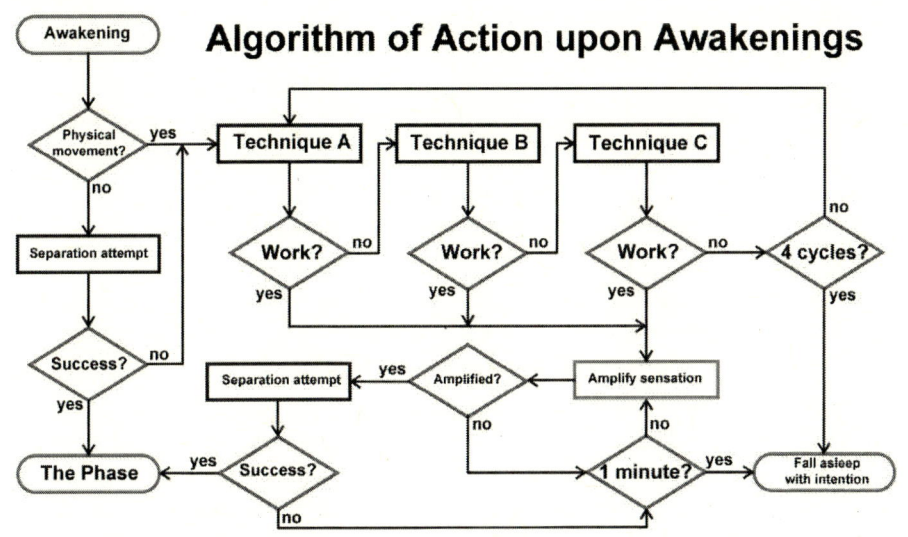

Algorithm of Action upon Awakenings

Having performed one cycle of techniques, one can easily go on to doing a second cycle, a third one, a fourth one, and so on. It is quite probable that during one of these cycles, a technique will suddenly prove itself, even though it had not been working at all just a few seconds beforehand.

A serious practitioner should commit to a minimum of 4 cycles. The problem lies in the fact that it is psychologically difficult to do something that has shown itself not to work, and one may give up taking further action, even though one could be at the cusp of falling into the phase. Keep trying, and then try again, and again! There have been cases where it took ten cycles to produce results. A monumental effort, yes, but one worth the outcome. But don't do it for more than one minute.

4. Falling Asleep with the Possibility of Trying Again.

If a practitioner is unable to enter the phase after performing cycles and attempts to separate, or even if everything worked out, it is still better to go back to sleep to facilitate subsequent attempts. Again, it is very important to go to sleep with a clearly defined intention of actually performing the cycles upon awakening. Such intention vastly increases the probability that the next attempt will occur soon. That is, one should not fall asleep with an empty head and the desire to simply get a good night's sleep. When using the deferred method, clear intention is mandatory, as several attempts are possible over the course of a sleep cycle.

Even if only a few attempts are made accompanied by decided and concentrated effort, then the four steps described in the algorithm will undoubtedly produce entrance into the phase.

It must always be kept in mind that one of the most common mistakes novices make is simply lying in bed while in the phase. Generally speaking, for each successful attempt novices have, there are 2 to 3 attempts where the phase had also occurred, but they didn't take advantage of the moment and missed separating by the skin of their teeth. For example, any technique working extremely well immediately after awakening is a sure sign of the phase. Instead of continuing to lie down in the phase and play with one technique or alternate through other ones, try as hard as you can to get out of your body. Any possible evidence of a technique working should be tested in the same way.

It is also important to immediately take advantage of a technique working. When something starts working, a novice will often, for some reason, fail to take immediate advantage of the moment. The phase is then already over within several seconds, and the techniques no longer work. If an opportunity to enter the phase isn't taken advantage of as soon as occurs, the window of time for leaving the body will simply close within several seconds. That's why it is necessary to try to leave your body immediately upon any technique working substantially well. Otherwise, the moment will be lost.

In order to more effectively use the system of indirect cycles, it is necessary to discuss what to do if one technique starts working, but progress then ceases during the cycle and phase entry does not occur.

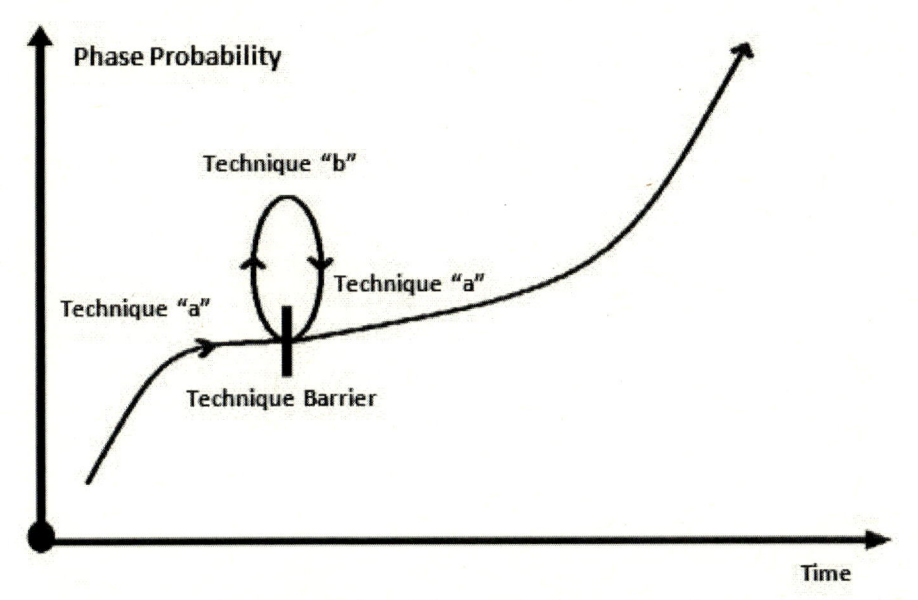

First, understand that if a technique has begun to work, only lack of experience and skill will prevent the phase.

Second, barriers are overcome by temporarily switching to other techniques. Let us suppose that noise arising when listening in grows louder and louder and then peaks in volume. It would surely be beneficial to switch to forced falling asleep or observing images for several seconds, and then return to listening in. The sound may then become much louder and provide an opportunity to proceed with the technique. Sometimes, it makes sense to break off several times into various techniques and then return to the primary technique that yielded some results.

The most important thing is to never give up on a technique that has begun working ever so slightly. In essence, it is a road sign to the shortest path to the phase, and should always be followed.

It is often possible to simultaneously perform two or even three techniques and experience no negative effect on results. It is also normal and natural to skip around from technique to technique, deviating from a specific plan of action. For example, sounds often arise during phantom wiggling. In this case, a practitioner may just simply switch over to listening in. Other oft-encountered results pairings are: images from sound, sound from rotation, sound from straining the brain, a strain on the brain from listening in, vibrations from rotation, vibrations from phantom wiggling, and so forth.

During initial attempts at using cycles of indirect techniques, the problem of confusion during a critical moment may arise, when a novice practitioner suddenly forgets exactly what to do and how to do it. This is normal, and the solution is to immediately do whatever comes to mind. Results can be achieved in this manner. When a practitioner is more relaxed about the practice, such problems will no longer occur.

HINTS FROM THE MIND

Varied cycles of indirect techniques is an almost mandatory precondition for getting the best result. There are some exceptions. Sometimes, through indirect indicators, a practitioner may be inclined to begin with certain techniques, regardless of what had been planned. These are a sort of hint from the body and the ability to use such cues plays an extremely important role in the use of indirect techniques because they enable a practitioner to substantially increase the effectiveness of his practice.

Hint No. 1: Images

If the practitioner becomes aware upon awakening that some images, pictures, or remnants from dreams are before him, then he should immediately proceed to the technique of observing images, with all of the results that arise from it. If this does not lead to anything, then cycling with a set of techniques should begin.

Hint No. 2: Noises
If the practitioner realizes upon awakening that he hears an internal noise, roaring, ringing, whistling, and so forth, then he should immediately begin from the technique of listening in. If this has no effect, then cycles of indirect techniques ought to commence.

Hint No. 3: Vibrations
If a practitioner feels vibrations throughout the body while awakening, they should be amplified through the use of straining the brain or straining the body without using muscles. When the vibrations reach their peak, the practitioner can try to separate. If nothing happens after several attempts, indirect technique cycles should start.

Hint No. 4: Numbness
If a practitioner wakes to numbness in a body part, phantom wiggling of that part should be attempted. If no result is achieved after several attempts, cycling should be tried. Of course, it is better to refrain from techniques if the numbness is very intense and causes substantial discomfort.

Hint No. 5: Paralysis
If the practitioner feels that his body is immobilized and that he is unable to move a muscle upon awakening, then he has encountered sleep paralysis (sleep stupor). This phenomenon is a sign that one is in the phase, and it only remains for the practitioner to somehow separate from the body no matter what, as well as overcome the night terror that often arises during sleep paralysis.

These hints may arise not only immediately upon awakening, but also upon an attempt to perform cycles of techniques. If the hints are more pronounced than the results of the techniques themselves, then it makes sense to turn one's attention to them or exploit them concurrently with techniques.

It is also necessary to simply understand what the hint is trying to tell you: for example, if some unreal sensation suddenly arises on its own upon awakening, then it is necessary to simply intensify it and leave the body right then. If you follow this general principle, then you don't need to know exactly what the hints are or what exactly to do when they occur. Everything should happen intuitively and easily. The point is that there are a large number of other phase manifestations in addition to the four hints above that one should be always ready for. However, it would be simply impossible to describe them all, let alone remember them.

AGGRESSION AND PASSIVITY

During the practice of indirect techniques, including technique cycles, unsuccessful attempts may result in falling asleep or becoming completely awake. These results indicate a deficiency or excess of aggression.

If a practitioner usually falls asleep while attempting to enter the phase, then more aggressive action is needed while performing indirect techniques. If, on the other hand, most attempts end in a full and alert awakening, then aggression should be curbed and techniques should be conducted more slowly and in a more relaxed manner. Balance between passivity and aggression is imperative; the phase state is easily attained by those practitioners who find a stable medium between passivity and aggression.

The issue of aggression requires a closer examination. *Quite often, attempts at indirect techniques are made leisurely, without desire or real effort, to "check them off the list". Results are more easily realized if the practitioner possesses an aggressive desire to enter the phase. More often than not, practitioners lack aggressive desire, instead of having too much of it. Thus, each effort requires a distinct want to succeed.*

THE BERMUDA TRIANGLE OF ATTEMPTS

Success at entering the phase depends on two factors: quantity and quality of attempts. Accordingly, the greater the quantity of high-quality attempts, the greater the odds of having a phase experience. However, practically all practitioners encounter certain psychological difficulties that deprive them of 30 to 75% of all attempts. That is, phasers often experience only half of what they could due to certain patterns of thought.

This mainly occurs during two common situations in which practitioners simply lose all desire to even try: a) excessively alert awakening b) awakening to physical movement. Even if a phaser suddenly decides to give it a try in such situations, his attempts are understandably performed waveringly and poorly, which is equivalent to not trying at all. However, in the absolute majority of such cases, no attempt is even made.

The hilarity of the situation consists in the probable falseness of the sensations of both excessively alert awakening and awakening to physical movement. For example, the thought, "I woke up way too alertly, nothing's going to work now" is usually immediately followed by falling back asleep. However, a substantial portion of movements upon awakening are false, even though it may seem that they are made with the physical body. But even if there is an actual alert awakening and actual physical movement, the likelihood of entering the phase does not actually decrease as much as one might think. That's why it is not only possible try to enter the phase in such situations - it is a must. Those who follow this simple principle alone may enjoy twice as many phase experiences as those who do not.

However, mindfulness of this principle alone is often insufficient to compensate for psychological certainty that nothing will work during a specific attempt. In order to solve this problem, one may use one a most effective psychological trick based on self-deception. If it seems to the practitioner that there is no sense in making an attempt as nothing will work anyway, he ought think exactly as follows: "Alright, entering the phase will hardly work out, but now I'm going to simply practice for future attempts and do everything as if these were ideal conditions". Afterwards, a high-quality "practice session" will occur, during which it might be easy to have a real phase experience. So, if it seems that nothing at all will happen upon an awakening, then simply give it a go and practice cycling indirect techniques, without worrying about the outcome.

It should also be noted that a phaser will often lose out on an attempt through the belief that he has to catch the right moment of being half-awake. Many think that catching that moment is a mandatory prerequisite for the indirect method. It generally is, but that moment of transition usually doesn't begin at the second one awakens - rather, it arises right when performing cycles of techniques! That is, the moment of being half-awake is not so much something to catch upon awakenings, but more something to induce using the techniques themselves - which is actually exactly what they're there for. That's precisely why there's no sense in giving up a chance for an attempt.

Every practitioner simply needs to be well aware that one may fall into the phase upon any awakening, no matter what it may seem and no matter what thoughts may cross one's mind. That's why you need to not over-analyze or over-think it, but simply to mechanically try, try, and try again.

FORCED FALLING ASLEEP - MAXIMUM EFFECT

There is a trick technique for making most phase entrances successful: forced falling asleep. It can be used with the following situations and variations: as an independent technique; when no other technique works; upon extremely alert awakening; when awakening to physical movement; in case of intense physical stimuli from one's physical surroundings; when getting a poorly working technique to yield results, and so on. In essence, this is a lifesaver technique for all those situations when something isn't working as one would like it to, or not as one had planned.

Interesting Fact!
Correctly using forced falling asleep in conjunction with indirect techniques can realistically bring odds of success to near 100 percent. That this, practically all attempts to exit the body upon awakening can become successful.

Odds of entering the phase diminish with every second when using cycles of indirect techniques upon awakening. Forced falling asleep, to put it simply, is a way to reel that receding lifeline to the phase back towards you. It tricks the brain, which will react automatically to all your actions and quickly thrust you into an intermediate state that is easy to use to enter the phase.

What the practitioner does is try to fall asleep as decidedly and as quickly as possible, but while maintaining the intention of not losing consciousness. The most important thing is to not get caught up in how to do it. Everyone intuitively knows how to do it, because everyone has had to force themselves to fall asleep at one point or another. You need only to get pulled in to a wave of sleepiness and catch it at the last second. It's quite similar to real life situations when there is very little time to sleep, and one nevertheless has to catch some rest. This technique is to be performed with that very determination to fall asleep quickly - but of course, here you do not fall completely asleep.

Independent Technique

This technique is used as an alternated technique when cycling upon awakening. Over the course of 3 to 5 seconds, the practitioner tries to abruptly, determinedly, and forcibly fall asleep, maintaining the intention of either not actually falling asleep or of coming back to himself at the last moment before losing consciousness. Afterwards, separation can often easily be successful. In addition, the following sensations may arise, which only need be intensified in order to definitively fall into the phase: vibrations, imagery, noise, and so on. In case of alert awakening or awakening to movement, it is recommend to begin cycling techniques from forced falling asleep.

Interesting Fact!

Some practitioners get forced falling asleep so well that they use nothing else besides alternating it with separation techniques upon awakening.

Periodic Adjustment of the State

This is used in-between any techniques or in-between full cycles of techniques. It is also called the Dnepropetrovsk method. In this case, the idea is that 3 to 5 seconds of credibly imitating falling asleep can not only conjure the phase all on its own, but also cause a kind of throwback to a more transitional state, thus increasing the effectiveness of all subsequent actions. Each time before performing techniques or full cycles of techniques, the practitioner simply throws himself back into a sleepier state via forced falling asleep in order to increase their effectiveness. Thus, in correctly implementing forced falling asleep, a situation occurs in which all actions are performed as if immediately upon awakening, when odds of success are highest.

Interesting Fact!

At an experimental seminar held August 21-23, 2009 in Dnepropetrovsk (Ukraine), 40 participants were asked to perform mandatory cycles of all the indirect techniques together with the technique of forced falling asleep. The success rate for the whole group reached 75% after only two nights, not counting those participants who made no attempts at all. This was the most successful seminar into 2011, and the system first tested out there took on the name "The Dnepropetrovsk Method".

Backdrop for All Techniques

This is to be employed simultaneously with all indirect techniques, as a backdrop to them. While performing any technique, the phaser should try to fall asleep simultaneously, as if the technique being performed (phantom wiggling, rotation, etc.) were necessary not for phase entrance, but for accelerating falling asleep. A phaser should simply try to fall asleep to the technique being performed without actually falling asleep. Any technique will usually begin to work at that moment, and it can be easily brought to the phase. One no longer needs to employ or continue on with concurrent forced falling asleep at this point. For example, if a practitioner's hand did not start moving within a few seconds of aggressive phantom wiggling, he will then begin trying to wiggle his hand while trying to fall asleep at the same time. The hand will usually yield to wiggling within several seconds, and the range of motion will begin to increase. Backdrop forced falling asleep may be included in the routine both from the start of attempts, as well as only when the techniques themselves are

www.obe4u.com

not working. *Such an approach often guarantees the greatest odds of success for indirect techniques.*

Interesting Fact!
When performed properly, backdrop use of forced falling asleep makes the choice of technique performed upon awakening inconsequential, as any technique will immediately start working.

Bringing the Techniques to Completion
This is to be used in cases when some indirect technique has begun working, albeit quite weakly or insufficiently. Here, in order to bring the working technique up to the right degree of manifestation, the practitioner should begin to perform forced falling asleep in parallel to it, just as is done with backdrop forced falling asleep. That is, the phaser should try to seemingly fall asleep to the technique being performed. As a result, the partially manifesting technique will start to work much better right then, and allow for the phase to be reached much sooner.

Despite all the merits of forced falling asleep and opportunities it offers, it quite rarely works at School of Out-of-Body Travel seminars for beginners. It is often put forward as an element for advanced practitioners who have reached the next level of sophistication. The problem consists in the fact that forced falling asleep is nearly always difficult for novices to conceptualize. In addition, information overload leads to an inability to digest additional information, and risks crowding out more elementary tasks at the start of one's practice.

This is primarily why forced falling asleep must be approached carefully. Ideally, the phaser himself should start to feel it approach on its own. This often occurs after one has already had a first experience. There's no sense in including it in the first things to be learned. Rather, it should only be used to fine-tune the effectiveness of attempts using indirect techniques. The exception would be situations where forced falling asleep is the last tool that hasn't yet been tried, and nothing else can be made to work upon awakening.

The most important thing is to never try this technique if you don't understand it. A practitioner may lose out on real experience in search of a silver bullet. He would waste time and energy on things obscure to him, and therefore, that which is bound to be ineffective. Conversely, if a practitioner immediately understands forced falling asleep and is familiar with it, then he may dive right into trying it in his practice.

What follows is a very characteristic example of how this technique can be incorrectly understood: Let us assume that a phaser tries to perform forced falling asleep in some way, but that it doesn't work. At the end of the attempt, the disappointed practitioner decides to fall fast asleep in order to catch the next awakening. And it's just at that moment that he begins to feel an imminent approach of the phase (vibrations, imagery, noise). On this the second try, he has done everything the right way - naturally and unaffectedly. Whereas before he had over-thought and over-complicated his actions when trying to do the technique, now he has been doing everything correctly - he simply begins falling asleep, as forced falling asleep should be done.

It's worth paying close attention to the fact that novices often get results from indirect techniques not while cycling them, but only when they want to fall asleep quickly after a failed attempt in order to catch one more awakening.

The main problem when performing forced falling asleep is the risk of easily falling asleep for real, no matter how awake one's mind seems before using this technique. This should always be remembered, and the length of time that this method is carried out should be carefully varied. In most cases, only several seconds are necessary in order to get results. Sometimes it needs to be done for longer, and sometimes the phaser falls asleep after two seconds of performing the technique, although it may seem to him that he had awoken too alertly and that nothing at all would work for him.

STRATEGY FOR ACTION

Some mistakenly believe that indirect techniques will produce quick, easy results, like a pill. Despite the fact that the techniques described in this guidebook are the best means to entering the phase, strong effort still needs to be exerted. This is not important for some, as everything comes quite easily to them, but for others this is of great importance.

Indirect techniques will definitely work if practiced consistently and as described. It has already been noted that in the majority of cases, making several concentrated attempts upon awakening without movement is sufficient enough to produce results. It may take a lot of time and effort to achieve phase entrance, so practitioners who set goals and work diligently will be presented with a crown of success.

Attempts are important in large measure not only for the final result, but also for the process itself. During practice, the practitioner independently learns and solves issues that may not have been understood in the guidebook. Other times, the practitioner will encounter situations that have never been described at all. It's impossible to prepare a student for every possible scenario, so as a practitioner moves deeper into practice, a unique, individual perspective and portfolio of experiences develops, which will certainly prove useful in the future. Until then, diligent practice of the information presented in this book will ready a practitioner for that personal frontier.

Actions in practice require strict attention. Study the techniques and select those that work best. Set the goal of consistent, conscious waking without movement. Set an objective of performing cycles of indirect techniques while waking up, day in and day out. *With such a clear course of action, the practitioner should never defocus his attention or dissipate his energy on other related actions, like, for example, on direct techniques for entering the phase.* If the indirect techniques do not work in the course of several days, continue trying. At latest, results occur in a matter of weeks - not months or years, like some sources maintain. Goals are to be stubbornly pursued - step-by-step, firmly, and diligently.

If no results occur after 10 to 20 attempts, it is better to cease practice for a week and take a rest, and then return with a fresh resolve to master the practice. Interestingly enough, it is exactly during such a break that spontaneous entrances into the phase through the most diverse methods occur.

If success is still elusive even after 2 weeks of trying, then a thorough analysis of the regimen should be conducted to root out any obvious mistakes or deficiencies. If overcoming them proves difficult or impossible, switching over to direct techniques is not recommended since they prove much more difficult than indirect techniques. Instead, techniques for entering the phase through conscious dreaming should be practiced.

It is also not worth skipping over problematic areas and trying to make up for mistakes by expending even more effort. For example, ignoring the precondition of awakening without moving will prove fruitless. Bypassing this requirement works for very few people. Facing every problem head-on and working hard to break through will be richly rewarded with unforgettable, treasured experiences. Keep trying!

TYPICAL MISTAKES WITH INDIRECT TECHNIQUES

- Internal certainty that nothing will happen instead of believing in positive results.

- Stopping the performance of techniques after an unsuccessful cycle when a minimum of four cycles should be practiced.
- Constantly awakening to movement instead of remaining still.
- Performing direct techniques in the evening. Performing indirect techniques in the evening, instead of upon waking up in the morning.
- Performing indirect techniques for an extremely long period of time (2 minutes or more). This is a complete waste of time in most cases.
- Switching from techniques that have begun to work instead of following them through to the end.
- Passively performing techniques instead of being determined and aggressive.
- Performing each technique separately for too long a period of time, even if the technique does not work, instead of switching to another technique within several seconds.
- Excessive thinking and analysis while performing indirect techniques, which require mental tranquility and inner stillness.
- Stopping and concentrating on unusual sensations when they arise versus continuing the technique that brought them about in the first place.
- Extremely long anticipation upon awakening instead of immediately performing techniques.
- Premature attempts at separating, instead of performing phase creation techniques through to the end of progress.
- Holding the breath when unusual sensations appear. Be calm instead.
- Opening the eyes when the only recommended movement is breathing or moving the eyes behind closed lids.
- Being agitated instead of relaxed.

- Ceasing attempts to separate even when partial success is met.
- Straining the physical muscles while performing the techniques versus remaining physically motionless.
- Not practicing after an alert awakening, when techniques are best applied - especially in the event of waking without movement.
- Merely imagining the techniques instead of really understanding them and performing them, if, of course, one is not performing rotation or other imagined techniques.
- Simply wiggling phantom limbs instead of employing a fixed determination to increase the range of movement
- Falling right asleep during forced falling asleep, instead of having the firm intention of continuing efforts within only 5 to 10 seconds.
- Scrutinizing the details of images when using the technique of observing images; the whole image should be observed panoramically lest it disappear.
- Intentionally trying to force pictures when observing images, instead of looking for what is naturally presented.
- Simply hearing noise when employing the technique of listening in, instead of attentively trying to pay attention, catch something, and listen in.

EXERCISES

Questions

1. Why are indirect techniques the easiest?
2. Why will one technique work for some people and not for others?
3. How many attempts are necessary in order to enter the phase?
4. When observing images, should a picture be conjured?

5. How is phantom wiggling different from imagined movement?
6. Where does sound come from while listening in?
7. How is forced listening in different from normal listening in?
8. When employing the technique of rotation, should one try to rotate or simply imagine the rotation?
9. What is physically strained when using the technique of straining the brain?
10. How is straining the brain different from straining the body without using muscles?
11. Should a practitioner fall asleep when using the forced falling asleep technique?
12. According to statistics from classes held at the School of Out-of-Body Travel, which indirect techniques are the most effective?
13. Why should one practice all of the primary techniques in a relaxed state?
14. What helps practitioners to enter the phase one-third of the time while using indirect techniques?
15. Is levitation the most popular separation technique?
16. What is the essential difference between indirect techniques and separation techniques?
17. How does the separation technique of rolling out differ from the indirect technique of rotation?
18. Is it necessary to imagine anything while trying to separate?
19. When is the best time to use indirect techniques?
20. Can techniques that are traditionally used upon awakening be attempted during the day? How effective are these techniques during the day?
21. Is becoming consciousness while dreaming the same as conscious awakening?
22. When employing indirect techniques, does an inability to awaken without moving have an effect on one's practice?

23. What are the components of the algorithm of cycling indirect techniques?
24. What first step must be taken while cycling through indirect techniques?
25. How many different techniques should a cycle consist of?
26. What is the minimum number of cycles that must be practiced?
27. If a lot of time has passed after awakening, is this good or bad for cycles of indirect techniques?
28. What must be done if a technique gets stuck at an unsatisfactory level of results?
29. If the cycles do not work, what should be done?
30. What are hints from the mind?
31. In what cases is it necessary to introduce aggressive effort when performing indirect techniques?

Task

1. Upon awakening, perform a full cycle of indirect techniques, and repeat this exercise until phase entrance is achieved.

Chapter 3 – Direct Method

THE CONCEPT OF DIRECT TECHNIQUES

Direct techniques for entering into an out-of-body experience are used without prior sleep by performing specific actions while lying down with the eyes closed. The advantage of direct techniques is that, in theory, they can be performed at any moment. However, a large drawback exists in the length of time it takes to master the techniques. Only 50% of practitioners achieve success after making attempts over a period of 2 to 3 weeks. For some, an entire year may pass before results are realized. The difficulty in achieving results with direct techniques is not a problem of inaccessibility, but the natural psychological characteristics of the individual. Not everyone is able to clearly understand the specific nuances involved, which is why some will continually make mistakes.

Many practitioners strive to master direct techniques right away because they appear to be the most convenient, straightforward, and concrete techniques. However, it is a grave mistake to begin attempting and mastering phase entrance from this level. In 90% of cases where novices begin their training with direct techniques, failure is guaranteed. Moreover, a vast amount of time, effort, and emotion will be wasted. As a result, complete disillusionment with the entire subject of phase experiences is possible.

Direct techniques should only be practiced after mastery of the easiest indirect techniques or how to become conscious when dreaming. In any case, difficulties will not wear one down afterwards, as it will be exceedingly clear from one's own experience that the phase is not a figment of the *imagination. Also, an advanced knowledge of indirect techniques will make it considerably easier to achieve direct entry into the phase.*

It is also worth always keeping in mind the average amount of time phasers spend on direct and indirect techniques to achieve results. For example, a novice expends an average of 5 minutes(5 attempts) on indirect techniques for each phase experience (averaging both successful and unsuccessful attempts), but 300 minutes(20 attempts) on direct techniques for each phase experience. An advanced phaser averages less than a minute(1-2 attempts) performing indirect techniques for each phase experience, but 30 minutes on direct techniques(2-3 attempts).

Quality of the phase experience is not dependent upon the chosen entrance technique. Direct techniques do not necessarily provide a deeper, more lasting phase over indirect techniques.

Direct techniques are better suited for some practitioners and not others, but this can only be said for a minority of the practicing population. Meanwhile, indirect techniques are accessible to absolutely everyone all of the time.

Interesting Fact!

In order to obtain best results at traditional 3-day School of Out-of-Body Travel seminars, instructors either completely omit the direct techniques, or wait until the last day to teach them, so as not to tempt novices to use them and subsequently ruin the group's success rate.

If a practitioner has decided to begin practice with direct techniques or has gained the necessary experience with indirect techniques, the underlying principles of the techniques must still be learned. Without these, nothing will occur, except coincidentally and in rare cases. The key to the successful use of direct techniques rests in achieving a free-floating state of consciousness. However, we will first examine a large variety of very useful aspects and factors that make direct entry into the phase much easier.

First, we will examine when it is best to perform the techniques and how intensively to exercise their practice. Then, we will examine the very important factor of body position, and the no less crucial issue of how long the techniques should be performed. Then, we will briefly investigate the issue of relaxation, and then we will immediately move on to the actual direct techniques. Only after covering all of the above are we able to delve into the issue of what a free-floating state of consciousness is and how to achieve it.

THE BEST TIME TO PRACTICE

The issue of time is not important with indirect techniques since the major prerequisite is that they are performed immediately after awakening occurs. In the case of direct techniques, the issue of timing is much more critical.

Naturally, the best method for finding the right time to perform direct techniques is the same as indirect techniques – *the deferred method*. However, there are some serious differences here. First of all, one may interrupt one's sleep at practically anytime of the night or early morning. Second, after having woken up (5-15 min.), one should not fall back asleep, but should immediately proceed to the techniques.

Direct techniques are many times more effective with the deferred method than at any other time. This is due to the fact that with the deferred method, the mind does not have time to become 100% alert, and it is easy to fall into the altered state of consciousness that will allow results.

When it comes to specific steps, one should awaken in the middle of the night either on one's own or with the help of an alarm clock. Then, one should get up and do something for 3 to 10 minutes, and then lie down again in bed and perform the techniques. If it is probable that the practitioner will wake up in too alert a state, and thus not even be sleepy, then the interval between awakening and performing the direct technique should be shortened, and fewer things should be done during that period of time. It should be noted that with this setup, a free-floating state of mind plays a far lesser role that with other procedures.

The second most effective window of time is before falling asleep at night, when the practitioner goes to bed. During this period of time, the brain needs to shut down the body and mind in order to renew its strength, which has been expended over the course of the day. This natural process can be taken advantage of by introducing certain adjustments to it.

Attempts at performing direct techniques during the day are less effective. However, if fatigue has already had a chance to build up by this time, this can be taken advantage of because the body will try to fall into sleep. This is especially suited for those who are accustomed to napping during the day.

Generally, other windows of time produce a substantially worse result, which is why one should start with performing direct techniques in the middle of the night, or before a night's sleep. Only after such techniques have been mastered will it be possible to experiment with daytime attempts.

INTENSITY OF ATTEMPTS

The degree of enthusiasm that is devoted to any pursuit is directly related to successfully reaching a goal. However, it is very important to know when to ease up, especially with the delicate matter of phase entry. One attempt per day using a direct technique is sufficient. If more attempts are made, the quality of each attempt will suffer considerably.

Interesting Fact!

www.obe4u.com

> *Many approach direct techniques as if digging a ditch: the more - the faster and the better. The result: dozens of attempts that yield no fruit.*

A lot of practitioners believe that dozens of attempts over the course of a day will yield the phase. This is not the path to success and will quickly lead to disillusionment with the practice. Even if after a week or a month no results are seen, direct techniques should be attempted only once daily (2-3 days per week). Persistent, analytical, and sensible, stubborn resolve to practice properly will produce the desired effect.

DURATION OF AN ATTEMPT

It is useless to attempt entering the phase using a direct technique by lying in bed and resolving neither to sleep nor get up until the phase occurs. Such coarseness in handling the delicate nature of the mind will produce nothing besides rapid emotional exhaustion.

Rigid timeframes apply while performing direct techniques before a sleep or in the middle of the night. Direct techniques attempts should only last 10 to 20 minutes. Longer durations inhibit sleepiness because the mind will concentrate too long on the techniques, and the desire to fall asleep will dissipate, resulting in insomnia that often lasts several hours. Overdone efforts negatively affect natural enthusiasm due to lost sleep and being tired the following day, which is compounded by the reality of a growing number of failed attempts.

If direct techniques produce no effect over the course of 10 to 20 minutes before sleep or in the middle of the night, then it is better to go to sleep with the thought that everything will work out another time. This is the positive outlook a practitioner ought to always maintain.

BODY POSITION

With indirect techniques body position isn't important since conscious awakening regardless of body position is the goal. However, the position of the body is crucial while practicing direct techniques.

There is not an exact body position that each practitioner should assume since, once again, individual characteristics and instincts differ widely. There are specific rules that allow one to select the right position, based on indirect indicators.

Many hold a belief that the correct pose is that of a corpse – lying on the back without a pillow, legs and arms straightened. This notion has probably been borrowed from other practices claiming that it helps achieve an altered state of mind. However, this position seriously impairs the efforts of the majority of practitioners. The corpse pose should only be used when it is probable that a practitioner will quickly fall asleep while performing techniques in this pose, even though it generally prevents sleep.

If a practitioner experiences difficulty falling asleep and is constantly awake while performing direct techniques, then the most comfortable position for the individual should be used.

If sleep comes quite easily to a practitioner, a less natural position should be taken. If a practitioner experiences fewer gaps in consciousness when the techniques are performed and has a harder time falling asleep, a more comfortable a position should be used. Depending on the situation, there are many possible positions: lying down on the back, on the stomach, on the side, or even in a half-reclined position. It is possible that a practitioner will have to change positions from one attempt to another, introducing adjustments related to a free-floating state of mind. Moreover, no more than 3 days per week should be spent on the direct techniques. The same goes for the practice of the phase itself. This limit may only be raised in case of a high level of experience and nearly all of one's attempts being successful.

RELAXATION

By nature, one should clearly understand that direct techniques are in and of themselves relaxation methods, inasmuch as no phase can occur without one being relaxed. Accordingly, one can go immediately into the phase without any prior relaxation.

Since the most effective window of time for using direct techniques occurs before sleep and at night, and lasts only 10 to 20 minutes in any case, additional time should not be wasted on trying to relax, nor should time for relaxation be subtracted from the requisite 10 to 20 minutes.

Correct and quality relaxation is a difficult pursuit and many go about it in their own way, producing an effect opposite to that of natural relaxation. For example, many endeavor to relax their bodies to such a degree that in the end the mind is as active as it would be while trying to solve a difficult mathematical equation. In this type of situation, entering the phase is impossible.

The body automatically relaxes when the mind is relaxed. The body, in turn, will never relax if the mind is active. Therefore, it is better for beginners refrain from the trouble of the nuances of relaxation and save their energies for more elementary matters.

Instead of forcing a technical relaxation, a practitioner should simply lie down for several minutes and this will provide the best relaxation. Lying down activates natural relaxation processes; the most powerful kind.

Complete, peaceful relaxation may only be coerced by those with specialized, in-depth experience. Generally, these are people who have spent a great amount of time and effort mastering trance and meditative states. Relaxation in these cases should take no more than 1 to 3 minutes and no longer, as when a practitioner is expert at relaxation it is sufficient to just think about it, and it occurs.

All quality relaxation techniques may well serve as direct techniques, if a free-floating state of mind occurs while they are exercised. After gaining the necessary experience with trance and meditation, a practitioner of these mental arts may proceed to mastering the phase.

VARIATIONS OF USING DIRECT TECHNIQUES

Techniques used to gain direct entrance to the phase are exactly the same as those used during indirect attempts. The only difference is in the method of implementation. However, since direct techniques mostly require passivity, not all techniques work equally well for both direct and indirect entries into the phase. For example, active techniques like straining the brain cannot be used to gain a smooth entrance into the phase.

Direct techniques differ from indirect techniques in their implementation because of the slow, halting production of results that occurs from the beginning of a direct attempt through the end of it. If upon awakening something happens to work, then this can practically always lead to entrance into the phase. For example, the same phantom wiggling before sleep can begin quickly enough, but range of movement will not be easy to increase, and the entire implementation of the technique will rely on protracted, rhythmic movement. Results take much longer: ten minutes instead of ten seconds. These differences also apply to every technique described in this guidebook.

Like with the practice of indirect techniques, to begin the practice of direct techniques, a practitioner should choose 2 or 4 of the most suitable techniques from those that prove most effective for the individual.

The primary difference in working with direct techniques is the time that it takes to exercise each. If testing a specific indirect technique takes only 3 to 5 seconds, then in this case several minutes will be spent. Duration varies depending on certain factors.

There are three primary ways of performing the techniques: classical, sequencing, and cycling - similar to the cycling used with indirect techniques. To understand which variant should be used, consider the following table:

Variations of Using the Techniques	When to Use It
Classical (passive) variation: One attempt of 1 technique. The technique may be alternated after each attempt.	- when learning direct techniques; - when a practitioner generally sleeps poorly; - if attempts lead to waking up; - if attempts with other variations occur without lapses in consciousness; - if the body and consciousness are in a relaxed state;
Sequencing (middle): One attempt with 2 to 3 techniques for 1 to 5 minutes. Techniques are alternated infrequently. Aggression fluctuates with the length of time that the techniques are performed.	- used if falling asleep occurs while using the classical variation, or if cycling results in becoming wide awake; - when a practitioner generally falls asleep quickly;
Cycling (active): Algorithm of cycling 3 techniques like with indirect entry to the phase, but performing each technique	- if the classical and sequencing variations put one asleep; - when one generally falls asleep very quickly;

| for 10 seconds to 1 minute, and not 3 to 5 seconds. | - can also be employed when exhausted or sleep deprived; |

A practitioner should always begin with the classical variation, i.e. using one technique over an entire attempt. Due to the unusual nature of the efforts involved, a beginner's enthusiasm may sustain a completely alert state. Later, however, strong, prolonged lapses of consciousness into sleep may occur. Here, it may be necessary to increase the level of activity by transitioning to the sequencing variation.

Sequencing is the primary variation used for direct techniques because of its elasticity in application. It can be passive if a practitioner alternates two techniques for five minutes each over the course of 15 minutes. It may also be aggressive if three techniques are sequenced for one minute each. Everything between these two extremes allows for proper practice of the techniques and selection of the best variation to achieve a free-floating state of mind.

If falling off to sleep stubbornly occurs even with the active form of sequencing, then one should start cycling through indirect techniques, but performing each technique for 10 seconds to 1 minute.

As work over many months with the techniques is implied, one should not torment oneself if on one day one does not want to do something. Otherwise, one may quickly tire out. Everything should be a pleasure to do and not cause any excessive emotional tension.

THE FREE-FLOATING STATE OF MIND

There are almost infinite descriptions of direct entry techniques offered in literature, stories, on the Internet, and at seminars. Sometimes, one description fundamentally differs from another. In the majority of cases, however, common threads exist that unite almost every description of a particular technique: short lapses in consciousness, memory gaps, and drifting in and out of sleep, all of which are hallmarks of the free-floating state of mind. After any of these phenomena occur, all manner of unusual pre-phase or phase sensations arise.

Lapses in consciousness may last for seconds, several minutes, or more than an hour. They may range from a simple loss of consciousness to entrance into a full-fledged dream. They may be singular and rare, or may occur several times over the course of a minute. Whatever a lapse entails, the mind attains a mode of operating that is ideal for phase experimentation, provided the practitioner is able to refrain from deep sleep and quickly return to a conscious, waking state.

Not every lapse of consciousness leads to the phase. The lapse must have sufficient depth to be effective. Thus, with every unsuccessful lapse, another deeper lapse should be incurred.

Free-floating State of Mind with Direct Techniques

The primary practical drawback of the free-floating state of mind is the possibility of falling completely asleep during lapses instead of only temporarily dipping into sleep.

Techniques are definitely necessary to ensure the desired result. Such techniques more or less fulfill an auxiliary function, and thus one need not be strict about them.

Interesting Fact!
It does not matter which direct technique is used; as long as it leads to lapses in consciousness, success is possible.

When performing the variations of the techniques, a practitioner can begin to vacillate between full alertness and complete asleep, coming to, and then nodding off again.

To avoid falling asleep requires a strong desire to return to wakefulness. This is accomplished by a strong resolve on the part of the practitioner, even if, while performing a direct technique, drifting in and out of sleep occurs. The practitioner must firmly assert that at the moment consciousness tapers off, awakening will immediately occur.

On the other hand, if lapses do not occur, and are replaced by complete alertness, the following tricks of the trade may help: full concentration on mental actions or, conversely, musing and daydreaming in parallel with the technique being used. It should be noted that these are only effective at the initial stages of working with direct techniques since such techniques have a strong sleep-inducing effect.

If direct techniques do not lead to light sleep or singular lapses after a long period of regular practice, then it must be assumed that the practitioner is dealing with some appreciable error in technique or in the length of performance.

The number of lapses that occur may be regulated by body position during practice or by changing the variation used while performing techniques.

Entering the phase with a free-floating state of mind most often occurs as the result of three key factors. First, one technique or another may begin to work well during a lapse. Second, nearness to the phase may unexpectedly manifest itself through sounds or vibration after a lapse. During this, transitioning to techniques that correspond to the above symptoms (listening in, straining the brain) may be applied. Third, when exiting a lapse, it is sometimes easy to separate or quickly find a working technique by paying attention to initial indicators.

Interesting Fact!
There is a theory that there is no such thing as a direct phase entrance method, and that all direct methods are actually a subcategory of the indirect method. The only difference would be that direct techniques involve inducing micro-sleep, which authentically mimics falling asleep, creating a physiological state closer to natural awakening, when it is easy to enter the phase.

Lapses in consciousness are not bound to occur in 100% of cases. However, striving to achieve lapses plays a very important role since they are not always perceivable, and a lapse occurrence is not always obvious. They can be very short in duration or shallow. Or, they may not occur at all. Nonetheless, properly applied techniques to produce lapses may give entrance to the phase. This is especially true of the deferred method for direct phase entrance. It is also worth noting that lapses in consciousness can be so shallow and brief that a phaser may simply be unable to recognize them.

AUXILIARY FACTORS

It can be categorically stated that there is one situation in which a practitioner will constantly have problems with the direct method, or never get it to work: excessive desire to get results right here and now. If a practitioner lays in bed with the thought that he will enter the phase no matter what using the direct method, then he might as well not make any attempt at all. Such excessive desire inevitably finds physiological expression in the form of a lack of lapses in consciousness, or their weak depth. The problem is that practically every new practitioner makes this mistake. Direct techniques are often considered difficult due to this seemingly inconsequential and barely perceptible mistake.

Interesting Fact!
For most practitioners, a key piece of advice is to let go of a burning desire to enter the phase no matter what when using the direct method.

That's why there should be an element of inner stillness and indifference to the end result before beginning an attempt, let alone during it. You need to let go of trying to control it, and simply commit yourself to entering the phase. One's mind should be completely still and almost completely indifferent as to how successful the attempt will be: if it works - great. If not - who cares? There should be intention to enter the phase, but that intention ought be kept inside, and not find expression in excessive desire or control over the situation.

Until a practitioner learns to have stillness in his approach to direct phase entrance methods, he cannot hope to obtain any real practical experience. In the best case, only one attempt in fifty will result in the phase, even though most of his attempts could have met with success. It's enough to consider that all advanced users of the direct technique benefit from ambivalence towards the result, whether or not deliberately. Conversely, all attempts by novices are accompanied by excessive desire to obtain a result that they have to have, and this is the main reason for lack of success.

Analyzing a typical example of how the direct technique can work should make the situation clearer: say someone accidentally described the direct techniques right away when telling another about the phase. His interest perked, the newly-initiated goes home and begins making an attempt just for laughs, without excessive desire. It turns out that this works on the first try. He experiences a turbulent and hyper-realistic phase. Now that he knows what all of the fuss is about, he longs to go there again. On the next day, he goes back to bed with a clear recollection of those electrifying events that he so desires to re-experience. But now, his mind craves results so much that his body is physiologically unable to fall into the state that had preceded his first successful attempt - an attempt made without any excessive effort. As a result, those same direct techniques no longer bring the phase. Anyone believing that getting results is a matter of technique (and not realizing it's a matter of attitude towards the process) would be dumbfounded.

Using direct techniques in the evening or in the middle of the night take advantage of the body's natural state of fatigue and for practical purposes this natural tiredness may be amplified. For example, direct techniques more easily lead to success if the practitioner is considerably sleep-deprived. Moreover, in such a state, inducing a free-floating state of mind may be forgone. The most important thing is simply not to fall asleep immediately, in addition to employing the appropriate variations with the techniques. Willful deprivation of sleep is torturous and useless even though great results may be achieved by an experienced and knowledgeable practitioner in a severely fatigued state. Beginners are better off approaching all forms of practice in a natural, balanced way.

An intense longing to sleep is not limited to long periods of sleep deprivation; physical and emotional fatigues also play important roles. In that case, the most important thing is not to fall asleep when performing the techniques, and thus one must select a more active technique variation than usual.

The above notwithstanding, factors such as fatigue and sleep deprivation are only to be used on those rare occasions caused by external circumstances. There's no sense in putting your body through intentional misery by trying to force fatigue or extended periods of sleep deprivation. Such situations are practically the exclusive domain of novices - an experienced phaser would always go to sleep when exhausted. Sacrificing the health in such a way is pointless when already having regular and easily-entered phases.

The direct techniques, after all, should only be performed when in a normal physiological state, and with enjoyment. A practitioner should take pleasure in the very process of using the method, and not regard it as a tiresome chore needed to enter the phase. This is the main reason why a practitioner should perform his favorite techniques when he's most in the mood for them. The phase should never be sought by trying one's will or body. With the direct method, there is a direct relationship between enjoyment and effectiveness: the more the process makes you irritable, the worse the free floating state of mind arises and the lower the odds of success - and vice-versa.

There are several signposts that will clearly indicate whether or not a phaser is on track to reach his goal of mastering the direct method. First, an unsuccessful attempt should not cause one to feel irritable or feel one is wasting time. That's the first sign of a strategic mistake regarding the process. There can be no talk of a having a solid direct-entrance phase experience as long as this happens. Next is enjoyment of the very process of performing the techniques. If a practitioner enjoys working with the techniques he is doing and finds them pleasant, then they will also work much better and be much more likely to lead to the phase. In addition, disappointment rarely accompanies unsuccessful attempts when one has such an attitude. One must always show respect for the techniques, and not treat them as a boring chore necessary to get into the phase. If such a problem exists, one should reconsider one's attitude towards the techniques and try to become interested in the mere performance of them. Although the techniques are not even of secondary importance for direct phase entrance, they can serve as a reliable gauge of the quality of the attempt.

STRATEGY FOR ACTION

If a novice begins his practice from the direct techniques, then he does so at his own risk and peril, having shunned recommendations based on work with thousands of people. When unsuccessful, practitioner himself would be solely to blame for the wasted time and effort. It should always be remembered that many even quite-accomplished practitioners try to avoid using the direct method to enter the phase.

Direct techniques seldom produce quick and clear results, unlike entering the phase via becoming conscious while dreaming or through the use of indirect techniques. At first, direct techniques produce sporadic results, which is why the path of practice should not begin with direct techniques hoping for fast reward. It is better to systematically practice a technique, working toward mastery on a consistent basis.

There is no cause for worry if results are not achieved after a month of attempts. A continual effort to analyze practice and improve should be the primary focus because failures are always caused by distinguishable mistakes.

Although difficulties may arise with direct techniques, one should never abandon what worked until then (i.e. indirect techniques), as this could temporarily deprive one of the experience that one has enjoyed so far.

A combination of direct and indirect techniques should never be used during the course of a single day since this would be detrimental to practical focus and enthusiasm. It is better to separately perform each type of technique on different days.

TYPICAL MISTAKES WITH DIRECT TECHNIQUES

- Lack of a free-floating state of mind, even though it is mandatory.
- Assuming an incorrect position when lying down.
- Performing direct techniques during the day when a practitioner is inexperienced, instead of in the evening or at night.
- Performing more than one attempt per day.
- Performing protracted relaxation before the techniques, even when this may play a negative role.
- Performing the techniques for too long when they should be exercised for no more than 20 minutes.
- Forgetting to affirm a strong intention of awakening during a lapse of consciousness.
- Falling asleep during lapses in a free-floating state of mind, instead of working toward multiple lapses while awakening.
- Forgetting separation techniques and awaiting some unknown event upon emergence from a lapse, instead of taking advantage of the moment.
- Excessively alternating the techniques in a primary repertoire, instead of testing them in a planned and systematic manner.
- Holding the breath when unusual sensations are encountered. Always be calm.
- Halting practice when unusual sensations occur when it is necessary to continue what brought about the sensations.
- Excessive excitement while performing direct techniques.
- Lack of aggression during attempts due to fatigue and sleep deprivation.
- Lack of a clear plan of action. Understanding and planning the use of distinct variations of the techniques

beforehand is crucial to the analysis of subsequent errors in practice.

EXERCISES

Questions

1. Which techniques should be mastered before proceeding to direct techniques?
2. Should results from the use of direct techniques be expected after several days or a week?
3. Is it better to practice direct techniques during the day or in the evening?
4. Is it correct to perform three direct attempts per day?
5. Which body position should be assumed when suffering from insomnia?
6. Which body position should be used by a person who falls asleep quickly?
7. How much time should be spent on a single direct attempt?
8. When can direct attempts be made for a longer period of time than usual?
9. What is the best way for an inexperienced practitioner to relax?
10. Can direct techniques substitute relaxation techniques?
11. Can relaxation techniques substitute direct techniques?
12. How many variations for performing direct techniques are there?
13. In what case is the variation of sequencing with direct techniques employed?
14. Which technique may not be used for direct entrance to the phase with the goal of creating a free-floating state of mind?
15. What happens to consciousness while in a free-floating state during direct techniques?

16. Should awakening be attempted if falling asleep occurred while using direct techniques?
17. What is the probability of entering the phase without a free-floating state of consciousness?
18. What do unsuccessful attempts using direct techniques most often end in?
19. Is sexual activity before an evening attempt using a direct technique beneficial?

Task

1. When performing direct techniques, try to achieve no less than three lapses in consciousness before 20 minutes elapse, or before you fall asleep. Repeat this challenge until phase entrance is achieved.

Chapter 4 – Becoming Conscious While Dreaming

THE CONCEPT OF TECHNIQUES INVOLVING BECOMING CONSCIOUS WHILE DREAMING

The techniques for phase entrance via becoming conscious while dreaming are based on reaching consciousness and self-awareness during a dream, which, regardless of dream quality, can be transitioned into a fully realized phase experience. Contrary to popular opinion, having an out-of-body experience through dreaming differs little from other techniques. The outcome is still categorized as a dissociative experience: being fully conscious while removed from the perception of a physical body.

The realism of a phase induced through becoming conscious in a dream does not differ from phases entered using other techniques, and, when deepened, the phase offers more vivid and lucid experiences than those of everyday life.

If a practitioner becomes aware of a dream while in it (usually accompanied by a clear realization that it is "just a dream"), then the phase is experienced from that moment forward.

Beginners often confuse the notion of becoming conscious while dreaming with induced dreaming. An induced dream is the dream of a specific topic, provoked on demand; this does not presuppose consciousness. Moreover, not all practitioners clearly understand what it means to be fully conscious while dreaming. Consciousness while dreaming is always present to some extent, but it is necessary to be as conscious as one would be in a wakeful state. Awareness is not possible as long as the plot of the dream continues. When full understanding occurs that everything around is just a dream, a person drops the dream and starts doing only what he wants to do at that very moment. And after awakening, he should not think that what happened was absurd or unexplainable.

During the process of becoming conscious in a dream, a practitioner's actions must be completely subordinated to the desire to experience a quality phase. This is why, upon becoming conscious in a dream, proceeding to techniques related to deepening and maintaining is crucial.

Techniques for becoming conscious in a dream differ very much in nature from other techniques, and there are good reasons why these methods are differentiated from other practices, like so-called *astral projection* or *out-of-body experience* (OBE). However, their characteristics differ very little in terms of results.

The technique-related peculiarities rest in the fact that specific actions are not required to produce immediate, concrete results. All technique-related elements are performed outside of when consciousness while dreaming occurs. This is because it is impossible to take some action if you are not conscious and do not realize that you are dreaming. All efforts are directed at making that very realization somehow occur.

Interesting Fact!
Even if a practitioner pays no heed to the techniques for becoming conscious while dreaming, but applies direct or indirect techniques, on average each third phase will still occur through becoming conscious in a dream. This has been statistically proven at seminars of the School of Out-of-Body Travel.

Many strive to achieve consciousness during each dream over the course of an entire night; however, this is rarely possible due to physiological barriers. There is a good reason that sleep and dreams are an important part of a human life. There is an important need to switch off not only body, but also consciousness, so that it may unconsciously sift and process the vast volume of information obtained in everyday life.

The timeframe for achieving conscious dreaming is very difficult to estimate due to the nature of required actions. Intensity and intention definitely exert heavy influence. A practitioner may become conscious in a dream when first lapsing into sleep, regardless of when it occurs. Or, with regular attempts, this could happen in two weeks to a month. Nevertheless, these techniques promise a much higher likelihood of success than direct methods, and can be compared with indirect techniques - inferior to the latter only in terms of the speed at which results are achieved and the amount of effort required.

Techniques used to attain dream consciousness should not be combined with other types of techniques. It is better to focus on one thing at a time. *Interestingly, when a technique is practiced on a regular basis, there is nearly a 100% guarantee that dream consciousness will spontaneously occur. A practitioner must know how to react when this happens.*

BEST TIME FOR BECOMING CONSCIOUSNESS WHILE DREAMING

As with other phase entrance methods, the best time for becoming consciousness while dreaming occurs when using the deferred method. That is, it's necessary to sleep for 5 to 7 hours, then wake up and perform physical activities for 3 to 50 minutes in order to consolidate the effect of the awakening, and finally go back to sleep with the intention of becoming consciousness during dream episodes to follow. The longer the interlude before going back to sleep, the higher the odds of success. There are some practitioners who are able to fall back asleep after a long interruption. Meanwhile, others are unable to fall asleep after only several minutes of being awake, and so they should make the break as brief as possible.

Consciousness while dreaming also arises easily during a daytime nap. It can also occur in the middle of the night, but for physiological reasons such experiences tend to be brief and are usually marginally lucid.

TECHNIQUES FOR BECOMING CONSCIOUS IN A DREAM

It is possible to simultaneously practice several techniques for becoming conscious in a dream since every technique is directly compatible with and complementary to others.

Remembering Dreams

There is a well-known and widespread of fallacy that supposes that dreams do not occur for some people. Everyone dreams, but not everyone remembers their dreams. Even those who actively dream remember only a small fraction of these nightly excursions. Hence, one should not think that it is impossible for someone who does not remember dreams to become conscious in one. Such a person should simply try to use the techniques.

At the same time, there is a direct correlation between the number of dreams remembered and the probability of becoming conscious while dreaming. That is why developing the ability to remember dreams is crucial. In essence, the ability to achieve dream consciousness rests with the conscious mind, which is very much interconnected with memory-related processes.

Consciousness is naturally inherent in dreams, but it lacks rapid, operative memory. Dreamers may know who they are, their names, how to walk, and how to talk, but may not know how surrounding events are related, or the nature of their significance.

By increasing the frequency of remembered dreams, short-term dream memory becomes more developed, which enables more realistic dream experiences followed by a higher probability of dream consciousness.

There are three techniques dedicated to increasing the number of remembered dreams.

The first is to simply recall the details of dreams upon awakening. Within the first few minutes of waking up, try to remember as many dreams from the night before as possible. This should be done with a great amount of attention and diligence because this exercise strengthens the memory. If possible, during the day, or, better yet, before going to sleep at night, recall the previous night's dreams once again as it is highly beneficial.

Writing dreams down in a special dream journal is much more effective than simple recall. Record dreams in the morning while memories are still fresh. The more details recalled when recording the dream, the better the ultimate results. This is a very attentive approach that demands a higher awareness than simple recollection. Writing dreams in a journal significantly increases awareness of actions and aspirations.

Another way of remembering dreams is to create a map of the dream world. This is called dream cartography and is similar to keeping a journal, though an enhanced level of awareness is developed by connecting dream episodes on a map.

First, record one dream, describing locations and events, which are plotted on the map. This cartographic process is repeated with each subsequent dream, and after several dreams an episode will occur that is somehow related to the location of a dream that has already been recorded. The two dreams that took place near each other are plotted next to each other on the map. Over time, more and more interrelated dreams will occur and the map will become increasingly concentrated rather than disconnected. As a result, the frequency and realistic quality of remembered dreams will increase, and the dreamer will increase the ability to achieve consciousness while dreaming.

It is best to set remembered dreams to memory after temporary awakenings versus waiting until morning. To accomplish this, it helps to have a pen and a piece of paper nearby so that a practitioner may quickly jot down a phase or several key words from the plot of the dream before falling back asleep. Using this information, the majority of dreams are quickly and completely recalled.

The initial result from exercising these techniques is a rapid increase in the number of remembered dreams. When this number becomes significant (anywhere between five and ten per night), dream consciousness follows on a regular basis.

Intention

Intention is crucial to the success of any technique. With regard to dream consciousness, its significance is multiplied. The creation of intention is inextricably linked to the creation of internal aspiration, which has reverberations in both conscious and unconscious states. In reality, an elevated degree of intention operates as a powerful method of mental programming.

This technique is performed before falling asleep by affirming a strong desire to become conscious while dreaming. For best results, alongside a strong, clearly defined intention, think through what actions will be taken when dream consciousness is achieved.

Creating an Anchor

Since dream consciousness is not linked to specific actions that take place within a dream and sensory perception continues to operate in the dream state, it is possible to develop and use an artificially conditioned reflex to achieve consciousness. The essence of this technique is to train the consciousness to uniformly react to certain stimuli that occur while being awake and when dreaming, establishing a habit of specific response every time a certain situation occurs.

For example, while awake, a practitioner may ask, "Am I dreaming?" every time they see an anchor. An anchor is any object that is often encountered while awake and while dreaming. Examples of anchors include a practitioner's own hands, red objects, or running water. When first using this technique, a practitioner will be unable to question whether a dream is in progress every time a pre-established anchor is encountered. However, with training and a strong desire this technique quickly produces results. Over time, subconscious questioning of the practitioner's state becomes habit, happening while awake and dreaming. The end result is dream consciousness.

It is important to note that one needs not only to simply ask this question, but that it is also important to answer it mindfully, trying to isolate oneself from surrounding events in order to be able to answer it in an as objective and unpredetermined way as possible. Failing to answer objectively will always result in a negative response ("no"), and dream consciousness will not be achieved.

Natural Anchors

In addition to creating deliberate anchors that induce conscious dreaming, natural anchors should be given focused attention. These are objects and actions that regularly cause dream consciousness, even when consciousness is not desired. Being aware of the existence of natural anchors actually doubles the chances of their appearance.

The following experiences are common natural anchors that are present in dreams: death, sharp pain, intense fear, stress, flying, electric shock, sexual sensations, and dreaming about phase entrance or the phase environment. When attempting dream consciousness, identifying natural anchors produces results nearly 100% of the time.

One may try to start flying each time that one answers the question. This is of course pointless when in waking reality. However, when dreaming, this will most likely lead to flight and once again prove that everything around is just a dream.

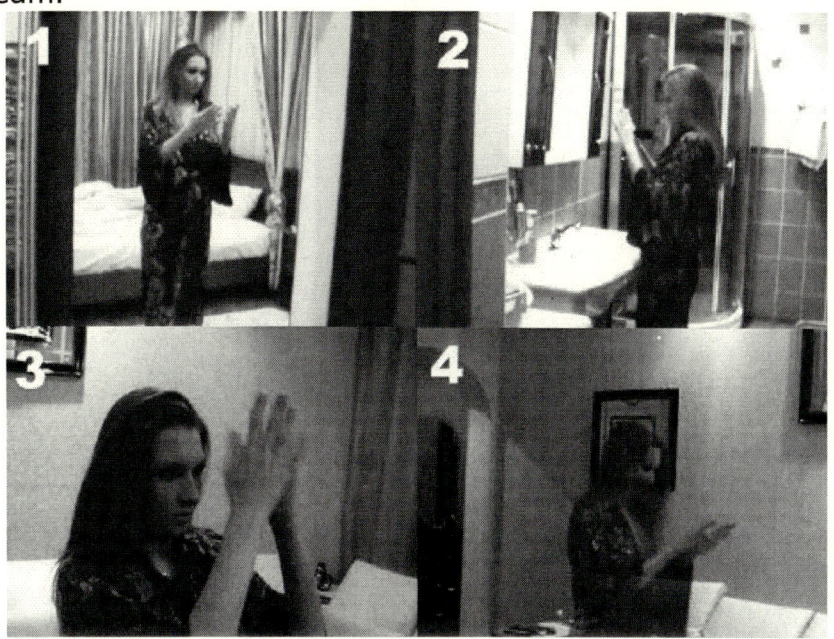

Self-Analysis

Consistent analysis of dreams helps to ascertain reasons for an absence of conscious awareness: these analyses are significant to attaining dream consciousness. Over the course of a lifetime, the mind grows accustomed to the paradoxical nature of dreams and pays less attention to them. This becomes apparent while trying to understand that a red crocodile is not only unable to talk to us, but that it also cannot be red, nor can it rent an apartment. While dreaming, these impossibilities are never called into question. The essence of self-analysis is remembering dreams and thinking hard about why their paradoxical features had not been adequately recognized in the dream state.

With experience, the everyday analysis of the correspondence of dreams to reality begins to have an effect on a practitioner's reasoning within the dream state. For example, that red crocodile's presence in a rented apartment could cause doubts that give pause for reflection, which could in turn lead to the understanding that everything happening is just a dream.

ACTIONS TO BE DONE WHEN BECOMING CONSCIOUS WHILE DREAMING

To ensure that dream consciousness leads to a fully developed phase experience, one of three specific actions must be taken.

The best is the techniques for deepening, which should be immediately applied once dream consciousness occurs. Deepening must be performed within the dream episode before all other techniques. Doing so virtually guarantees entrance to the phase. The choice of actions that follow deepening is dependent upon a practitioner's predetermined plan of action in the phase.

When becoming conscious while dreaming, it is quite dangerous to try to return to one's body in order to roll out of it right away unless one has deepened beforehand. This could result in a situation where, after having easily returned to one's body, one would not be able to separate from it, as the phase becomes significantly weaker when physical sensations coincide with the position of a real body. If one is to employ such an option, then in order to return to one's body one should simply think about it, which is often sufficient to make the transition occur almost immediately.

Another option is the use of translocation techniques to arrive at a desired place within the phase world. It is also dangerous to employ this variation without first deepening;

translocating in a shallow phase makes a return to the wakeful state very likely. Translocation is often accompanied by a substantial decrease in the depth of the phase state.

STRATEGY FOR ACTION

To achieve dream consciousness, constant practice is highly necessary because sporadic practice will fail to develop the requisite background thought processes.

As a rule, employing phase entry techniques within the context of dream consciousness produces results after several weeks, and the effects of the techniques are increasingly pronounced with time. If there are no results within a month or two, refrain from these techniques for a period of time, take a break for a week or two, and resolve to assume a fresh start later.

Practitioners often stop using these techniques after initial results as later effects become elusive and the frequency of dream consciousness rapidly declines. These techniques should not be abandoned after first yielding results, though a gradual decrease in practice is generally acceptable.

TYPICAL MISTAKES WHEN PRACTICING BECOMING CONSCIOUS WHILE DREAMING

- Perceiving the state of dream consciousness as a non-phase state even though this phenomenon is one and the same with the phase.
- Attempting dream consciousness while performing other phase entrance techniques when it is better to focus on dream consciousness alone.

- When falling asleep, lacking sufficient desire to experience conscious dreaming even though this is critical.
- Continuing to yield to the plot of a dream even after achieving dream consciousness, whereas subsequent actions must be independent and based on free will.
- Incorrectly answering the question "Am I dreaming?" while dreaming.
- Forgetting to immediately begin deepening techniques when dream consciousness has been achieved.
- When exercising memory development, recalling the most vivid dreams instead of every dream.
- Inconsistent concentration while practicing dream consciousness techniques.

EXERCISES

Questions

1. What is the difference between an out-of-body experience and dream consciousness?
2. After attaining dream consciousness, does the realistic quality of the surroundings differ from that of wakefulness?
3. Which technique can be used in a dream to become conscious in it?
4. Is it possible to achieve dream consciousness after the first attempt?
5. Is it true that not all people dream?
6. Why is learning to remember as many dreams as possible important for becoming conscious while dreaming?
7. What is dream cartography?
8. To experience dream consciousness, what must be done while falling asleep?
9. Could a tape measure become an anchor used to achieve dream consciousness?

10. What experiences in dreams often spontaneously give rise to a state of conscious awareness?
11. What must immediately be done after becoming conscious while dreaming?

Task

1. Try to achieve at least one instance of dream consciousness.

Chapter 5 – Non-autonomous Methods

THE ESSENCE OF NON-AUTONOMOUS METHODS
FOR ENTERING THE PHASE

Non-autonomous methods of entering the phase are various types of external influences that are able to help put a practitioner into the phase state. Computer programs, devices, various physical actions, the aid of a helper, or even chemical substances are examples of non-autonomous methods. In rare cases, these methods actually help, while some hinder the possibility of a genuine phase experience.

Never count on a magical substance or machine to automatically eliminate the difficulties associated with phase entrance. If such a substance existed, the whole topic of phase experimentation would exist at an advanced level of development and prevalence in society.

In actuality, there are no devices or methods able to consistently provide access to the phase state. At best, these exist in a largely supplementary capacity, and the more a practitioner is able to do on his or her own, the more helpful and effective these supplements are. If phase entry has not been mastered autonomously, then results through the use of supplements will be totally accidental.

The reason behind the weak effectiveness of non-autonomous methods of phase entrance rests in the fact that the physiological process responsible for the phase experience cannot be exactly defined. Only generalities are known, nothing else. In order to gain a clear understanding of the state, the processes that give rise to it must be discerned and analyzed. All existing technologies have either blundered down a clearly mistaken path (synchronizing the hemispheres of the brain), or traveled toward the detection and use of indirect indicators (cueing technologies).

CUEING TECHNOLOGIES

Of all non-autonomous assistance methods, cueing technologies yield the best results. The operating principle behind cueing technologies is quite simple: a device detects rapid eye movement (REM) and sends signals to a sleeping practitioner, prompting dream consciousness or an awakening that may be followed by indirect techniques. Cueing programs or devices may also send indicators over specific intervals of time; these are received during REM sleep and are meant to cause a sleeping practitioner to awaken and attempt indirect techniques.

More sophisticated REM-detecting technologies may be purchased at specialized stores or through online merchandisers. REM-detecting technologies work by virtue of special night mask equipped with a motion sensor that detects the frequency of specific eye movements that occur during REM sleep. When the eye movements reach REM quality, the device sends discreet signals to the practitioner through light, sound, vibrations, or a combination of these. In turn, the practitioner must discern the signal and react to it while sleeping with the goal of phase entry through dream consciousness.

The effectiveness of REM-detecting devices is more plausible in theory than in practice. The mind quickly develops a tolerance for these types of external stimuli and stops reacting, and, as a result, such technologies are hardly used more than one or two nights per week. Secondly, a practitioner will detect only a small portion of the signals, and conscious reaction occurs in even fewer instances.

Cueing technologies are best used to send signals that allow a practitioner to awaken without moving during REM sleep, which facilitates a high probability of phase entrance through indirect techniques.

Pricing of these "mind-machines" (the common moniker of any device that purports to produce altered consciousness) widely varies and is determined by quality of REM detection and signaling. Available models include: DreamStalker, DreamMaker (NovaDreamer), REM-Dreamer, Astral Catapult, among many others. Since the use of these devices does not guarantee increased success in practice, investing money in the technology is not recommended. If a practitioner is curious about cueing technologies, similar devices may be constructed at home using a special computer program and a run-of-the-mill optical mouse. Designs for a homegrown setup are easily located on the Internet.

Another do-it-yourself way of experimenting with cueing is through the use of a computer, a music player, or even the alarm clock function on a mobile phone. The practitioner saves short sounds or phrases, played as an alarm every 15 to 30 minutes while sleeping. These sounds will signal the practitioner to wake up and attempt indirect techniques.

If the practitioner decides to use cueing technology, several fundamental principles should be considered as results will be less likely if they are ignored. First, mind-machines should be used no more than twice a week. Otherwise, too high a tolerance will be built up, rendering the machines ineffective. Second, use cueing technology in combination with the deferred method, which was covered in the section on indirect techniques. It is better to sleep for six hours without distraction and then, after sleep has been interrupted, put on a sleep-mask or earpiece and continue sleeping. Sleep will be light for the remaining two to four hours as there will be more REM sleep, making it easier for the mind to detect cueing signals. Finally, master indirect techniques before making use of cueing technologies to attain dream consciousness and subsequent phase entrance.

WORKING IN PAIRS

Working in pairs is considered the second most effective non-autonomous method of entering the phase. One practitioner is to be the active one, and the other fills the role of helper. The active practitioner attempts to enter the phase while the helper provides various types of support to this end.

For example, the active practitioner lies down in bed while the helper stays nearby, waiting for the active one to fall asleep. When sleep occurs, the helper observes the eyes of the active, watching for the signs of REM sleep, which is mainly characterized by quick eye movements. When REM is apparent, the helper whispers to the sleeper, communicating that everything the practitioner is experiencing is a dream. The helper may vary the volume of the whisper, use touch to strengthen the signal, or shine a flashlight on the sleeper's eyelids – which is very effective.

The active practitioner should detect the signals without waking and indicate a state of conscious awareness by performing quick, cyclical eye movements. If no such indication is given, the helper continues to rouse the active practitioner, who may finally wake.

If the active practitioner is unable to stay in the dream, indirect techniques should be performed. The active practitioner should under no circumstances move upon awakening or waste valuable seconds before transitioning to indirect attempts. If phase entrance does not occur after exercising the techniques, the practitioner should again fall asleep with the intention of making another attempt.

Generally, several such attempts are enough to glean results. Working in pairs is best performed just prior to a daytime nap, or with the same deferred method used for indirect techniques - an early-morning interruption of a practitioner's nighttime sleep.

TECHNOLOGIES FOR INDUCING THE PHASE

The ambition to create a device that facilitates quick and easy phase entrance has led to the appearance of assorted technologies that claim to fulfill such a role. As already stated, none of these devices has been proven effective.

The most famous of these is the Hemi-Sync system, which purports to synchronize the two hemispheres of the brain. Hemi-Sync was developed by Robert Monroe, an American esotericism expert and researcher. The idea behind Hemi-Sync is that out-of-body sensations may be induced by achieving synchronization of the brain's two hemispheres. However, this type of approach yields a paradox for the lack of scientific (or pseudo-scientific) evidence that hemispheric synchronization influences sensory perception. Actually, it is the cerebral cortex and constituents that are primarily responsible for sensory perception. At the beginning of the 20th century, it became clear that the key roles in sensory processes are played by varying levels of inhibition and activity in the cerebral cortex. Synchronization devices have no effect on the operation of the cerebral cortex.

The idea of using sounds of various frequencies to induce a specific level of electrical activity in the brain is, so far, considered impossible. Thus, the sounds and noises used to assist separation from the body cannot directly affect the process, but merely serve as cueing signals. Such a system works only after having been used for a long time, if it works at all. Moreover, it might only work once or twice. Usually, it never works at all. Nevertheless, synchronization systems are able to help practitioners reach a free floating state of consciousness since the systems prevent sleep or induce wakefulness, providing fertile ground for direct phase entry.

The idea of inducing various phase states through sound has gained wide attention. Many other programs and technologies have appeared as a result, including, for example, the Brain Wave Generator (BWG), which allows the practitioner to independently experiment with a wide array of sounds and frequencies and various methods of transmission. The effect is the same: cueing during sleep or the maintenance of a transitional state. Thus, there is no noticeable difference between using machines and listening to similar sounds or musical compositions.

Inasmuch as the devices described above have not delivered notable result, the search for new technologies continues unhindered. The number of ideas for exerting noninvasive influence over the brain and its constituent parts is increasing. For example, there is a theory that phase experiences may be induced by electromagnetically stimulating the left angular gyrus. However, this, like all other non-autonomous methods, is strictly based on theory. At present, consistent, focused, and unassisted practice is the simplest and only guaranteed means to achieving phase entrance.

HYPNOSIS AND SUGGESTION

Hypnosis is a little-studied method of entering the phase. The idea is that a hypnotist is able to cause a person to enter the phase through suggestion or affirmation. There is no doubt that hypnosis is an interesting concept, especially for persons who easily yield to power of suggestion. However, such individuals account for only 1% of the population.

Due to specific characteristics of human perception, the chances are nil that hypnosis is a likely conduit to phase entrance. So, it seems unlikely that hypnotic techniques will become well-known, or that a top-notch hypnotist would, through suggestion, easily be able to lead a subject directly into the phase.

However, it is completely feasible that hypnotic suggestion may promote increased frequency of dream consciousness or awakening without moving (and remembering to do indirect techniques). Here again, this method is only a facilitator, while actual phase entrance depends on the efforts of the practitioner.

PHYSIOLOGICAL SIGNALS

The simplest way to supplement the practice is establishing a reminder that prompts conscious awakening and subsequent indirect techniques. This may be accomplished by blindfolding the eyes or tying a cord taut around an arm or leg. The idea is that the reminder is immediately felt when the practitioner wakes, prompting the attempt of indirect techniques. In actuality, mind-machines work using the same principle since these are most effective as cues that arouse an intention to perform a specific action.

A more sophisticated example of a reminder is when a practitioner dozes off in a position meant to cause numbness to a certain body part. While awakening, the practitioner will take the physical numbness as a cue to practice indirect techniques. A secondary benefit to this method of physiological signaling is that the numb body part may easily be used to perform phantom wiggling. Falling asleep while lying on the back with an arm behind the head, or by lying directly on an arm are effective examples. These and other postures will impede circulation, cause numbness, and promote awakening. Naturally, the numbness should not be excessive.

Diverse experiments that exploit physiological needs are especially popular for inducing conscious awakening or becoming conscious while dreaming. For example, a practitioner may forgo water over the course of the day before attempting to enter the phase. The effect is an acute thirst while dreaming, which may be used to communicate that the dream state has taken over. Or, thirst causes repeated awakenings, during which the practice of indirect techniques may commence. An alternative to depriving the body of water is including more salt in foods consumed before going to sleep.

Another method is to drink a lot of water before sleep, causing the practitioner to awaken, naturally producing an opportunity to perform indirect techniques. Using this has been known to result in dream consciousness.

Another popular method helps with direct techniques. It works by falling asleep while keeping the forearm propped up at the elbow. When the practitioner falls asleep, the forearm falls to the bed as the body shuts down. Feeling the arm fall signals a lapse of consciousness, after which direct techniques may be attempted. If this method fails to produce results on the first try, it may be repeated by raising the forearm before falling asleep again. This method helps some, but rarely on the first try. It should not be counted on as panacea.

Like all other non-autonomous methods, practicing phase entrance using physiological signals should not be done on a regular basis. There are more pleasant, autonomous techniques that only require natural willpower and healthy desire.

THE COFFEE METHOD

Out of all of the substances used for practicing the phase, only coffee is readily obtainable. However, it should only be taken by novices who sleep too hard. For everyone else, there's no sense in using it, as one's practice should be natural.

The essence of the this tactic is to use the deferred method in conjunction with taking coffee. For example: a practitioner sleeps for 6 hours, gets up, drinks coffee, and goes back to sleep with the intention of catching the next awakening in order to use indirect techniques or in expectation of becoming consciousness while dreaming. Thanks to coffee's invigorating properties, one will be at a higher state of awareness during subsequent awakenings, and awakenings themselves will be more frequent. There will also be a high likelihood of becoming consciousness while dreaming.

While some hold it's best to take a double dose of the drink, such things are purely individual, and everyone has to find what works for them. Some enjoy the same level of success when drinking black tea instead of coffee.

CHEMICAL SUBSTANCES

Since the beginning, the history of advances in phase entrance methodologies has included a direct link to the use of consumable supplements, starting with plants and mushrooms in ancient times. The use of specialized herbs, mushrooms, and cacti is still practiced in isolated cultures: Siberian shamans and North American Indians, for example. Amid the hunger for altered states of awareness, these chemical supplements have reached every corner of the developed world. However, the proliferation of these substances has caused a marked degradation in the progress of modern phase practice.

The names and descriptions of these various chemical concoctions, herbs and plants included, are not worthy of inclusion in this text. They are officially considered illegal in some countries while still available in the pharmacies of others; nevertheless, they are all dangerous.

There are two primary problems with using such supplements. First, practicing the phase through the consumption of chemical substances and various herbal supplements is not a path to development, but to ruin. Drug abuse and personal development are polar opposites, in no way compatible. Cheap thrills are consistently followed by chemical dependencies and health problems.

Second, although a user may experience phase sensations under the influence of such substances, the quality of experience is completely different. It is not only the stability or depth of the phase that are affected by these supplements, but also a user's consciousness and awareness. The use of substances and the resultant alteration of mental processes negatively impact self-awareness. The phase must be accompanied by two things: out-of-body sensations and a complete, conscious awareness. If one of these is missing, then the state experienced, by definition, is not the phase. When descriptions of these chemically "enhanced" experiences are studied, the hallmark of every one is a complete lack of control.

Using any type of chemical or herbal substance to reach the phase must be ruled out. Summarily, these make it impossible to experience the phase and ultimately destroy physical and mental health.

THE FUTURE OF NON-AUTONOMOUS METHODS FOR ENTERING THE PHASE

Even though no beneficial non-autonomous technologies currently exist, the future is wide open for them.

With the development of effective technologies, the phase will cease to be the exclusive domain of the initiated and become a widespread practice. Only then will the (sometimes justified) stereotypes and prejudices connected to the mystical nature of the phenomenon be dispelled, and only then will the phase gain the necessary attention from researchers needed to ably develop the science of phase practice.

When externally applied methods that cause phase entrance are discovered, the human experience will drastically change. Those technologies for inducing and monitoring phase experiences will open up incredible possibilities. For example, it will be possible to participate in a movie instead of just watching it; people will be able to try and evaluate products without leaving home; travel throughout designed worlds will take place; computer games will be substituted with analogous experiences including real physical sensations.

The ultimate step would be the unification of phase experiences into a collective, parallel world integrated to existent digital networks: the Matrix (the Mindnet). Using this Matrix, it will be possible to communicate with someone on the other side of the planet - not just through a broadband video link, but literally *tête à tête*.

This vision of the future is a drop in the ocean of possibilities that will open with phase entrance technologies. The first step toward the future is a thorough, pragmatic, and correct application of the techniques now available.

TYPICAL MISTAKES WITH NON-AUTONOMOUS TECHNIQUES

- The belief that devices are able to cause phase entrance if autonomous techniques fail, even though it is much easier to enter the phase through strictly individual efforts.
- Wasting a large amount of time and effort on various technologies to create a phase state.
- Using cueing technologies on a daily basis, even though they aren't supposed to be used more than twice a week.
- Using cueing technologies all night long, when it is much better to use these in conjunction with the deferred method.
- Using cueing technologies without affirming a personal intention of appropriate reaction to the signals: this is crucial to cue effectiveness.
- Working in pairs during the first hours of nighttime sleep, even though REM sleep occurs infrequently during them, and at that for only short periods of time.

- While working in pairs, the helper giving an active practitioner too strong a signal. Signals should be kept discreet to prevent waking the sleeper.
- Employing an amateur hypnotist to increase the frequency of dream consciousness.
- The use of hypnotic suggestion on a practitioner who is not susceptible to hypnosis.
- Using physiological signals on a daily basis and thus causing physical discomfort versus getting enjoyment out of the practice.
- The belief that chemical substances are the normal path to dissociative experiences. Acting on this belief is equivalent to drug abuse.

EXERCISES

Questions

1. Are techniques based on breathing be considered non-autonomous methods of entering the phase?
2. Which non-autonomous and non-chemical means allow phase entrance after the first attempts?
3. Why is it still not possible to create a device that causes phase entry?
4. Are cueing technologies beneficial to overcoming difficulties with conscious awakening?
5. What happens if a practitioner uses cueing technologies for seven days in a row?
6. Can cueing technologies make use of light signals?
7. Can feasting on peanuts before sleep help the process of phase entry?
8. Will putting a tight rubber band around an ankle promote phase entry?
9. While working in a pair, are both practitioners required to enter the phase?

10. Can the helper be compared to a cueing device while working in a pair?
11. When should the helper give the signal that the active practitioner is dreaming?
12. Would a hypnotist making suggestions about entering the phase be helpful to every practitioner?
13. Why do phase-inducing technologies sometimes work, even though these are based on flawed theories?
14. What is absent in a phase induced by chemical substances?

Managing the Out-of-Body Experience

Chapter 6 – Deepening

THE CONCEPT OF DEEPENING

Deepening refers to techniques that induce realistic perception and awareness in the phase state.

The phase is not an exact, fixed state where a practitioner is either present or not. It is a realm of states characterized by a transition from the usual perception of the physical body to a complete alienation from it, while maintaining consciousness and reality of perception, albeit in a different frame of space. The transition begins with perception of the natural, physical body followed by a moment of ambiguity where a clear experience of body is intermingled with a sense of the perceived body. Afterward, the perceived body enters the phase space, while the physical body becomes a memory. At this point, the perceived senses may be quite dull; for example, vision may be blurred or completely absent. Deepening techniques solve the problem of diminished or absent sensory perception in the phase.

Sensory experiences within a fully realized phase experience are as realistic as those in everyday reality. In almost one-half of all cases, practitioners observe that reality-based surroundings pale in comparison to the vibrant detail and color of the phase space. To this end, after entering the phase, a practitioner must perform deepening techniques to enhance and solidify the degree and quality of phase reality.

Clarity of Perception and Phase Space at Various Stages of Phase Depth

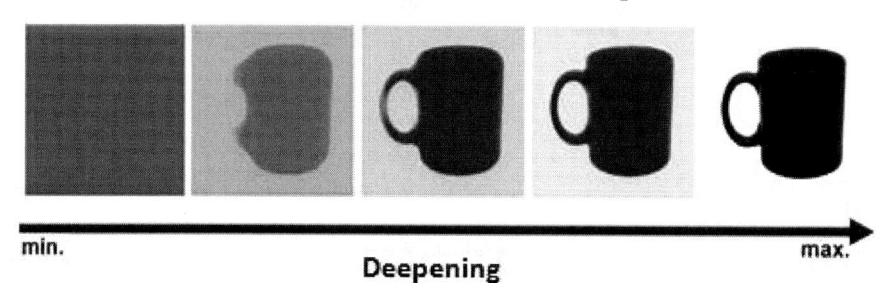

min. ──────────────────────── max.
Deepening

Full spatial perception in the phase only occurs after deepening techniques have been applied. There would be no point to remaining in the phase without deepening. For example, what is the point in finding a person in phase, if it is not even possible to discern his or her eyes there?

In a considerable number of cases, deepening is not necessary, since the phase experience is completely realistic, if not hyper-realistic. In cases like these, deepening may be bypassed.

Deepening is also related to the length of time a practitioner may remain in the phase. If an action is taken without a deep, realistic phase, the experience will always be several times shorter in duration than a phase where deepening techniques had been applied. The properties of the phase space very much depend on its depth. When surroundings are blurry and unclear, the stability of objects is very weak.

There is a direct correlation between the realism of a phase and a practitioner's level of awareness, so it is extremely important to ensure a deep phase in order to promote maximum awareness.

Interesting Fact!

The realism of a deep phase space is often so great that it causes uncontrollable fear or shock.

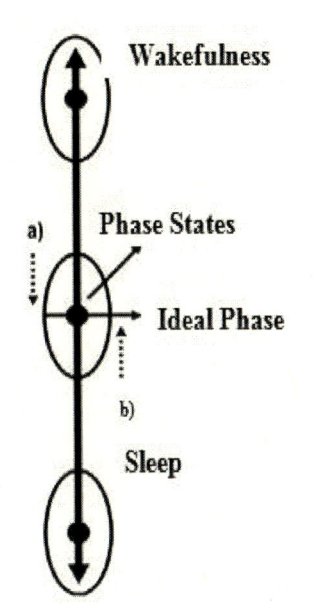

Phase deepening consists of:

a) increasing the clarity and realism of the phase space
b) increasing of the level of background awareness

Deepening should only be performed following complete separation from the body. If initiated before separation, the phase may end prematurely. If complete separation does not occur, primary deepening should be used. As regards the deepening techniques themselves, there is one main one and there are several subsidiary ones. The main technique, which does not present any difficulties, is sufficient for having a successful practice.

Interesting Fact!
Ignorance of deepening techniques has led to a great number of baseless theories and superstitions. Some practices treat differing phase depths as various states and even worlds. In reality, there are simple actions that ensure a singular phase experience.

PRIMARY DEEPENING TECHNIQUES

The goal of primary deepening is to achieve complete separation from the body, allowing further actions within the phase. Primary deepening entails achieving two principal objectives: complete separation from the physical body and anchoring the perceived body within the phase space.

When separation from the body occurs through the use of a separation technique, a posture must be assumed that is completely different from the posture of the real, physical body. The greater the degree of postural similarity between the physical and perceived bodies, the more shallow and brief the phase will be. For example, in the case of horizontal levitation, a 90· turn must immediately be performed, arms and legs spread, adopting a vertical posture. Under no circumstances should a practitioner in the phase remain in a posture identical to that of the physical body.

If a practitioner is pulled back toward the body after separation, anchoring should be initiated that facilitates standing or sitting in the phase. Resisting the gravity of the physical body is paramount to remaining in the phase. The result of willful resistance is directly proportional to the degree of applied effort. It will help to grab hold of surrounding objects and hold on to them; any means of anchoring the perceived body within the phase are appropriate. It is possible to start rotating around an axis; not simply imagining the rotation, but performing it with the perceived body as well.

DEEPENING THROUGH SENSORY AMPLIFICATION

The more a phase is experienced by the sensory faculties, the deeper and longer the phase will be. Sensory amplification in the phase is the most effective deepening technique precisely because it allows the activation of primary internal sensations during the transition from reality to the phase. There are several ways to perform sensory amplification.

Palpation is the first deepening technique that should be recalled when entering the phase.

Vision may be absent at the beginning of a phase experience, but the sensation of occupying a defined space is almost always present. In the case of a completely absent sense of sight, only tactile-kinesthetic perception is possible. That is, movement throughout a space and touching objects there is the only option when vision is absent. The sense of touch plays a key role in the perception of everyday reality. This is eloquently demonstrated by Penfield's cortical homunculus featuring the parts of the body that correspond to cortices of the brain responsible for their operation. It demonstrates how our actual self-perception is completely disproportional to the size of parts of the body. Accordingly, if the sense of touch is actively used in the phase space, it is only natural that the phase will deepen and reach its maximum potential.

Penfield's Cortical Homunculus

Palpation is performed by fleetingly touching anything that may be found in the immediate surroundings. This should be done by quickly but carefully perceiving the feel of surfaces and shapes. Hands should not remain on a particular place for more than one second, remaining constantly in motion to locate new objects. The goal of palpation is to touch and also to learn something about encountered objects or shapes. For example, if one feels a mug, one may touch it not only from the outside, but also from the inside. Once a practitioner has rolled out of the body, the bed may be touched, as well as the floor, the carpet, nearby walls, or a bedside table.

Another palpation technique is performed by rubbing the palms against each other as if trying to warm them on a cold day. Blowing on the palms also produces sensations that will help deepen the phase. Since tactile perception of the world is not limited to the palms, the hands should be moved over the entire body while in the phase to excite and fully activate the sense of touch.

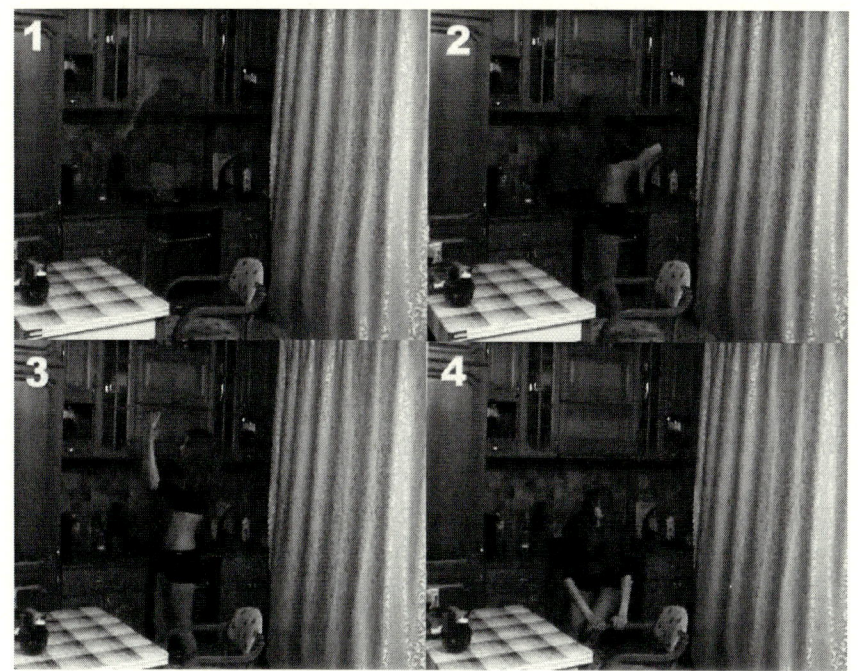

As soon as palpation begins, the feeling that the phase is deepening and becoming fixed soon follows. Usually, it takes five to 10 seconds of palpation exercises to reach the maximum level of deepening. After performing this technique, the pseudo-physical sensations will be indistinguishable from those of everyday reality. If vision is absent on phase entry, it quickly emerges during palpation.

Peering is the primary technical variation of sensory amplification. However, it is not always initially accessible since it requires vision, which may begin as absent in the phase. Once vision appears or has been created using special techniques (see Chapter 8), peering may begin. The effectiveness of this technique originates in the fact that vision is the human's primary instrument of perception. Therefore, by exciting vision to its maximum potential within the phase, it is possible to attain a fully immersive phase state that is completely apart from normal reality.

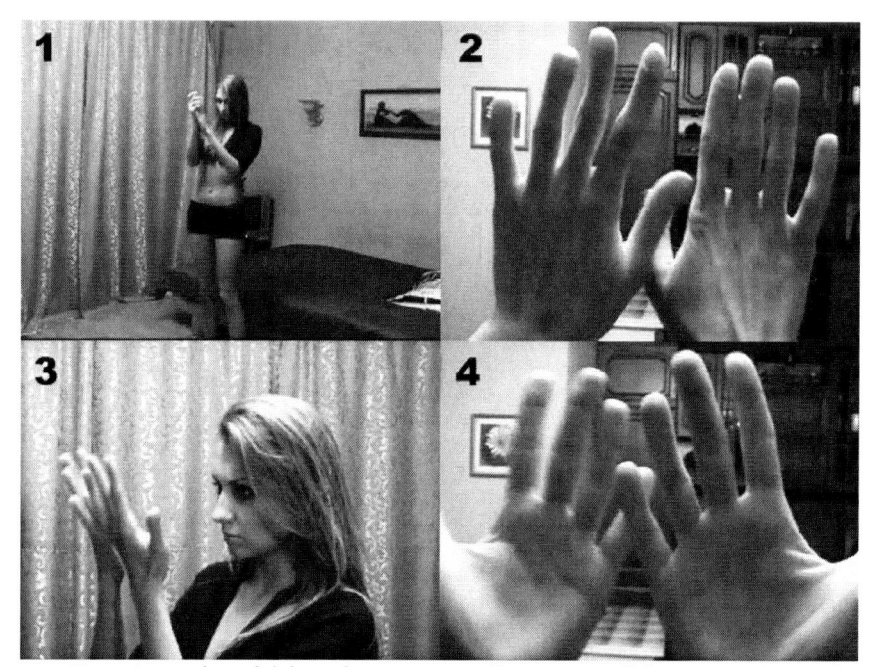

Peering should be done at a distance of four to six inches from objects within the phase. A practitioner should glance over the minute details of objects and surfaces to bring definition to the phase space while increasing the quality of vision. When looking at hands, the lines of the palm or the fingernail and cuticles should be examined. If observing a wall, study the texture of its wallpaper. When looking at a mug, one should look carefully at its handle, the curve of its rim, or any inscriptions. Attention should not remain on one area of an object for more than half a second. Active observation should constantly move to new objects and their minute details, approaching objects or picking them up to draw them nearer. It's best when objects are near one another; otherwise, too much time is spent moving around.

Peering brings quick and clear results. Usually, if vision is blurry and there is a yearning to return into the physical body, with just 3-10 seconds of peering all of this will be gone without a trace. After peering, vision adjusts as quickly and clearly as if a camera lens was correctly installed in front of the eyes, capturing the image in the sharpest of focus.

Simultaneous peering and palpation provide the maximum possible deepening effect in the phase. This method of sensory amplification engages the two most important perceptions, thus the effect is twice greater than when the two actions are separately performed. If vision is present in the phase, simultaneous peering and palpation is an absolute necessity because it facilitates good phase depth in the quickest and simplest manner.

The combination of palpation and peering must not only be performed simultaneously, but also upon the same objects. For example, a practitioner may look at his hands and simultaneously rub them against each other; or while looking at a coffee mug, all of its parts may be observed and touched at the same time. It is necessary to maintain dynamism of action, remembering that feelings should be experienced not half-heartedly, and remembering that full concentration on sensory amplification is an excellent means to a deep, quality phase.

Palpation and peering should be performed not only simultaneously, but preferably also on the same objects. For example, when scrutinizing your hands, you can also rub them together at the same time. When scrutinizing a mug, you should simultaneously palpate all of its features, and vice-versa. Also keep the action dynamic and obtain sensations engagingly, and not "for the sake of appearances".

Sensory amplification comes intuitively when you remember a simple rule: if some sensations are lacking or if one of the five senses is dull and vague, then that sense needs to be heightened as much as possible using the phase space. The previously lacking sensation will become intense and highly-charged. In case of dim vision, for example, one ought to scrutinize something more and more fixedly from a close distance. When experiencing weak bodily perception, palpate your body and move it in as many different ways as you can.

SECONDARY DEEPENING TECHNIQUES

Diving Headfirst

Diving headfirst is used if sensory amplification techniques do not work, or when the practitioner in the phase is located in an undefined space where there is nothing to touch or look at. This technique works thanks to the unusual vestibular sensations that it causes, which help to enhance perception. This technique is performed with the eyes shut if vision is available and the practitioner literally dives headfirst into the floor or space at the feet. A feeling of movement away from the physical body will immediately arise during the flight down, and the dive itself will be experienced as if it is really happening. Simultaneously, the surrounding space may darken and become colder. Agitation or fear may also appear. After 5 to 15 seconds of flight, the practitioner either arrives in an undetermined place in the phase or hits a dead end, like a wall. In the case of a dead end, a translocation technique should be used. Translocation may also be attempted if deepening does not occur during the flight, if sense perception stops improving, or if a good degree of realism has already been achieved. An alternative to the translocation technique: hold the hands about four to six inches in front of the face and try to observe them without opening the eyes; this will move the practitioner to another random location.

When falling headfirst, do not think about the floor; assume that it will be penetrated. This very effective if the phase has not reached a fullness of depth.

A desire to not simply fall down observing one's perceptions, but instead race swiftly downward while trying to move away from the body is extremely important. In case of failure to do so, instead of deepening, such a fall may lead to a return to the state of being awake, i.e. to a foul.

Vibration

Like falling headfirst, the vibration technique should be used if sensory amplification techniques do not work, or when the practitioner in the phase is located in an undefined space where there is nothing to touch or look at. This technique works thanks to the unusual vestibular sensations that it causes, which help to enhance perception.

After separating from the body, it is normally quite easy to create vibrations by thinking about them, by straining the brain, or by straining the body without using muscles. The occurrence of vibrations provides a significant opportunity to deepen the phase. An advantage of this technique is that it does not require any preliminary actions and thus may be practiced at any moment.

The brain is strained to the maximum extent possible, which causes vibrations that may be intensified and managed through spasmodic or prolonged straining.

If this technique does not produce deepening after 5 to 10 seconds, the technique has to be changed or action should be taken at the practitioner's current depth in the phase.

Aggressive Action

This technique may be used as an alternative to any other deepening technique since it can be used at any moment. Practicing this technique only requires aggressive action of the perceived body. A practitioner may run, roll on the floor, perform gymnastics, or move the arms and legs. Maximum activity and aggression are paramount to the successful use of this technique.

If the practitioner is stuck in a dark space, waving the arms and legs from side to side is appropriate. If the practitioner is in water, swimming with determined, powerful strokes would be suitable recourse. The type of action very much depends on the specific situation along with an aggressive desire on the part of the practitioner.

As a rule, the effect of such movements and relocations comes quite quickly, especially if attention is focused on all the accompanying sensations.

Imagining Reality

This interesting technique should be used by experienced practitioners, or if all other deepening techniques fail.

A practitioner aggressively imagines being located in the physical world, experiencing its intrinsic reality of perception, and not in the phase. This should be done while in a state of separation from the body with a sense of vision present. If successful, the surrounding phase space will immediately brighten and sensory perception of the phase will exceed the normal experience of reality.

If this technique produces no clear results after a few seconds, another technique should be used.

GENERAL ACTIVITY

All deepening techniques should be practiced with a high level of aggression, and with no pauses, only continuous, deliberate action. If techniques are practiced in a calm, relaxed manner, then deepening attempts will most often result in falling asleep or returning to the body.

Any deepening technique should be performed quite intensely. The entire process should be somewhat hurried and aggressive. There should be no pause, but only active, fluid, and concentrated effort, preferably coupled with constant maneuver and movement around the space one is in.

In addition, it should be kept in mind that no deepening technique should be performed "as a chore", but with the intense desire and intention of deepening. If this is done, the techniques will be start to be performed in an ideal way. The phaser must try no matter what to merge into the phase world with all of his senses- it will become all the more realistic.

Interesting Fact!
There are known cases of certain swear words being used as a deepening technique to help express out one's intention to deepen. Such an approach may be used during phase entrance in order to maintain and control the phase space.

TYPICAL MISTAKES DURING DEEPENING

- Forgetting to perform deepening techniques when necessary.
- Halting deepening techniques before reaching maximum realism in the phase.
- Carrying out unnecessary deepening while at a sufficient depth.
- Carrying out main deepening techniques prior to having become completely separated from the body, although at this time only primary deepening should be used.
- Continuing deepening techniques when results have already been achieved.
- Alternating too quickly between deepening techniques instead of concentrating on each of them for at least 5 to 10 seconds.
- Performing the techniques slowly and calmly instead of aggressively.
- Observing objects located too far from the eyes during visual sensory amplification instead of the required four to five inches.
- When peering, scrutinizing a single detail of an object for too long when it is necessary to quickly switch from one detail to another.
- Taking in a whole object when peering while only parts of it should be observed.

- Concentrating too long on the details of a single object instead of focusing on different objects in quick succession.
- Long palpation of a single object during sensory amplification instead of rapidly switching from one object to another.
- Deepening while standing in place when it is important to maintain constant motion.
- Falling headfirst with the eyes open, although the eyes must be shut to avoid crashing into the floor.
- Falling headfirst without the desire or intention of falling far and quickly.
- Forgetting to use translocation techniques after hitting a dead end.
- Forgetting to alternate deepening techniques if some of them are not working.
- Fear of the hyperrealism of the experience and halting deepening instead of calmly continuing with the technique.

EXERCISES

Questions

1. After which phase entrance techniques is deepening necessary?
2. Why is phase deepening necessary?
3. Are there cases where phase deepening is unnecessary?
4. What level of reality should be achieved by deepening?
5. When should deepening begin after entering the phase?
6. Does deepening influence the length of a phase experience?
7. Why is primary deepening necessary?
8. May one touch one's head when the performing sensory amplification?
9. Should a practitioner look at curtains while peering?

10. Is it effective to apply peering at phase objects from a distance of 1 to 1.5 yards?
11. Can peering be used during palpation?
12. When should the eyes be closed while falling headfirst?
13. Would throwing punches like a boxer help a practitioner to deepen?
14. How calmly should the deepening techniques be performed?

Tasks

1. Devote the next three successful phases to perfecting deepening techniques, using all of the methods described in this chapter.
2. Try judging which technique suits you best from personal experience.

Chapter 7 – Maintaining

THE GENERAL CONCEPT OF MAINTAINING

Phase maintenance or "maintaining" refers to techniques that allow a practitioner to remain in the phase for the maximum amount of time possible. Without knowledge of "maintaining" techniques, the duration of the phase will be several times shorter than it could otherwise be. The shortest phases last just a few seconds. Beginning practitioners usually fear not being able to exit a phase; this shouldn't ever be a concern because the real challenge is being able to maintain the phase state, which is easily lost unless phase maintenance techniques are used.

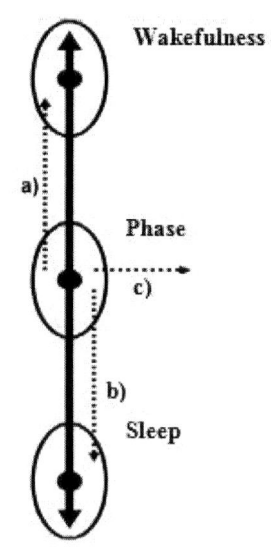

Staying In the Phase Consists of:

a) resisting ejection into wakefulness
b) resisting falling asleep
c) resisting an unrecognized phase

Phase maintenance consists of three primary principles: resisting a return to the wakeful state (known as a foul), resisting falling asleep, and resisting a false exit from the phase.

Resistance to returning to the body is self-explanatory, whereas resistance to falling asleep is unclear to many. Not everyone knows that almost half of phase experiences usually end in a quite trivial way - falling asleep. A person usually loses attentiveness, his or her awareness dissipates, and everything around gradually loses clarity and turns into what is for all intents and purposes a usual dream.

Resisting a false exit from the phase (false awakenings) is a lot more surprising and dramatic. Sometimes a practitioner detects an impending exit from the phase and subsequent deepening techniques fail to work, resulting in what seems to be a return to the body and physical reality. Sure that the phase has ended, a practitioner may stand up and then fall asleep after perceiving a few steps. In such cases, falling asleep most often happens without any movement, but while still lying in bed. The problem is that the difference between the phase and reality can be so subtle that in terms of internal or external indicators, the phase practically can't be distinguished from reality. Therefore, one must know the necessary actions to take in the event that the phase ceases, since the end of a phase could actually be a trick and purely imagined.

There are specific solutions for the three problems described in addition to general rules that apply to any phase experience. Studying these rules should be given just as high a priority as studying the specific solutions, since only some of them, when applied separately, may help one to remain in the phase several times longer than usual.

In some cases, techniques for maintaining are not applicable. However, knowledge of how to maintain is useful for the majority of experiences. Also, there might be situations when someone need only resist a foul, while someone else may need to resist falling asleep. All of this is very specific to each case and can be determined only in practice.

With perfect knowledge of all the techniques for maintaining, a phase may last two to four minutes, which doesn't sound like an extended duration, but really is. A particularity of the phase space is that achieving something and moving around in it takes a minimum amount of time, mere seconds. Thus, so much can be done during 3 minutes in the phase that one literally needs a list, so as not to waste any time.

There are theories that have neither been proven nor disproven claiming that time in the phase contracts and expands relative to real time. Thus, one minute of real time while in the phase may feel much longer in terms of phase time.

Perception of time varies from practitioner to practitioner. Novices especially perceive a real minute as more like 5 to 10 minutes in the phase. This is determined by the particularities of individual psychology, state of mind, and the type of events that occur in the phase.

In order to understand how long a phase really lasted, one does not need to try using a stopwatch in the real world. It is better to count how many actions took place in it and how much time each of them could have taken. The result will differ from one's first rough estimate several times over.

The maximum duration of the phase depends heavily on the ability to apply phase maintenance techniques. Some practitioners have difficulty breaking the two-minute barrier while some find it easy to remain in the phase for 10 minutes or longer. It is physically impossible to remain in the phase forever because even a 20-minute phase is unheard of.

TECHNIQUES AND RULES AGAINST RETURNING TO THE BODY

Of the following techniques, constant sensory amplification and as-needed sensory amplification are applied the most often while performing phase maintenance. However, unlike with other technical elements of phase exploration, secondary techniques of maintaining often become the most used and the most appropriate for certain individuals. Thus, all the techniques should be studied, but the first two should be considered very carefully.

Constant Sensory Amplification
The same sensory amplification described in the chapter on deepening (Chapter 6) also applies to "maintaining". In essence, having achieved the necessary depth of phase, one should not stop to actively agitate his or her perception, but should keep on doing this all the while, albeit not as actively as during deepening.

The idea is that during the entire duration of the phase, all action should be focused on experiencing the maximum possible amount of tactile-kinesthetic and visual perceptions. This entails constantly touching and examining everything in minute detail. For example, if passing by a bookcase, touch and examine some of the books in it, including their pages and corners. Tactile observation should be performed on every encountered object.

Palpation may be applied separately as a background sensation. This is done in order not to overload the sense of sight. The hands should be touching something all the time, or better still, rubbing each other.

As-Needed Sensory Amplification
Applying the as-needed sensory amplification technique is no different than constant sensory amplification. It is used only when a foul (a return to a wakeful state) is imminent or when phase vision starts to blur and fade. For example, while traveling in the phase everything may start to blur, signaling a weakening of the phase. At this moment, the practitioner should touch every available object and observe everything in

fine detail. As soon as everything returns to a clear and realistic state, actions may be continued without needing to perform amplification.

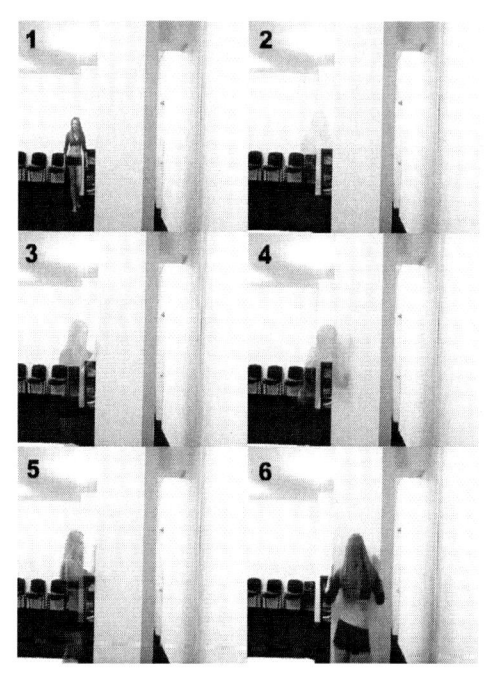

Constant Vibration
This technique is used to maintain constant, strong vibrations in the phase. As previously noted, vibrations are generated by straining the brain or tensing the body without using muscles. Maintaining strong vibrations will have a positive effect on the length of the phase.

Strengthening Vibrations as Needed
In this case, vibrations are created and strengthened only if signs of a foul become apparent. Examples of foul indicators include duality of perception or blurred vision. Strengthening vibrations will help to deepen the phase, allowing a practitioner to stay and continue within the phase.

Diving Headfirst

This technique is the same as the deepening technique of the same name. If a phase is about to dissolve, dive headfirst with the eyes shut and a desire to dive as quickly and deeply as possible. As soon as phase depth returns, translocation techniques may be used to keep from arriving at a dead end.

Forced Falling Asleep

As soon as indicators of a foul appear, immediately lie down on the floor and attempt forced falling asleep; the same as the phase entry technique. After successfully performing the technique (3-10sec.) , a practitioner may get up and continue to travel through the phase since the perception of reality and its depth will most likely be restored. Resist actually fall asleep.

Rotation

If indicators of a foul appear, the practitioner should start rotating around the head-to-feet axis. Unlike the phase entry technique of the same name, the movement does not have to be imagined. This is an absolutely real rotation in the phase. After several revolutions, depth will be restored and actions may be continued. If indicators of a foul persist, rotation should continue until proper depth is achieved.

Counting

During the entire phase, count to as large a number possible - not just for the sake of counting, but with a strong desire to reach the highest number possible. Counting may be performed silently or out loud.

This technique works by creating a strong determination to remain in the phase by providing a goal that requires action in the phase.

Listening in

If there are any background sounds similar to those heard while entering the phase - rumbling, whistling, ringing, buzzing, or sizzling – these sounds may be used to prolong duration of the phase by aggressive attempts at listening in, hearing the entire range of internal sounds. The forced listening in technique may also be used for phase maintenance.

Hooking onto the phase

Another interesting method of "maintaining" is hooking onto the phase. In the event of an impending foul, grab onto an object in the phase actively palpate or squeeze it. Even if a return to the body occurs during this technique, the hands will continue to hold the phase object and the physical hands will not be perceived. Beginning with these phantom feelings in the hands, separation from the body is possible. Any nearby object may be hooked: the leg of a chair, a drinking glass, a doorknob, a stone, or a stick. If there is nothing to grab hold of, clasp the hands together or bite down on a lip or the tongue.

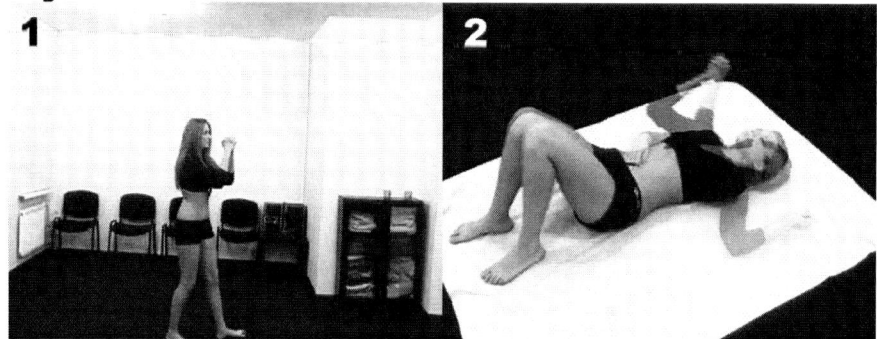

Two rules apply to using the techniques that help to resist a phase exit. First of all, never think that the phase might end and result in a return to the body; thoughts like this are like programming that immediately send the practitioner to a wakened physical state. Secondly, do not think about the physical body. Doing so will also instantly return the practitioner to the body, every time.

TECHNIQUES AND RULES FOR RESISTING FALLING ASLEEP

Constant Understanding of the Possibility of Falling Asleep

Most of the time, falling asleep while in the phase can be overcome by a constant awareness that sleep is possible and detrimental to a continued phase. A practitioner must always consider the probability of falling asleep and actions must be carefully analyzed to ensure that they are based on real desires and not on the paradoxical notions common to dreams.

Periodic Analysis of Awareness

Periodically asking the question, "Am I dreaming?" while in the phase helps appraise situations and the quality of the actions being performed at any moment. If everything meets the standards of full phase awareness, actions may be continued. Asked on a regular basis, this question becomes habit automatically used while transitioning to the phase state. If you keep asking this question regularly, sooner or later it will arise automatically at the moment when you are actually transitioning into a dream. This will then help one to "wake up", after which it is possible to continue to remain in a full-fledged phase.

The frequency of the question should be based on a practitioner's ability to consistently remain in the phase. If a phase usually lasts five to 10 minutes or more, it is not necessary to ask the question more than once every 2 minutes; otherwise, this question has to be asked frequently, literally once a minute, or just a little less often.

Be Observer

There is another important rule related to resisting falling asleep: no practitioner should engage or participate in spontaneous events occurring in the phase. Events that are not planned or deliberate lead to a high probability of being immersed in the side action, which results in a loss of concentrated awareness.

TECHNIQUES AGAINST FALSE AWAKENINGS

Since the techniques for testing the realness of the end of the phase are a little awkward and demand additional attention to actions, they should only be used in those cases when they are indeed required. Until then, one should simply bear them in mind and use them only in moments of doubt. The same methods may be used to safely determine whether or not the practitioner is in the phase when using techniques for entering it.

Hyper-Concentration
Since the cessation of the phase experience may be simulated and no different in terms of perception from a real exit, differences between the physical world and the phase world must be actively discerned. In other words, a practitioner must know how to determine whether a genuine phase exit has occurred.

At present, only one experiment is known almost to guarantee an accurate result. The phase space cannot withstand prolonged close visual attention to the minute details of objects. Within several seconds of acute examination, shapes begin to distort, objects change color, produce smoke, melt, or morph in other ways.

After exiting the phase, look at a small object from a distance of four to six inches, and remain focused on it for 10 seconds. If the object does not change, a practitioner can be assured that the surroundings are reality. If an object is somehow distorted or askew, a practitioner knows that the phase is intact. The simplest option is to look at the tip of the finger since it is always close at hand. It is also possible to take a book and examine its text. Text in the phase will either blur or appear as alphabetical gibberish, or be full of incomprehensible symbols.

Auxiliary Techniques

There are a variety of other procedures to test for the occurrence of a foul. However, since any situation, any quality, or any function can be simulated in the phase, these procedures are not always applicable. For example, some suggest that it is sufficient to attempt doing something that is realistically impossible, and, if a practitioner is in the phase, the impossible action will be possible. The problem with this suggestion is that the laws of the physical world may be simulated in the phase, and so flying, passing through walls or telekinesis may not be possible in even the deepest phase. It has also been suggested that looking at a clock twice in a row may help a practitioner determine whether or not the phase is intact; allegedly, the clock will display a different time each time it is observed. Here again, the clock's display may not change in the phase.

One of the most undeservedly popular reality checks consists of trying to breathe out through a pinched nose. If you are able to do so, consider yourself in the phase. However, if there is serious doubt regarding the nature of the space you are in, this method may yield a false positive over one-third of the time. That is, you may be unable to breathe out through a pinched nose even when in the phase.

Of all the auxiliary procedures, one deserves mention and works in the majority of cases: searching for inconsistencies with reality in the surroundings. Although the usual surroundings of a practitioner may be 100% accurately simulated in the phase, it is very rare. Therefore, it is possible to figure out whether a phase is intact by carefully examining the room where everything is taking place. In the phase, there will be something extra or something will be missing; the time of day or even the season will be inconsistent with reality, and so on. For example, when verifying whether a foul occurred, a room may be missing the table supporting a television set, or the table may be there, but be a different color.

There is also a quite logical method for determining whether or not a practitioner is in the phase. If an experienced practitioner experiences doubt as to whether the phase has really ended, then that one doubt is nearly always sufficient to conclude that everything around is still the phase.

GENERAL RULES FOR MAINTAINING

The rules for maintaining the phase deal with resisting all or most of the problems which cause a phase to end. Some of these rules are capable of increasing the length of stay in the phase by many times and must be followed.

The practitioner should not look into the distance. If faraway objects are observed for a long period of time, a foul may occur, or one may be translocated towards these objects. In order to look at distant objects without problems, a practitioner has to employ techniques for maintaining. For example, from time to time the practitioner should look at his hands, rub them against each other, or maintain strong vibrations.

Constant activity. Under no circumstances should a practitioner remain passive and calm in the phase. The more actions performed, the longer the phase is. The fewer actions – the shorter the phase. It is enough to pause for thought, and everything stops.

Plan of action. There should be a clear plan of action consisting of at least 2-3 tasks to be carried out in the phase at the earliest opportunity. This is necessary for several important reasons. First, the practitioner must not pause in the phase to think about "what to do next", which frequently results in a foul. Second, having a plan, the practitioner will subconsciously perform all of the actions necessary for staying in and maintaining the phase to carry out all the tasks that have been planned. Third, intelligent and pre-planned actions permit focused advancement of purposeful actions versus wasting phase experiences on whatever comes to mind at a given moment. Fourth, a plan of action creates necessary motivation and, consequently, pronounced intent to perform the techniques to enter the phase. In other words, having a clear and very interesting plan of action can substantially increase odds of landing in the phase, sometimes manyfold. Meanwhile, the plan itself should be actually interesting, curious, or extremely important, as well as - and this is vital - specific.

> ***Interesting Fact!***
> *Upon three-day School of Out-of-Body Travel seminars achieving consistently high effectiveness (a 60 - 70% success rate), group success began being evaluated not only by the fact of phase entrance, but also completion of the group's shared plan of action. Up to a third of participants usually achieve both. Such emphasis during training sessions has been able to double the average duration, quality, and frequency of novices' initial attempts.*

Stopping the ID. The less internal dialogue (ID) and reflection that occurs in the phase, the longer it lasts. All thinking must be concentrated on what is being achieved and perceived. Talking to oneself is completely prohibited. The reason for this is that many thoughts may act as programming in the phase and even announcing them internally may introduce alterations, including negative ones. For example, thinking about the body cause a return to it. The practitioner may also get lost in thought, which will lead to a foul. Also, sporadic thoughts usually and quite easily cause the practitioner to simply fall asleep.

Intention. Any technique or method for maintaining the phase must be accompanied by fixed and clear intent to stay in the phase for as long as possible. Sometimes the mere intention of having a long-lasting phase is enough, and no maintaining procedures are necessary.

A practitioner must try to re-enter the phase after experiencing a foul. Always remember that a typical phase experience consists of several repeated entries and exits. Essentially, in most cases it is possible to re-enter the phase through the use of separation or phase state creation techniques immediately after returning to the body. If the practitioner has just left the phase, the brain is still close to it and appropriate techniques may be applied in order to continue the journey.

TYPICAL MISTAKES WITH MAINTAINING

- Forgetting to try to re-enter the phase after it is over, although doing so greatly helps to increase the number of experiences.
- Staying focused on techniques for "maintaining" instead of performing them as background tasks.
- Getting distracted by events and dropping phase maintenance techniques instead of continually performing what's needed to maintain the phase.
- Succumbing to the idea that maintaining is not necessary when the phase appears very deep and stable, even though these could be false sensations.
- Using the necessary techniques too late.
- Stopping due to uncertainty about further actions, while there must always be a plan.
- Forgetting that it is possible to fall asleep in the phase without realizing it. Recognizing the risk of falling asleep must be a primary focus.
- Getting pulled into events occurring in the phase instead of observing and controlling them from the outside.
- Forgetting that techniques for "maintaining" must always be used to remain in as deep a phase as possible, and not just for maintaining any odd state.
- Stopping the use of techniques for "maintaining" during contact with living objects, when the techniques must be used constantly.
- Counting without the desire to count as high as possible.

- Performing imagined rotation instead of real rotation.
- Passiveness and calmness instead of constant activity.
- Excessive thinking and internal dialogue when these should be kept to an absolute minimum.

EXERCISES

Questions

1. What is a foul?
2. What is the minimum duration of the phase?
3. What do phase maintenance ("maintaining") techniques counteract besides fouls and falling asleep?
4. Why might a practitioner think that the phase has ended when it actually is still in progress?
5. Should "maintaining" techniques always be used?
6. What primary techniques work against the occurrence of fouls?
7. How can a practitioner hook onto the phase?
8. While in the phase, what do thoughts about the body lead to?
9. What question should be asked in the phase in order to reduce the probability of falling asleep?
10. What happens to an object during hyper-concentration?
11. How else, apart from hyper-concentration, might a practitioner effectively recognize a false foul?
12. While in the phase, is it permitted to look into the distance for a long time?
13. What is ID and how does the degree of it affect the duration of a phase experience?
14. What should a practitioner always do after an inadvertent return into the body?

Tasks

1. During the next few phases, dedicate yourself to the single goal of maintaining as long as possible, using as many maintaining techniques as you can.
2. Figure out which techniques have proven the most effective and comfortable for you, so that you may use these later.
3. Increase the duration of your average phase to at least 2 minutes (evaluated objectively).

Chapter 8 – Primary skills

THE ESSENCE OF PRIMARY SKILLS

When dealing with a fully-realized phase, requisite knowledge is not limited to entry techniques, deepening and maintenance of the state, translocation, or finding and interacting with objects. In order to feel comfortable, a practitioner has to master or at least acclimate himself to a whole series of techniques to correctly react in any number of situations. For example, a practitioner needs to know how to create vision, if it is absent. Actions including passage through a wall or taking flight in a deep phase do not happen easily, although these actions may be assumed natural occurrences, since the phase exists apart from the physical world. In addition to techniques that allow interaction with the physical setting and surroundings of the phase, methods must learned and applied to counteract fear if it forces a practitioner to consciously and consistently leave the phase.

A practitioner does not have to know all the primary skills by heart, but it is necessary to pay close attention to some of them: emergency return, creation of vision, translocation through objects, and contact with animate objects. For many, skills dedicated to fighting fear will also prove extremely relevant.

The final choice of methods that require added focus on the part of the practitioner must be made on the basis of personal experiences and problems faced while in the phase, since different practitioners often have completely different types of problems.

DISCERNING THE PHASE

Problems with phase identification during entry often arise at the initial stages of studying the phase. A practitioner simply cannot understand whether or not he or she is already in the phase. This uncertainty can manifest while lying down or while practicing in other postures.

If a practitioner is simply lying down, physically perceiving his own body, and doing nothing, then it is indeed difficult to determine whether or not he is present in the phase. It is sufficient to note that there might be no signs of a phase state. On the contrary, there may be a host of signs and unusual sensations, but they by no means necessarily indicate the onset of the phase.

The problem of the uncertainty of a phase state is always solved through actions. If the practitioner is lying down, then standard separation techniques may produce indication of phase achievement - in the majority of cases – since such techniques may often be incorrectly performed.

It is possible to perform techniques that are only achievable in the phase state. If a practitioner stands up and does not recognize his surroundings, then it can be assumed that the practitioner is standing up in the phase. However, often based on the observation that "everything is as in reality", a practitioner may stand up and note that everything is in fact "as in reality" simply because the practitioner is still in "reality". In answer to this dilemma, the phenomenon of hyper-concentration has been previously mentioned in relation to maintaining phase. By using hyper-concentration, it is always possible to ascertain whether the practitioner is in the phase. However, as a rule, hyper-concentration is rarely necessary. Most often, the following signs indicate that separation has occurred in the phase: unusual sensations in the body during movement, extreme tightness during movement, a strong physical urge to lie back down, disjointedness of surroundings, and blurred or complete absence of vision.

Often, the problem resides in the use of direct techniques where the practitioner expects fast results and attempts to determine whether the phase has been achieved. As a principle this should not be done. When using direct techniques, the phase manifests itself clearly; therefore, if an attempt to determine its presence is made, it is an indicator that the phase is quite likely still far off.

EMERGENCY RETURN. PARALYSIS

Statistics show that in one-third of initial phase experiences, a practitioner is faced with a degree of fear that forces a return to the body. Periodically, even experienced practitioners face situations that require an abrupt return to wakefulness. This presents a number of concerns.

In and of itself, returning to the body is almost always unproblematic; remembering and thinking about the body often suffices and within moments the practitioner is returned to the body from whatever location in the phase. Admittedly, it is advisable during this type of situation to shut the eyes and abstain from touching anything. As a rule, when these actions are performed, simply standing up in the physical world is all that is required to complete a return; however, this is not always simply achieved.

Sometimes after reentering the body, the practitioner suddenly realizes that physical functionality has ceased due to the onset of sleep paralysis, or the sensation that the body has been switched off. During sleep paralysis, it is impossible to scream, call for help, or even move a finger. In the majority of cases, it is also impossible to open the eyes. From a scientific point of view, this is a case of an abrupt, unnatural interruption of the rapid eye movement (REM) phase of sleep, during which this paralysis is always present, and it can persist for some time after the phase is interrupted.

This is where it gets interesting. People in the physical world are accustomed to an important rule: if you wish to achieve something, then do it, and do it as actively as possible. This rule, though good, is not always applicable to certain conditions linked to the phase, and applies least of all to exiting the phase. Sometimes extreme effort makes it possible to break through sleep paralysis and resume movement, though most of these efforts tend to exacerbate immobility.

Due to the unusual nature of a negative situation following a deliberate, fear-induced return to the body, the depth of the phase may greatly increase because of the body's natural, protective inhibition of functions originating in the cerebral cortex; this results in even greater agitation and greater fear. The paralysis grows stronger. This is a vicious circle that leads to unpleasant feelings and emotions, which may evaporate any desire to practice the phase.

Ignorance of correct procedures has led to the widespread opinion that such adverse situations may make it impossible to come back from the phase at all. These opinions suppose that it is, therefore, dangerous to get involved with the practice. However, the solution to this problem rests in very simple actions and procedures that can prevent a large number of negative experiences:

Complete Relaxation

In the section on deepening and maintaining, it was noted that the more active a practitioner is while in the phase, the better. Conversely, if there is less activity, the quality of the phase declines, allowing for an easy exit. Thus, in order to leave the phase, the practitioner only needs to completely relax and ignore any perceived sensations, actions, or thoughts. A practitioner may also recite a prayer, mantra, or rhyme, since that helps the consciousness to be distracted from the situation more quickly. Of course, one needs to calm down and try to get rid of the fear, which in and of itself is capable of keeping such a state going. Periodically, the practitioner should try to move a finger in order to check whether attempts at relaxation have had an effect.

Concentration on a Finger
A practitioner experiencing sleep paralysis should try moving a finger or a toe. At first this won't work, but the practitioner has to concentrate precise thought and effort on the action. After a little while, the physical finger will begin to move. The problem with this technique is that the practitioner may accidentally start making phantom motions instead of physical movements, which is why an understanding of the difference between the two sensations is necessary, since it is often not very obvious.

Concentration on Possible Movements
The physiology of sleep paralysis, the phase state, and dreams are such that when the practitioner is in one of these states, some actions are always associated with movements made in the real body. This is true when moving the eyeballs, the tongue, or while breathing. If the practitioner concentrates attention on these processes, it is possible counteract inhibitions to physical movement; as a result, a sleep-paralyzed practitioner will become able to move in reality.

Reevaluating the Situation
Under normal circumstances, deliberate exit from the phase is not the norm. Deliberate exit is commonly caused by certain fears and prejudices. If a practitioner is not able to activate the body using other emergency return techniques, a careful consideration of the possibilities offered by the phase is recommended. There are many interesting and useful things that can be experienced in the phase. Why ruin the possibility of great opportunity because of a baseless fear?

To be fair, it must be noted that emergency exit techniques do not always work. As a rule, after a long period of sleep deprivation, or at the beginning of or in the middle of a night's sleep, the urge to sleep is so great that it is difficult to resist the sleep paralysis phenomenon. In this respect, reevaluating the situation is highly recommended so that a practitioner is able to take advantage of the situation versus suffering by it. Sleep paralysis is easily transmuted into a phase state by means of indirect techniques.

By the way, knowing how to exit paralysis is important not only for practitioners of the phase, since such paralysis occurs even without the phase for approximately one-third of the human population at least once in a lifetime. It usually happens before or after sleep.

FIGHTING FEAR

Fear in the phase is a very common occurrence. The practitioner may experience fear at any stage, although it is expressed much more clearly during initial practice. The causes of fear are very diverse: a feeling that returning to the body is impossible; a fear of death; worrying that something bad is going to happen to the body; encountering something scary and terrible in the phase; painful sensations; overly sharp, hyper-realistic sensations.

> ***Interesting Fact!***
> *Fear is often specific in the phase and depends on the practitioner's current life situation. For example, young mothers often begin to fear entering the phase just as they're entering it out of a sense that they would risk leaving their children behind. It often worry that they simply might not return or undergo an unsafe situation.*

One fear dominates all others: the instinct of self-preservation, which, without any apparent reason, can induce a feeling of absolute horror – a feeling that cannot be explained or controlled.

For a novice stricken by insurmountable fear that causes paralysis, there is only one way to gradually overcome it. Each time a novice enters the phase, an attempt should be made to go a step further than the previous time. For example, in spite of feeling terrified, the practitioner should try to raise the hands and then move them back to the initial position. The second time, the practitioner should attempt to sit down. The third time, standing up should be attempted. The fourth time, walking around in the phase is advised. Then, after incremental steps toward experiencing the harmlessness of the phase state, productive, calm action may ensue.

Interesting Fact!
Fear itself can be used to enter the phase and remain there for a long time. Once the phase is entered, fear should be allayed if it begins to cause problems for the practitioner.

For a practitioner who faces periodical fears, realizing that there is no real danger encourages progress in practice. Urges to rapidly return to the body are then made baseless. Sooner or later, calmer thought dominates events in the phase, and fear happens less often.

When dealing with momentary fear caused by events in the phase, the simplest solution is to tackle it head-on and follow through to the end in order to avoid a fear-driven precedent. If a practitioner always runs away from undesirable events, the events will occur more and more frequently. If a practitioner is incapable of facing fear in the phase, it is best to use the translocation technique to travel elsewhere, although this solution only produces temporary relief.

PHASE OBJECT AGGRESSION AND ATTACKS

It's worth taking a moment to go into detail on phase objects behaving aggressively towards practitioners, as many are concerned about this issue. However, one fact that says a lot should be considered immediately: these types of issues usually concern or are encountered by the esoterically-minded, or those who have read much eclectic literature on the subject of phase states. Such issues are rare among those with a materialist outlook.

Here, phase objects are provoked to react adversely by incorrect behavior on the part of practitioners. It's enough to note that many authors writing on the phase devote up to half of their books to the subject of protection from such attacks. Of course, a negative experience is sure to follow a close reading of such material. Moreover, the negative experience would occur without adequate understanding of the occurrence - and such understanding which would otherwise remedy the issue.

The first thing to know in this regard is: no thing and no person in the phase presents any real threat. The practitioner himself is able to control everything that occurs. That's why there's no point in fearing anybody or anything in the phase, no matter how threatening they may seem or what someone may have said or written about it.

The second thing to know is: the only thing that can and does attack is the practitioner's own fear, be it conscious or unconscious fear. The properties of the phase space are such that a novice's inability to control the process will lead to his subconscious expectations causing much to happen to him. That's precisely why a still "green" phaser who has read much about "astral attacks" will encounter materialized and hyper-realistic fears that not only terrorize, but also cause true pain: beatings, abuse, torture, suffocation, and the like. Until the reason for them is understood, the problem will remain unsolved. Moreover, all kinds of absurd theories about evil beings thus find confirmation, which is why old wives' tales continue to have wide currency, even in our modern era.

An experienced practitioner controls his entire experience from beginning to end, and his subconscious expectations don't interfere with the behavioral mechanisms of the phase space. Thus, attacks are a rarity. And even if they occur, this problem is easily resolved by counteractive assertiveness or a simple attempt to face the unpleasantness head on.

CREATION OF VISION

Vision is often available at the very beginning of a phase, especially when the practitioner uses image observation and visualization techniques to enter. Sometimes vision appears within the first few seconds. Other times, it manifests during the deepening process. However, there are cases where vision is not available and must be created quickly, at any cost. Vision may arrive as soon as it is thought about, but if this does not occur, a special technique is necessary.

To create vision, a practitioner needs to bring the hands four to six inches in front of the eyes and try to detect them through the grayness or darkness. Peering aggressively and attentively at the minute details of the palms will cause them to become visible, much like if they were being developed on Polaroid film. After several seconds, vision will become clear, and along with the palms, the surroundings will also become visible.

Under no circumstances should the physical eyelids be opened. Vision will appear on its own and will not differ from that of reality; meanwhile, the physical sensation of opened eyes will emerge. It is possible to shut the eyes in the phase an infinite number of times, even without having opened them at all, since the latter is not needed for creating vision. However, the eyelids may only be opened while experiencing a very deep phase, as opening the eyes will cause a return to wakefulness during a shallow phase.

The practitioner must also keep in mind that vision should only be created after a complete separation from the body and a subsequent translocation has been achieved. Attempting to view the hands during flight or while hovering in an unidentified space leads to arbitrary translocation.

CONTACT WITH LIVING OBJECTS

Two problems may surface while conversing with animate objects in the phase: silence or a return to the body. In view of the fact that many phase applications are based on contact with people for one purpose or another, it is necessary to understand how to correctly manage contact with living objects.

In order to avoid a foul (ejection from the phase into reality), the elementary rules of "maintaining" must be observed. For example, actively observe the facial features or clothing of a person you want to communicate with. While communicating, the practitioner should constantly rub the hands together or maintain strong vibrations by straining the brain. Remember to perform the techniques to avoid becoming absorbed in communication.

A more complex problem is overcoming the communicative unresponsiveness of objects in the phase. In many cases, the speech of an object is blocked by the internal stress of the practitioner. Sometimes the problem stems from an expectation that an object will not be able to communicate in the phase.

It is important to treat the objects in a calm manner. There is no use trying to shout or beat the object to force communication. On the contrary, it is much more effective to treat the object gently, without applying pressure. Do not peer at an object's mouth expecting sounds to emerge. It is better to look elsewhere; taking a passive interest in communication generally yields the best results.

As a rule, after the first time that communication with a living object is successful, future attempts go unhindered.

Communication methods in the phase should be no different than those used in ordinary life: talking, facial expressions, gesturing with the hands, body language. Telepathy may be used too.

READING

Reading text in the phase may be accompanied by a number of difficulties. First, small print becomes illegible because the effects of hyper-concentration may distort text. This problem is solved by using large-font textual sources of information. For example, the text of a normal book blurs when observed too attentively, but the large font on the cover of a book is easily read since its size is sufficient for rapid reading without detailed scrutiny.

The second problem encountered while reading in the phase is when text is legible but is completely meaningless in composition, i.e. gibberish. This problem is solved by turning over the pages, looking for a readable message. It is also possible to find another copy or create it anew using the object-finding techniques. The same applies to cases where the text is seen as a set of incomprehensible symbols or signs.

While reading in the phase, the practitioner should not forget about performing "maintaining" techniques to prevent a foul by becoming too relaxed.

VIBRATIONS

The phase is often accompanied by an unforgettably unusual sensation that may be used successfully to enter, deepen or maintain it. It is difficult to describe it better than the sensation of a heavy current passing through the entire body without causing any pain. It may also feel like the whole body is contracting, or a tingling sensation similar to numbness. Most often, the sensations are similar to high-frequency vibrations of the body, which explains the origin of the term "vibration".

If the practitioner is not sure whether or not he experienced vibrations, then there is a good method to solve his problem: realize that if he really did, he will not have any doubts about it. In all other cases, when there are doubts and uncertainty, the practitioner is definitely not dealing with vibrations, or is dealing with another form thereof.

If you have experienced vibrations at least once, the recollection of these sensations helps greatly during the simultaneous application of indirect techniques. Vibrations are created, supported and strengthened by straining the brain or tensing the body without using the muscles. For vibrations to appear, it often suffices merely to think about them. During the first experience, one should experiment with them for a while by rolling them around the body and its parts, as well as strengthening and weakening them.

However, one should not think that the presence of vibrations is a necessary condition for being in the phase. Many novices often strive not for the phase but for vibrations, after which the former must supposedly follow. That should not be the case. There are indeed specific techniques that make it possible to get into the phase by creating vibrations, but in all other cases they are not necessary and some practitioners may never have them at all.

TECHNIQUES FOR TRANSLOCATING THROUGH OBJECTS

In a deep phase, the properties of the surrounding environment become very similar to the physical world. However, it may sometimes be necessary to pass through a wall or translocate to avoid a physical barrier in the phase. There are two basic options for passing through barriers like walls. Usually, mastering these requires several attempts.

> ***Interesting Fact!***
> *If a practitioner concentrates on the physical sensations associated with passing through a wall, it is possible to get stuck. A practitioner may even experience the feeling of obstructed breathing when this happens.*

Rapid Defocused Penetration
Run or jump at a wall with a burning desire to penetrate it. Don't focus on the wall; instead concentrate on the immediate surroundings. Do not try to take anything from the

current location since this may impede a successful passage through the wall.

The Closed Eyes Technique
When approaching a wall, the practitioner must close his eyes and completely focus on a desire to pass through it while imagining that the wall does not exist, or that it is transparent and penetrable. Surface resistance should be pressed through, continuing on with the aggressive desire and concentration.

FLIGHT

Taking flight in the phase is a simple matter of remembering past dreams of flight. Nothing needs to be tensed, no word needs to be said. Attempting flight with closed eyes produces a high rate of success, but presents an increased probability of inadvertent translocation.

If a flight attempt is unsuccessful, a practitioner may try jumping from a high elevation or from a window. The natural instinct of dream flight takes over and the fall becomes a controlled flight. However, jumping from windows or other elevations is advisable only to practitioners with experience, since novices may not always be able to determine whether they are in the phase or in reality.

In case of difficulties with take-off, you can also try to jump up and stay airborne for as long as you can. It's better to do it in incremental bounds, as that keeps you more active - which is safer in terms of maintaining the phase.

When flying in a deep phase, another problem besides taking-off may arise: maintaining the phase state. In order to avoid a return to the body or sleep, flying has to be as energetic and sensation-infused as possible. To that end you can also keep up vibrations, as well as periodically rub together and scrutinize your hands. In certain conditions, flying in the phase can not only keep the state stable, but also even deepen it. This happens during aggressive flight with sharp turns and constantly flying close-by various objects in order to visually inspect them.

The most important thing is to try not to fly in a relaxed, laid-back manner or take in the scenery, as this will quickly lead to the end of the phase.

SUPER-ABILITIES

The realism of the phase space does not impose limits on the ability to perform actions that cannot be performed in the physical world. It is important to remember that only a practitioner's apprehension places limits on what may be done in the phase.

For example, if a practitioner needs to get to a location - even very far away - it may be reached by teleportation. If an object needs to be moved from one side of the room to the other, it may be moved by telekinesis. One of the major benefits of the phase experience is unencumbered freedom of action.

To master unusual abilities, only a few phases need to be spent on concentrated development of the methods.

Telekinesis

In order to learn telekinesis (moving objects by thought), the practitioner concentrates on an object while experiencing a deepened phase, and attempts to move the object by thinking about the movement. The only required action is aggressively willing the object's movement. No specific external actions are required. Everyone inherently knows how to do this. If attempts are unsuccessful at first, press on. Before too long, the full effect of the practitioner's will yields results. Using this ability helps to encourage a good phase experience by providing a tool for carrying out planned tasks.

Pyrokinesis

Igniting an object in the phase just by staring at it requires a strong desire to heat up and set fire to the object. Performed successfully, an object will smoke, distort, darken and then burst into flames.

Telepathy

To develop telepathy in the phase, it is necessary to peer at animate objects while listening in surrounding external and internal sounds with the intention of their hearing thoughts. Even experienced practitioners encounter difficulty while developing telepathy, but when successful, contact with people in the phase is substantially simplified. Using telepathy, discerning the thoughts of people, animals, and objects is possible. However, this should not be taken too seriously, since it is merely the nature of the phase to simulate what is expected.

THE IMPORTANCE OF CONFIDENCE

A crucial factor in developing phase abilities is self-confidence in the ability to use the skills. Initially, these abilities are absent because the human brain, tuned in to ordinariness, blocks confidence in the ability to do anything unusual. As soon as strong confidence is reached in the performance of phase abilities, everything becomes easy to achieve.

Although confidence in phase abilities may grow strong, practitioners should remain soundly aware that abilities in the phase are limited to the phase. Attempting telekinesis, pyrokinesis, or transmutation in the real world may waste time and energy.

TRANSMUTATION INTO ANIMALS

Many practitioners actively experiment with their bodily form during the phase, which can take on any appearance thanks to the properties of the phase space. Such experimentation, despite being somewhat difficult, is quite popular and interesting. Nearly every advanced phaser experiments with it sooner or later.

Interesting Fact!
People appear in human form while in the phase only because they are accustomed to it from everyday life. Actually, you can feel every fine detail while inhabiting any body or any thing, as there is no personal "body" as such in the phase.

A distinctive trait of experiments with altered physical perception is the unbelievably fine detail of sensation. If a phase practitioner takes on the form of a lizard, he will be able to feel not only his tail, but also that his tongue is now forked. Meanwhile, if a practitioner takes on the form of a wolf, then he will feel the nails on his paws, and experience incredibly heightened sense of smell. The same applies to every possible sense, the true-to-lifeness of which depends on one's mastery over incarnating in the phase.

One feels as if new parts of the brain activate that are responsible for the sensory perception of body parts that humans don't have. Such body parts can then not only be felt, but also controlled. For example, if a practitioner has become a bird in the phase, then he will not only feel his wings, but also be able to control them as if he had been born with them. Such reorganization of perception is possible for all human sensations and this applies not only to animate objects, but also to inanimate ones: stones, trees, furniture, etc.

Without further ado, here are the techniques for transforming one's embodiment:

Transmutation upon Separation

Immediately after separation, the practitioner's attention is focused on his already having achieved his desired embodiment. This must not merely be imagined - instead, one must try to feel the new embodiment immediately. For example, if a phaser wants to transform into a snake, then after rolling-out he must try no matter what to immediately feel himself rolling out while in the elongated body of a snake, and not of a person. If this is not successful, then other transmutation techniques need to be tried, as this one is to be used only at the beginning of a phase entrance. If transmutation is successful, then one should immediately move on to deepening the phase while in the newly obtained embodiment, like after a conventional separation.

Dynamic Transmutation

While still in human form in the phase, one should briskly imitate the movements of the target animal while taking on its external appearance. During this process, it's important to not only imitate the movement of the creature, but also try to feel oneself being it. The practitioner will gradually take on all of the anatomical sensations and external appearance of the target form. For example, if the practitioner has decided to become a tiger, then he should try to run in leaps on his four extremities, trying to feel the entire body of the big cat along with its sensations, starting from the touch of its paws and claws on the earth to the tip of its tail.

Transmutation upon Translocation

When using the technique of translocation via teleportation with eyes closed, you need to focus your attention not so much on the translocation destination as on your external appearance and internal sensations. Once translocation has taken place, the phaser will turn up in the right place and in the right form. For example, if a practitioner has decided to become a disembodied sphere, then he should close his eyes in the phase and focus on both the thought-form of the place where he wants to appear and on his sensations. An immediate sensation of flight and gradual feeling of transformation of bodily perception will arise. Depending on the degree of concentration, the flight may come to an end at the desired place within several seconds, and the practitioner would immediately have spherical vision and corresponding bodily sensations.

Transmutation through Intention
Experienced practitioners or those who can easily concentrate their will are often able to take on the form they want without using any special techniques. It is often enough for them to simply intensely desire to take on one form or another, and that form comes to them, be it abruptly or gradually. Ultimately, this is what all phasers should strive for. For example, if a practitioner has decided to transform into a dragon, then he will concentrate his intention on that desire, and his bodily sensations will go into a state of flux, and then stabilize again once he has already transmutated. Alternatively, he will simply begin to perceivably mutate into a fire-breathing dragon. Also of good help when performing this technique are elixirs, tablets, and potions that can be programmed in the phase to have a specific effect when taken.

With all such techniques - and the entire practice of the phase itself - intention, self-assurance, desire, and purposefulness have significant importance. Knowing specific techniques is often unnecessary if you have a firm desire that you unhesitatingly want to achieve no matter what. Problems with intention and self-assurance always lie at the root of lack of success at transmutating in the phase. Phasers often simply lack confidence in their ability to transmutate, which finds expression in failed attempts to take on another bodily form.
Any lack of confidence when performing the transmutation techniques in the phase will always be evident

in the final result. Meanwhile, lack of confidence indicates a certain level of self-analysis, which in turn is a symptom of insufficient concentration on the technique. That's why total concentration on and putting one's all into a technique practically guarantees successful results.

When it comes to deepening and maintaining, it is important to make the transformation of one's external appearance quickly, or when feeling constantly vivid sensations and actions. Otherwise, a foul will occur if one drags out transmutation or otherwise performs it slowly.

CONTROLLING PAIN

Along with all the positive experiences and sensations that may be enjoyed in the phase, experiences of a painful nature may also manifest. Punching a wall in a deep phase state will cause the same pain as if a wall had been struck in physical reality.

Some actions in the phase may unavoidably cause unpleasant feelings of pain; therefore, it is necessary to know how to avoid painful actions. Focusing on an internal confidence that pain will not result from an action will alleviate the problem. A practitioner may experiment with this type of focus by pummeling a wall while resolving that there is no pain. If the experiment succeeds, then obtaining the same result will never again require the same level of effort; thinking that the phase is painless will suffice.

MORAL STANDARDS IN THE PHASE

From the very beginning, it should be understood that the moral compass of the phase space has nothing in common with the societal norms and laws of the physical world. The phase space seemingly imitates the physical world with all its properties and functions only because we are accustomed to them and are not expecting anything else. Moral principles and rules apply only to the place where they were developed. It does not make sense to profess them while in the phase.

The practitioner should not refrain from certain actions in the phase because some would be unacceptable, improper, or bad in the real world. These are merely behavioral patterns that are hardly suited to the world of the phase, where everything operates on the basis of entirely different laws.

The only moral rules that might exist in the phase are those that the practitioner establishes. If desired, complete, unhindered freedom may be experienced.

STUDYING POSSIBILITIES AND SENSATIONS

Novice practitioners should not immediately rush towards a single specific goal if long-term practice is desired. It is better to extensively investigate the phase and its surroundings before focusing on accomplishment. This will build intimacy with the experience and allow unhindered entry and interaction with the phase.

As in reality, learning whatever first reveals itself is the key to increasing and specializing knowledge. A beginning practitioner should at first enjoy the simple fact of actually being in the phase, then glean its details and functions. Once inside the phase, a practitioner should explore it, examining and interacting with everything encountered.

He should also try to fully sharpen all the feelings possible in the phase in order to fully understand how unusual it is in its realism. A practitioner must experience movement: walking, running, jumping, flying, falling, swimming. Test the sensations of pain by striking a wall with a fist. The simplest way to experience taste sensations is to get to the refrigerator and try to eat everything that you find there, at the same time not forgetting to smell each item. Walk through the walls, translocate, create and handle objects.

Explore. All these actions are very interesting in and of themselves. The possibilities really are infinite. However, only when they are well understood and thoroughly explored can it be said that the practitioner really knows what the phase is about.

TYPICAL MISTAKES WITH PRIMARY SKILLS

- When trying to discern whether or not a phase is intact, judgment is based on similarity to the departed physical environment. In the phase, physical attributes are simulations.
- Hyper-concentrating on an object for too short a time while trying to determine whether the surroundings are in the phase or in the physical world.
- Deliberately attempting to end the phase prematurely when the entire natural length of the phase should be taken advantage of.
- Panic in case of paralysis instead of calm, relaxed action.
- Refusal to practice the phase because of fear, though this problem is temporary and resolvable.
- Opening the eyes at the initial stages of the phase, since this frequently leads to a foul.
- Premature attempts to create vision in the phase, whereas separating from the body and deepening should occur.
- Excessive haste while creating vision, as in the majority of cases vision appears naturally.
- While concentrating on the hands to create vision, doing so at an excessive distance versus the recommended four to six inches.
- Forgetting about the techniques for "maintaining" while in contact with living objects.
- Forgetting to shut the eyes or defocus vision when translocating through walls or other solid objects.

- Desiring to do something superhuman in the phase without the required internal desire and confidence.
- Fear of experiencing pain in the phase instead of learning to control it.
- Observing moral standards in the phase when they do not apply.
- A tendency to immediately use the phase for something practical instead of first thoroughly exploring and interacting with the surroundings.

EXERCISES

Questions

1. Are there skills in the phase that must first be mastered before the phase may be used to its full extent?
2. Is it possible to understand whether a phase is intact by attempting to fly?
3. Has a practitioner most likely gotten up in the phase or in reality if there are doubts about this?
4. Is it sufficient to think about the body in order to return to it, and is it only required to return into the body in order to control it?
5. Which arm should be actively and aggressively moved to overcome sleep paralysis?
6. Is it possible to tell jokes to oneself to overcome sleep paralysis?
7. Is it possible to move the physical eyes while in the phase?
8. What should be done if sleep paralysis cannot be overcome?
9. Can sleep paralysis occur without practicing the phase?
10. What if fear is not addressed and conquered?
11. Is it possible to gradually master the phase in order to overcome fear?
12. Is there cause for fear of anything in the phase?

13. At what point can vision be created in the phase by opening the eyelids and not through the use of special techniques?
14. What would happen with an attempt to open the eyes after sitting up in bed, i.e., before becoming completely separated from the phase?
15. Why may contact with living objects in the phase cause a return to the body?
16. What problems might occur if a practitioner studies the mouth of a talking object?
17. In the phase, how quickly can small text be read?
18. Which is easier to read in the phase: text in a newspaper or text on a large billboard?
19. Is it possible to see hieroglyphs instead of text while reading in the phase?
20. Is it possible to burst through a wall after running up to it with the eyes shut?
21. Which muscles of the body must be tensed to start flying in the phase?
22. Are there any extrasensory abilities that are inaccessible in the phase?
23. Can a practitioner transform into a ball while in the phase?
24. How does pain in the phase differ from pain in the physical world?
25. Should a practitioner give up a seat to an elderly person while in the phase?
26. Due to moral considerations, what is prohibited in the phase?

Tasks

1. During your next phase session, walk around your home investigating the rooms, kitchen, and bathroom in detail.
2. Learn to pass through walls. Completely dedicate one long phase experience to perfecting this skill.

3. Learn to fly in the phase.
4. While in a deep phase, learn to control pain by hitting a wall with your fist.
5. While in the phase, learn telekinesis (the ability to move objects by thought) and pyrokinesis (setting objects on fire, also performed by thought).
6. Dedicate a lengthy phase experience to an experiment with vision: create it if it is not already available, and then shut your eyes and recreate vision. Do this at least ten times over the course of a single phase
7. Dedicate a long phase to searching for different kinds of texts in order to experiment with reading various size fonts.

Chapter 9 – Translocation and Finding Objects

THE ESSENCE OF TRANSLOCATION AND FINDING OBJECTS

Like everyday reality, the phase space cannot be used for certain purposes if it is not known how to move around and find necessary things. In a wakeful state, it is more or less known where something is located and how to reach it. In the phase, the same assumptions cannot apply since phase mechanisms work by different principles.

The reason for addressing translocation and finding objects in the same chapter is because both techniques rely on the same mechanics. In other words, the same methods - with minor exceptions - can be applied to both translocation and finding.

After studying the techniques described in this chapter, a practitioner in the phase will be able to go to any location and find any object. The only limitations that exist are those of the imagination and desire; if these are unlimited, so are the possibilities.

Regarding translocation, attention should not be focused on methods for traveling through nearby spaces. For example, a practitioner may simply walk into an adjacent room, or out to the street via the corridor or through the window. These are natural, easy actions. A practitioner should instead concentrate attention on how to move to remote destinations that cannot be quickly reached by physical means.

It is important to mention the necessary safety procedures for translocation. Sometimes, due to a lack of experience, a practitioner may mistake the phase for reality, and reality may be mistaken for the phase. Mistaking the phase for reality implies no danger since a practitioner simply believes that an entry attempt was unsuccessful. However, if reality is mistaken for the phase, a practitioner may perform dangerous or even life-threatening actions. For example, after getting out of bed in a wakeful state, thinking that everything is happening in the phase, a beginner may approach a window and jump out of it, expecting to fly, as is customary in the phase. For this reason alone, shortcuts to flight should only be taken after gaining a level of experience that makes it possible to unambiguously distinguish the phase from a wakeful state.

If a glitch occurs when practicing translocation techniques (for example, landing in the wrong place), a practitioner should simply repeat the technique until the desired result is obtained. Either way, initial training is a must in order to make everything easier for you later on.

As far as object-finding techniques are concerned, these are used for both inanimate and animate objects. In other words, these techniques are equally effective for finding, for example, a person or a utensil. However, there are several techniques that are only suitable for finding living objects.

BASIC PROPERTY OF THE PHASE SPACE

All methods for controlling the phase space stem from a primary law: the degree of changeability of the phase space is inversely proportionate to the depth of the phase and the stability of its objects. That is, the deeper and more stable the phase, the more difficult it is to perform something unusual in it because in a deep, stable phase, the laws of it begin to closely resemble those of the physical world.

All translocation and finding objects techniques are based on knowledge of methods that exploit this primary law. The secret lies in the fact that not only phase depth affects the controllability of the phase, but so does phase stability, which in turn depends to a large extent on the number of sensations experienced in the phase. The techniques for translocation and finding objects are used when these experienced sensations are weakened through certain actions.

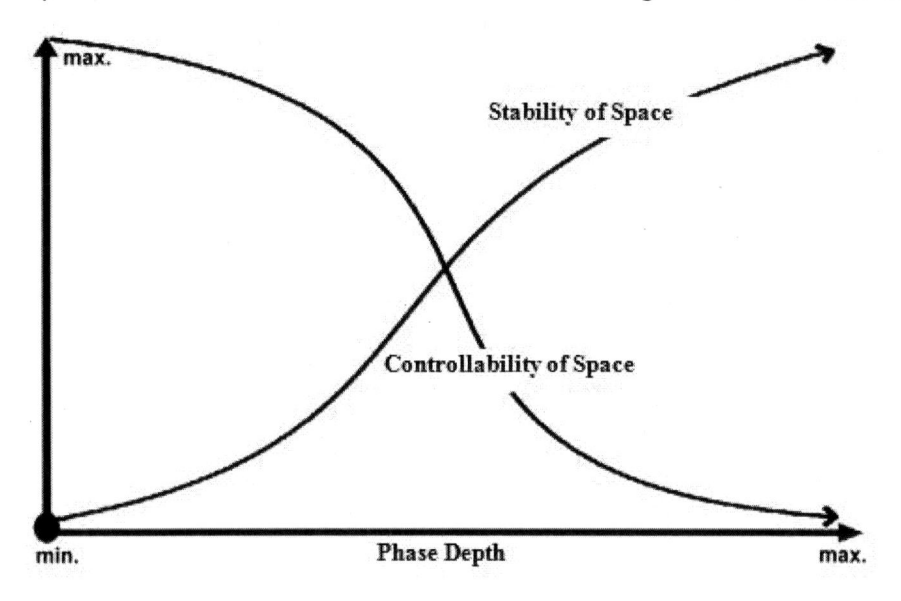

[Graph: Stability of Space increases with Phase Depth (from min to max), while Controllability of Space decreases with Phase Depth. X-axis: Phase Depth (min to max). Y-axis: min to max.]

In other words, if a practitioner located in the phase holds a red pencil and examines it, tactile and visual perceptions are engaged, which under sharp agitation cause the object to exist in its complete form. However, as soon as the eyes are shut, the stability of pencil image weakens. In this situation, it will be enough for the practitioner (after sufficient training) to concentrate on believing that the pencil is dark-blue in order for it to appear dark blue after opening the eyes. This phenomenon occurs because the color of the pencil is no longer determined by perceptual areas of the brain and, therefore, it is possible to change it.

If a red pencil is placed on a table and the practitioner's eyes are shut, and there is concentration on a thought that the pencil is no longer on the table, then after opening the eyes, the practitioner will find that the pencil has disappeared.

In essence, when the pencil is lying on the table and the practitioner's eyes are closed, no perception is being invested in the pencil - the practitioner's eyes do not see it and his skin does not touch it. The pencil only remains as a memory, which the practitioner modifies using autosuggestion.

Components of Phase Space Stability

Memory & Expectation	Visual Perception	Tactile Perception	Vestibular Perception	Auditory Perception

Using certain technique-related methods, a practitioner may cause the stability of the phase state to remain in flux using techniques that best suit the practitioner's individual personality.

TECHNIQUES FOR TRANSLOCATION

Translocation during Separation

The easiest way to translocate is to do so while separating from the body. Employing this technique is extremely simple and convenient. It may be combined with almost any separation technique and is performed by focusing on the image and feel of a desired location during the initial stages of exiting the body. It is even better to imagine that phase entry will occur and separation will complete in a chosen location.

Interesting Fact!
After having changed place of residence, the practitioner will very often continue for some time to separate from the body in the same house where he was used to doing this previously.

A drawback of this technique is that separation occurs only in the beginning of the phase experience and, therefore, can only be used once. Other options should be considered after the first translocation.

Translocation through a Door
In order to use this technique, approach any door with the strong belief that it leads to the required location. After opening the door, the practitioner will see and be able to step into the destination. If the door was originally open, it must be completely shut before applying the technique.

A drawback to this technique is that its practice always requires a door. If there is no door, users of this translocation technique should create one using an object finding technique.

Translocation through Teleportation
To apply this technique, shut the eyes (if vision is present), and then concentrate attention on a thought-form or image of a location elsewhere in the phase. At this moment, there will be a sensation of swift flight and within 2 to 10 seconds, the destination will be reached.

The success of this technique depends on a strong concentration upon a single goal: the desired location. The technique must be performed very clearly, confidently, aggressively, and without distractions. Any unrelated thoughts have a profoundly negative influence on its performance. They unnecessarily prolong the flight, cause a foul, or result in arriving at an undesired location.

Translocation through Teleportation with the Eyes Open

This technique is difficult because it requires an unstable phase space caused by a strong desire to translocate to another location. Whereas during teleportation by flight with eyes shut the practitioner disentangles himself from the current location, that is not the case here. Therefore, this technique should be used only by experienced practitioners who are confident that they are capable of remaining in the phase.

As far as implementing the technique is concerned, the practitioner simply needs to stop and concentrate on the thought that he is already present in the desired location and focus on its image. It is important to not stare at or touch anything during the thought. Surrounding space will dim, blur and then disappear during this time, and then the intended location will gradually start to appear. The rate of space metamorphosis depends on the degree of desire to reach the required location.

If concentration is weak or phase depth is poor, then after space destabilizes, it might not be restored - and a return to the wakeful state will occur.

Translocation with Closed Eyes

This is one of the easiest techniques. To use this technique, the practitioner simply needs to shut the eyes and have an intense desire that, when the eyes are next opened, the required location will be reached. In order to considerably increase the effectiveness of this technique, it would be useful to imagine, at the moment you close your eyes, that you have already reached the desired location. In order to stay in the phase, it's better to perform this technique while moving, i.e. walking, running, or flying. For example, in order to get to "point a", close your eyes, focus your attention on already being in "point b", and then open your eyes there.

Translocation by Concentration on a Remote Object

To perform this technique, the practitioner should peer from a distance at a minor detail of the desired location. The greater an intention to see an object's detail, the quicker the arrival at the object's location.

A drawback to this technique is that this type of translocation is possible only for places that are already visible, albeit from a great distance.

Translocation by Passing through a Wall

This technique is performed by walking or flying through a wall with the eyes shut and a firm conviction that the required location is behind the wall. The barrier does not necessarily have to be a wall. It can be any non-transparent object through which a practitioner may walk or fly: a screen, a wardrobe, and so on.

The main drawback of this technique is the necessity of appropriate skills for penetrating through solid objects of the phase. Another necessary condition for applying this technique is the presence of barriers to pass through.

Translocation through Diving

This technique is identical to passing through walls with the only difference being that instead of a wall - which may not always be available - the practitioner will use the floor or the ground. The practitioner must dive headfirst with the eyes shut and have complete confidence that the required location is underneath the solid surface. The ability to pass through solid objects is, naturally, also required.

A practitioner may dive through the floor or the ground, and also into any flat horizontal surface: a table, a chair, a bed, and so forth.

Translocation through Rotation

To apply this technique, a practitioner in the phase will start rotating on an axis while simultaneously concentrating on a belief that a desired location will be reached once rotation is stopped. The eyes must be shut during the rotation, or vision must not be focused on anything in particular. As a rule, two to five revolutions on an axis are sufficient. Once again, everything depends on the ability to fully concentrate on a desired goal without any distractions.

Translocation through a Mirror

Due to the special properties of mirrors and people's superstitious beliefs about them, they can be used to easily translocate in the phase. To that end it's enough to jump or dive into any large mirror encountered along the way. Meanwhile, you can focus your attention on the location you want immediately being behind it. Due to the properties of mirrors, you often don't even have to close your eyes or turn around when penetrating their surface.

Interesting Fact!

When novices at School of Out-of-Body Travel seminars are asked to take a look in the mirror during their first phase, it is rare for two descriptions of the event to be similar, as everything happens differently for each person: some see their actual reflection, others see nothing, still others see different people, and in some cases the movements of the reflection don't match those of the practitioner, etc. Once at a seminar, 16 were able to look at a mirror while in the phase, and no two people had similar experiences.

OBJECT FINDING TECHNIQUES

Technique of Translocation

All translocation techniques are also applicable to object finding techniques since the use of both techniques requires altering the surrounding space. Instead of concentrating on a location, the practitioner is to focus on the specific detail of a space that is to be found or changed. As a result, finding the necessary object (provided this technique has been mastered) is guaranteed, but maintaining the original location where the action begins is not guaranteed.

If the goal is to find an object while remaining in the present location, use the specialized techniques described later on: techniques that change only a portion of the phase space.

Finding by Calling a Name

This technique is only used to find living objects. The practitioner must call a person or an animal by name to cause the animate phase object to enter or appear nearby. The call should be loud, nearly a shout, otherwise it will not always work. Generally, it is often enough to pronounce a name several times to achieve results.

If the desired animate object does not have a name or the practitioner does not know it, then any name or general summoning will do, like, "Come here!" This should be done while mentally focusing on a clear image of the desired person or animal.

Finding by Inquiry

To perform this technique, approach any person in the phase and ask him (or her) where to quickly find a desired object. An accurate answer is usually given straight away, and it should be followed. However, to avoid wasting time, do not forget to mention that the object must be found "quickly", or specify that the object should be "nearby". During this communication, under no circumstances should there be a doubt about the accuracy of the information, since otherwise it may lead to a simulation of what is expected.

The drawback of this technique is that it requires the presence of an animate person and good skill at communicating with objects in the phase, which can prove difficult.

Finding by Turning Around

In order to use this technique, the practitioner must concentrate and imagine that the required object is located somewhere behind his back, and after turning around he will actually see it there, even if it was not there just a moment earlier. This works best if the practitioner, prior to turning around, has not seen the place where the object is expected to appear.

Finding Around a Corner

When approaching any corner, concentrate and imagine that the required object is just around the corner. Then, after turning the corner, the object will be found. Anything that limits space visibility may be regarded as a corner. This does not have to be the corner of a house or another type of building; it could be the corner of a wardrobe, the corner of a truck, etc.

The drawback of this technique is that it requires the availability of a sufficiently large corner that blocks the view of anything around the other side of it.

Finding in the Hand
This technique is, in essence, only applicable to finding objects that can fit in or be held by the hand. To perform this technique, concentrate on the idea that the object is already in hand. At that moment, the practitioner must not look at it. Soon after beginning to concentrate on this idea, the practitioner will at first feel a slight sensation of the object lying in his hand, followed by a full sensation and appearance of the desired object.

Finding by Transmutation
This technique distorts the phase space while not completely disengaging a perception of the space. The practitioner must give strong attention to a thought that a required object is going to appear in a desired location. There must be sufficient confidence that the practitioner's desires will be realized. At this moment, the process of metamorphosis will begin: space will distort and dim, and the required object will begin to manifest itself. After this, brightness and focus will be restored with necessary alterations made present in the phase space.

This technique is relatively difficult to perform in comparison to others, and, therefore, it is better to use it only after a high level of experience has been reached, as it is difficult to remain in the phase during any metamorphic process.

As is evident in the name of this technique, it can be used to find objects and also create new objects from found objects.

TYPICAL MISTAKES WITH TRANSLOCATION AND FINDING OBJECTS

- Applying translocation and object finding techniques without the precondition of a steady phase.
- Insufficient concentration on a desire to travel to a location or to find an object.
- Doubting that results will be achieved instead of having complete confidence.
- Passive performance of the techniques instead of a strong desire and high level of aggression.
- Forgetting to repeat translocation or object finding techniques when the technique did not work or worked incorrectly during the first attempt.
- Getting distracted by extraneous thoughts during the lengthy process of teleporting with eyes shut. Total concentration is required at all times.
- Applying the technique of teleportation with eyes open without adequate experience.
- Failing to immediately translocate when using the closed eyes technique; this may induce flying a la teleportation technique.
- Glossing over minute details or only observing the broad features of a remote object while applying translocation by concentration.
- A delayed desire to move while translocating during separation. An instantaneous desire to immediately move is necessary.
- Forgetting to first shut a door completely when using translocation through a door; otherwise, there will be contact with what is already behind it.
- Using a translocation technique to go through a wall without knowing how to pass through solid objects.
- Paying too much attention to the process of translocation through a wall; this leads to being trapped in the wall.

- Forgetting to shut the eyes while translocating diving headfirst. The eyes should remain closed until after the technique is complete.
- Insufficient internal association with an animate object while finding it by calling its name.
- Trying to find an object via interrogation instead of passively communicating with living objects of the phase.
- Using distant corners when applying the technique of finding an object around the corner. Choose nearby corners to avoid wasting precious travel time.
- Applying transmutation techniques without possessing sufficient experience in managing the phase space.

EXERCISES

Questions

1. What becomes possible with the ability to translocate in the phase?
2. What becomes possible with the ability to find objects in the phase?
3. What do translocation and finding objects techniques have in common?
4. What is the sole limitation on the possibilities offered by translocation and finding objects?
5. How may one translocate across very short distances?
6. When may the technique of flight by jumping out of a window be attempted?
7. What should be done if translocation and object finding techniques do not yield the required result?
8. Is it possible to find a person from real life using the technique of finding objects?
9. Does the stability of space decrease in a deep phase?
10. What are the fundamental components of space and object stability?

11. How large is the role of auditory perception in the stability of space?
12. What is most important while using a teleportation technique?
13. What does speed of movement depend on during teleportation?
14. Should a novice apply the technique of teleportation with open eyes?
15. What technique might the translocation with closed eyes technique turn into?
16. Should large or small details be scrutinized while translocating by concentration on remote objects?
17. Is the technique of translocation during separation applied after separation or while beginning to separate?
18. When applying the technique of translocation through a door: is it better if the door is open or closed?
19. Why might translocation by passing through a wall fail?
20. When using translocation by diving, is it important to be in a place where there is something to stand on?
21. While applying the technique of rotation, should rotation be imagined or real?
22. Is it possible to use a translocation technique to attempt finding objects?
23. When using the technique of calling by name, what should be done if the name of a desired person in the phase is unknown?
24. While looking for an object using the method of inquiry, is it important to specify that the object needs to be found "quickly"?
25. How far back must a turn occur when the technique of finding objects by turning is being used?
26. Would the corner of a fence be suitable for applying the technique of finding objects around the corner?
27. Is it necessary to shut the eyes while using the transmutation technique?

Tasks

1. Dedicate the next three phases to experiments with translocation techniques, using all of them and traveling wherever you want.
2. After experiencing three phases dedicated to translocation, select the techniques that work best for you.
3. During the next phase, travel to the Eiffel Tower, to the Moon, and to the homes of some of your relatives.
4. Dedicate the next three phases to experiments with the full range of techniques for finding objects, including translocation techniques.
5. After three phases dedicated to finding objects, select the techniques that you are most comfortable with.
6. In the next phase that you experience, find your mother, and then at the same location locate this textbook, a red globe, and a green rose.

Chapter 10 – Application

THE ESSENCE OF APPLICATIONS OF PHASE STATES

Phase perception initially causes so much emotion and variety of experience that the practitioner is often not concerned with the question of how the phase might be purposefully used. The critical question of application becomes even more crucial as experience increases. Application of the phase becomes more vivid against the background of understanding how the phenomenon can provide a means of gaining information and new experiences.

Some approach the phase practice with a predetermined goal, uninterested in anything else. With a specific goal, the problem of where the goal came from might arise, as the phase phenomenon is wrapped in a thick layer of prejudices and stereotypes, which often have no bearing on the reality. The primary purpose of this chapter is to precisely separate reality from fiction. Its second purpose is to provide a detailed description of what may be obtained from the practice of phase experiences.

Every proven and accessible practical application of the phase is based on three qualities: a) application founded on the phase's ability to simulate any object and any space with any properties and functions; b) application based on the opportunity to connect with the subconscious mind in order to obtain information; c) application based on the phase's ability to impact a practitioner's physiology.

Most importantly, nothing described in this chapter is difficult to achieve. Any application may be achieved during the very first phase if a practitioner manages to focus and apply the appropriate techniques for translocation or finding objects. Regardless of whether the practitioner adheres to a mystical or pragmatic worldview, a full range of access is inherently possible.

Possible applications of the phenomenon certainly exceed the scope of descriptions related through this chapter. It is possible that other applications simply have not been proven yet, and, so far, the correct methods of practicing these are still unknown. Only the practitioner may determine the limits of possibility within the phase. Of course, common sense should be applied - otherwise, it would be logically and psychologically difficult to disengage misconceptions. *The goal of this book is to provide a real (though minimal) foundation that is firm and unyielding, whatever the circumstance. If the practitioner follows a strict approach to practice, it will be much more difficult to become lost during further practical and theoretical studies.*

APPLICATIONS BASED ON SIMULATION

Many wonder about the nature of the phase state in relation to the brain, i.e. whether or not the phase is all in one's head. But in the context of applying the phase, this is not a valid concern. Perception of the entire physical environment is performed through sensory organs. In the phase, perception is the same, sometimes even more realistic. Whether everything described in this chapter occurs in reality or is merely simulated makes no difference in terms of the encountered sensations.

Traveling
- *Around the world:* It is possible to reach any point of the planet, and it is particularly interesting to revisit places where the practitioner once lived or visited, and visit places that the practitioner has a strong desire to visit. Every sight and beauty of the Earth become accessible, be

it the Eiffel Tower or an island in Oceania, the Pyramids of Egypt, or Angel Falls.
- *Through Outer Space:* Although humankind is not going to reach Mars any time soon, any practitioner may stand on its surface and experience its unique landscape through the use of translocation in the phase. There is nothing more amazing than observing galaxies and nebulae, planets, and stars from the vantage point of deep space. Of all phase applications available, this one provides practitioners with the most striking aesthetic experiences.
- *To different places in time:* This makes it possible to visit a childhood, to see what a person will look like in the future; a pregnant woman in the phase may see what her child will look like. Travel far back in time and witness the construction of the Pyramids at Giza, see Paris in the 17th century, wander among the dinosaurs of the Jurassic period.
- *Through different worlds:* Travel a world that has been described in literature or just invented by the practitioner, developed in the imagination. These could be extraterrestrial civilizations, parallel worlds, or universes from fairy tales and films. Any destination is nearby.

Encounters
- *With relatives:* Since relatives cannot always see each other, there is the remarkable possibility to meet each other and talk in the phase. Of course, this does not entail mutual presence. It is enough for one person to possess the required desire - the second person may never even know. Realizing the desire to contact a close relative and exchange information is a treasure.
- *With acquaintances:* Circumstances often prevent seeing people who are important. This is an opportunity to realize a desire and finally meet that certain person again.
- *With the dead:* Regardless of the nature of the phase phenomenon, nothing else yields the possibility to see,

talk to, and embrace a deceased loved one. These are vivid, personal experiences, accessible to everyone, and achieving these encounters does not require major difficulty. Courage is the only necessity. From a technique-related point of view, a stable phase and application of the finding objects technique sets the stage for what at first may seem impossible. It should be noted that when a deceased person is encountered in the phase, the distortions caused by the object finding technique may lead to some very undesirable occurrences.
- *With celebrities:* Through the use of object finding techniques, a practitioner has the opportunity to meet any famous person. This could be a historical persona, a contemporary politician, or an artist. In the phase state, they are all accessible for any type of interaction. For example, a practitioner could meet Julius Caesar, Jesus Christ, Napoleon, Churchill, Stalin, Hitler, Elvis Presley, Marilyn Monroe, and a great many others.

Realizing Desires
- Everyone has dreams. Regardless of whether they ever come true in reality, their realization may at least be enjoyed in the phase. Some dream of a visit to Las Vegas, some to drive a Ferrari, some visit Outer Space, others would like to bathe in a pile of money, and some desire sexual experiences without limits. All of these may finally be experienced in the phase.

Alternative to the Virtual World
- In the phase, young men may participate in game battles as if the battles were real. A practitioner can visit unusual worlds and places while enjoying completely realistic sensations, feel a weapon in his hands, and even the smell of gunpowder. If desired, even the sensation of battle wounds may be experienced. Gaming possibilities in the phase are not limited by the power of a microprocessor, but the extent of a practitioner's imagination.

APPLICATIONS BASED ON CONTACT WITH THE SUBCONSCIOUS MIND

If obtaining access to information in the phase seems natural from a mystical or esoteric point of view (in light of various fields of information and other such phenomena), then how would it be for a materialist who doesn't even believe in such things?

Assume that the phase state is just an exceptionally unusual state of brain and that perception within it is no more than an unusually realistic play of its functions. Assume that a practitioner in the phase decides to travel to a forest. To do so, the translocation with closed eyes technique is used, and, as a result, a forest appears.

What happens if the vision contains very detailed knowledge of forests, what forests consist of, and where forests originate? The brain creates a hyper-realistic space superior to that of everyday reality, consisting of millions of blades of grass, leaves, hundreds of trees, and a multitude of sounds. Each blade of grass has depth and build, not just a point. Each leaf also consists of component parts. A unique, natural pattern makes up the bark of each tree.

Suddenly, a wind begins to blow through the forest, and millions of leaves and blades of grass, following a mathematical model of the propagation of air masses, begin oscillating in a wavelike fashion. Thus, a certain resource inside us is capable in mere seconds not only of creating millions of details in the desired scene, but also to control each of those details individually!

Even if the phase is just a state of mind, this does not mean that there are no sources of information within it. The mind possesses great computing ability and is equipped to imagine the full extent of the impossible. No computer, however powerful, is capable of similar feats. A practitioner is able to somehow tap into amazing resources while in the phase. It only remains to learn exactly how to achieve mastery.

It is possible that the phase space is governed by the subconscious mind. This means that the practitioner is able to contact the subconscious while in the phase state. During everyday life, the subconscious mind sends information based on calculations determined by enormous capabilities. However, humans neither hear nor perceive these signals because people are accustomed to receiving information linguistically. The subconscious mind hardly operates within the limitations of language. Communication with the subconscious mind on a conscious level is only possible within the phase. If all phase objects are created and controlled by the subconscious mind, then it is possible to use them as translators. For example, when talking to a person in the phase, normal words are heard while the object and communicated information is controlled by the subconscious mind.

An explanation of how information is obtained in the phase can hardly be unequivocally proven. Perhaps there are other undiscovered resources. But that is not so important. The most important thing is definitely known: how to obtain information in the phase.

Algorithm for Obtaining Information from the Phase

Clearly define the information that needs to be obtained	Enter into a full-fledged deep phase	Create the required object	Obtain the information
Apply the information	Verifying the information in real-life	Exit the phase	Verify the information in the phase

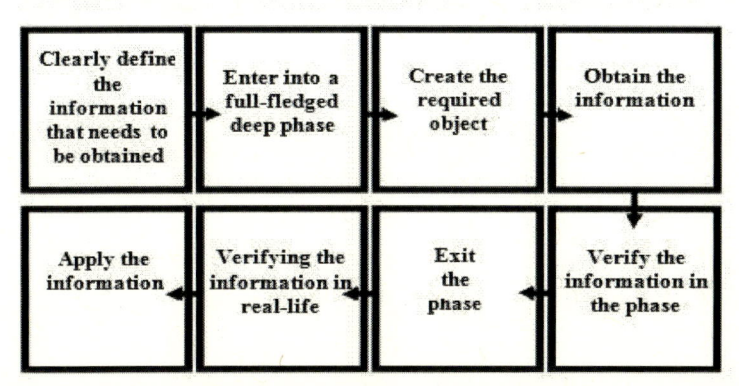

The algorithm for obtaining information from the phase is not complex. After entering the phase, only the techniques for obtaining information and the methods of verifying it need to be learned in order to increase the amount of knowledge gleaned from the phase.

Based on the pragmatic explanation of the nature of the phase as an unusual state of brain controlled by the subconscious, it may be assumed that the amount of information obtained in the phase is limited. If the phase exists within the confines of the brain, then the brain can only operate on data that has been received by it since birth. Indeed, it appears that everything perceived through the sensory organs is remembered and correlated with other data. This is true not only of the perceptions we are aware of, which comprise only a small fraction of total sensory input, but also the enormous volumes of information registered at the subconscious level.

If any event is actually a consequence of other events, which were, in turn, also consequences of previous happenings, then nothing occurs by chance. The initial data is known - therefore it is possible to calculate what is implied by it.

As a result, if everything is based solely on the resource of the subconscious mind, then information may be obtained about everything that is related to an individual life: the practitioner's experiences and the experiences of those with whom the practitioner experiences life. Both our own future and past, and the future and past of others can be figured out. All in all, in order to approach knowing the whole of the information available in the phase, personal knowledge capacity would need to increase by 100 or even 1,000 times.

The only information that is not available in the phase is that about which the subconscious mind does not have any preliminary information. For example, where to purchase a winning lottery ticket that will win millions of dollars cannot be learned since there is no data that could support the necessary calculation. The subconscious mind will also not be able to show the practitioner what a random street in a small town on the other end of the Earth looks like. A practitioner should not try guessing what information the subconscious mind has to offer and what it doesn't because mistakes are easily made. For example, if a practitioner has never been to Paris and never seen the Eiffel Tower, it might be assumed that the practitioner's subconscious mind knows nothing about it either. However, over the course of his life, his mind has already received an enormous quantity of information about it from pictures, photographs, stories, videos, books, and so forth.

There are three basic techniques for obtaining information in the phase. Each of them has its advantages and disadvantages that must be studied and learned before use.

Animate Objects Technique

To perform this method of obtaining information, the practitioner, in a full deep phase, must locate a person by techniques for finding objects and procure the necessary information from that person through the use of simple questions. If the required information is linked to a certain person, then that person should be located in the phase. If the information is not related to anyone in particular, then it is possible to create a universal information source, which must be associated with wisdom and knowledge. For example, this could be a wise recluse, a well-known philosopher, or a guru.

The advantage of this technique is that it is easy to pose additional questions and it is also easier to verify whatever information is obtained. A drawback of this technique is that, for many, it is difficult to communicate with living objects in the phase because of an object's unresponsiveness or a practitioner's problems with maintaining the phase while talking with objects.

Inanimate Objects Technique

Use techniques for finding objects in order to locate information from sources like inscriptions, books, or newspapers. While trying to locate the source of information, remember to concentrate on a belief that what is found will have the desired information. Source types are not limited to paper media; even radios or televisions may be watched or listened to, and computer search engines and file systems also may produce results.

A huge drawback of this technique is that considerable complications arise if an additional or a follow-up question emerges, which may cause the practitioner to have to stop and repeat the searching process.

The upside to this technique is that if a practitioner has problems communicating with animate objects, this technique can temporarily serve as a reasonable alternative.

Episode Technique

In order to receive information using this method, imagine an event or series of events that will communicate the desired information. Then, move to the area where predetermined events are expected to take place by using translocation techniques. After arriving at the destination, use visual observation to understand what is taking place and the information that the events are communicating. The episode technique is suitable only for cases where information can be obtained by observation.

How to verify the information? The techniques for receiving information in the phase are not complex and prove successful after just a few attempts. However, as was already mentioned earlier, the properties of phase spaces that do not fall under the category of vivid perception are not particularly stable - not only in terms of appearance, but also in terms of their properties. Correctness of information also depends on the objects themselves. The problem rests in that the practitioner may not be able to properly control the object in question and may receive false information.

Interesting Fact!

> *The phase space is not everyday reality; therefore, it should not be treated with the normal belief that every observation should be regarded as fact.*

Even when a practitioner has learned to find animate and inanimate objects with an absence of doubt, there is still no guarantee that the received information is always accurate. A few technique-related tricks are able to test an object's ability to speak the truth.

For example, an object can talk about something with absolute confidence, but that does not mean that what it communicates is all true. If doubt is experienced while finding the object, then doubt may have an effect on what the object says. This is why doubt must be avoided at all costs - although beginners are bound to initially have problems with this.

To determine whether an object is able to give accurate information, *a control question* should be asked. It essentially consists of asking some very simple questions and observing the object's reaction. For example: "How much is two times two?", "What's my name?", "How old am I?", and "Where do I live?", and so on. If the object is unable to answer even such simple questions correctly, then there is no sense in trying to obtain further information from it. The practitioner must have made committed some errors when creating the object. A proper object will remain silent or say that it does not know the answer to the control question.

After any information is obtained, it must be confirmed. This is done by means of *a clarifying question*. The practitioner needs to ask the object where the information came from to find out the details that offer proof of the information's authenticity in the real world. The object may also be asked the same questions more than once, provided they are reworded. The answers to reworded questions must be identical.

Remember, the more important the nature of the information and the more serious action it implies, the more effort needs to be invested in verifying it in the real world since a certain percentage of the information is bound to be incorrect despite correct performance of information-related techniques.

Approaching the obtainment of information with as simple questions as possible is also extremely important. The simpler the information that needs to be found out, the better. As soon as a phaser becomes able to do this in his practice, he can move on to more difficult and more important tasks. There's no sense in beginning such experiments with something incredibly difficult. If a practitioner is unable to count how many pairs of shoes there are in his foyer, then he'll hardly be able to find out how to become a millionaire.

In addition to everything else, it's important to consider how specific the needed information is. Practitioners quite often seek answers to totally vague or abstract questions while in the phase, which leads to a lack of success. The more specific the question, the greater the odds of obtaining an answer to it. For example, it hardly makes sense to expect a specific and clear answer to a vague and all-encompassing question like, "what awaits me in the future?" It's many times better to ask a question regarding how to achieve some extremely specific goal in the future. Other examples: instead of "how do I get a raise at work?" ask "how can I make my current project as successful as possible?" Instead of "how do I get healthy?" ask, "how do I get rid of my headache?" and so on.

The ability to obtain undistorted information from the phase is considered to be a masterful skill of nearly the highest order. So where do problems occur? As has already been noted, obtaining information is not anything difficult from a technical point of view - it suffices to get into the phase and find something out from objects or the phase space. Problems occur on a completely different plane, one that is much more difficult for people to control - the plane of thought, mood, and belief - both the superficial and deep-founded variety.

One of the most exciting and interesting tasks of ongoing modern research is the study of how the phase space, its properties, and functions depend on the internal mental background of the practitioner. This task is made particularly clear by the following example. This example will assume that the phase space is controlled by the subconscious mind. It will also assume that a practitioner has gotten into the phase using an indirect technique and has rolled out of his body while in his bedroom. It turns out that the subconscious was able to generate the entire room along with millions of minute details with exact precision in a matter of seconds, perhaps in a mere fraction of a second. Unimaginable is the amount of computation that had to occur in order to so quickly generate everything, up to every thread in the curtains and every dot of ink on the wallpaper, without violating any laws of physics. It's difficult to even fathom. Next, the practitioner decides to perform a well-known test with a calculator. To this end, he needs to find that computational tool and punch in the numbers to be crunched. He will then verify the calculator's answer in the real world. And so, he uses the technique of finding and finds a calculator. He finds the real thing, and not just a mere representation of it. This object, despite its size, is quite complicated - yet the phase creates it with singular accuracy and precision. All of its lines, buttons, and curves are generated - all much more accurately than could ever be drawn. Moreover, this calculator can even be taken apart, and its internal components may be examined. Everything here is generated in only an instant.

But then the trouble starts. The practitioner multiplies 2 by 2 and gets some odd result, e.g.: AP345B, 5?eE74047... etc. That is, the result is anything but the correct product.

A paradoxical situation now arises: the subconscious mind generates a space around the practitioner, accurate to an impossible degree and up to the minutest detail. However, this very same subconscious mind is unable to multiply simple numbers together, a simple math problem that the practitioner himself can solve within a second. Doesn't this situation seem strange? Actually, not at all. The phase space and its computing resources are not at issue here. For the phase, this calculation is not difficult at all. This is really a mere trifle for the resource that the practitioner has at his disposal, even if he himself has difficulties with multiplication tables.

The crux of the problem lies in the mind of the practitioner when he is performing this given test. He may simply lack confidence (and this doubt will be reflected in the result). In addition, there may be a mass of other thoughts and feelings going through his head, which may bring all of his efforts to naught. For some reason, it sometimes seems that a similar phenomenon pertains not only to the phase, but also to the everyday physical world...

A quite similar situation arises with the technique of translocation in the phase with eyes closed. It is enough to think of something extraneous, enough to have some doubt in the outcome of the flight, and that flight will then take much longer, or even eject one into a different place, or simply return one back to the physical body. The very same mechanisms and systems are at play when obtaining information. While with teleportation it's enough to translocate several times in order to understand the essence the answer sought, or to feel it, more protracted problems may develop with obtaining information.

One of the proven properties of the phase state is that its stability and steadiness are directly proportional to those of the person experiencing the sensations it offers. For this reason, the external characteristics of objects tend to be very stable and unchanging. For example, one cannot put one's arm through a wall when in a deep phase. But at the same time, the properties and invisible functions of those same objects can be very unstable and sensitive to any mental disturbance. That is why it is difficult to instantly evaporate water or turn it into blue brick while in the phase, but water can easily be turned into vodka - a transubstantiation accompanied by change not only in taste and smell, but even in properties which affect the mind of a person who drinks it. After all, water and vodka have the same outward appearance, but only differ in terms of properties. And just as well, an object created in the phase for the purpose of obtaining information is extremely dependent on the internal state of the practitioner. A polluted mind muffles just what the practitioner wants to learn, and blocks what phase objects could easily convey to him.

For that very reason, a practitioner desiring to obtain information in the phase should remember one important thing: one must be not only externally, but also internally as indifferent as possible to the information one obtains. In parallel with this, it is necessary to have full and complete confidence that everything will work. Otherwise, the object will vacillate between what one wants to hear and what one is afraid to hear, instead of a simple transmission of information occurring. This problem is overcome in large measure through practice, but there are some tricks that facilitate this task. The simplest of these is as follows: the practitioner asks the object his question neither point-blank nor right away, but unexpectedly during conversation on a side topic. This approach simply allows the practitioner to relax and remain indifferent to what is happening, if at least for a short while.

CREATIVE DEVELOPMENT

Surely, any creative person reading this textbook has had ideas occur more than once regarding the broad possibilities of using this phenomenon for artistic and cultural purposes. And indeed, it is difficult to imagine any limitations in this field. In addition to there being no boundaries from a technical standpoint, there are also no limits regarding the type of creative output. The artist, the musician, the sculptor, and the designer will all be able to apply the practice of the phase to their purposes. The experiences offered by the practice of the phase are sufficient in and of themselves. They indeed allow one to gain access to the gushing fountain of inspiration that is the human imagination.

- *Creating works of art:* Using the methods of object finding or translocation, an artistic practitioner can purposefully seek an object in the phase that may be composed in real life. If necessary, it is possible to easily return to study an object in the phase. For example, a painter may find a stunning landscape and put it to canvas in the real world while periodically returning to the same landscape in the phase.
- *Viewing future completed works of art:* If an artist is in the process of realizing an idea, then a preliminarily look at the end result of a design may be seen in the phase. A painter can examine a painting in advance; a sculptor may see a completed sculpture, and an architect will be able to wander through a house that is still in the early stages of design. Any creative work can be simulated in the phase.
- *A source of inspiration and fantasy:* The phase practice imparts ideas and desires that positively affect creative endeavors. Furthermore, the realization of desires and travels through unusual spaces evoke great emotions, which provide excellent inspiration.

The idea of employing the phase to model creative output is obvious, as absolutely everything may be created in this state. The artist may create a landscape that he is only just preparing to paint, or has already partially sketched out. This gives him an opportunity to assess the result in advance, and introduce any changes as necessary. Or he may review all of the landscapes that he intends to paint, and then choose the most promising one to start work on. Or, he can simultaneously examine all the landscapes that he has ever seen, as the phase space easily reproduces them for him in fine detail.

This possibility offered by the phase is quite useful for the musician, as it allows him to create musical scores of any complexity, including those making use of an orchestra or chorus, whose members can led be easily and freely, without worrying about how difficult it is to do this or that, and without having to avoid over-straining those musicians who must comply to his every demand. Also, he does not have to worry about whether the orchestra, for example, will able to immediately play the notes just as he wants, because the output will always comply with his wishes. Naturally, to this end the student must first master how to control the phase, but is that really an obstacle?

A sculptor or an architect can easily create anything in the phase and review it in every detail, and thus have an advance opportunity to uncover any weak aspects of his design. There's no point in describing how artists of every medium can make use of the properties of the phase, because such people can figure out those uses for themselves. Undoubtedly, an artist working in any medium can find something there for himself.

It must also be emphasized that works of art created in the phase state won't disappear anywhere. That is, there is no need to worry about recasting works of art already created in previous phase experiences. They are preserved there forever, and can always be found there again. In other words, any and all information can be stored with perfect fidelity.

The only thing a creative person may have to worry about is how, in the real world, to reproduce those wonderful masterpieces that he creates so easily in the phase. The fact is that the phase space is much more powerful than our waking conscious awareness - that is, our capabilities are much reduced during waking life. However, there will always be a chance to go back into the phase and work out the details. In essence, everything is limited only by our primitive memory, which is often unable to recall such large amounts of information during waking life.

SPORTS

In many spheres of human activity, skill at complex physical movements is quite important - sometimes everything can depend on it. Meanwhile, motor skills are the most important factor in the majority of sports, from martial arts of any kind to fencing, gymnastics, weightlifting, figure skating, and so on. In many ways, playing these sports depends on learning to perform certain moves automatically. And so, gymnasts perform somersaults or some other feat dozens of times over the course of a training session, and boxers devote half of their workouts for months on end to practicing one and the same punch.

For such people, there is one additional type of movement training that may be performed in the phase. The potential for such training in the phase may not initially be obvious, but movement in the phase sets off the same brain activity as it does in wakefulness, only nerve impulses are not sent to the muscles. Accordingly, any movement that has been well practiced in the phase will remain almost equally well practiced in the real world. This phenomenon allows the training routine to be supplemented, or even substituted when injured or unable to train for any reason.

Of course, one will never become an Olympic champion by training exclusively in the phase, but doing so is still extremely effective.

It turns out that practitioners of East Asian martial arts are especially drawn to the phase. Thus, many karate enthusiasts either perfect techniques while in the phase, or simulate going up against stronger rivals. Even more interestingly, some find world-renowned masters for personal instruction. Especially popular phase trainers are Steven Seagal, Jackie Chan and, of course, Bruce Lee.

Sport in the phase can be combined with the technique for obtaining information, which is described in this book. The student can use that very technique to find out exactly how to train, and which technologies and opportunities can be taken advantage of in order to improve and become more successful at a given sport. This assumes, of course, that the student plays sports, something always recommended.

THE PHASE - AN ALTERNATIVE TO NARCOTICS

When in search of new sensations and adding color to life, a practitioner can fully counter any inclination to take narcotic substances. The phase is essentially an independent and safe way to have far more powerful experiences than could be had using any narcotic. The same may also partially apply to alcohol, as interest in it might be dislodged by self-development through the phase.

The opportunity to use narcotics while in the phase and have the same sensations and experiences might also serve as a way get out of a drug habit in real life.

Even more pressing is the need for the phase to make inroads into mystical schools whose practices are often much based on various herbal or chemical substances. People often do not scorn controlled substances in the pursuit of "personal development", "spirits", or "getting in touch with their higher selves". However, this is nearly always due to the simple reason that such people are simply unaware of the existence of other methods for experiencing a profoundly altered state of consciousness. Talk with any mystic burned-out by the use of various powders, tablets, grasses, cacti, or mushrooms, and they'll freely admit that they would never have undertaken such experimentation if they had known that there are simple and easily-accessible phase entrance techniques.

People have grown accustomed to the belief that ancient shamans and Magi knew something special and that their techniques were quite advanced. However, in nearly every culture they manifested their abilities nearly exclusively thanks to the use of various stimulants. They were essentially always taking the easy route of degradation, interpreting narcotic-fueled hallucinations instead of the pursuing the kind of personal development that modern people strive for.

Unfortunately, lack of widespread knowledge regarding indirect techniques for entering phase states has led to a situation where a market has formed in the West for chemical substances for the practicing the phase. Even though success is guaranteed 90% of the time when correctly performing indirect techniques, people are indoctrinated to believe that experiences are not a matter of technique or method, but rather of the presence or absence of some substance or another in the body. As a result, purely psychological dependence on the use of such substances develops, and progress using techniques to enter the phase is stunted. There can't be any talk of a real practice at an advanced level when any auxiliary substances are being used. The most important characteristic of the phase is the fact that it can be achieved independently.

UNPROVEN EFFECTS

People often approach the practice of various phase states with deep-rooted misconceptions about what can actually be achieved through practice. Everything listed in this section refers to these misconceptions. It has not been proven that any of these things is impossible; however, actions should be based on proven and verified methods in order to avoid making mistakes and wasting time.

Physical exit: If the first experience with the phase phenomenon happens by accident, it is almost impossible not to interpret it as a real separation of the soul from the body – a physical exit. This is how the initial phase experience really feels. With experience it becomes easily noticeable that certain things in reality do not match things in the phase, like the placement of objects or furniture in the house where a phase is first encountered.

No actual physical exit from the body has ever been proven through scientific experimentation and observation. For example, in the phase, it is not possible to fly around to locations in physical world, although it may seem so; the locations that are experienced are produced within the mind. Nor is it possible to pinch someone in the phase and then to find a bruise on the person while in reality.

Other worlds: The phase space is similar to the physical world, and a practitioner may be inclined to think that the soul has left the body. Sometimes the phase takes on an absolutely unnatural form. As a result, the practitioner may decide that a parallel world has been entered: the world beyond, the astral plane, mental space, or the ether. Although travel in the phase can lead to many places, this does not mean that the phase allows travel through or use of actual, alternate worlds. The practitioner should be reasonable.

Development of super-abilities: It is partially correct to consider the practice of the phase as an extrasensory ability since it is an actual development of extremely unusual skills that have always been considered mystical. Times have changed, and the phase should hardly be shuttled off to the esoteric, obscure corners of knowledge.

There exists an unproven theory that the practice of the phase can impart unusual abilities. While literature is full of references to this effect, these abilities have not yet been proven by anyone. The same applies to intentionally developing unusual abilities in the phase. Yes, these may be trained while in the phase, but this does not mean that training in the phase will yield the same results in the real world. Practice should not be for the sake of achieving super-abilities since there are many proven applications that do translate to reality in valuable ways. Be realistic.

USE OF THE PHASE BY THE DISABLED

While practicing the phase may still be viewed by the majority as entertainment or an element of self-development at best, phase practice takes on a whole new meaning for the physically disabled. For them, the phase may be the only place where the handicaps of reality dissolve and disabled practitioners experience a range of possibility greater than that of the life experienced in reality.

A blind person will see again in the phase, even more clearly than seeing people do in reality. Someone who is paralyzed will be able walk, run, and also fly. A deaf person will hear the murmur of streams and the chirping of birds. For the disabled, the phase practice is a chance to discover new, incomparable worlds free of physical limitation.

Naturally, there are some nuances that must be understood. First, for example, if a person was born blind, then there is the question as to whether or not they would be able to see in the phase in the same way ordinary people see. However, this issue has not been fully studied, and blind people should simply carry out their own independent research. Second, some types of disabilities can negatively affect the practice of the phase states. For example, people who have gone blind have greater difficultly catching the intermediate state between sleep and wakefulness since, unlike seeing people, they may awaken without opening their eyes to the perception of sound. Third, psychological factors may play a pronounced negative role. Certain beliefs and attitudes that may present an obstacle.

Whatever the individual issues, this particular area of phase applications requires additional study. It deserves significant attention because it is a valid tool for the rehabilitation of the disabled. It is workable, unique, and extremely surprising in terms of the experiences that it offers.

APPLICATIONS BASED ON INFLUENCING PHYSIOLOGY (SHORT VERSION)

There are three main elements that, with the help of the phase, may influence the physiology in very beneficial ways. First, it is possible to contact the subconscious mind to learn how to influence physiology. Second, the brain reacts more strongly to sensations than to real events. For example, if running while in the phase, the physical processes of the body would be consistent with the processes occurring in the body of a person running in reality: respiration accelerates, blood pressure increases, the heartbeat quickens, and even blood flow to the feet becomes greater. Third, while the practitioner experiences profound changes of consciousness in the phase, this is where all direct and indirect forms of autosuggestion are most effective.

Not all influences on physiology are 100% effective. However, even without a guaranteed rate of success, the effort to influence physiology is worthy of attention because amazing results can be obtained. Always remember that achieving a good result may require repeated influence from the phase. Even in the physical world, medications require repeated ingestion.

If the goal is to affect the course of a disease, do not place all your hopes on the phase. The services of medical doctors must be the first recourse. The more serious the illness, the more strongly this rule applies.

Obtaining Information

Information on health problems may be obtained using the same techniques used for obtaining information. It is also possible to learn methods to remedy health problems, if such methods exist. Both of these possibilities apply to third parties being helped by efforts in the phase. Information gathering is the only proven way to influence the physiology of other people by using the phase. For example, it is possible to find a well-known healer in the phase and ask about personal health problems or the problems of a friend or family member. A clarified answer may be used in the assistance of traditional medical treatment.

Attention from Doctors
Find a doctor in the phase by using the technique of finding objects and ask the doctor to take examine or treat a known illness or other health problem. For example, in case of abdominal pains the doctor may palpate the belly, apply pressure to various points, and perform a special massage. Any actions are possible, including an operation. After leaving the phase, the practitioner will feel a positive result.

Taking Medicines
The placebo effect is much stronger in the phase than in reality since all actions occur in a highly modified state of consciousness and are perceived directly. Object locating techniques may be used to find medications used to treat existing problems. It is also possible to create self-made substances to produce the desirable effect. For example, in case of an acute headache in reality, a practitioner may take a painkiller while in the phase and its effect will be partially felt in the wakeful state.

Direct Effect
An illness or problem may be directly affected by actions in the phase. For example, a sore throat may be warmed by envisioning a burning sensation in the throat or by moving to a hot location, like a sauna. If a practitioner would like to increase physical flexibility, then stretching in the phase will cause the body to adjust to the nonexistent action by relaxing and tensing the corresponding tendons and muscles.

Programming
This is nothing more than normal autosuggestion or auto-training in the phase, which is more potent in the phase than reality. A practitioner should repeat a desired goal

silently or aloud and, if possible, should imagine experiencing the desired result. For example, if the aim is to alleviate depression, a practitioner should attempt to recreate a happy mood in the phase, experiencing it to the fullest extent possible. Simultaneously, silent repetition of a goal with complete understanding and expectation that everything will be alright and that everything is wonderful will undoubtedly produce the desired effect.

Useful Experiences
Everything with useful properties in reality should be experienced as useful in the phase since the body will react in practically the same manner. Useful experiences may include exercising, going to the gym, having a massage, taking mud or salt baths, and experiencing pleasant emotions.

Psychology
Practicing phase-related techniques favorably affects the psychology because it offers new opportunities and evokes new emotions. However, there are specific applications of the phase that produce differing psychological effects. For example, it is possible to use the phase space as a bridge for dealing with phobias by facilitating a setting where a practitioner may confront and deal with certain fears. Various complexes may be defeated in a similar manner. The use of a well-known technique called re-visiting (recapitulation), where a person re-experiences adverse events while trying to relate to them in a new way, has been used successfully in the phase.

APPLICATIONS BASED ON INFLUENCING PHYSIOLOGY (FULL VERSION)

Obtaining information
Actions. The essence of this technique is to obtain useful information in the phase that can be applied to self-healing.

The information obtained may pertain not only to actions to be implemented in real life, but also to actions to be performed directly while in the phase. It's possible to learn how to help another person, or learn what that other person needs to do to in order to overcome his illness. For example, if the practitioner has some illness or other health-problem, he can learn in the phase which medicines would have the best effect in the physical world, or which actions taken in the phase could help him to recover from his illness or affliction.

Therapeutic indications. The therapeutic indications are endless. As the technique concerns obtaining information and knowledge, it can be used for any self-healing case, no matter what its gravity or variety, and no matter whether the intent is to heal in reality or while in the phase.

Example. For example, a practitioner has hurt his leg while at work. There's a bad painful bruise, and it's taking a long time to heal. And so the question arises as to how to get the bruise to start healing faster and become less painful. The practitioner enters the phase and employs the technique for obtaining information through animate objects, and to that end summons a surgeon. He briefly describes the problem and asks for advice. The surgeon recommends that the practitioner first go for a short run in the phase in order to get rid of the pain or simply stop feeling it, and then, before returning to reality, smear some cooling-agent onto the bruise and inject a large dose of novocaine into it. The phase surgeon might also advise him to apply a compress using ingredients that he had never even thought of, or take a specific medicine. The result is that all of the above is implemented both in the phase and in reality, achieving a result commensurate with the quality of those actions.

Effectiveness. Effectiveness (in this context: the accuracy of knowledge obtained through the phase) is highly dependent on one's level of mastery - that is, on the ability of the practitioner himself to obtain information from the phase. For a novice, no more than 20 to 40 percent of advice obtained may be accurate, but with experience that number may reach 70 or even 100 percent. Considering this, it is vital to use the techniques for verifying obtained information.

Difficulties. The main difficulty with this type of healing using the phase lies in the fact that the practitioner must posses an additional skill: the ability to obtain correct information from the phase and, by corollary, the ability to verify that information. It's usually necessary to simply enter the phase, deepen it, and then perform the actions one planned to do, all the while maintaining the phase. But in this case, everything is much more difficult.

The very accuracy of knowledge obtained is highly dependent on how impartial the practitioner is to the information he is receiving, and how confident he is that he will be able to obtain accurate information. He should not make the source of information feel pressured to say what he wants to hear. By doing so, the practitioner would choke off the flow of accurate information. It's hard for the average person to "turn-off" habits like this without serious training, as everyone is accustomed to contemplating something in the back of one's mind, or having some desired outcome for a conversation.

Accessibility. Of course, obtaining information in the phase for the purpose of healing is one of the most difficult processes of all, and so the novice is better off shying away from it if he doesn't have a pressing need to go through with the process. Unlike many other methods for healing through the phase, it is necessary here to master the separate and difficult technique of obtaining information.

Taking medicines

Actions. Most people are aware of the so-called placebo effect that occurs when sugar-pills administered instead of real pharmaceuticals work just as well as drugs about one quarter of the time. In the phase, this feat can be pulled off much more impressively and with much greater effectiveness, as not only may any pill (or other dosage form) be generated, but its effects can also be felt immediately. The physical body simply has no other choice when it is given a pill with ascribed properties. All of this forces the physical body to react to the events taking place in the phase and recreate the effect in every possible way in the practitioner's real-life organism. This is a great method.

The physical body is totally fooled, and forced to work in a one way or another, solve a specific problem, or complete a certain task. The key to understanding how this occurs lies in the following fact: the physical body reacts to all experiences in the phase state as if they were actually occurring in reality, and attempts to physically adapt to phase events by trying to create the needed and hitherto insufficient effect.

This is made clear by the following simple lab experiment: when observing a practitioner who is running while in the phase, changes in breathing patterns are recorded, as is increased heart-rate, elevated blood-pressure, and even blood rushing to the legs. And these are only external indicators. Along with them come the same internal endocrine secretions that would occur if the practitioner were actually running a race. These internal processes can be understood through the following example: taking a shot of vodka in the phase. One not only smells and tastes the vodka, but also instantly feels the corresponding effect of having a shot, which may partially linger on after having returned to the waking state. But the vodka may have no influence if the practitioner focuses on it having the same properties as water. That is, the vodka itself can thus lose its natural properties. And so, when taking medicine in the phase, one ought try right then and there to feel its effect, and as intensely as possible.

For a long time, there was no explanation as to how taking medicine in the phase in the form of placebos could be effective and work. This is especially considering that the practitioner knows that he is taking a placebo, no matter how vivid the sensations and reactions that accompany it. The answer came in late 2010 when yet another test on placebos was performed at Harvard Medical School on patients suffering from irritable bowel syndrome. The experiment was unique in that the patients knew that they were taking a placebo - that is, a sugar pill. Nevertheless, the group taking the pseudo-medicine experienced nearly twice the symptom reduction as the control group not given anything. And in a 2008 Duke University experiment on placebos, people were given fake pain relievers of supposedly different price ranges. It turned out that the "expensive" pain-killers worked on 85% of test subjects, while the "cheap" ones were effective only for 61 percent. It is interesting to note not only the difference in effectiveness between the same sugar pills, but also that they were so effective to begin with. This experiment demonstrates that it's actually better to take well-known, well-advertised, and expensive drugs in the phase in order to obtain maximum effect.

    The procedure for self-healing in the phase through taking medicine is as follows: the practitioner must find (using the techniques for finding objects) specific medicines or create them, and then take them in the usual way, actively trying right then and there to immediately feel the corresponding effect. If it is not possible to feel the primary effect of a medicine, then the most strongly associated side effects ought be felt. The medicine or healing substance itself may take any form: tablets, pills, drinkable infusions, balsams, potions, etc. When a person takes these substances in the phase, the body will begin to reproduce their effect and associated sensations. In addition, a corresponding reaction will occur at the level of internal bodily functions - the same effect that the medicinal substance was to have brought about. This is all quite simple.

    Of substantial significance is the ability to create one's own remedies with the desired set of healing properties. For example, one can create and take a pill that has been programmed with the finding objects technique to simultaneously treat two or more diseases, even if no such drug exists in the physical world. Meanwhile, it is worth noting the regularity with which invented substances are less effective than existing or well-known ones - this phenomenon is due to practitioners having psychological blocks.

Of course, in most cases it is not enough to take a single dose of a medicine while in the phase. Therefore, it's a good idea to go on a kind of treatment regime, taking doses at regular intervals, just as if with a real pharmaceutical prescription. In some complicated situations, it is necessary to take medicine regularly in the phase over one's whole life - just as in the physical world.

It is worth mentioning one important item on the subject of dosage: it is in fact possible to still obtain a desired effect without taking any medicine in the phase. However, it is difficult for a practitioner to make his organism work in the desired way without a supporting anchor. The medicines themselves are what greatly facilitate the activation of the desired self-healing program by acting as anchors. As it turns out, the dosage amount does not have any importance at all. However, it's better to follow established norms at the beginning of one's practice, as this activates subconscious programming correlating quantity with quality. Nonetheless, an overdose may have adverse effects. Once a practitioner learns to independently reproduce the effect of medicines on his body, it will be possible to use preparations in minute amounts.

When choosing among various medicines, the question may arise as to whether or not the side effects that many of them have will also occur in the phase. It can be confidently stated that the incidence of side effects is reduced here by 50 to 100 percent, because as far as the subconscious mind is concerned, any medicine should heal first and foremost. Meanwhile, the body may not be programmed to produce side effects. Given this situation, it is better not to use medicines whose side effects are well known, as in that case side effects may not only arise, but also be dominant when certain technique-related mistakes are made. That is, the medicine may do more to cause harm than to heal in the phase.

Therapeutic indications. Therapeutic indications for taking any medicine in the phase know practically no limits. As with obtaining information, the phase can be employed towards accomplishing any objective or tackling any illness.

Example. Suppose a practitioner catches a bad cold, resulting in the symptoms of headache, runny nose, cough, and fever. He enters a deep stage, and, using the technique for finding objects, finds on the nightstand a box of well-advertised cold relief medicine, the kind that is dissolved into a glass of water. He then goes into the kitchen and drops a tablet into a glass of water, which starts fizzing and dissolving. As soon as the tablet dissolves, he drinks down the entire glass, trying at the same time to immediately feel its effect: warmth courses through his body, a certain feeling of well-being arises, his temperature goes down, post-nasal drip eases, and so on. After returning to the physical world, the practitioner either immediately feels better, or the relief comes gradually from that point on. The procedure is then carried out several times over the course of the next several days. The practitioner may then separately implement a preventative course of treatment, making future colds milder and much less frequent.

Of course, the technique for finding objects can be employed towards a variety of ends. For example, you may find a glass with a cold-relief tablet already dissolved into it, and thus save time.

Effectiveness. For the novice, the effectiveness of taking medicine in the phase as a means for healing ranges from approximately 50 to 70 percent. That is to say, in the majority of cases there is a clear and stable effect. Considering that pills, for example, are rarely this effective in real life, it turns out that in many cases this is the best of all available ways to heal oneself. For experienced practitioners, effectiveness reaches 90 to 100 percent. It is necessary at times to adjust the regularity with which medicines are taken while in the phase, as dosage increments are often crucial to optimizing the effect.

Difficulties. There are no substantial difficulties with taking medicine in the phase. Required here are the basic skills of finding objects and the ability to reproduce medicine's effect when taking it - this is accomplished by simply deepening one's desire for this to happen. If this is not achieved on the first try, then it will work by the second or third attempt.

Accessibility. Medicines are the basic means of influencing the organism while in the phase state. As this technique is both accessible and easy to master, even for novices, one should add it to one's repertoire right away and try to achieve results from the very first attempts. This is especially true, in view of the technique's high level of effectiveness.

Direct influence

Actions. Direct influence on the organism while in the phase is attributed to the effect of the body reacting at all levels to the impact of phase experiences, as was described in the section regarding the technique of taking medicines. That is, when something is done to the organism while in the phase, the effect is immediately felt there, and, at the same time, there is a real effect on the body in the physical world, just as if everything were happening in real life. The main difference with techniques for direct influence is that the problem is approached not through an intermediary (medicine), but is instead tackled directly. This is essentially a more thorough method, but also a more difficult one.

In practice, it works like this: a person goes into the phase state and begins to directly influence the sick organ or organism using all means at his disposal - both those that exist in the physical world and those that do not. Moreover, he can influence the body simply at the level of perception, without external contact. The very perception of direct influence is the key factor here. Without it, there's no real point to applying the technique - nota bene.

There are many options for directly influencing the organism as a whole or influencing its individual parts: heating, cooling, releasing energy, numbing, massaging, administering injections, smearing ointments, radiation treatment - in general, everything that is possible or impossible in real life. This process requires both taking the initiative and a creative approach.

One may influence either the entire organism as a whole, or any separate part of it while in the phase. For example, one can easily warm up the entire body, heat up only the brain, or even massage it, as incredible as that may sound. Though this may strike some as unbelievably strange, one may actually put one's hand through the body while in the phase, feel any organ, and influence or affect it as necessary. Doing this feels so realistic that people are often long unable to bring themselves to attempt it, if only out of the fright that strikes them when they feel their own hand passing through their own body and touching their internal organs. For example, if a person wants to have an affect on the liver, he will be able not only to hold it with his left hand, but also to directly feel the liver itself, as well as the sensation of holding it. This may be particularly frightening when acting on the heart or the brain. The phase is the only place where one may do all this. And this is truly more than just an incredible experience that leaves an emotional impression lasting one's entire life. Significantly, one can affect not only a disease, but also its symptoms. By alleviating and eliminating symptoms, one will likewise influence their source. This is especially important when the source of the symptoms themselves is not well understood.

Of course, as with most other techniques for influencing the body while in the phase, a single direct treatment is often not enough. As a rule, the procedure should be performed several times by entering the phase for several days in a row, or even implementing a treatment regime. Either way, all this depends on a practitioner's level of skill in employing the technique. It goes without saying that an experienced practitioner need perform far fewer procedures than a novice.

Therapeutic indications. Directly influencing the organism is easiest when it comes to a problem whose localization is known. It is very difficult to directly influence an imperceptible illness of an unknown nature that exhibits few symptoms.

Example. The example of an injured leg will now be taken up again. The practitioner enters a deep phase and immediately begins manipulating the leg in every way possible. First, he concentrates on his leg not hurting and being already healed, and tries to circulate internally-generated therapeutic heat and vibrations about it. The healing effect must be felt immediately. If there is time left, the practitioner uses the technique for finding objects to summon a syringe loaded with painkillers and fast-acting bruise-treating medication. He injects the entire does into his leg, trying to immediately feel the effect of the preparation. This comes easily: the practitioner feels numbness and pleasant sensations emanating from the shot. If possible, he finally rubs in a specially created ointment onto his leg, further accelerating the healing process. When the practitioner returns from the phase, he is likely to immediately feel that his leg hurts a lot less, and that it will soon begin to recover. Nevertheless it's best to perform the same procedure several times.

Another example: kidney stones. The practitioner enters into a deep phase, and for several minutes tries to "blast" the kidneys with warm vibrations that dissolve the stones. To do this, he first tries to simply feel his kidneys, and then invokes the necessary processes in them by force of a strong desire to do so. Afterwards, he slips his hands into his abdomen, holds one kidney in each hand, and starts massaging them in such a way as to dissolve the stones in them. Then, he carefully slips his fingers into his kidneys, and uses them to rub the stones into a harmless powder. For maximum effect, the practitioner should carry out this procedure regularly and consistently on this problem, as it is not one that is quickly resolved.

Effectiveness. In most cases, the technique of direct influence is a very effective means of treatment. This is especially true when the problem is palpable and obvious. Effectiveness can reach 60 to 80 percent even for a novice, to say nothing of what more experienced practitioners can achieve.

Difficulties. Directly influencing the organism while in the phase involves no substantial difficulties. It is only necessary to feel the effect of such influence, which is easy to do when desire is strong enough, even without prior training. There remains the minor problem of fear arising when hands are inserted into the body, a phobia that tends to be difficult to overcome. However, the fear often becomes surmountable when one's goal is serious enough. Sometimes curiosity alone is not enough to bring oneself to hazard the venture.

Accessibility. Directly influencing an illness or health problem is sufficiently easy in the phase, in addition to being quite effective. Therefore, even beginners are encouraged to use this technique from their very first attempts and never forget about it, even after having mastered other techniques for healing themselves while in phase states. This technique is one of the fundamentals.

Programming

Actions. The effectiveness auto-training, self-programming and self-hypnosis have been long established. They have been proven to bring results even when performed while awake. The deeper the trance state that they are implemented in, the more effective they are. From this perspective, the idea cannot but occur of also using similar techniques to heal through the phase, as the phase state is the deepest hypnotic trance state that can be achieved consciously and independently. Moreover, the usual trance state in which self-hypnosis is performed does not even begin to compare with the phase in terms of substance or effectiveness. Therefore, self-programming is many times more effective in the phase than in any other state. This is, for all effective purposes, a new era of development for these kinds of technologies.

Programming in phase consists of creating self-fulfilling subconscious resolutions. Since a person in the phase is in the deepest of all possible altered states of consciousness, this is the most effective place for such programming. Given the fact that much human illness is psychosomatic in nature, and yet still causes real suffering, programming techniques employed in the phase can destroy such "diseases" at the root.

In practice, one gets into the phase and introduces a resolution directly at the subconscious level to remedy a specific health problem. There are several variations of this action in the phase. First, one simply can firmly state one's resolution aloud regarding remedying a problem or regarding one's well-being. Second, programming can also be effected wordlessly, at the level of speechless understanding and intention. This second variation is much more difficult than verbal suggestion, so it is better for the novice to shy away from it.

The duration of one attempt should not take up an entire phase, as what matters here is not the length of an attempt, but it's quality. What's important is that the programming occurs in the subcortex at the deepest and most meaningful level, even if it lasts for only 10 to 15 seconds. Don't assume that several words pronounced half-heartedly will do all of the work on their own, as if this were the same thing as casting a spell. These words need to be experienced and felt at all levels of perception and consciousness awareness.

When programming your subconscious, it is very important to note that verbal formulas should not contain negations. For example, one should not say, "I do not have insomnia." Instead, it is much better to affirm, "I sleep deeply and soundly, I fall asleep quickly." As with other techniques for self-healing in the phase, acting on a problem just once is often not enough when programming. It is better to introduce resolutions several times on different days. Sometimes it's advisable to implement an entire treatment regime.

Therapeutic indications. Programming for self-healing in the phase can be applied to almost any disease or ailment, but it works best of all for problems of personal psychology or general well-being. For example, one may use it to improve overall working capacity, alleviate fatigue and anxiety, increase stamina, improve overall health, bolster the immune system, and much more.

Example. A practitioner has an illness that is at a serious stage and accompanied by fatigue as well as irritated mood, but has no possibility of taking sick-leave to get better, as he needs go to work every day. And so, he enters a deep phase and begins to say aloud the following words: "Once I exit the phase, within a day I will feel buoyant, healthy, and active. I will be in a good mood and have ideal overall well-being. I am healthy. I am active. I am happy. I have boundless energy, and I am full of vitality." Meanwhile, he does not merely utter these words, but also tries to feel them, to experience them. Of course, it's better for him to initiate further procedures to treat the disease itself before exiting the phase. In any case, repeating such an affirmation almost immediately after returning to reality may also bring solid results.

Effectiveness. The effectiveness of programming for self-healing through the phase is not very high, as most people are unable to feel the self-programmed resolutions fully and deeply. Effectiveness for beginners is somewhere within the bounds of 30 and 50 percent. Effectiveness increases with practice. Interestingly, a single session is very often enough for experienced practitioners - unlike the case with other methods for self-healing through the phase.

Difficulties. The main difficulty arising when using programming techniques occurs with being able to sincerely feel the resolution being made. This can be an insurmountable obstacle for many due to their psychological makeup or difficulties in understanding what is going on. It is also necessary to make separate note of the fact that the process of programming may eject a practitioner from the phase, as it tends to be relaxing. Thus, it is important not to forget to employ some of the techniques for maintaining the phase while programming. For example, one might constantly rub the hands together, scrutinize something up-close, or keep vibrations going the whole time.

Accessibility. Considering likelihood of effectiveness and technical difficulties, self-healing in the phase through programming is often not very accessible for beginners. Therefore, unless there is some specific goal that can only be solved only in this way, it is better to use other techniques.

Psychological impact

Actions. Whenever it is necessary to solve problems related to psychological or psychosomatic illnesses, using the phase for psychological impact is the most effective, clear, and proven way to influence the organism. It's not for nothing that science has documented its effectiveness in studies on lucid dreaming.

The operational principles of this technique are simple:
> *-The physical body adapts to events experienced in the phase;*
> *-Re-experiencing negative events of the past erases the impression made by them at the physiological level;*

It would serve well to start by noting that practicing the phase, even outside the context of self-healing, in and of itself has a powerful, positive, and favorable effect that will manifest itself in any individual pursuing it. The point is that once someone has experienced the phase and realized the true expanse and endlessness of the world's horizons, he or she begins to relate to real life in a different way. He becomes more open, has fewer issues with himself and the world, and more sociable. Moreover, practical mastery of the phase builds inner centeredness - though it's real work. Practicing the phase cannot but have a beneficial effect on the individual, as it is a real form of self-actualization in and of itself. It is both authentic and lasting self-actualization - unlike other practices that verge on delusion and conjecture.

Therapeutic indications. The following types of problems may be acted upon with the help of psychological impact in the phase: mental illnesses and other problems (including phobias, fears, complexes, indecision, depression, social anxiety, and much more). This technique for self-healing in the phase is ill suited for conditions that are not of a psychological nature. The exceptions to that rule are illnesses caused by factors of a psychosomatic nature (according to some reports, up to 50% of all diseases fall into this category, but such distinctions are difficult to categorize on a case-by-case basis).

Example. A person is afraid to travel by airplane (aerophobia). To solve this problem, the person should enter a deep phase, and, by employing the technique of translocation, find himself in an airplane going through rough turbulence. Despite the fact that all this is not really happening in the physical world, the fear experienced will be 80 to 120 percent that of a similar real-life situation, as the realism of the phase state is extremely elevated. There is practically no difference between sensations experienced in the phase and those of real life. However, there is no actual threat to life and limb in the phase - the practitioner understands this subconsciously, and tries to stay in the airplane as long as possible, getting used to its swaying, shaking, and sudden dips. Only a couple of such riveting simulations are usually enough to at least take any phobia out of the forefront of one's mind and stop it from causing further distress, if not indeed banish it.

The next example to be considered is a scenario where a person had a very stressful experience while still a child: the death of a favorite puppy. In such cases, an age-old method works quite well - communicating with the geist of the departed (this also works with human beings). This is quite a sure method, especially considering that there is nothing difficult about it from a technical point of view. One need only enter a deep phase and apply the technique for finding objects. The exact same puppy remembered from childhood will appear. It will also lick one's face, play, bark, and look at its owner with loyal eyes, wagging its little tail all the while. The practitioner will be able to once again pick it up, pet it, touch its fur, and feel its weight and warmth. The puppy will be just the same as if encountered in real life. Even when it playfully nips at the hand, the owner will feel it. The first such meeting will naturally cause some sadness and tears, but from then on, once one realizes that one can continue to meet with this pet in phase, sadness will quickly recede to the background (as will all psychosomatic complications caused by the death of the beloved animal). The practitioner will begin to feel that the puppy is really alive. After all, perception arises from sensory input, and not deductive reasoning.

Effectiveness. The instruments for psychological impact in the phase are quite effective. As psychology is being discussed, it is difficult to compare the effectiveness of this technique with other methods of treatment. Nonetheless, even for beginners the rate of success reaches 100% during the very first applications. That's something that really stands out.

Difficulties. As it is the psyche and the mind that are being impacted by these techniques for self-healing, a certain amount of internal effort is necessary to achieve results. For example, if a person is trying to overcome claustrophobia, then real fear will arise when he finds himself in enclosed spaces while in the phase. He will still have to confront his phobia on his own. The phase here only provides a springboard for working on oneself. It should never be assumed that the incredible effectiveness of this method comes out of thin air, without effort on the part of the practitioner.

Accessibility. Self-healing in the phase using the technique of psychological impact is readily accessible to beginners, starting from their first phase entrances. This is because it does not require any special skills except the ability to translocate, and so this course can be taken right from the outset.

Healing Others

In addition to self-healing, the phase state of the mind also provides some possibilities for having an influence on the health of others.

It's not news that most people are firstly interested not in self-healing, but in helping others. This is understandable, as perhaps they have loved ones who are for whatever reason unable to use the phase, or are extremely negatively prejudiced against such things. Perhaps the reader of this book is a professional who treats diseases in non-traditional ways, or is a novice healer himself.

It is well to first emphasize that only one of the wide variety of theoretical ways to have an influence on another person in the phase is proven and absolutely practicable, and it is techniques for obtaining information. While the effects of all the other techniques on the practitioner himself are beyond doubt and have been proven experimentally, their influence on other people remains theoretical - as of yet, no one has been able to prove remote influence on another person in a controlled experiment. For example, if you find a friend in the phase and give him some medicine, the effect of that medicine on him will remain theoretical.

It is important to realize that trying to employ anything but the technique for obtaining information risks time and energy being spent in vain. Some certainly will claim to have proven that it is possible to have a direct affect on another person through the phase. However, only what each and every person can accomplish - literally from the first time - will be discussed here. Whatever the case may be, it can be definitively stated here that either influencing another person remotely is impossible, as few have reported results, or it simply remains unclear how to do it. Either way, in embarking upon such hitherto unproven experiments, one does so at one's own risk and peril. If remote influence through the phase nevertheless shows itself to be working, then it is already the practitioner himself who will have to know what needs to be added so that the impact on the other person brings stable results.

One's theoretical view on the nature of the phase phenomenon will play an enormous role in one's choice of a course of action. The materialist will not have any way of helping another person besides obtaining information. The occultist is hardly likely to encounter barriers to his practice. This is a choice for each person to make. It should be understood that even if other techniques allow some influence on others, the results are clearly far from stable - as many will doubt the results due to a lack of empirical evidence, and not out of their own views or theories. That very lack of empirical evidence forbears a definitive statement here. Scientific experiments have delivered no confirmation to date.

Of course, if one wishes to help another person, there is another proven way to do so besides obtaining information: convincing him to practice the phase and employ the appropriate techniques for self-healing himself. From a pragmatic point of view on the phenomenon, this is a much surer way than trying to influence another person from the phase.

The technique of obtaining information will be of help for the practitioner who has decided to heal another person. This technique is described in detail in this book, along with how to use it. The only difference is that information must be sought on a particular person, and not on oneself. The practitioner may learn not only how to provide treatment in real-life, but also how to obtain a comprehensive diagnosis.

It works like this: using the technique for obtaining information, one finds a specialist who will help deal with the problem that one's acquaintance is experiencing. One then speaks with this doctor about how to help him, about what can be done in reality, and so on... The phase doctor's prescriptions and/or advice are then relayed to the person for whom they were obtained. Alternatively, the entire phase experience is related to the person in need.

From a materialist point of view, it is necessary to note the fact that far from everyone can be helped using the phase. Without going into detailed explanations, it will simply be stated that the more one knows about a person, the more one will be able to find out about him in the phase. Even if one has only seen the person's picture, it is possible that one will nonetheless find out something about him, and be able to help him in some way. But if one knows this person personally, then the amount of information obtained about him through the phase will increase drastically. A practitioner should at least talk for a short while with a person before attempting to obtain information in the phase about his health, or treatment methods best suited to his condition.

Theoretical ways to heal others
The following methods have in no way been proven to work in practice. One may experiment with them at one's own personal discretion. Moreover, if a practitioner intends to help people in these ways, he should never under any circumstances promise to solve all of their problems, because they should not forgo more traditional methods of treatment. A student ought be sensible and realistic in evaluating his capabilities, especially if he is only just starting out with his practice, and most of his views are based on borrowed theories, rather than on personal experience.

Also, all of these techniques require the ability to find objects. To better understand the essence of techniques for treating other people, it is best to learn them by practicing on oneself. This chapter will only briefly describe adapting some techniques for work with others.

Almost everyone asks the question, "Who are these subjects that we are to find in the phase and heal?" This question arises for one simple reason: there are no clear common definitions regarding the nature of the phenomenon itself that would allow one to speak confidently on its particulars. Many people (up to 25% of the world population) still do not know that the Earth revolves around the sun, rather than vice versa. So it's quite a transition from there to the phenomenon at hand...

Upon discovering who or what these phase subjects and objects were, the explanation for the nature of the phenomenon itself would at last be at hand. For the materialist, people in the phase, no matter what their external realism or believability of behavior, would be merely simulated clones that have no relation to people or objects in the real world. For the esoteric, the person or object in the phase would be the soul of a real person. So it's the same as usual: each person sees the world in accordance with his assumptions and knowledge. But caution is always advised in such matters, as people all too easily succumb to the power of pitfalls of various kinds, some of which they cannot escape for the rest of their lives.

Taking medicines. Adapting this technique to treating another person means that that person must first be found in the phase (using the technique of finding). It is then necessary to administer appropriate medication depending on the nature of the health problems. Possibilities include not only pharmacy drugs, but also any possible folk remedies. For example, if the other person has prolonged headaches, then he should be given powerful painkillers to swallow, as well as other drugs that strike at the headache's cause (if known).

Direct Influence. With direct impact on another person, after first finding him in the phase, it is necessary to work directly and fixedly on the problematic organs, or on his general condition. To this end, one may use official prescriptions or folk remedies, various kinds of massages, as well as anything else that comes to mind. For example, a patient has bad sunburn. In addition to all the other options for treatment, one might run one's hand over his damaged skin, thus restoring it (this comes easily), give him injections to accelerate the healing, or use ointments, and so on.

Programming. After having found someone in the phase, one simply looks him in the eye and impresses upon him that he does not have a particular problem, that it will pass quickly, that he is healthy, vigorous, happy, etc. Perhaps a practitioner's friend is chronically fatigued. In that case, after finding him in a phase, the practitioner needs to convince him that he is full of energy, active, has boundless energy, strong motivation, is more goal-determined than ever, and so on. All this must be said right to his face with a firm voice. There will hopefully be an immediately change to his countenance, thus confirming the instant effect. One may also obtain verbal confirmation from him that the programming is working.

Psychological Impact. In adapting this healing technique to work with another person, one need first find that subject, and then immerse him in the necessary feelings and experiences. For example, a person is afraid of dogs. So, the practitioner finds him using the techniques for finding objects, and then places him in a situation where there are many dogs and they all are friendly to him, nuzzling up to one another, and playing. Conversely, the practitioner could place him in a situation where there are dogs behaving very aggressively, threatening to bite. However, the aim here is to ensure that the person being helped doesn't get nervous, but instead coolly beats off the dogs without experiencing fear. It might not be that easy, but the practitioner should try to change the attitude of the other person to the problem.

It is also worth noting again that this technique can be applied in the most pragmatic way possible - asking the person with health problems to take up the practice of the phase himself. Simply having the phase itself in one's life has an indelibly positive effect, not to mention the possibilities for self-healing that come with it. Practicing the phase is one of the most interesting experiences one will ever encounter.

If the goal is to affect the course of a disease, do not place all your hopes on the phase. The services of medical doctors must be the first recourse. The more serious the illness, the more strongly this rule applies.

TYPICAL MISTAKES WHEN USING APPLICATIONS

- Attempting an applied use of the phase without reaching a good depth. Deepening must always be performed before applications are attempted.
- Being so involved in phase applications that "maintaining" techniques are forgotten.
- Forgetting to consider how to breathe when traveling through Outer Space or underwater, which may lead to a feeling of asphyxiation.
- Concentrating on a certain object while traveling through time instead of concentrating on time travel, which should be the focus since it is the point of performing the application.
- Forgetting techniques for "maintaining" when animate objects are encountered, when these techniques must always be kept in mind.
- An inability to overcome fear during contact with deceased people. This fear must be overcome once and it will never resurface again.
- Limiting desires while practicing the phase. There is no limit to desire within the phase.
- Limiting the performance of certain actions, although there are no customary norms of behavior in the phase, unless the practitioner decides upon specific limits.
- While looking for information in the phase, attempting to obtain knowledge which clearly exceeds the scope of the subconscious mind.

- Applying the technique of obtaining information from animate objects without knowing how to communicate with them.
- Forgetting to check the ability of an object to convey valid knowledge. The probability of bad information is much higher if it is not verified.
- Failing to verify information in the phase before using it in reality.
- Forgetting to verify serious information in reality before using it. Verification absolutely must be performed to avoid using bad information in reality.
- A single attempt to influence the physiology through the phase. In the majority of cases, results are gained through repeated effort.
- An attempt to cure some disease only using the phase, whereas it is compulsory to seek medical advice.
- Initially believing that the phase is the exit of the soul from the body, while this is easily refuted in practice.
- Concentrating only on unproven applications, despite all the evidence out there that this is most likely a waste of time.

EXERCISES

Questions

1. What are the three basic applications of the phase?
2. Are proven practical phase applications accessible to any practitioner?
3. While in the phase, is it possible to travel through Africa?
4. Is it possible to walk on the moon in the phase?
5. Is it possible, while in the phase, to appear at the time of the Earth's creation?
6. In the phase, is it possible to appear in the magical world behind the looking glass?
7. Which relatives can be met in the phase?

8. Is it possible to meet and talk to your favorite actor in the phase?
9. Where can one realize any cherished dream?
10. Can a practitioner appear in the computer game Doom?
11. Can a musician use the phase for creative purposes?
12. Does the practicing the phase influence a person's imagination?
13. What most probably governs the phase space?
14. What kind of information is obtainable in the phase?
15. While in the phase, is it possible to find out where the lost key to an apartment is located?
16. What kind of people can discover where treasure is hidden in the phase?
17. Should any information obtained in the phase be construed as accurate?
18. Should information obtained in the phase be verified after waking up, even if it's already verified in the phase?
19. Should obtaining information occur before deepening has been performed?
20. To obtain information while using the animate objects technique, who should be talked to if the goal is to find out the thoughts of a boss at work?
21. How might information from an animate object be obtained?
22. Can an inscription on a wall be used as an inanimate source of information?
23. Is it possible to use the episode technique to learn where one has lost the key to one's apartment?
24. Should a doctor be consulted before trying to cure a disease through phase practice?
25. Are results from influencing physiology in the phase always 100% guaranteed?
26. What phase techniques might be used to influence the bodies of other people?
27. Is it possible to obtain information that can be used to influence the body and its functions?

28. Is it possible to take a well-known painkiller in the phase and feel its effects on exit?
29. Is it possible to use autosuggestion in the phase?
30. Can athletes use the phase to develop their skills?
31. Is it realistic to expect that the soul will exit the body while practicing the phase?
32. Is it possible to enter a parallel universe through the phase?
33. Should a practitioner hope to develop super-abilities in the phase?

Tasks

1. Meet your favorite singer and travel to your dream house in the phase.
2. While in the phase, find a wise person who is an authority on matters of the phase and learn from them what entrance techniques will best suit your practice.
3. Try to perceive heat throughout the entire body by translocation to a sauna or through auto-suggestion.
4. Learn to move objects by simply staring at them in the phase, and appreciate the extent to which this skill is reflected in reality.

Auxiliary Information

Chapter 11 – Useful Tips

A PRAGMATIC APPROACH

The only sure way to get practice without unnecessarily wasting time is to have a pragmatic and rational approach to the nature and possibilities of the phase phenomenon.

The majority of available information regarding dissociative phenomena is inaccurate. This becomes obvious during initial entries into the phase. This is why practice should begin from the perspective of a clean slate, using a logical bearing in thinking: *everything not confirmed by personal experience should be taken with a grain of salt.* This means only personal experience should be taken seriously, not the experience of acquaintances, authors, teachers, blogs, or forums.

To err is human; thus, it is also human to pass on errors. As a result, many paradoxical old wives' tales concerning the phase phenomenon have become accepted a priori.

Not everything written in esoteric literature should be thrown out. Some things may possibly be drawn from it. After reading such literature, a practitioner should not assume that the new knowledge is a universal truth.

For a house to stand firm, it needs a solid foundation. The only way to build a good foundation for phase practice is to approach the phenomenon in a down-to-earth manner, from a scientific perspective, discounting any purported supernatural phenomena. Once a solid foundation has been established, everyone has the right to build their own truth on it.

INDEPENDENT ANALYSIS

If a practitioner is only interested in having phase experiences, then the simple study of this guidebook and other materials may suffice. However, if a practitioner wants to achieve the best results, ample focus must be given to individual thought and formation of opinion based on personal analysis.

Until all questions are answered through a search for answers in various sources of information, no real progress should be expected. Many things cannot be described or explained. The resolution of many issues will always remain up to individual judgment and understanding. Finding all of the answers is impossible. Moreover, trying to possess all of the answers is a serious inhibitor to real progress because the practitioner would have to digress into dubious literature and conversation aside from real, formative practice.

The advice and experiences of others may lead to error. In no case should there be any authorities or unachievable ideals. A logical, even skeptical approach should be taken during research and practice. The goal of this guidebook is to provide the reader with linear, factual information sufficient for the development of independent analysis.

Each time a practitioner encounters some incomprehensible phenomenon or problem when performing phase techniques, an independent analysis of the phenomenon should be formed before looking elsewhere for the cause. If a seeker looks for answers outside of personal reasoning, there is a high risk of assimilating and acting upon a fallacy.

Many practitioners are not willing to analyze personal successes and failures, and instead search all sorts of books, which often contradict one another. Using a hodge-podge of extraneous, unverified information can only lead one to further, and quite infectious, fallacy.

	Indirect method	Becoming consciousness while dreaming method	Direct method
\multicolumn{4}{c}{**Scale for Discovering and Analyzing Mistakes in Phase Entrance Methods and Phase Experiences**}
1	Have an attempt upon awakening	Have a firm intention	Have lapses in consciousness
2	Have any technique work when alternating through techniques (already in the phase!)	Have a dip into sleep	Have a deep lapse in consciousness (already in the phase!)
3	Have a separation	Have an episode of consciousness while dreaming (already in the phase!)	Have a separation
4	Have a deepening of the phase		
5	Have a plan of action realized		
6	Have a phase maintained for a long time		
7	Have a secondary exit from the body		
\multicolumn{4}{c}{In case of problems entering the phase or controlling it, steps that were skipped or not completed should be determined using the scale.}

APPROACH TO LITERATURE

Literature of every sort has always been the main vehicle for disseminating information about the phase state. The phase phenomenon is referred to by other terms: astral projection, out-of-body travel, or lucid dreaming. In addition to disseminating information, many books are often vehicles for disseminating fallacies.

This is easy to recognize when researching several such books and comparing described events and theories. The information is more often than not contradictory and based on opinions that have never been verified by anyone, including the authors. The result is a mass of speculation that has no bearing on reality, nearly always accompanied by a false certainty about the subject matter. However, unlike the real world, the phase is not a place where one can believe one's eyes or feelings. The phase's appearance and qualities depend very much on the person experiencing it.

For example, if a practitioner believes upon entering the phase that his body will be lying nearby on the bed, then it will always be there. If a practitioner believes that the perceived body should always be tethered to the physical body, then the practitioner will always see and even feel a tether in the phase. This is a simple case of expectations becoming reality. Similarly, someone who has entered the phase by accident and thinks that the time of death has arrived may see angels and a tunnel with a light at the end. If someone is extremely religious, there may be a perception that something holy, even God, has appeared. If entry to the phase is construed as a result of being abducted by aliens, then that is exactly what will happen.

This would all be quite funny if it were not encountered all of the time. If one has no doubts going in, then the only thing left to do is to believe. To believe, to tell others about it, and write books about it...

www.obe4u.com

There are authors who impart no illusions, but it is often difficult for a novice to separate the truth from illusion or open fabrication, which is why a skeptical approach to the contents of any book is warranted. The only truth conveyed in any book is that which has been verified by personal experience. The rest should simply be noted and possibly taken into consideration.

In conclusion, books should be studied to discover technique-related information that allows a practitioner to enter the phase and control the experience. This is the only point of intersection among all beliefs and theories.

PRACTICE ENVIRONMENT

Since techniques used to enter the phase are associated with a specific type of mental operation, it is necessary to create comfortable conditions so that external distracters are kept to a minimum. A room should neither be too cold or too hot, nor too bright. Performing techniques at a comfortable temperature in a darkened room or while wearing a sleeping mask are ways to promote unhindered practice.

> ***Interesting Fact!***
> *In bright rooms, wearing a sleeping mask over the eyes can double the success rate of attempts, and also help one to enter a much deeper and longer phase.*

Interfering noises are often also major distracters and isolation from such noises is necessary to successful practice. It is often sufficient to turn off the phone and close doors and windows. If this does not help, or if it is extremely loud outside the window, one can use standard earmuffs.

It is also helpful to give advance notice to people so that they are not alarmed. It is also preferable that no one is in the bed with the practitioner. Most often, domestic animals interfere with the performance of techniques, which is why they should be fed beforehand and kept out of the room where direct or indirect techniques are practiced.

TALKING WITH LIKE-MINDED PEOPLE

Great benefit is derived by discussing personal experiences with other practitioners. This leads to an exchange of information, new knowledge, and mutual help concerning certain problems and issues.

The greatest effect comes through communication in person, and not solely through mail, forums, and blogs. Meeting face-to-face with like-minded people promotes camaraderie and a useful knowledgebase to consider during individual practice.

Due to the fact that knowledge of the phenomenon is underdeveloped, difficulties may arise in finding someone to talk to. This can be solved by personally sharing phase experiences with friends and family members, regardless of whether they are fellow practitioners. It is even better to pass on training literature, like this guidebook.

Interesting Fact!
More and more families all across the world enjoy the phase together. Out of all those registered with the OOBE Research Center, the most interesting is a family in which 6 members representing three generations (ages 14-65) competitively practice the phase. In another case, an 8-year-old actively practices with his parents.

The website www.obe4u.com also has a discussion forum devoted to the phase, making it possible to obtain and exchange a large amount of information. The site also has the contact information for the coordinators of Phase Practitioner

Clubs all around the world, which are non-commercial associations of enthusiasts who meet to exchange and discuss experiences.

THE RIGHT WAY TO KEEP A JOURNAL

Keeping a journal can be of much help while learning and practicing the phase. When properly kept, a journal can help a practitioner to develop an analysis that will increase the quality of phase experiences. By and large, keeping a journal helps to iron out a sporadic practice, turning it into a structured discipline that can be mastered.

An effective diary should contain a massive amount of indicators that allow a statistical study to uncover patterns. It is essential that each entry include the date, time of day or night, and a detailed account of entries into the phase and phase experiences. Descriptions of mistakes and a plan of action for the next phase should also be recorded. During the novice stages of practice, even noting unsuccessful entry attempts is beneficial. Later on, only successful phase experiences may be recorded.

Here is an example of a proper journal entry:

Data:
Experience No. 12
January 5th, 2008
2:13 PM

Experience:
I woke up early in the morning. After exercising, I took a shower and ate breakfast. I watched TV and read books until lunch.

I laid down for a nap at 1 PM, right after lunch. I felt like performing indirect techniques, and affirmed this intention. I woke up the first time to movement, but after trying to employ forced falling asleep (in order to negate the effects of the movement), I fell asleep. I woke up the second time without movement and tried to roll out. This didn't work and I tried levitating and getting up. After that, I moved on to phantom wiggling. Movement occurred in my right hand. After doing this for several seconds, I decided to try listening in. Sounds started, but I was unable to make them louder. However, images appeared before my eyes and I started to view them. After they became realistic, I decided to try rolling out and it worked without a hitch.

My vision was dim, as if through a veil. But then, the rest of the sensations I felt reached the verge of reality. This is when I went to the window. For some reason, it was summer outside, and not winter. There was a red fire-truck outside the window. There were really low clouds in the sky. The sun was above them.

Next, everything quickly faded away and I found myself back in my body. Then, I got up and looked at the time. It was 2:15 PM.

Mistakes:
1. When the phantom wiggling worked, I should have aggressively tried to increase the range of movement, and not simply done wiggling, let alone change to another technique. After all, if wiggling occurs, the phase can always be entered. 2. The same with the sounds. I had no great desire to amplify sounds or even listen in. Everything was done lackadaisically. 3. I should have started with deepening and not actions, as visual sensations were not vivid. 4. I should have employed techniques for maintaining. 5. You can't look down for long without simultaneously using techniques for maintaining, yet I took in everything outside the window and in the sky. 6. I forgot about the plan of action. 7. I should have tried re-enter the phase.

Plan of action for next time:

1. Definitely deepen the phase as much as possible. 2. I should try to go through a wall. 3. Translocate to my Auntie in New York. 4. Translocate to the Statue of Liberty and examine her crown.

Chapter 12 – A Collection of 45 Techniques

GENERAL PRINCIPLES REGARDING THE TECHNIQUES

The techniques detailed below may be used both with a direct method of entering the phase without prior sleep, and with an indirect method performed upon awakening. The exceptions are the dream consciousness techniques, which are listed separately, although they cannot but have a direct influence on the probability of success of the other methods. Conversely, all of the other techniques cannot but have the side effect of increasing the probability of dream consciousness arising. With a few exceptions, the list does not include non-autonomous phase entrance techniques based on external physical factors or chemical influences.

The specifics of using each method are described in detail in its corresponding section. All of the techniques listed below are to be used in accordance with the instructions for each method. However, it is necessary to first understand a fundamental difference here. With an indirect method upon awakening, the goal is to find a technique that works by quickly alternating through the most interesting and intuitive ones. As soon as a technique starts working, keep with it and intensify the effort, and then try to separate right away. It will become apparent how well a technique is working by the intensity of its effects. For example, some imagined movement may become real. Any real sensations arising from the techniques upon awakening mean that they are working, and that the practitioner is already in the phase.

The techniques play a secondary role with the direct method, and serve to create a free-floating state of mind (fading out or activating consciousness, depending on the type of technique being performed) that is conducive to brief lapses in consciousness. The deeper a lapse, the better the chances of immediately entering the phase when resurfacing from it. Meanwhile, techniques may work from beginning to end. However, this means nothing without lapses in consciousness, unlike with indirect techniques.

It's also important to remember that direct techniques performed without prior sleep have one-tenth the success rate of indirect ones performed upon awakening. That's why all the techniques below can easily bring results upon awakening, but be useless for novices when used at other times.

Each technique is described only in general terms, and it is assumed that the practitioner already has a basic understanding of all of the mechanisms by which the phase occurs and is able to fill in all of the additional nuances on his own.

Several technique-based tricks can be used to substantially improve the odds of success of practically all of the techniques listed below. First, you should try to not simply perform the techniques "for the sake of appearances", but rather give them your all, trying to become one with them and put all of your sensations into them. Next, you can move your gaze up slightly, as naturally as possible. Third, begin to use the techniques by first imagining yourself doing a 180 degree turn along your head-to-toe axis. Fourth, while you're performing your techniques always try to recall sensations of how they had already worked in the past, or of past phase occurrences. Fifth, you should always have a clear motivation for entering the phase. That motivation may perhaps arise from the most interesting plan of action you can think of.

TABLE FOR CREATING YOUR OWN TECHNIQUES

Table for Creating Phase Entrance Techniques and How They Work in Practice

		A Active (sensory perception)	B Active (imagined)	C Passive (detection)
1	Sight	Observing images (hint)	Visualization	Observing images
2	Hearing	Noise (hint)	Imagining sounds	Listening in
3	Kinesthesia	Phantom wiggling	Imagined movement	
4	Vestibular sense	Real rotation	Imagined rotation	
5	Tactile sensation	Vibrations	Cell phone	

Examples of mixed techniques:
Visualizing the hands technique	1A, 3B, 2B(C);
Swimmer Technique	3B, 5B(C);
Alien Abduction Technique	4B, 5B;
Rope Technique	1B, 3B, 4B, 5B;
Sensory-Motor Visualization Technique	1-5B;

Notes: This table does not include the sense of smell due to its rare use, nor emotional sensations due to difficulty in conjuring them. Meanwhile, some other elements are also left out.

The techniques described below are but a drop in the ocean of their myriad possible variations. It suffices to say that practically every phaser will come up with some technique elements independently and be successful at using them in practice. Considering the many variations of certain techniques and the fact that several of them can be used at the same time, the total number of possible techniques numbers in the thousands. However, all of them only differ in several fundamental ways, and knowing how they differ will allow you to easily create as many techniques as you want on your own. Moreover, understanding the principles of creating techniques makes it substantially easier to conceptualize and understand the techniques themselves.

A table for creating techniques is presented below, but it is not to be overused - after all, technique is in the end a matter of secondary importance when it comes to entering the phase. The most important thing is to understand how the phase state arises, and then all of the techniques will work. Otherwise, you could know dozens or hundreds of them, but to no practical end.

TECHNIQUES BASED ON MOVEMENT

Separation technique
The practitioner tries to immediately separate from his body without using any techniques for creating the phase state: simply roll out, levitate, stand up, crawl out, etc.

Phantom wiggling technique
The phaser tries to move some part of his body without moving a muscle, and meanwhile without imagining or visualizing anything. For example, this could be an arm, leg, shoulder, the head, or even the jaw. When movement arises, the main aim is to increase the range-of-motion as much as possible, but not necessarily the speed of movement or the portion of the body part being wiggled.

Imagined movement technique
A phaser tries to realistically feel some movement that he starts off by simply imagining. For example, this could be swimming, running, walking, flying, or peddling with the legs or arms. The practitioner doesn't have to visualize the technique when performing it, as movement itself is most important here.

TECHNIQUES INVOLVING SIGHT

Observing images technique
The phaser peers into the void before his eyes without opening them. As soon as he begins to see any imagery, he tries to discern it better by defocussing his sight, as if he were looking beyond the imagery. This makes it become steadier and more realistic.

Technique of visualization
The phaser tries to realistically see and discern an object no more than 6 inches from his eyes.

TECHNIQUES BASED ON VESTIBULAR SENSE

Technique of imagined rotation
The phaser tries to imagine that his body is rotating along his head-to-toe axis. The end goal is to replace imagined sensations with real ones. Rotation may generally take place on any plane, but one shouldn't try to visualize it or try to see oneself from the side, as the main emphasis is on one's own vestibular sensations.

Technique of real rotation
The phaser tries to rotate the sensation of his physical body along his head-to-toe axis. In this case, the process need not be visualized or imagined. You should start off from real sensations, although the plane of rotation may be changed at will.

Swing-set technique
The phaser tries to feel that he is riding a swing-set, or that his body itself is rocking with the same range of motion. The primary goal is to achieve the realistic sensation of swinging and try to make 360o revolutions.

TECHNIQUES INVOLVING HEARING

Technique of listening-in
The phaser listens inside his head, trying to hear if there is any noise or background static. If sound is heard, one must try to amplify it as much as possible through the same passive listening in.

Technique of forced listening-in
The phaser tries actively, and even strainingly, to hear sounds inside his head or background static with all his might. If this works, he tries to amplify those sounds as much as possible using the same active listening in.

Technique of imagining sounds
The phaser tries to hear some specific sound inside his head. Someone's voice, familiar music, and the sound of one's own name being called work best of all. If such sound arises, then the practitioner tries to make it as loud as possible.

TECHNIQUES BASED ON TACTILE SENSATIONS

Cell-phone technique
The phaser tries to feel some object lying in his hand, e.g. a cell-phone, an apple, a TV remote control, etc. Meanwhile, one should try to achieve realistic sensations in full detail.

Technique of imagined sensation
The phaser tries to feel tactile sensations on his body, starting with the sensation that someone or something is lying on him, and ending with the feeling of touching someone or something.

Straining the brain technique
The phaser tries to strain his brain either spasmodically or continually, as if it were a muscle. This brings a feeling of real strain inside the cranium, in addition to pressure, noise, and vibrations. This is essentially a technique of creating and intensifying the vibrations that enable phase entrance.

Technique of straining the body but not the muscles
Like straining the brain, but with the whole body. One tries to strain the body, but not the physical muscles. This causes internal tension, noise, and vibrations, which can eventually lead to the phase.

Technique of bodily perception
The phaser tries to authentically feel that his body is being stretched apart, compressed, inflated, deflated, twisted or otherwise distorted in some way.

TECHNIQUES BASED ON REAL MOVEMENTS AND SENSATIONS OF THE PHYSICAL BODY

Technique of eye movement
The phaser makes abrupt left-to-right or up-and-down eye movements. The eyes are kept closed the whole time. When properly performing the technique, vibrations and possibly separation will occur.

Forehead dot technique
Without opening his eyes, the phaser directs his gaze towards a dot on the center of his forehead. This is not to be a forced or excessively aggressive movement. This will bring the eyes into a position they naturally take during deep sleep, which may lead to a reflexive entrance into the phase or facilitate the performance of other techniques.

Technique of breathing
The phaser focuses his attention on the process of breathing and all of its aspects: the expansion and contraction of the chest cavity, the lungs filling with air, and the passage of air through the mouth and throat. A fluid transition to the phase may occur or vibrations may arise.

Raised hand technique
The phaser raises his forearm from the elbow while lying down and simply falls asleep. Once the practitioner fades out of consciousness, his forearm will drop, notifying him that he can perform another technique or immediately separate, as the right transitional state may have occurred during the lapse in consciousness.

Tactile irritation technique
The practitioner loosely ties his ankle or wrist with a cord, or puts on a sleeping mask. The sensations created by these foreign objects can remind the practitioner to perform the right actions either upon awakening or immediately after a lapse in consciousness.

Technique of physiological discomfort
The practitioner eats little throughout the day or drinks little water while eating lots of salty things. Conversely, the practitioner might drink too much water over the course of the day before making an attempt to enter the phase. The resulting physiological discomfort will often awaken the practitioner, induce consciousness while dreaming, or keep him from falling into deep sleep when performing the direct techniques.

TECHNIQUES BASED ON INTENTION AND FEELINGS

Technique of forced falling asleep

The phaser mimics natural sleep while maintaining control of his conscious mind, and then either employs techniques or immediately tries to leave his body at the last second before fading out. This technique can be used either on its own, or in parallel with any other technique.

Technique of intention
The practitioner enters the phase only through an intense and focused intention of immediately experiencing the phase. Alternatively, this may also be a calm but constant desire felt over the course of the day. Intention is especially effective not only during an attempt or long before one, but also every time you fall asleep, as this moment can be taken advantage of using the direct or indirect method.

Technique of recalling the state
When attempting phase entrance with or without techniques, the practitioner tries to recall - and thus induce - the sensations of a previously had phase experience.

Technique of recalling vibrations
In order to induce vibrations, the phaser tries to simply recall the sensation of them in as much detail as possible. Intensely desiring vibrations can also induce them.

Technique of translocation
The practitioner immediately tries to employ the translocation technique in a stubborn and self-assured manner without using a phase creation or separation technique.

Technique of motivation
In order to have a phase entrance occur spontaneously or get techniques work better, the practitioner creates a most interesting and important a plan of action for the phase that he wants to carry out no matter what.

Technique of fear
The phaser tries to recall something as scary, awful, or graveyard-like as possible, and imagines it right next to him - this is meant to evoke pure terror and horror, which will elevate to a phasic state at the right moment. The main deficiency of the technique is that fear can linger on into the phase, and the practitioner might subsequently try to get out of the state.

Technique of flight
Without using a phase creation or separation technique, the practitioner tries to conjure the sensation of flying right from the start.

Technique of counting
In order to enter the phase, the practitioner counts down from 100 to 1. Depending on the phase entrance method to follow, he should either try to keep his attention focused on counting, or, conversely, try to achieve lapses in consciousness.

Technique of dotting
The practitioner moves his attention to points on the skin atop of the largest joints of the body, or moves his awareness to inside the joints themselves. You should pause at each point for several seconds or breaths, trying to feel them as distinctly as you can.

BEST OF THE MIXED TECHNIQUES

Swimmer technique
The phaser tries to imagine the process of swimming in as much detail as possible, trying to feel all of the physical sensations of the process and even feel the water surrounding his body. Any swimming style may be used. (Best technique of 2010 and 2011 at School of Out-of-Body Travel seminars)

Rope technique

The phaser imagines that a rope is dangling above him, and that he is climbing up it. Meanwhile, one should try to feel one's own arm movements, the touch of the rope, and the sensation of height. Visualization of the process may occasionally be added in.

Technique of visualizing the hands

The phaser tries to feel that he is rubbing his hands together, as if trying to warm them. Meanwhile, it's important to try to feel the movement of your hands, the feeling of them coming into contact, the sound of rubbing, and also try to see the whole process in front of you. The imagined hands should be rubbed at a distance of no more than 6 inches from your eyes.

Sensory-motor visualization technique

The phaser should try to imagine as fixedly and actively as possible that he has already separated from his body and is employing a technique for deepening the phase, including the intensification of every sensation possible. He should imagine that he is walking inside a room, scrutinizing everything from a close distance, touching something, and so on. That is, he should immediately deepen the phase without using techniques to create the state or separate.

UNCONVENTIONAL TECHNIQUES

Alien abduction technique

The practitioner imagines that aliens have invaded his bedroom and are grabbing his ankles and pulling him out of his body. Alternatively, he imagines that he is being pulled out by a beam emanating from a spaceship.

Sex technique

The practitioner tries to feel the intimate sensations of the copulative act in as much detail as possible. This works better for women in the passive form.

Toothbrush technique
The practitioner tries to feel that he is brushing his teeth. He tries to feel the movement of his hand, the sensation of the brush in his mouth, and the taste of toothpaste. He can also try to add in sensation by imagining himself standing in front of a mirror in a bathroom.

Whispering pillow technique
Lying with his ear to his pillow, the practitioner tries to hear sounds, melodies, and voices coming from it. He can try to hear specific sounds, or simply passively listen in to what's there.

TECHNIQUES FOR BECOMING CONSCIOUS WHILE DREAMING

Anchor technique
During wakefulness, the practitioner develops the habit of analyzing his state whenever he encounters specific anchors: his hands, the sound of water, people's faces, etc. This practice will gradually transition over into dreaming, giving him a chance to react to an anchor and realize that everything around him is a dream. An anchor should be something encountered neither rarely nor frequently both when dreaming and during wakefulness. In order to get a clearer understanding of whether one is surrounded by reality or the dreamscape, one should try to levitate or go into hyperconcentration whenever an anchor is encountered.

Dream memory development technique
The practitioner recalls all of his latest dreams both in the morning and in the evening. For more solid results, one

should keep a dream journal and try to enter as many dream episodes into it as possible. The more dreams that the practitioner remembers, the more vivid future ones will become, and the more frequently he will become conscious during them.

Technique of dream map-making

Here, the practitioner not only keeps a dream journal, but also tries to mark all of the places he dreamt he was in on a special map. The main goal is to create an integrated plane where dream places merge together into a unified world.

Technique of dream analysis

Whenever performing dream analysis, be it mentally or when keeping a dream journal, the phaser should take as critical a stance as possible towards the logical inconsistencies that go unnoticed while dreaming, as they can serve as a clear marker that one is in a dream. Such critical awareness will gradually work its way into one's dreams, enabling one to turn dreams into the phase. This technique is especially effective when analyzing dreams immediately upon awakening.

THE HIGHEST TECHNIQUE

The highest universal technique

A practitioner well acquainted with the phase will try to not use techniques to create the necessary state. He will attempt to obtain it immediately. This is similar to intense intention to experience the phase coupled with focused recollection of the sensations associated with it. This technique is only suitable for phasers who have formidable experience.

Chapter 13 – Putting a Face on the Phenomenon

STEPHEN LABERGE

Stephen LaBerge was born in 1947 in the United States. At the age of 19, he received a Bachelor's Degree in mathematics from Arizona State University, after which he enrolled as a graduate student in the Chemistry program at Stanford University. In 1969, he took an academic leave of absence.

He returned to Stanford in 1977 and began studying the human mind, including subjects related to dreaming. LaBerge received his Ph.D. in psychophysiology in 1980. He founded the Lucidity Institute in 1987.

Stephen LaBerge has made the largest scientific contribution to the study of phase states. It suffices to say that LaBerge was the first in the world to prove during a full-fledged scientific experiment that it is possible to become conscious while dreaming This was done through logging specific signals made with the eyes by a person dreaming while sleeping under measurement instruments. These experiments also proved that eye movement in the physical body and perceived body are synchronous.

Lucid Dreaming, first published in 1985, is LaBerge's most well-known book. *Exploring the World of Lucid Dreaming*, a book that LaBerge wrote with Howard Rheingold, was published in 1990. It was mainly thanks to the efforts of LaBerge that mind-machines for achieving dream consciousness were created, such as DreamLight, NovaDreamer, and DreamMaker.

The key feature of LaBerge's work and achievements is an absolutely pragmatic approach to the nature of the phenomenon. Arguably, he is one of the few authors and researchers totally lacking in irrationality. Everything that can be read and learned from his books is verifiable and accessible for everyone, with no peddling of out-of-this-world superpowers.

CARLOS CASTANEDA

Due to Carlos Castaneda's desire to follow the spiritual practice of the Warrior's Path, which entails erasing one's personal history, the details of his biography are unclear. As far as Castaneda's early years are concerned, it can only be stated that he was born outside of the United States sometime between 1925 and 1935. He enrolled at the University of California, Los Angeles (UCLA) in the 1960s, where he received a Ph.D. in anthropology on the basis of his books.

Castaneda's entire life path was devoted to studying the teachings of a certain Juan Matus or Don Juan Cachora. It is more than likely that his persona is a composite-image of an Indian Shaman, a sorcerer, and an heir of the culture of the ancient "Toltecs".

Castaneda wrote a dozen books; however, the book *The Art of Dreaming* (1993) has the most to do with the phase state. It contains several effective techniques for entering the phase through dream consciousness. His subject matter is soaked in a large amount of mysticism and virtually devoid of any pragmatism.

www.obe4u.com

Despite the fact that the main orientation of Castaneda's work did not touch upon the phase state, he nevertheless became one of the founding fathers of this field, as his general popularity reached massive proportions worldwide.

Carlos Castaneda passed away in 1998.

ROBERT A. MONROE

Robert Monroe was born in the United States in 1915. In 1937, he graduated from Ohio State University with a degree in Engineering. He worked for some time as a radio program producer and director until he established his own radio company in New York, which rapidly expanded.

In 1956, his company also conducted a study about the effect of sound waves on the abilities of the mind.

In 1958, Monroe had an accidental personal experience with the phase phenomenon, which strongly stoked his interest in the subject to which he would devote his entire career. In 1974, he founded the Monroe Institute, which was entirely devoted to studying unusual states of consciousness and the ability to influence them through audio stimulation and other technologies. One of its main achievements was the creation of the Hemi-Sync system, which was designed to help a person reach altered states of consciousness, including out-of-body states, by synchronizing the two hemispheres of the brain.

His first book, *Journeys Out of the Body*, was published in 1971. Two books then followed: *Far Journeys* (1985) and *Ultimate Journey* (1994).

Robert Monroe has, so far, made the largest contribution toward popularizing the phase state. However, he understood the phase more as an actual exit of the mind from the body, which is why the term "out-of-body experience" (OBE) was introduced. The book *Journeys Out of the Body* was such a massive success that Monroe quickly became an undisputed authority in the field.

However, the large influence of mysticism on Monroe's work and views cannot be ignored. This is especially apparent after his second book. The majority of phenomena described in the book have not been verified in practice. The only attempt at conducting a full-fledged scientific experiment proving that the mind left the body was unsuccessful. In the end, typical misconceptions about the phase became widespread, as did awareness of the existence of out-of-body experiences.

Robert Monroe passed away in 1995.

PATRICIA GARFIELD

Patricia Garfield was born in 1934 in the United States. From the age of 14, she kept an uninterrupted daily dream journal that would allow her and all of humanity great insight into dream phenomena associated with the phase.

She was one of the founders of The Association for the Study of Dreams. Dr. Garfield holds a Ph.D. in clinical psychology.

She is the author of a great number of books, with the 1974 best-seller *Creative Dreaming* being the most widely lauded. It was one of the first pieces of literature to approach the phase state in a practical and non-specialist way, and received worldwide interest and appreciation. The book contains good practical guidelines and also describes the dreaming practices of various cultures.

SYLVAN MULDOON

Sylvan Muldoon was born in the United States in 1903. He is considered to be the American pioneer in the study of the phase, although he used the esoteric term astral. He inadvertently woke up in the phase at the age of 12, where he saw a cord connecting his perceived body to his real body. Muldoon first thought that he was dying during the experience, although he eventually concluded that this was an instance of "astral projection". He had repeated experience with the phenomenon, but was still unable to become an advanced practitioner due to a lack of full control over the practice.

After coordinating efforts with Hereward Carrington, the famous American investigator of the unknown, the two published the sensational, jointly authored book *The Projection of the Astral Body* in 1929. The authors published two other books: *The Case for Astral Projection* (1936) and *The Phenomena of Astral Projection* (1951).

Despite a large serving of esotericism, Muldoon's books, (especially the first one) contain a lot of helpful, practical information and explanation of the most diverse phenomena that can occur during the phase. However, Muldoon is considered to be the greatest popularizer of irrational esoteric terms and theories, which subsequently became quite widespread.

Sylvan Muldoon passed away in 1971.

CHARLES LEADBEATER

Charles Leadbeater was born in England in 1847 (1854 according to some sources). After dropping out of Oxford due to hard times, Leadbeater became an ordained priest, but then became quite active in the occult. This led to his becoming a member of the Theosophical Society in 1883. Leadbeater became one of its most famous participants.

The combination of a bright mind, scientific knowledge, and interest in the paranormal led him to publish many books on many diverse topics. One of them, *Dreams: What They Are and How They Are Caused* (1898), was one of the first works to touch upon the phenomenon of the phase. Leadbeater's writing is saddled with a ton of esoteric terms and theories. In it, the term astral plane is predominantly used for the phase. Nevertheless, the book is not without some helpful guidelines concerning techniques.

Charles Leadbeater passed away in 1934.

RICHARD WEBSTER

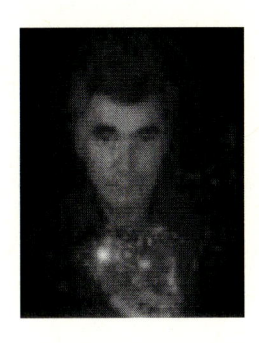

Richard Webster was born in New Zealand, where he still resides. He is the author of about 50 publications that have sold many millions of copies around the world. Some of them, like *Astral Travel for Beginners*, are completely devoted to the phase state. However, the book is saturated with widespread misconceptions about the phase phenomenon and misguided theories trying to explain it. The technique-related aspect of the book is also presented ineffectively.

It is quite likely that the author himself has no practical experience, which can also be said for the contents of his other dozens of books devoted to various topics.

ROBERT BRUCE

Robert Bruce was born in England in 1955. He has performed his life's work while living in Australia. After studying and promoting dissociative phenomena for many years, by the beginning of the 21st century he had become one of the leading authorities in the astral projection field. He is also a specialist in many other paranormal fields of study.

Robert Bruce wrote several books, the most important and well known of which is *Astral Dynamics* (1999). The author holds quite open esoteric views, which are very strongly reflected in his theories and terminology. The helpful, practical guidelines in his books are quite often loaded with a large amount of information that has not been verified or proven by anyone. Robert Bruce is also a propagator of typical superstitions and stereotypes concerning the phase phenomenon.

CHARLES TART

Charles Tart was born in the United States in 1937. He received his Ph. D. in psychology in 1963 at the University of North Carolina. Tart also received training at Stanford University. He was one of the founders of transpersonal psychology.

He became one of the most preeminent researchers of unusual states of awareness after the publication of *Altered States of Consciousness* (1969), the first book that he worked on. It was one of the first books to examine entering the phase through dream consciousness. The book received popularity when the use LSD and Marijuana were often viewed as vehicles to elevated consciousness, and the book even describes the use of chemical substances in the context of phase states.

Chapter 14 – Final Test

The questions on the test may have one or more correct answers, or none of the answers may be correct. Thus, the questions must be read completely through, and attention must be paid to their implications and finer points.

A student's theoretical knowledge is considered to be satisfactory if the correct answers to at least one-half of the questions are given. If a score of less than 50% is received, a student should study the weak points again or re-read the entire guidebook. Otherwise, it is quite probable that fundamental mistakes will be made, which will in turn interfere with individual practice.

If a score of at least 80% is achieved, then a theoretical knowledge of the practice is at an advanced level, which will surely have a positive effect on the practitioner's direct experiences in the phase.

Answers are in the appendix at the end of the guidebook.

1. Noise and realistic images unexpectedly arise when performing the indirect technique of phantom wiggling. What can be done?

A) Continue with phantom wiggling.
B) Switch to observing images or listening in.
C) Try to do all or some of the techniques simultaneously.
D) Choose the technique with the strongest precursors and continue with that one.

2. A practitioner unintentionally opens the eyes for several seconds upon awakening. What is the best way to start indirect techniques in this case?
A) Attempting to separate.
B) The observing images technique.
C) The rapid eye movement technique.
D) The forced falling asleep technique.
E) It's best to not start any technique and fall back to sleep with the intention of reawakening and trying to do everything again without first moving.

3. Which actions are preferable for performing a direct technique before falling asleep for the night after a long period of sleep deprivation or exhaustion?
A) Monotonously performing the observing images technique.
B) Being attentive and concentrating on actions.
C) The absence of a free-floating state of consciousness.
D) Quickly alternating techniques.
E) High-quality relaxation.

4. Mild vibrations occur when performing a direct technique. Can the straining the brain technique be used to amplify the vibrations?
A) Yes.
B) No.
C) It may be used, but for practical purposes - only when a practitioner is exhausted or sleep-deprived.
D) It may be used, as long as the attempt to enter the phase is not being made during the day.

5. Which of the actions given below increase the likelihood of entering the phase through dream consciousness when used right before falling asleep?
A) Performing direct techniques.

B) Intending to perform indirect techniques upon awakening.
C) Recalling dreams from the night before.
D) Creating a plan of action for use in case of entrance to the phase in such a way.

6. If awareness occurs at the very last moment of a dream that fades away, which of the actions given below should be undertaken in order to enter the phase as soon as possible?
A) Try to fall asleep again in order to once again become self-aware while dreaming.
B) Immediately perform indirect techniques.
C) Take a break and perform direct techniques later.
D) Start to recall that night's dreams.

7. Which of these are most likely to produce a quick phase entry when awakening in a state of sleep paralysis?
A) Relaxation.
B) Falling asleep with the intention of becoming self-aware while in a dream.
C) Moving the physical eyes and tongue.
D) Direct techniques.

8. What should be done when spontaneously thrown from the body while lying down or waking up in the middle of the night?
A) Return to the body and perform appropriate separation techniques.
B)B) Implement a predetermined plan of action for the phase.
C) Deepen immediately.
D) Try to quickly establish vision, if it is not already present.
D) Employ the forced falling asleep technique.

9. While trying to enter the phase, rolling out works at first, but only partially, and the movement cannot be extended any further no matter what effort is made. What is it best to do in this situation?
A) Try to turn back and roll out further once again, and repeat several times.
B) Start doing cycles of indirect techniques.
C) Take a break and try to separate after several minutes.
D) Try to separate by levitating, getting up, or climbing out.
E) Use any indirect technique for phase entry and attempt rolling out again.

10. A practitioner unexpectedly gets stuck in the floor or wall while rolling out. What should be done to resume the phase?
A) Force through the obstacle.
B) Employ translocation techniques.
C) Attempt to return to the body and roll out again.
D) Perform sensory amplification.

11. How may a practitioner deepen the phase while flying through a dark formless space while separating?
A) Employ the technique of falling headfirst.
B) There is no way to do this.
C) Create and amplify vibrations.
D) Begin self-palpation.
E) Translocate to another area in the phase and deepen it through sensory amplification.

12. If deepening techniques do not completely work within 15 to 30 seconds, what can be done?
A) Continue trying to go deeper.
B) Exit from the phase.

www.obe4u.com

C) Attempt to return to the body and once again use phase entrance techniques.
D) Proceed to performing predetermined actions.

13. Which technique or way of maintaining the phase should be used when teleporting somewhere with closed eyes?
A) The technique of amplifying and maintaining vibrations.
B) Tactile sensory amplification, feeling the sensation of rubbing the hands together.
C) No technique.
D) The technique of rotation.
E) Repeating aloud the desire to remain in the phase.

14. In which situations is falling asleep in the phase most likely?
A) When looking for a desired person.
B) When communicating with animate objects.
C) When completely calm, having completely halted all activity.
D) When traveling aimlessly.
E) When taking part in side events.

15. Which of the following indicators guarantees that the phase has been exited and the practitioner is in reality?
A) A clock shows the right time, and the same time even if a practitioner turns away from it and then looks at it again.
B) Sensations are completely realistic.
C) The presence of friends or family in the room who communicate with the practitioner.
D) An inner feeling that the phase has ended.
E) Nothing happens after staring at the end of a finger from close distance for five to 10 seconds.

16. In which situations should traveling in the phase be deliberately discontinued?
A) When a fear that a return will be impossible, or a direct fear of death arises.
B) When there is a real possibility that the practitioner will be late for something in the physical world.
C) When frightened by some strange events or objects.
D) When there is an inexplicable mortal fear of something unknown or incomprehensible.
E) If someone in the phase strongly insists that the practitioner should return to reality.
F) If sharp pain occurs in the body that is not caused by interaction with objects in the phase world.

17. What will most likely occur when trying to evade some awful being or dangerous person?
A) The object will get bored and stop.
B) Fear of the object will go away.
C) The phase will occur more frequently, as well as be longer and deeper than usual.
D) The practitioner will become calmer and unnerved less frequently.
E) The more fear there is, the more often the object will chase the practitioner.

18. When should establishing vision in the phase be considered, if it has not occurred on its own?
A) Immediately upon separation without deepening.
B) Immediately after deepening.
C) While flying through dark space during translocation.
D) When there is a desire to immediately explore the surroundings after separation has occurred.

19. How is it possible to pass through a wall while standing close to it, without stopping to look at it from close range?

A) By gradually pushing the hands and arms through it, and then the entire body and head.
B) By gradually pushing the head through it at first, and then the entire body.
C) By trying to put a hole in it, and then expanding the hole and climbing through it.
D) By ramming it with a shoulder, trying to bring it down.

20. While in the phase, a practitioner is in a situation where the arms are totally paralyzed and immobilized. This happens in a room with a single exit: a door that has started to close. What are the two easiest ways to keep the door open?
A) Order the door to stay open in a loud, imperious, and assertive manner.
B) Free the arms and hold back the door.
C) Stop the door with telekinesis.
D) Create a person through the method of finding.

21. What difficulties may arise for a practitioner in the phase while using the door technique of translocation?
A) The door will not open.
B) The wrong place is behind the door.
C) It is not possible to use the hand to pull the door handle because the hand goes through the handle.
D) Difficulties with internal concentration occur at the critical moment.
E) A black void often appears on the other side of the door.

22. What are necessary conditions for getting results when translocating in the phase after rolling out during initial separation from the body?
A) Absence of vision.
B) Practicing after sunset.

C) A firm intention to end up somewhere.
D) Certainty of the final result.
E) The presence of vibrations.

23. A practitioner is in a dark room in the phase where everything is poorly visible. There is a chandelier, but no light switch. What is the fastest way to turn on the chandelier to light the room?

A) Translocate through teleportation to the place where the toggle or switch for the light in question is located.
B) Find a flashlight through the method of finding and illuminate the room with it.
C) Rub the light bulbs in the chandelier with the hands.
D) Create a light switch in the room using the method of finding an object.
E) Close the eyes and imagine that the room is already lit, and then open the eyes.

24. When communicating with an animate object in the phase, a desire to add a specific person to the scene arises. Which of the following actions are advisable only for beginners in this case?

A) Propose going to a neighboring room where the needed subject will be presented through the use of the door or corner technique.
B) Summon the needed person by calling their name loudly.
C) Translocate back to the same place, and have both animate objects present there upon your return.
D) Add the needed person through the closed eyes technique.
E) Ask the animate object that you are talking to if it does not mind adding someone to the scene.

25. Where is one not allowed to go using translocation techniques?

A) Inside a mammoth.

B) To the past or the future.
C) To heaven.
D) To an episode of the movie Star Wars.

26. How will a deceased person in the phase differ from their living self when correctly performing the technique for finding the person?
A) Only the practitioner himself can conjure up differences, or not see or perceive them.
B) The deceased will have a different timbre of voice.
C) There will be a radiant halo around the deceased's head.
D) Physical perception of the deceased will be less realistic than in real life.
E) The deceased will not remember anything.

27. What difficulties can arise in the phase while obtaining information from animate sources of information?
A) Inability to remember information obtained.
B) Sources of information are silent.
C) Inadequateness of the sources of information.
D) Sexual attraction, if the source of information is of the opposite or desired sex.
E) Being given false information.

28. How might a practitioner accelerate the healing process of a cold that is characterized by a stuffy nose and a sore throat?
A) Maintaining and amplifying vibrations for the entire length of the phase, and entering it over several days in a row.
B) Taking aspirin and entering the phase over several days in a row.
C) Traveling to hot places in the phase and entering it over several days in a row.
D) Experiencing stressful situations over several phases.

E) Finding a doctor in the phase and asking him what it is best to do in real-life or even in the phase itself.

29. Which of the following achievements belong to Stephen LaBerge?
A) Founding the Lucidity Institute.
B) A Ph.D. in anthropology.
C) Scientifically proving that lucid dreaming is possible.
D) A Ph.D. in psychophysiology.
E) Proving that eye movements in the phase and in reality are synchronized.

30. Who of the following approached the study of the phase state from a pragmatic point-of-view that was totally devoid of occultism?
A) Stephen LaBerge
B) Robert Monroe
C) Sylvan Muldoon
D) Charles Leadbeater
E) Patricia Garfield
F) Carlos Castaneda

Chapter 15 – The Highest Level of Practice

THE PROFESSIONAL-CLASS PRACTITIONER

Being generally acquainted with the indirect techniques as well as the elementary rules of deepening and maintaining the phase may be considered the threshold level of practice. Detailed knowledge of the technical aspects of the practice may be considered the basic level. To be discussed now is the higher level of practice, which differs substantially from lower levels on every front.

If a practitioner is still unable to intentionally enter the phase at least several times a week, then he should not read this section. It may cause his mind additional confusion and distract him with things that are not yet necessary and difficult to understand. If he decides to read on anyway, he does so at his own risk and fully responsible for the consequences of his decision.

When mastering the practice of the phase, the process is sequential: one starts with simple background knowledge and techniques, and then works one's way up to increasingly difficult things. However, once a certain level is reached, the process goes back the other way: one's entire approach simplifies as one discerns the underlying principles. One cannot start off from those principles, as they can only be discerned through individual practice upon having mastered the basics. This comes naturally for many practitioners. The aim of this section is only to highlight things that will be realized consciously or subconsciously by a person constantly practicing the phase.

If a practitioner's mind and attention-span become inevitably overwhelmed with a large body of theoretical knowledge, no need to worry - everything with become simpler with experience, and the discipline of practicing itself will bring much more enjoyment. Perhaps only the discipline in its higher form should be considered the real practice of the phase, as only then does it harmonize with real life and bring no discomfort.

A high level practitioner can achieve the following:

- *Indirect techniques work no less than 90% of the time.*
- *Consciousness while dreaming can be obtained 80% of the time that one desires it.*
- *Direct techniques work no less than 60% of the time.*
- *Deepening takes a minimal amount of time and is performed while accomplishing a plan of action.*
- *Maintaining is less energy-consuming and its effects more prolonged.*
- *The phase can be applied in one way or another as soon as one desires to do so.*
- *Even a moderate-level practitioner can enter the phase many times a day (3-6 times, not counting secondary entrances). At a high level of practice, this should be normal.*

If a phaser has not reached such a level in every aspect, then he is still making some fundamental mistakes and therefore has something to work towards. If he has reached a high level, then he is already living in two worlds, and before him lies an unlimited Universe, where now only he alone can determine his actions and find meaning in them. He is at a point where no one or anything can make any substantial corrections to his experience.

THE ABSOLUTE PRINCIPLE

Pure desire is one of the core principles of a high level of practice. The practitioner already knows what exactly he needs from one technique or another. He strives to directly achieve his aim through a combination of specific, focused desire and recall of the state. In other words, the phaser now strives towards a desire to accomplish or experience something, and not towards going through rituals in pursuit of some vague goal.

In order to achieve something, the practitioner now simply wills it. It is obtained without any other actions. There is no longer any point to most of the techniques, which only become necessary in special cases when they are the only way to achieve a result in difficult situations.

INDIRECT TECHNIQUES

When at a high level of practice, a phaser is not surprised by the phase itself (as is the case at other levels). The only surprise comes from unsuccessful attempts when he is unable to enter it. This is especially true regarding indirect techniques. Three key factors lead to such a success rate.

If techniques performed upon awakening do not work due to an aggressive approach, this is always remedied by correct use of forced falling asleep in parallel to the techniques. They always start to work, and so choice of technique is not important here. And if a technique has started working upon awakening, then that's a clear sign of a deep phase. That is, working techniques are markers of the phase. Many experienced practitioners immediately begin to use forced falling asleep in parallel with performing the indirect techniques, which is why they are either immediately able to exit the body, or the first technique that they use works.

An experienced phaser does not perform indirect techniques in order to obtain the right state. He moves directly towards that state, and might perform some technique in order to control his conscious mind. The task is to obtain the right state - a certain physiological process - upon awakening. And if that state's already there, and if that state is already quite familiar, then it only remains to go for it! That's the whole secret. It's almost impossible to describe how it feels in words, yet many do it intuitively in practice. It's usually more a combination of recollection of the state, forced falling asleep, and an intense desire to enter the phase no matter what. The most important thing is to aim right for the phase.

Understanding a logical fact dramatically increases the effectiveness of indirect techniques: practically every time a practitioner is waking up, he is already in the phase, be it a deep or shallow form of it. Physiologically speaking, a person who has just woken up is in the phase by definition. Once a practitioner understands this, he will act in a much more self-assured and focused manner during attempts, and results will follow. It's no secret that a substantial portion of unsuccessful attempts - if not 90% of them - are unsuccessful due not to any action, but because lack of confidence finds expression in the results. This is due to the phase's tendency to model expectations. You expect nothing to happen, and so even if you are in the phase - nothing will happen. Believe that you will do it right here and now because you are already in the phase - and enjoy the result! We are actually already in the phase upon every awakening. One can even take the following approach to this understanding: when waking up, our task is not to enter the phase, but to deepen it. This is easily observed with the technique of sensory-motor visualization, which essentially consists in performing deepening without any separation or prior employment of techniques. There's a reason why this technique works well for experienced practitioners, and novices have a hard time getting it.

DIRECT TECHNIQUES

The main conclusion that an experienced practitioner will come to is that direct techniques are actually easy, and not much more difficult than any other ones. The problems only lies in understanding certain subtleties. As soon as they become clear, results are easy to obtain.

Despite it being constantly emphasized that the free-floating state of mind is of decisive importance, nearly all novices stubbornly look through all the various techniques in search of a silver bullet. However, an advanced practitioner will hardly ever use techniques. He will immediately go for the free-floating state of mind with practically no effort or strain. That's why the same phrase always comes from the mouths of experienced practitioners: "That's right, I don't do anything at all. I simply lie down and wait for the phase." And it just comes 50-70% of the time. This comes in sharp contrast to some novices who simply waste much time and energy banging their heads against the wall trying to leave their bodies, and as a result only 1-2% of their attempts result in success, which is at best purely incidental.

Let's take up an example of direct phase entrance by the advanced practitioner. The phaser determines the interesting things he will do in the phase, lies down at bedtime in an uncomfortable position for sleeping, and simply tries to fall asleep while holding on to the thought that it'd be swell to enter the phase. That's all! Three to ten minutes later, and he's already caught a lapse of consciousness into the phase. Meanwhile, if he felt that he would fall asleep quickly, he'd use cycles of techniques to keep his conscious mind focused. If, on the other hand, his mind were excessively active, then he would monotonously perform some technique while lying in as comfortable a position as possible for sleep. But in most cases, the quintessence of direct techniques consists in attempting to fall asleep in an uncomfortable position, all the while having the thought of the phase in the back of one's mind. Or at least that's how it's supposed to be, and that's just how it often works - for the simple reason that those are the best conditions for having the right kind of prerequisite lapses in consciousness, on the rebound from which the phase arises. If ten or fifteen minutes go by without result, then the phaser simply goes to bed or stops with the attempt, as a direct phase entrance attempt should be done with enjoyment. If the phaser is not enjoying himself, then that's a sign that he's making mistakes.

Meanwhile, the most important improvement a phaser can make is in his attitude towards the end goal of an attempt. There's a reason why he holds on to the thought, "it'd be swell to enter the phase". That should be in the back of his mind, but not at the center of his attention. The practitioner should be indifferent as to whether or not anything happens. He should let go of control, desire, and the feeling that it's important - and then everything will work. If he lies down to perform a direct technique with intense desire to enter the phase right then and there and no matter what, then nothing will happen. There won't be any phase without a cool, indifferent attitude. If there is anxiety or expectation, nothing will happen. An advanced practitioner would not even attempt direct techniques if he felt excessive anxiety or desire regarding phase entrance. He only makes attempts when he's cool and collected, as well as more or less indifferent to the result. Deep down, of course, he's not indifferent. His desire is deeply held - it is not of the superficial type that physiologically interferes with obtaining results. As soon as the practitioner understands the significance of this principal, the effectiveness of his phase entrance attempts will suddenly improve.

The only exception might be using the direct method to enter the phase in conjunction with the deferred method. In this case, the techniques can take on substantially more importance, and deeply-held intention less importance. This depends on how long one has been awake after sleeping. Such attempts are more similar to the indirect method in terms of effectiveness.

BECOMING CONSCIOUS WHILE DREAMING

For the experienced practitioner, becoming conscious while dreaming requires the least effort and attention of all. He essentially only does two things in order to guarantee dream consciousness during the middle of the night, or better yet - with the deferred method. First, he creates an interesting plan of action that will lure him into a dream. Next, while falling asleep, he simply desires to experience dream consciousness, but without dwelling on it too much or being obsessive about it. That's all! The practitioner would be quite surprised if nothing worked at all.

Once again, everything depends on correctly forming an intention. An experienced practitioner forms an intention in a fundamentally different way than a novice. A novice would think to himself, "I want to become conscious in a dream", while a phaser would tell himself, "I'll soon become conscious during my dream", which allows for the programming to make it much deeper into his subconscious mind. Moreover, his prior practice has already trained him for that moment, and there's nothing else that he needs to do.

NON-AUTONOMOUS METHODS

Experienced and advanced practitioners who have achieved a high level of control over phase entrance never use any auxiliary means, be they devices, working in pairs with friends, audio files, chemical preparations, herbal substances, etc. There's simply no need for them. If it's much easier for a novice to enter the phase by his own efforts alone, then the same is true for an advanced phaser, but all the more so. The use of non-autonomous methods is always the lot of those who search for an extraneous solution to their own common mistakes in using regular techniques, instead of correcting those mistakes like everyone else.

DEEPENING

The deepening techniques used by an advanced practitioner essentially differ little from those used at the basic level. However, there are two fundamental differences in the way these techniques are performed. First, an experienced phaser will prefer to perform deepening at the same time he begins to implement his plan of action. That is to say, he doesn't do as a novice does: separate, deepen, and then implement the plan of action. Instead, he separates and immediately implements his plan of action, in parallel to intensifying the realness of his sensations. This has beneficial effect on the quality of the deepening, and it simply saves time for other things in the phase.

Second, advanced practitioners and novices differ in their intent to deepen and how it they realize it. If, when performing a deepening technique, a novice will often expect results from the simple fact of mechanically performing some action, then an advanced phaser will perform deepening techniques with the focused aim and desire of obtaining a hyperrealistic phase, as if being pulled towards it by the techniques themselves, all while recalling the sensations of previous experiences. The techniques merely serve to help him better express his intention.

MAINTAINING

Perhaps the only thing that an advanced practitioner might still have to struggle with is maintaining the phase. However, it's only a struggle in a relative sense, and more of a struggle for perfection. An essential way that an experienced phaser differs from a novice is that the length of time that he stays in the phase is fully sufficient for his needs. No matter how long he stays in the phase, this duration is multiplied by his many phase entrances over the course of even a single day. As a result, he always accomplishes all of the tasks he has set for himself, and often quite quickly. And if a practitioner accomplishes all his objectives, why should he be dissatisfied with the duration of a phase?

The first sign of an advanced practitioner is that he always has a plan of action for the phase. An interesting and useful one. He always knows what he will do in the phase and how he will apply it. He always wants to enter the phase, as he always has many things to do in it, even if they sometimes have nothing to do with the physical world. Moreover, many advanced practitioners undertake their own studies of the phase, which serves to further stimulate their own practice and personal development.

The main problem novices have in maintaining the phase paradoxically consists in fear of a foul, i.e. an involuntary return to the body. This usually causes them to perform the maintaining techniques incorrectly, and they nearly always lack the intention of maintaining, not to mention confidence In their own abilities. But this is a decisive factor when it comes to maintaining the phase.

A novice performs maintaining techniques in order to not be returned back to the body or not fall asleep, while an experienced practitioner performs maintaining techniques in order to maintain his presence in the phase.

As a result, the former is often soundly thrown out of the phase, while the latter has experiences that are many times longer and more relaxed. Even thinking of one's own body while in the phase is fraught with the danger of returning to it, to say nothing of techniques which are focused on the conscious ability to reenter the body.

While in the phase and when performing any maintaining technique, a practitioner should be extremely confident that he will be in the phase for just as long as he needs to be.

Such confidence alone is sufficient to substantially prolong the average phase.

However, when maintaining the phase, advanced practitioners have to face the real issue of keeping their minds out of their bodies - and this means false fouls. The absolute majority of returns to the body from the phase are false. Depending on one's personal characteristics and level of practice, from 50 to 90% of all returns to the body can be false. That's precisely why the mandatory rule is: upon returning to the body, one must try to separate from it again. Even when following this rule, the experience nonetheless often ends in a false awakening that is only recognized some time after the fact.

The problem is partially resolved by understanding that a return to the body from the phase means nothing at all. If it happens, it's but a trifle for one's practice not worthy of the slightest attention. If you were just in the phase, then it can't end so easily or quickly. *An experienced practitioner should always (always!) try to re-enter the phase and do it with as much self-assurance as possible. And if one is at last unable to leave the body again, then one must perform at least two reality checks (hyperconcentration, breathing out through a pinched nose, looking for inconsistencies, etc.), as there is a high likelihood that one is still nevertheless in the phase.* Reality checks alone can prolong a phase experience by up to 20 percent. In summary, at higher levels of practice, a phaser must try to re-exit his body. If he is unable to, then he must perform reality checks.

There are several reasons why practically all practitioners have such problems with false returns to the body. One of the main ones is a certain lack of confidence in one's own powers when maintaining the phase, which is remedied by intensifying one's intention and concentration. However, there is also a certain problem that is practically resistant to controllable solution and is brought about by the astounding characteristics of human consciousness during altered states: false memory.

Sometimes, a cluster of false memories - yet quite detailed and emotionally-charged ones - will suddenly appear in a phaser's memory during a phase experience. This indicates that he has long been in the phase, and thus quite a psychologically accepting state. As a result, a phaser may not put up much resistance to a foul, or even control the foul himself. As soon as he returns to the body, he'll realize that the phase was actually much shorter than it seemed to his mind. Sometimes only a detailed analysis can uncover this uncommon problem and bring the practitioner to understand that he was not in the phase for the seeming 5 minutes, but merely 10 seconds. The prescription for this strange trick of the human mind is nevertheless the same: mandatory re-exits from the body no matter what it seems or what one thinks, and if this is unsuccessful - reality checks.

CONTROL

A professional practitioner will translocate within the phase and find objects in it upon first attempt when using any technique, or just pure willpower without using techniques at all. It's not hard at all for him to lift a house or a mountain with one finger, as his mind no longer harbors the biases and patterns of the everyday world. He can take on any bodily form and conjure any sensation, including those alien to human existence or human knowledge. In other words, if there is something a practitioner can't do in the phase, that means he hasn't reached a high level of control over it, and has something to work on.

The things he has to work on are quite clear: intention, self-assurance, and desire. Those are the very factors that determine every facet of controlling the phase. If something doesn't work out, then mistakes are to be sought not in one's technique, but in how it is performed internally, inside one's subconscious mind - which will never grow accustomed to the fact that the limitations of the physical world no longer always apply.

APPLICATION

Despite the fact that it's not difficult for an advanced phaser to apply the phase towards any well-known practical application, he's unlikely to do this often. There are several reasons for this. First, when your tally of phase experiences numbers in the thousands, and you do it many times per day, your needs simply cannot keep up with your experience. Simply put, the phaser has already accomplished everything that he needed to, and returns to practical application only rarely. Second, advanced practitioners rarely see the phase as a means to solve some task or problem. For them it's simply a life to live. After all, we don't live here in the physical world for the sake of achieving something in the phase world. We live for this world. It's the same with the phase. It's good, miraculous, and magical only because it exists, and we can inhabit it. That's why advanced practitioners seek nothing in the phase. They are content with the very fact of living in two worlds.

Obtaining information from the phase is its most difficult application. All of the other applications present little difficulty, even for moderately advanced practitioners. However, mastering the skill of obtaining credible information is a job that's never finished.

Techniques have been simplified as much as possible here. After all, techniques for obtaining information are needed to create intermediaries between the practitioner and his subconscious mind (or fields of information, as some believe them to be). These intermediaries are necessary in order to better understand and clearly "see and hear" the information. But in the end, all these are intermediaries and rituals for novices who don't understand what's going on internally. However, they do understand what's going on externally, and so there's no other way to explain it to them. In most cases, an experienced phaser will use the most clear-cut way of obtaining information: getting it directly. The practitioner's question is raised as a thought-form, and the answer to it instantly appears in his memory, as if it were something already known. This is similar to the long-recognized phenomenon of false memory, but in this case the memory doesn't have to be false - it can contain truly useful information. Otherwise, the task of finding something out can be set before entrance into the phase, and the answer to it can be found in one's mind immediately upon separation.

Influencing physiology occurs in the same way. The desired effect is achieved not by taking pills or other measures in the phase, but through directly inducing it. Meanwhile, due to the special ways in which the subconscious mind works, it's still sometimes recommended to use additional "crutches" in the form of pills or the like in order to increase the effectiveness of the physical body's reaction.

THE PLACE OF THE PRACTICE IN LIFE

A high level phaser lives in proper balance between the practice and real life. This is reflected in a successful and content physical life that neither interferes with the practice nor detracts from it, but instead enriches it with emotion. The phase enriches physical life, and physical life enriches the phase. Problems in day-to-day life have a catastrophic effect on one's practice. Thus, even when in pursuit of a better phase practice, one should never forget the real world, where consciousness first arose. In the same vein, the phase itself can be used with wide application for one's career or business.

An experienced practitioner always knows when it's time for real life and when it's time for the phase. Everything goes best when the two are kept separate, and not intertwined. For example, during the working day one must try not to think of the phase, but instead concentrate on more vital matters. When the time comes to enter into one's practice, it is necessary to turn one's attention to only it, and put aside any pressing problems. A practitioner will feel most comfortable when he clearly separates his two lives, and thus avoid the gaps in practice that inevitably occur unless this philosophy is followed.

However, this is not to give the impression that advanced phasers must enter the phase every day without exception. They too take breaks, whether by choice or due to external circumstances. They're sometimes simply not up to it for physical reasons. On a good week they'll devote maybe 3-5 days to it, and be able to enter the phase from 3 to 6 times or more on each of those days. That's about five hundred full-fledged phase experiences per year, enough to take long strides towards mastering the phenomenon.

ABILITY TO TEACH

Once a phaser has achieved a higher level of practice, he's now a new type of person, and perhaps - in terms of the evolution of human consciousness - a man or woman of the future. He is the keeper of rare knowledge regarding techniques that is augmented by his personal practice. He must realize and understand that his is a quite rare and precious skill, one that most can only dream of. This knowledge should not be applied merely towards personal betterment and living fully in two worlds at once. The world is wonderful only when internal and external harmony are in synergy.

A practitioner should therefore always pay more attention to those around him and their take on the phenomenon. The more people there are around the practitioner who understand and practice the phase, the more comfortable he himself will feel. Of course, knowledge of such hidden human abilities should only be passed on under the banner of theoretical neutrality and as pragmatic a position as possible, ensuring the widest possible reception and avoidance of the societal rejection that has been the bane of the practice since time immemorial.

One can not only teach one's friends and family, but also head a local Practitioners' Club, open a branch of the School of Out-of-Body Travel, write books and articles, launch websites, and volunteer to participate in OOBE Research Center experiments. As your achievements grow, you could even undertake your own research at the Center.

The most important thing is not to let your experience and knowledge go to waste! Find a way to apply them towards helping all of humanity. You're now a special person, and it's your turn to change this world!

Appendix

SEND IN YOUR EXPERIENCES!

If you've been able to experience out-of-body travel (enter the phase), then the OOBE Research Center is always interested in studying your experience, as well as possibly using it in its work. Please send your the first and most interesting journeys by email to obe4u@obe4u.com Don't forget to include your full name, age, country and city, as well as profession.

ANSWERS TO THE FINAL TEST (CHAPTER 14)

1. A,B,C,D;
2. D;
3. B, C, D;
4. C;
5. A,B,C,D;
6. B;
7. -
8. C;
9. A, D, E;
10. B, C;
11. A,C,D,E;
12. A,D,A+D;
13. C;
14. D, E;
15. E;
16. B, F;
17. C, E;
18. B;
19. -
20. A, C;
21. A, B, D;
22. A, C, D;
23. E;
24. B;
25. -;
26. A;
27. B,C,D,E;
28. B,C,E;
29. A,C,D,E;
30. A, E;

A SIMPLIFIED DESCRIPTION OF THE EASIEST METHOD

Upon awakening, without moving or opening the eyes, immediately try to separate from the body. The separation attempt should be carried out without any imagining, but rather with the desire to make a real movement without straining the muscles (rolling out, levitation, standing up, etc.).

If separation does not occur within three to five seconds, immediately try alternating several of the most effective techniques for three to five seconds each. When one of the techniques works, continue it for a longer period of time:

Observing images: Try to examine and discern the pictures arising before closed eyes.
Listening in: Attempt to hear sounds in the head and make these louder by listening in or strengthening the will;
Rotating: Imagine rotating around the head-to-foot axis;
Phantom wiggling: Try to move a part of the body without straining the muscles, and try to increase the range of movement;
Straining the brain: Try straining the brain, which will lead to vibrations that may also be intensified by further straining the brain.

As soon as one technique clearly starts to work, continue with it as long as progress is apparent, and then try to separate. If separation fails, return to the technique that was working.

Do not give up alternating through techniques until one minute has elapsed. Separation from the body may be attempted periodically, especially if interesting sensations occur.

ATTENTION!

When making attempts to enter the phase, the practitioner should have complete confidence that he will be immediately successful in everything. Even a shroud of doubt will keep the practitioner in his body, this is especially true when it comes to indirect techniques.

Four typical barriers to mastering the phase encountered by 90% of practitioners are:

1 - Forgetting to deepen the phase;
2 - Forgetting to maintain the phase;
3 - Absence of a plan of action when in the phase;
4 - Forgetting to try to re-enter the phase after a foul;

COPYRIGHT

Due to the nature of this practice, the techniques in this book are not copyrighted. Up to 25% of the techniques in this book may be encountered piecemeal in other sources. Meanwhile, even the procedures developed by the author and the OOBE Research Center cannot be copyrighted, as in most cases they are intuitive and have probably struck somebody's mind in the past.

This book contains a composition of both compiled and independently developed methodologies whose main distinction consists in having tested them under real conditions when teaching them to a mass audience of novices and experienced practitioners. In other words, this book contains only verified information on techniques that will be the most up-to-date until the next edition of the book. With such an approach, copyright is not even a secondary concern - it's practically a moot point.

THE SCHOOL OF OUT-OF-BODY TRAVEL

Michael Raduga's School of Out-of-Body Travel conducts training seminars in many countries around the world. The coursework allows students to master the phase phenomenon and hone their skills at traveling in the phase. Information on existing branches and seminar schedules are available on the website www.obe4u.com. We also welcome potential partners interested in organizing School of Out-of-Body Travel branches and seminars. All correspondence regarding seminars, partnerships, and proposals related to the translation of this book may be handled by e-mail at obe4u@obe4u.com.

OOBE (OUT-OF-BODY EXPERIENCE) RESEARCH CENTER

The OOBE Research Center was founded in 2007. Its initial task was to conduct mass experiments at the School of Out-of-Body Travel aimed at developing simplified methodologies for teaching the phase phenomenon. This book is the result of that research. It subsequently took up the study of all aspects of this phenomenon, and is currently undertaking experimental work on: determining and working with the fundamental properties of the phase, seeking out and developing the best methods for controlling the state, practical applications of the phenomenon, and its popularization, among other projects.

Volunteers for experiments are always being sought! In order to participate, ability to enter the phase at least once a week and basic knowledge of the English language are necessary. Thanks to modern means of communication, you can be located anywhere. Don't let your experience go to waste - put our experiments on your plan of action!

For more information, visit:
http://research.obe4u.com/

BRIEF GLOSSARY OF TERMS AND DEFINITIONS

Out-of-body experience (OBE), lucid dreaming (LD), astral projection – a number of terms united by **the phase** that refer to the state in which a person, while being fully conscious, realizes consciousness outside the normal range of physical perception.

Indirect techniques – entry into the phase within five minutes of awakening from sleep of any duration - provided there has been minimal physical movement.

Direct techniques – entry into the phase without any prior sleep, after excessive physical movement upon awakening, or having been awake for at least five minutes.

Dream consciousness – entry into the phase through becoming consciously aware while a dream episode is happening.

Cycles of indirect techniques - the easiest way to enter the phase, employed by rapidly alternating certain techniques upon awakening from sleep until one of them works.

Dissociation – separation; in this case, a scientific term describing experiences in the phase.

Sleep paralysis – a stupor; the complete immobilization that often occurs when falling asleep, awakening, and entering or exiting the phase.

Stencil – the real physical body that is no longer perceived while in the phase.

Deepening the phase – methods for making the phase as realistic as possible by stabilizing the surrounding space.

Maintaining the phase – methods for maintaining the phase state by preventing a lapse into sleep, a return to reality, or an imagined return to reality.

REM – rapid eye movement sleep (REM phase); a sleep phase characterized by increased brain activity that is accompanied by rapid eye movement and dreaming.

SOBT – *School of Our-of-Body Travel*.
Foul – an inadvertent termination of the phase through a spontaneous return to everyday reality.
FFA – forced falling asleep.

PART IV: CONSCIOUS EVOLUTION 2.0

Or What the Bible, Alien Abductions and Near-Death Experiences All Have in Common

FOREWORD

This article is not about God, aliens or life after death. It is about a phenomenon that left huge traces to be seen in all these topics, as well as in many others, but usually people cannot see this fact.

I think that sometimes when people claim to see God, aliens or have near death experiences, they made incorrect interpretations of our hidden ability. We should know the truth and think about explanations of the phenomenon.

I know almost everything about the OBE because I live in this topic 24/7. It is my life. I analyze dozens of out-of-body experiences every day that is why I can see obvious traces of the phenomenon in many aspects of everyday life. I can prove it in this article.

Actually, the out-of-body phenomenon is so normal that it may be a sign of the next step of the evolution of consciousness. Maybe, in the future our consciousness will be present not only in the wakeful state of the physical body but even outside of it. It seems that we are really very close to the next step of our conscious evolution.

Sources:

1 – Quotes from the Bible;
2 – Well-known cases of abductions by aliens from the site www.ufocasebook.com;
3 – Quotes from *Life after Life* by Raymond A. Moody;
4 – One long thread about first-time out-of-body experiences (500+ cases) from a discussion board on the website www.aing.ru;

Michael Raduga
Founder of the OOBE Research Center
www.obe4u.com

Chapter 1. Biblical Astral Travelers

Right from the start, I should make it perfectly clear that I'm not going to say there is no God. I'll simply be discussing specific individual cases in which a misinterpretation of events has possibly occurred, and nothing more. I would have written a different article if I had wanted to discuss the existence of God.

I first read the Bible when I was 9 years old out of sheer curiosity and personal desire. Even back then, a natural question occurred to me: don't the protagonists of biblical stories very often if not almost always encounter higher beings while dreaming or when in states close to that of sleep?

(*Second Book of Samuel*, Chapter 7)
4 And it came to pass that night, that the word of the LORD came unto Nathan, saying,

(*Acts of the Apostles*, Chapter 16)
9 And a vision appeared to Paul in the night; There stood a man of Macedonia, and prayed him, saying, Come over into Macedonia, and help us.

(*Acts of the Apostles*, Chapter 18)
9 Then spake the Lord to Paul in the night by a vision, Be not afraid, but speak, and hold not thy peace:

(*First Book of the Torah: Genesis*, Chapter 46)
2 And God spake unto Israel in the visions of the night, Jacob, Jacob. And he said, Here [am] I.

(*First Book of Chronicles*, Chapter 17)
3 And it came to pass the same night, that the word of God came to Nathan, saying,

I haven't even bothered to list examples where it was written out in black and white — The Lord appeared to him in a dream and said... There are multitudes of such passages. I would just leave it at that, but for the fact that my students and I already use techniques for leaving the body upon falling asleep and awakening, as well as becoming conscious while dreaming.

(Al Magico)
...This night it finally happened consciously!...

(Amigo)
...I was awakening at night in my bedroom. It was dark. I tried to turn on the lights, but the light-switch wasn't in

its usual place, and I realized that I was dreaming. It was so dark that I started to get really scared...

(Azimut)
I was unable to do astral projection for over a year, until I started doing indirect techniques more often and more intensely. It happened this morning at 9 AM...

But that's just the beginning. Most interestingly, I have found at least four clear descriptions of spontaneous exits from the body upon falling asleep or waking up in the Bible. Meanwhile, there are clearly more of them, but the rest are only described in brief and are thus less obvious examples. The four passages we will look at simply contain the most detail, and everything adds up in them.

(*First Book of Kings*, Chapter 19)
4 But he himself went a day's journey into the wilderness, and came and sat down under a juniper tree: and he requested for himself that he might die; and said, It is enough; now, O LORD, take away my life; for I [am] not better than my fathers.
5 And as he lay and slept under a juniper tree, behold, then an angel touched him, and said unto him, Arise [and] eat.
6 And he looked, and, behold, [there was] a cake baken on the coals, and a cruse of water at his head. And he did eat and drink, and laid him down again.
And the angel of the LORD came again the second time, and touched him, and said, Arise [and] eat; because the journey [is] too great for thee.

Sound familiar? Do you remember your parents ever waking you up to go to school, and then having dressed and gotten your books together, only to have your parents wake you up again? This may have happened to you several times. Or do you remember ever having turned off the alarm clock, only to have it buzz once again and wake you up? That's a typical false awakening. You encounter false awakenings nearly every day, but they are far from always vivid. This lack of vividness is why people often do not recognize that a false awakening has occurred. Up to one-third of all sensations and movements that occur upon awakening do not happen in the real world, they just seem to be.

(<u>Edgaras</u>)
...I was somewhere between 8 and 10 years old. The alarm clock went off, I was having a hard time getting out of bed. I thought for a few moments about how it was time to go to school... Then I got up out of bed, already wide awake, and went to the bathroom... All of the sudden mom came into the room and asked me to wake up and go to school... And this happened more than once...

Let's imagine that Elijah fell asleep not under a juniper tree, but in a comfortable apartment, and that his thoughts upon falling asleep had turned not to God, but to the fact that he had to go to school the next day. Would an angel have visited Elijah in that case? Or imagine Edgaras in Elijah's place. Thinking about leaving the body while falling asleep is one of the key secrets to having an out-of-body experience upon later awakening. Meanwhile, you can think not only about leaving the body, but also about what you want to obtain from the experience itself... That's why it is not at all surprising that the angel came to Elijah - who had been pondering his relationship with God - not during an afternoon walk, but just after he had fallen asleep. But Elijah did not recognize that his subsequent awakenings were false, because an out-of-body experience can outmatch waking life in terms of vividness of sensation.

(*First Book of Samuel*, Chapter 3)

1 And the child Samuel ministered unto the LORD before Eli. And the word of the LORD was precious in those days; [there was] no open vision.
2 And it came to pass at that time, when Eli [was] laid down in his place, and his eyes began to wax dim, [that] he could not see;
3 And ere the lamp of God went out in the temple of the LORD, where the ark of God [was], and Samuel was laid down [to sleep];
4 That the LORD called Samuel: and he answered, Here [am] I.
5 And he ran unto Eli, and said, Here [am] I; for thou calledst me. And he said, I called not; lie down again. And he went and lay down.
6 And the LORD called yet again, Samuel. And Samuel arose and went to Eli, and said, Here [am] I; for thou didst call me. And he answered, I called not, my son; lie down again.
7 Now Samuel did not yet know the LORD, neither was the word of the LORD yet revealed unto him.
8 And the LORD called Samuel again the third time. And he arose and went to Eli, and said, Here [am] I; for thou didst call me. And Eli perceived that the LORD had called the child.
9 Therefore Eli said unto Samuel, Go, lie down: and it shall be, if he call thee, that thou shalt say, Speak, LORD; for thy servant heareth. So Samuel went and lay down in his place.
10 And the LORD came, and stood, and called as at other times, Samuel, Samuel. Then Samuel answered, Speak; for thy servant heareth.
11 And the LORD said to Samuel, Behold, I will do a thing in Israel, at which both the ears of every one that heareth it shall tingle.

According to my research, no less than 50% of those surveyed have reported hearing similar voices at least once in their lives when falling asleep. Moreover, they remember hearing recognizable albeit imaginary voices. We're not even taking into account that all of you have heard unreal sounds hundreds of times when falling asleep and upon awakening, but thought nothing of them, as you thought that they were real (assuming them to be neighbors talking or sounds from outside the window). This is all normal for when consciousness is fading out or coming back on again.

(<u>Goodman</u>)
...I decided to lie down at about 2PM. About 2 minutes later, after I had just started lying in bed, I heard a voice. I somehow sensed that someone was sitting on the chair next to the couch...

(<u>Slider</u>)
...Literally just seconds before I fell asleep, it was as if someone was calling me... Please note that I was not yet asleep. At first it was a normal "voice"... then it got bossier, and then it started ordering me about. And then it was as if something was pulling me into the bed...

There is even a special technique for inducing such sounds and using them to exit the body. It is called the technique of listening in. There are many variations to it. They include trying to hear someone calling your name when you are falling asleep, and especially upon waking up. If you hear your name called, you can separate from the body. Practitioners usually set themselves goals other than meeting God. On the other hand Samuel received a clear order from his mentor to do just that: ("Go, lie down: and it shall be, if he call thee, that thou shalt say, Speak, LORD; for thy servant heareth.")

Now it's time for the next two biblical passages. They are both very similar. For no less than a third of us they recall a completely familiar situation that we have found ourselves in at one time or another: sleep paralysis (sleep stupor, catalepsy), which is nearly always accompanied by a wild terror and often occurs when falling asleep or waking up.

> (*Book of Job*, Chapter 4)
> 12 Now a thing was secretly brought to me, and mine ear received a little thereof.
> 13 In thoughts from the visions of the night, when deep sleep falleth on men,
> 14 Fear came upon me, and trembling, which made all my bones to shake.
> 15 Then a spirit passed before my face; the hair of my flesh stood up:
> 16 It stood still, but I could not discern the form thereof: an image [was] before mine eyes, [there was] silence, and I heard a voice, [saying],

> (*First book of the Torah: Genesis*, Chapter 15)
> 12 And when the sun was going down, a deep sleep fell upon Abram; and, lo, an horror of great darkness fell upon him.
> 13 And he said unto Abram, Know of a surety that thy seed shall be a stranger in a land [that is] not theirs, and shall serve them; and they shall afflict them four hundred years;

We'll examine a select few modern accounts out of hundreds that I have. They will surely strike you as quite similar to the Bible passages cited above, especially in terms of the emotions felt.

> (Stress)
> ....There was a sharp crack, and the feeling of falling down. Someone's unintelligible whisper in my right ear changed into a scream, which died down for a second, only to blast in again from all sides. I was panicking in mortal fear.

(<u>Skyer</u>)
...I was being awoken by an acute fright that had begun while I was dreaming... A wild terror suddenly overcame me. Something started to make a lot of noise in the distance...

(<u>Sol</u>)
....Last time, having been struck by sleep paralysis together with an awful fear, I rolled out of bed...

Fear and darkness upon awakening or falling asleep... These are all completely typical things for the practice of out-of-body travel. Novices report experiencing them in a third of all cases! Meanwhile, they rarely expect an encounter with God afterwards, which is why he usually doesn't appear to them.

This gets right to the essence of the phenomenon. During a spontaneous and uncontrolled out-of-body experience, you get exactly what you fear or expect at the moment. This will be demonstrated again and again below. Meanwhile, in the bible excerpts above, the reason why the protagonists met the Lord is completely clear and understandable - if they but only think of God, they cannot but meet him. It was completely normal for them to have seen God.

And here's what's most important - this all may seem to be empty talk or senseless theory, but hear me out: not only biblical characters have had encounters with God. How many similar stories are there in other sources? Tons. And they all contain the same telltale characteristics - lying down, falling asleep, waking up, and so on. Moreover, one can meet God each and every time one engages in the practice of leaving the body. The procedure is simple: use techniques to go out-of-body, and then use techniques to find the objects that you are looking for. That's all there is to it... Back in my youth when I was first getting into out-of-body travel, I met God several times out of sheer curiosity. I've met scores of practitioners who have done the same. You can even try it yourself.

But who or what is being encountered? Is it really God? That's for you to decide. Some practitioners would say that it is a simulation generated by the subconscious mind, which controls everything during the out-of-body experience. Others maintain that they visit a parallel world inhabited by many Gods. Yet others say that the same God that everyone talks about is encountered during all of these experiences. Here everyone interprets what occurs as they see fit. The most likely explanation is that no real god is at play in such phenomena. God may very well exist, but in these cases something a little different is going on.

Conclusion: at least a portion of the accounts of the Lord appearing in the Bible were hardly visitations by the creator himself. The most likely explanation is that they were spontaneous and unrecognized experiences of the out-of-body state, with ensuing numinous episodes induced by faith in and expectation of the Almighty. The weightiest argument supporting this stance is the fact that anyone can reproduce such experiences himself. Who knows, were it not for spontaneous out-of-body experiences, perhaps the Bible itself would never have been written.

And isn't the Bible itself a hint at our possessing latent abilities? Abilities so important and special that we cannot but associate them with the divine.

Chapter 2. Application to Be Abducted by Aliens

The question of whether or not extraterrestrial civilizations exist is outside of the scope of this article, but I would like to note that the majority of UFO abduction reports involve the same incorrect interpretation of the spontaneous out-of-body state as is the case with the Bible. Each era has gods of its own. I do believe that there are other civilizations out there, but doubt that they are as involved in home visitations as one would infer from reading thousands of "abduction reports".

As with God's appearances in the Bible, I have always been made uneasy by alien abduction stories, because both nearly always occur when the subject is falling asleep or awakening.

(Christina C, ufocsebook.com)
...I woke up because I heard him crying, it was dark, just a little light shining through the drawn window shades. I went to his crib and reached down to pick him

up, but he was not there! I yelled to his father but he never moved. I went to the other side of the room to turn on the light, but it would not come on! I went back to the crib, a bright light flashed on and was beaming through the window, and there he was, still crying, very upset, I picked him up and hugged him close... Directly above the house was a very large triangle shaped object...

(Whitley Strieber, ufocasebook.com)
...After a couple of hours, he was awakened by an unusual sound. He felt that the security of his cabin had been breached. He was soon shocked to see a creature in his bedroom...

If you are still harboring hope that I was in error with the conclusions reached in the chapter above, then what I'm about to say may totally unnerve you. At age 15 I was also "abducted". However, two years later, after having gained significant out-of-body and lucid dreaming experience, I came to the realization that it had all been a spontaneous exit from the body. Had the experience not repeated itself and had I not started experimental research on the phenomenon with diabolical persistence, then to this very day I would still be 100% convinced that I had been abducted by aliens. After all, it felt totally real - and how can one not but believe one's senses? I had always had quite vivid and lucid dreams, but this was nothing like a dream by any measure.

The awakening, falling asleep, fear, and paralysis that I encountered during the "abduction" are typical features of alien abduction stories that you will read over and over again across many sources. For example:

(Anonymous, ufocasebook.com)
...One night I awoke about 3:00 A.M., terrified. I sensed two beings in my bedroom at the foot of the bed. I did not try to look at them because I was afraid of what I

would see. I saw the glow of the clock and Jeff, (my husband) sleeping next to me. I tried to turn (I was on my stomach) to wake him up but I was paralyzed. I then tried to scream but no sound would come out...

(Anonymous, ufocasebook.com)
...During the last part of June (1987) as she was lying down on her bed, she felt somewhat uneasy, as if someone was watching her. The time was 10:00 PM. She then heard a voice say, "We have come for you... You will not be hurt." She then realized that her entire body was paralyzed, and that she could only move her eyes...

(Anonymous, ufocasebook.com)
...I was sitting outside one night reading. All of the sudden it felt as though...as though something was smothering me. I started to panic because I couldn't breathe. I tried to scream but nothing came out...

(Peter Khoury, ufocasebook.com)
...While lying on his bed, he felt something grab his ankles. He suddenly felt numb and paralyzed, but remained conscious. Then he noticed three or four small hooded figures alongside the bed...

Meanwhile, the characteristic features of the above accounts are also typical for out-of-body travel and lucid dreaming! Isn't that strange? Isn't it a little odd that my practitioners also encounter beings during experiences that exhibit the same characteristic traits? The difference is simply that my practitioners don't sensationalize what happened, as they already understand that an out-of-body traveler might experience anything during his or her first adventures. The following are only a sampling of legion examples to be found on our internet forum:

(Lilia)
...I had only just fallen asleep when something changed. I heard the sound of what seemed to be someone jumping from the chair in the bathroom, but there were no cats in the house. And then I heard steps. I had never experienced such mortal fear before in my life, nor would I ever thereafter. I was sleeping in the living room, and could see my home's front door. The door started to open, but I couldn't see who it was. Only once they started coming towards me from the left was I able to catch sight of them by looking to the side. They were about 6 feet tall and translucent, I could see the wall through them. They had radiant almond-shaped eyes that were of a beautiful turquoise color. I wanted to get up or call for help, but I couldn't even move a finger...

(Skyer)
...I was sleeping on the floor. I woke up. Like on any other morning, I was lying in bed half-awake and looking up at the ceiling, planning out my day. I suddenly heard someone walking in the hallway. I had spent the night in the office... The armored door was locked from inside... The windows were reinforced with steel webbing. I was paralyzed with fear... The door started to open slowly, and a being about 6 feet tall came into the room. He had yellow-greenish skin and a large, slender head...

(Roman 26)
...I had just shot up awake at night after sleeping on the couch. Still not quite understanding what had happened, suddenly an ominous and frightening dwarf-like being appeared in the corner away from me. Everything was so real that I froze out of fright and got goosebumps everywhere.

(Stress)

There was a sharp bang, and then the feeling of falling down... I was panicking, afraid for my life, and also had the feeling that they were going to take my soul. Attempts to get up, open my eyes, or move yielded no results. I could feel that my whole body was paralyzed, which just magnified the fear...

The above is just a small sampling of the first-hand accounts posted on our forum, but no one would say that our website was devoted to UFOs. People are simply developing new abilities. I would suggest that the difference between "abductions" and the practice of exiting the body consists only in the interpretation of events. Of course, you may say that the phenomena are not mutually exclusive, and that extraterrestrials might be using this ability of ours to facilitate "abductions". However, if you left your body of your own free will, and then proceeded to look for the aliens yourself and have a conversation with them, would that be "abduction"? Meanwhile, there's nothing stopping you from doing whatever you want with the aliens... Once I understood that I really hadn't been abducted, I went out of my way to encounter extraterrestrials in a bid to overcome my fear of them. And what does it say if a solid majority of my practitioners have deliberately encountered aliens at least once?

In at least a third of all reported UFO and alien encounters, you'll find telltale evidence of a spontaneous out-of-body experience. In at least another third of such reports, even though an out-of-body experience is clearly the underlying phenomenon, details are either missing or omitted (often on purpose, in order to cover up discrepancies). Here is the most simple example of how it can happen:

(Kelly Cahill, ufocasebook.com)
...After midnight the Cahills were on their journey home when they first noticed the lights of a rounded craft with windows around it. Within what seemed only a second or two, Kelly was now very relaxed, suddenly calmed by

the disappearance of the intense, glowing light that had turned night into day for a brief few moments. The first words out of Kelly's mouth [to her husband] were, "What happened, did I blackout?" Her husband said nothing, as he had no answer to give his wife. He cautiously drove his family home.

I think that by now it has already become obvious that Kelly had simply dozed off back at the very beginning of the story, lulled into sleep by the night drive, and that everything happened outside of the physical world, and only to her alone. However, the sensations were so realistic that she had a different interpretation: her husband had simply had his memory erased. And the result is shocking: one of the most widely circulated accounts substantiating the existence of extraterrestrial civilizations.

But why do these "abductions" happen? The mechanism is quite simple: sometimes the conscious mind awakens before the body, or the body falls asleep before the conscious mind. At that moment, people find themselves outside of the physical world, even though nothing may have changed in terms of sensory perception. It is spontaneous out-of-body experiences. If one's suspicions are aroused by what's going on, then internal fears and expectations immediately come to the surface and materialize in the most realistic way. If angels and gods previously visited the living, then in an era when talk of extraterrestrials fills the TV airwaves, there is nothing else to expect.

We have already discussed what a spontaneous exit from the body leads to when one expects God or guests from Mars. But now, as evidence of what happens when one's mind is occupied by things other than aliens or angels, let's introduce an account given by a child who also spontaneously fell into such a state:

(Azwraith)

...It happened late at night in wintertime when I was 8 years old. I woke up and was surprised at how light it was outside for the middle of the night. I walked to the bathroom... I got some water and went to the window, and then I almost dropped the glass once I saw something the size of a dwarf noisily running across the windowsill. It was about the same height as the window. The creature had a humanoid form, it was wearing small black boots, striped bright green stockings, a bright red jacket, and a hooded cap of the same color... I was so scared that I figured I should run and hide, but out of sheer curiosity I decided to move closer to the window and ascertain whether or not I had just been seeing things. Going to the window, I saw how a strange object flew out from one corner of the house. I immediately recognized it from its outline and shape: this was Santa's sleigh!

Thousands of people have attended my seminars, and a great deal of them had initially become interested in out-of-body travel after having experienced sleep paralysis, spontaneous exit from the body, or even "alien abduction". The ET abduction interpretation of the spontaneous out-of-body experience is just as widespread as the experience itself. According to surveys in the United States alone, 10% of Americans claim to have been abducted by aliens at least once.

Conclusion: in most cases, this phenomenon is not proof of the existence of curious extraterrestrials, but does prove that we are more than simply the physical body in which we are usually trapped. Meanwhile, this is all easily proved in practice. Anyone can make contact with extraterrestrials using out-of-body travel techniques

Chapter 3. How to See the Bright Light at the End of the Tunnel while You're Still Alive

Near-death experiences are indeed the only more or less straightforward glimpse of life after death. Unfortunately, we will now be discussing just that phenomenon. "Unfortunately" because you will have to examine its nature from a completely different point of view. Simply put, it is clear that both out-of-body travel and lucid dreaming are of the same nature as near-death experiences at clinical death. However, the first two somehow fail to prove the existence of an afterlife. They even refute some commonly advanced claims. **Before examining the issue, I would like to start by saying upfront that I am not trying to prove that there is no afterlife.** I would only like to demonstrate that one of the phenomena associated with the life-after-death issue may possibly be of a wholly other essence and significance.

Perhaps we could start by saying that from a purely logical point of view, it would be incorrect to consider "near-death" experiences to happen near the moment of actual death, as accounts of them are always related by living people... Maybe this all has more to do with life than death. I would also like to note that Raymond Moody, whose book we will be citing, did not go so far as to state that the accounts he gathered were unambiguously conclusive evidence of the survival of the soul and life after death. He merely made a hypothesis and backed it up using the excellent testimonies he collected.

You'll have to admit that if you hadn't known beforehand that the following accounts belonged to people who were at the edge of death, it would have been easy to assume that they were written by alive-and-well practitioners of out-of-body travel:

(*Life after Life* by Raymond A. Moody)
...I could feel myself moving out of my body and sliding down between the mattress and the rail on the side of the bed-actually it seemed as if I went through the rail-on down to the floor. Then, I started rising upward, slowly...

(*Life after Life* by Raymond A. Moody)
... At that point, I kind of lost my sense of time, and I lost my physical reality as far as my body is concerned-I lost touch with my body. My being or my self or my spirit, or whatever you would like to label it-I could sort of feel it rise out of me, out through my head. And it wasn't anything that hurt, it was just sort of like a lifting and it being above me...

(*Life after Life* by Raymond A. Moody)
... I was above the table, and I could see everything they were doing. I knew that I was dying, that this would be it. Yet, I was concerned about my children,

about who would take care of them. So, I was not ready to go...

Conversely, when reading the experiences of out-of-body practitioners, one might simply assume that they are descriptions of situations experienced at the moment of death, especially considering the fact that the feeling of imminent death is one of the most common sensations experienced while out-of-body.

During an uncontrolled exit from the body, that which you fear or expect the most is exactly what will happen to you. And that's where reports of gods, flights of the soul, and UFOs come from. To put it simply, exit from the body occurs when the conscious mind is "on", but the body is "off". Apparently, the same thing can happen while under anesthesia or dying, and often does. That is, people fall into the same state that practitioners of out-of-body travel do. If you happened to find yourself in such a situation while on the operating table or during a serious illness, in the overwhelming majority of cases your thoughts would turn to God, angels, and a tunnel with a bright light at the end - which is exactly what you would get.

There is no trait characteristic of near-death experiences that is not also characteristic of out-of-body travel. For example, seeing one's own body on the bed:

(*Life after Life* by Raymond A. Moody)
...He were "able to see everything around me -including my whole body as it lay on the bed without occupying any space"...

(Mister SIGMA)
...I felt like my body was going through the ceiling, and even so I was pulled up higher and higher. I was afraid that this was already death, and was afraid not so much of death as of the unknown. Everything was happening

so rapidly, and I wasn't ready for such changes... I flew about my room and saw myself lying in my bed...

Flying orbs radiating light:

(*Life after Life* by Raymond A. Moody)
...When I woke up in severe pain. turned over and tried to get in a more comfortable position, but just at that moment a light appeared in the corner of the room, just below the ceiling. It was just a ball of light, almost like a globe, and it was not very large, I would say no more than twelve to fifteen inches in diameter... I had the feeling of being drawn up and of leaving my body, and I looked back and saw it lying there on the bed while I was going up towards the ceiling of the room...

(Ruklinok)
...I was levitating about one foot over the bed... I couldn't figure out why everything was lit underneath my back. I looked over my left shoulder and saw a small, bright, white orb about six inches from my shoulder blade - that's what was illuminating the room...

Periodic lack of bodily perception:

(*Life after Life* by Raymond A. Moody)
...Dying persons whose souls, minds,consciousnesses (or whatever" you want to label them) were released from their bodies say that they didn't feel that, after release they were in any kind of "body" at all....

(Tolik)
...It was incomprehensible, there was no feeling, I couldn't see my own hands. I was like an orb, transparent and hanging on the wall over the bed...

Meanwhile, even the vaunted tunnel of light is not the exclusive domain of near-death experiences:

(*Life after Life* by Raymond A. Moody)
...I was moving through this-you're going to think this is weird-through this long dark place. It seemed like a sewer or something. I just can't describe it to you. I was moving, beating all the time with this noise, this ringing noise...

(Igor.L)
...When flying through the tunnel, I noticed that it had a lot of spurs and paths. There was a bright light at the end. I became interested in what was going on, and fell into another reality...

The similarity between the two experiences is inescapable. It is obvious even to someone who has experienced neither firsthand. As the number of out-of-body practitioners continues to increase, I have been meeting more and more people who have had both types of experience. And do you know what they say? That the experiences are one and the same! There is no fundamental difference between them, except that there is no risk of death when one practices on one's own.

There is another strong argument in favor of near-death experiences and out-of-body travel being the same thing: false near-death experiences. There is no difference whatsoever between them and their bona-fide near-death counterparts. For example, once a person came up to me and started telling me about how he had experienced clinical death, an exit from the body, travel through a tunnel, etc. But after asking him some questions, it became clear that no clinical death had occurred, and that the rest of the experience had happened during a standard, spontaneous exit from the body. This is because clinical death is when doctors establish the fact of cardiac arrest, which is different than dozing off after a sumptuous breakfast of jam doughnuts.

What's more, it's easy to come to the conclusion that you're dying when having an out-of-body experience. Such thoughts occur in about a fifth of all exits from the body. Even after having had thousands of OBEs, I still fall into such terror myself from time to time. That's to say nothing of novices, who often cower back into the body after having just left it:

(Budushee)
...I actually fell onto the floor, but felt no physical sensation from it, just a panicky fear and omen of looming death...

(Yuri)
...Upon becoming fully aware of my nature, I clearly understood that I didn't have a body, it was simply gone! My first thought was, "so this is what death's like!"

(Lilia)
...That's when it hit me that I was dying. I ran to the living room and saw myself lying on the bed. And I jumped back into myself...

However, you might argue that with all of the above I have just proved that there is life after death. Actually, the correct deduction is that we can have near-death experiences without the threat of dying. Meanwhile, there is one more kicker here. During my first years of practicing out-of-body travel, I was sure that my soul was actually leaving my body and that I was therefore immortal. But after undertaking endless experiments, it turned out that my "soul" was not travelling through the physical world at all, but throughout something else entirely. It's possible that this is all just a mental projection, albeit a more realistic one than the physical world. Many believe that it's a parallel world. But that's not important here. What's important is that this is a very complicated question and that many answers are possible.

Conclusion: it's possible that near-death experiences are important not as proof of life after death, but as evidence that we all have a great many more abilities in the physical world than we are aware of, even if we only realize this in critical situations. This is reinforced by the fact that any person can experience such a "near death" by following special technique-based procedures, and without any threat to life or limb.

Chapter 4. Evolution

THE MASS NATURE OF THE PHENOMENON

What would happen if we combined three excerpts: one from a biblical appearance of God, one from an alien abduction story, and one from a near-death experience testimony?

> *...In thoughts from the visions of the night, when deep sleep falleth on me, fear came upon me, and trembling, which made all my bones to shake. Then I heard a voice say, "We have come for you... You will not be hurt." I could feel myself moving out of my body and sliding down between the mattress and the rail on the side of the bed-actually it seemed as if I went through the rail-on down to the floor. Then, I started rising upward, slowly...*

Having had thousands of my own out-of-body experiences and having analyzed those of thousands of others, I can definitively state that the above would be a classic example of a first-time exit from the body typical for novices.

It's very likely that such phenomena are very closely interrelated. It's possible that they are of one nature. And that's not considering hundreds of mystical and occult schools in which the same practice, under the most diverse names, stands apart from all the others as the pinnacle of development.

A few words on the mass scale of the phenomenon, which is not without importance. One person in four has experienced leaving their body upon falling asleep or waking up. One in three has experienced sleep paralysis at least once. One in two has reported having become conscious while dreaming. And everyone has encountered this hundreds of times in a superficial or unrecognized form. For example, up to a third of all actions and sensations upon awakening are not real. And how many times have you woken up, done something, and then gone back to sleep, not even suspecting that none of this occurred in the physical world?

By all accounts this is clearly a mass phenomenon, an ability inherent in each person. I can vouch for this as I am able to teach anyone to have an out-of-body experience.

A NEW STAGE IN THE EVOLUTION OF CONSCIOUSNESS

This ability of ours has always accompanied us, influencing us all the while. But it wasn't until now that we have looked in the right direction and finally seen this elephant in the room, a hitherto secret phenomenon confounding the minds of millions. Isn't it time we recognized its due and logical role as the common denominator of a long list of phenomena that had until now always seemed unrelated? Wouldn't the world become simpler, and wouldn't we then understand ourselves much better?

As it turned out, certain commonalities of several completely different, but hitherto uncompared, phenomena became clear and straightforward to me, thanks to both my activities and personal experience in the field. I couldn't but conclude that there was some common denominator at work.

Man has extraordinary ability to adapt and is constantly evolving. Although it's hard to imagine now, just several thousand years ago our consciousness and self-awareness looked totally different. They simply did not exist in their now familiar form. What is going on today can be alternatively interpreted as either natural evolution or social (cultural) evolution.

It's entirely possible that conscious awareness, once having developed and then having proceeded to consume our entire waking life, is actually evolving into those states of consciousness where it would seem to have been impossible: those occurring while our body is asleep. To put it bluntly, consciousness ran out of room in our waking mind and continues its expansion into the brain. There is only one piece of evidence of this process: half of all people report experiencing 100% conscious awareness flaring up into their dreams.

Meanwhile, another take on the origin of the out-of-body phenomenon looks to fundamental transformations in science and culture. Even three or four hundred years ago, the average level of intelligence was hardly one-half of what it is today. Thanks to modern education systems, enormous floods of information, and lightning-fast communication, our conscious minds have had to use their resources to their full capacities. Perhaps those capacities are not enough. Our craniums are overfull, and perhaps that's why consciousness is overflowing to where it seemingly wasn't meant to be or couldn't have been. With the overloads introduced by modern society, it simply has nowhere left to go. That's why spontaneous dissociation when awakening and throughout dreaming occurs increasingly often. It also happened in the past, but rarely. But now it's taking on an incessant nature.

By all accounts, we are now at the breakthrough stage of a new era: the entrenchment of a new state of mind and consciousness, which has become the next logical outcome of human evolution.

Children, with their predisposition for out-of-body experiences, deserve special attention. Most adults simply forget that having out-of-body experiences was the norm for them during early childhood. I've met many people over the course of my practice who remember how often it happened for them at an early age. I've had the opportunity to speak with children who maintain that they were able to do it on command before they could even speak, but that later it started happening increasingly rarely with age and that they gradually forgot about it. This speaks either for the natural evolution of consciousness, or, conversely, for regression...

Either way, we may turn our attention to this new state of consciousness that we have. And it has possibly just begun to develop. If earlier we only had three primary and completely different states - wakefulness, REM sleep, and non-REM sleep - then now we have something in-between wakefulness and REM that includes features of both. The first steps in scientifically proving the existence of this state were taken by Stephen LaBerge at Stanford University in the beginning of the 1980s. A successful experiment was conducted regarding consciousness while dreaming. Meanwhile, today it is clear that the experiment's result has implications for a far greater number of phenomena. It has become fully apparent that consciousness while dreaming is practically the same thing as out-of-body travel, but that it occurs as a result of different method. And we have already identified spontaneous exit from the body in a whole slew of phenomena.

However, when you see the word "dreaming" in the context of all of the above, don't think that experiencing the phenomenon itself feels like being in a dream. We have identified a whole number of cases in which super-realistic sensations made people think that they were dying, seeing God, or encountering aliens. The term "hyper-realism" is often brought in to describe the experience: in most exits from the body, every sensation is so heightened that the physical world seems like a faint dream in comparison.

I have no interest at all in discussing where we actually go when we leave our bodies. My task is only to inform people of the opportunity to do so and to teach them how to take advantage of it. Meanwhile, practitioners can decide for themselves what is actually going on. Some believe that they are travelling in spirit form through the physical world. Others hold that their soul travels about parallel worlds. Still others consider it all to be only a mental state.

THE FUTURE

It is entirely possible that we will all be living in two worlds within a certain period of time. In fact, practitioners of out-of-body travel and lucid dreaming already do. But here we're not discussing the practice, but rather an ordinary ability that will be completely normal for us.

For example, when someone goes to bed in the evening or in the afternoon, he will easily be able to leave his body immediately and then do a whole number of interesting things. And before morning awakening, he will sometimes be able to consciously spend time outside of his physical body, and then return to it. Practically speaking, we would have 2 to 3 extra hours in our lives each day. Considering the hypertrophied perception of time outside of the body, those two hours would be more like a double life. We should call it nothing other than living in two worlds at once. And this will be a completely ordinary phenomenon.

How long will this process take and when will it become natural for all of humanity? Perhaps a few decades. Maybe a century or another millennium. That means that in any case we will have to wait for the passing of a number of generations for this ability to become inborn and normal for everyone. However, thanks to technique-based procedures it is already accessible to all. It only requires a certain amount of effort. All of the instructions are available on my website at www.obe4u.com.

We will use this skill for the most diverse purposes, which are already a reality for out-of-body travel practitioners: travelling in time and space; meeting any person, living or deceased; obtaining information; self-healing; artistic applications, entertainment, and much more. In essence, a new world is opening up in front of us, the one which we read about in fairy tales. It is limitless and ideal, there all things are possible and accessible. And this is all with full conscious awareness and with bodily perceptions more vivid than in the physical world. Perhaps this is heaven itself?

Some believe that we enter some parallel world when exiting the body, one where everything is controlled by informational fields and other such things. A pragmatic position would lean more in favor of calling it a newly developing mental state and for all events in it being controlled by our own exceedingly powerful subconscious, which wields fantastic computational resources. No supercomputer has a fraction of the computational power of our own subconscious mind. Seeing it in action will electrify you. This is such a profound state that the ancients seemed to have ascribed its occurrence to God. This was nearly directly alluded to in key Bible verses that specify the ideal time for having a spontaneous out-of-body experience:

(*Book of Job*, Chapter 33)
14 For God speaketh once, yea twice, [yet man] perceiveth it not.
15 In a dream, in a vision of the night, when deep sleep falleth upon men, in slumberings upon the bed;
16 Then he openeth the ears of men, and sealeth their instruction...

Michael Raduga

TABLE OF CONTENTS

PART I: GET PHASE WITHIN 3 DAYS

THE PHENOMENON..6
THE INDIRECT METHOD: STEP-BY-STEP INSTRUCTIONS.................8
STEP 1: SLEEP 6 HOURS AND THEN WAKE UP WITH AN ALARM CLOCK.......9
STEP 2: GO BACK TO SLEEP WITH AN INTENTION.............................10
STEP 3: SEPARATE THE INSTANT YOU AWAKEN...............................11
STEP 4: CYCLING TECHNIQUES AFTER ATTEMPTS TO SEPARATE.........12
STEP 5: AFTER THE ATTEMPT..16
PLAN OF ACTION IN THE PHASE..16
DIDN'T WORK?...18
THE FOUR PRINCIPLES OF SUCCESS..22
IT WORKED!..23

PART II: 100 PHASES

CHAPTER 1. MY FIRST PHASE..25
    SEPARATION IMMEDIATELY UPON AWAKENING.........................25
    EMPLOYING THE INDIRECT TECHNIQUES....................................29
    HINTS FROM THE MIND...35
    BECOMING CONSCIOUS WHILE DREAMING..................................37
    DIRECT EXIT FROM THE BODY WITHOUT PRIOR SLEEP............40
    SPONTANEOUS EXPERIENCES...50
CHAPTER 2. FULL-FLEDGED TRAVELS IN THE PHASE.................59
CHAPTER 3. JOURNEYS OF WELL-KNOWN PRACTITIONERS....119
CHAPTER 4. THE AUTHOR'S EXPERIENCES...................................135

PART III: A PRACTICAL GUIDEBOOK

CHAPTER 1 – GENERAL BACKGROUND..170
    THE ESSENCE OF THE PHASE PHENOMENON..............................170
    SCIENCE AND THE PHASE..172
    ESOTERIC AND MYSTICAL EXPLANATIONS................................174
    WHY ENTER THE PHASE?...176
    THE LIFESTYLE OF A PRACTITIONER...177
    PRACTICE REGIME: 2 TO 3 DAYS PER WEEK................................180
    ALGORITHM FOR MASTERING THE PHASE...................................182
    TYPES OF TECHNIQUES..185
    CONTRAINDICATIONS...188
    RECOMMENDATIONS FOR USING THE GUIDEBOOK..................189
    EXERCISES...190

CHAPTER 2 – INDIRECT METHOD...192
    THE CONCEPT OF INDIRECT TECHNIQUES..................................192
    PRIMARY INDIRECT TECHNIQUES..194
    SELECTING THE RIGHT TECHNIQUES..200

www.obe4u.com

SEPARATION TECHNIQUES..202
THE BEST TIME TO PRACTICE..210
CONSCIOUS AWAKENING..212
AWAKENING WITHOUT MOVING...217
CYCLES OF INDIRECT TECHNIQUES...219
HINTS FROM THE MIND..226
AGGRESSION AND PASSIVITY...228
THE BERMUDA TRIANGLE OF ATTEMPTS...229
FORCED FALLING ASLEEP - MAXIMUM EFFECT..............................231
STRATEGY FOR ACTION..236
TYPICAL MISTAKES WITH INDIRECT TECHNIQUES........................237
EXERCISES...239

CHAPTER 3 – DIRECT METHOD..242
THE CONCEPT OF DIRECT TECHNIQUES..242
THE BEST TIME TO PRACTICE..244
INTENSITY OF ATTEMPTS...245
DURATION OF AN ATTEMPT...246
BODY POSITION..247
RELAXATION...248
VARIATIONS OF USING DIRECT TECHNIQUES................................249
THE FREE-FLOATING STATE OF MIND..251
AUXILIARY FACTORS..254
STRATEGY FOR ACTION..258
TYPICAL MISTAKES WITH DIRECT TECHNIQUES...........................259
EXERCISES...260

CHAPTER 4 – BECOMING CONSCIOUS WHILE DREAMING...............262
THE CONCEPT OF TECHNIQUES INVOLVING BECOMING CONSCIOUS WHILE
DREAMING...262
BEST TIME FOR BECOMING CONSCIOUSNESS WHILE DREAMING......................264
TECHNIQUES FOR BECOMING CONSCIOUS IN A DREAM...............265
ACTIONS TO BE DONE WHEN BECOMING CONSCIOUS WHILE DREAMING........270
STRATEGY FOR ACTION..271
TYPICAL MISTAKES WHEN PRACTICING BECOMING CONSCIOUS WHILE
DREAMING...271
EXERCISES...272

CHAPTER 5 – NON-AUTONOMOUS METHODS.....................................274
THE ESSENCE OF NON-AUTONOMOUS METHODS..........................274
FOR ENTERING THE PHASE..274
CUEING TECHNOLOGIES..275
WORKING IN PAIRS...277
TECHNOLOGIES FOR INDUCING THE PHASE..................................278
HYPNOSIS AND SUGGESTION..279
PHYSIOLOGICAL SIGNALS...280
THE COFFEE METHOD..281
CHEMICAL SUBSTANCES...282
THE FUTURE OF NON-AUTONOMOUS METHODS FOR ENTERING THE PHASE...283
TYPICAL MISTAKES WITH NON-AUTONOMOUS TECHNIQUES....284
EXERCISES..285

CHAPTER 6 – DEEPENING..287
THE CONCEPT OF DEEPENING..287

PRIMARY DEEPENING TECHNIQUES..290
DEEPENING THROUGH SENSORY AMPLIFICATION.....................290
SECONDARY DEEPENING TECHNIQUES...296
GENERAL ACTIVITY...298
TYPICAL MISTAKES DURING DEEPENING...299

CHAPTER 7 – MAINTAINING..302
THE GENERAL CONCEPT OF MAINTAINING......................................302
TECHNIQUES AND RULES AGAINST RETURNING TO THE BODY...........304
TECHNIQUES AND RULES FOR RESISTING FALLING ASLEEP.....................309
TECHNIQUES AGAINST FALSE AWAKENINGS..................................310
GENERAL RULES FOR MAINTAINING..313
TYPICAL MISTAKES WITH MAINTAINING 315
EXERCISES..316

CHAPTER 8 – PRIMARY SKILLS..318
THE ESSENCE OF PRIMARY SKILLS...318
DISCERNING THE PHASE...319
EMERGENCY RETURN. PARALYSIS...320
FIGHTING FEAR..323
PHASE OBJECT AGGRESSION AND ATTACKS..................................325
CREATION OF VISION..326
CONTACT WITH LIVING OBJECTS...327
READING...328
VIBRATIONS...329
TECHNIQUES FOR TRANSLOCATING THROUGH OBJECTS...........330
FLIGHT...331
SUPER-ABILITIES...332
THE IMPORTANCE OF CONFIDENCE 333
TRANSMUTATION INTO ANIMALS...333
CONTROLLING PAIN...337
MORAL STANDARDS IN THE PHASE..337
STUDYING POSSIBILITIES AND SENSATIONS..................................338
TYPICAL MISTAKES WITH PRIMARY SKILLS..................................339
EXERCISES...340

CHAPTER 9 – TRANSLOCATION AND FINDING OBJECTS.........343
THE ESSENCE OF TRANSLOCATION AND FINDING OBJECTS...........343
BASIC PROPERTY OF THE PHASE SPACE..344
TECHNIQUES FOR TRANSLOCATION...346
OBJECT FINDING TECHNIQUES..351
TYPICAL MISTAKES WITH TRANSLOCATION AND FINDING OBJECTS.........354
EXERCISES...355

CHAPTER 10 – APPLICATION...358
THE ESSENCE OF APPLICATIONS OF PHASE STATES 358
APPLICATIONS BASED ON SIMULATION...359
APPLICATIONS BASED ON CONTACT WITH THE SUBCONSCIOUS MIND.........362
CREATIVE DEVELOPMENT...371
SPORTS 374
THE PHASE - AN ALTERNATIVE TO NARCOTICS............................375
UNPROVEN EFFECTS..376
USE OF THE PHASE BY THE DISABLED..378
APPLICATIONS BASED ON INFLUENCING PHYSIOLOGY (SHORT VERSION).......379

www.obe4u.com

APPLICATIONS BASED ON INFLUENCING PHYSIOLOGY (FULL VERSION).........381
TYPICAL MISTAKES WHEN USING APPLICATIONS...................................402
EXERCISES...403

CHAPTER 11 – USEFUL TIPS...406
A PRAGMATIC APPROACH..406
INDEPENDENT ANALYSIS...407
APPROACH TO LITERATURE..409
PRACTICE ENVIRONMENT...410
TALKING WITH LIKE-MINDED PEOPLE..411
THE RIGHT WAY TO KEEP A JOURNAL..412

CHAPTER 12 – A COLLECTION OF 45 TECHNIQUES....................415
GENERAL PRINCIPLES REGARDING THE TECHNIQUES................415
TABLE FOR CREATING YOUR OWN TECHNIQUES.........................416
TECHNIQUES BASED ON MOVEMENT..418
TECHNIQUES INVOLVING SIGHT..419
TECHNIQUES BASED ON VESTIBULAR SENSE.................................419
TECHNIQUES INVOLVING HEARING...420
TECHNIQUES BASED ON TACTILE SENSATIONS.............................420
TECHNIQUES BASED ON REAL MOVEMENTS AND SENSATIONS OF THE PHYSICAL BODY...421
TECHNIQUES BASED ON INTENTION AND FEELINGS..................422
BEST OF THE MIXED TECHNIQUES..424
UNCONVENTIONAL TECHNIQUES...425
TECHNIQUES FOR BECOMING CONSCIOUS WHILE DREAMING............426
THE HIGHEST TECHNIQUE..427

CHAPTER 13 – PUTTING A FACE ON THE PHENOMENON..........428
STEPHEN LABERGE..428
CARLOS CASTANEDA...429
ROBERT A. MONROE..430
PATRICIA GARFIELD..431
SYLVAN MULDOON..431
CHARLES LEADBEATER...432
RICHARD WEBSTER...433
ROBERT BRUCE...433
CHARLES TART..434

CHAPTER 14 – FINAL TEST..436

CHAPTER 15 – THE HIGHEST LEVEL OF PRACTICE...................446
THE PROFESSIONAL-CLASS PRACTITIONER..................................446
THE ABSOLUTE PRINCIPLE...447
INDIRECT TECHNIQUES...448
DIRECT TECHNIQUES..450
BECOMING CONSCIOUS WHILE DREAMING...................................452
NON-AUTONOMOUS METHODS...452
DEEPENING...453
MAINTAINING..453
CONTROL...456
APPLICATION...457
THE PLACE OF THE PRACTICE IN LIFE..458
ABILITY TO TEACH..459

APPENDIX 461
    SEND IN YOUR EXPERIENCES! 461
    ANSWERS TO THE FINAL TEST (CHAPTER 14) 461
    A SIMPLIFIED DESCRIPTION OF THE EASIEST METHOD 462
    ATTENTION! 463
    COPYRIGHT 463
    THE SCHOOL OF OUT-OF-BODY TRAVEL 464
    OOBE (OUT-OF-BODY EXPERIENCE) RESEARCH CENTER 464
    BRIEF GLOSSARY OF TERMS AND DEFINITIONS 465

PART IV: CONSCIOUS EVOLUTION 2.0

    FOREWORD 468
CHAPTER 1. BIBLICAL ASTRAL TRAVELERS 470
CHAPTER 2. APPLICATION TO BE ABDUCTED BY ALIENS 479
CHAPTER 3. HOW TO SEE THE BRIGHT LIGHT AT THE END OF THE TUNNEL WHILE YOU'RE STILL ALIVE 486
CHAPTER 4. EVOLUTION 493

www.obe4u.com

Proposals regarding translating and publishing this book and other works of M.Raduga may be sent to obe4u@obe4u.com